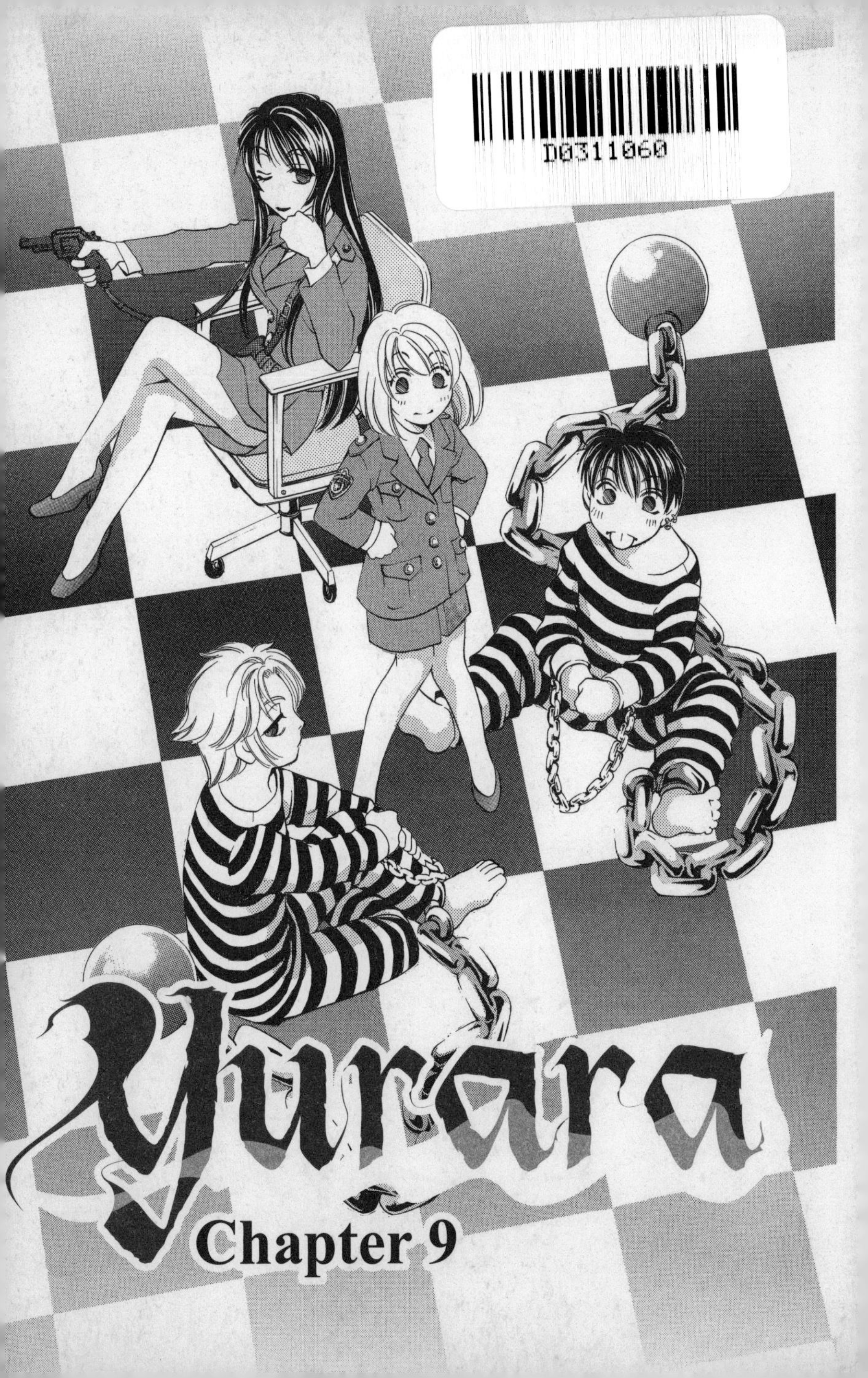
Yurara
Chapter 9

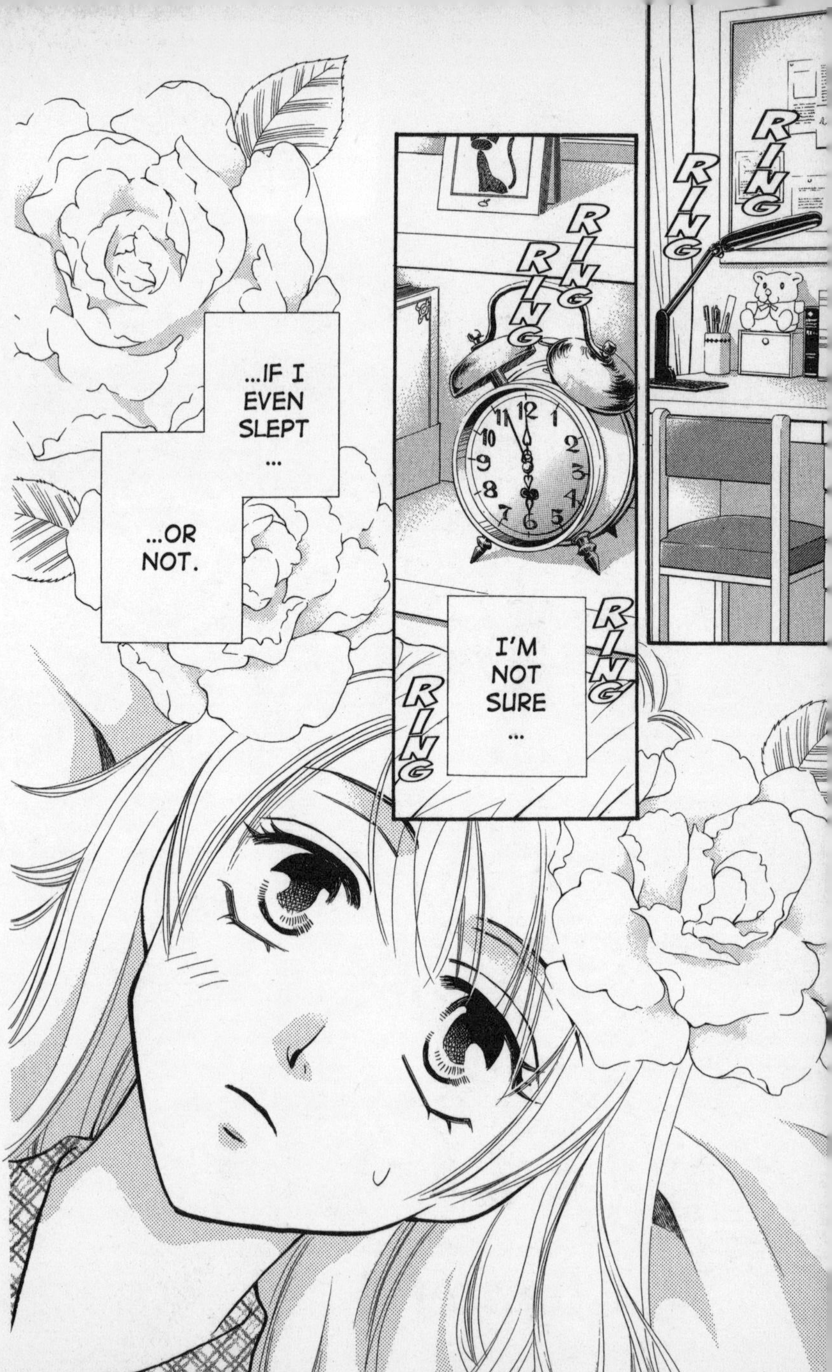
RING
RING
RING
RING
RING
I'M NOT SURE...
RING
...IF I EVEN SLEPT...
...OR NOT.

Shojo Beat

Yurara™

Volume 3

If you so much as touch me, you're dead!
Oh, come on, Yurara...

Story & Art by

Chika Shiomi

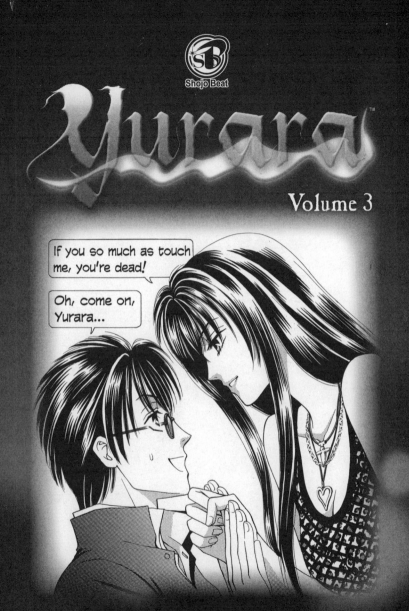

Contents

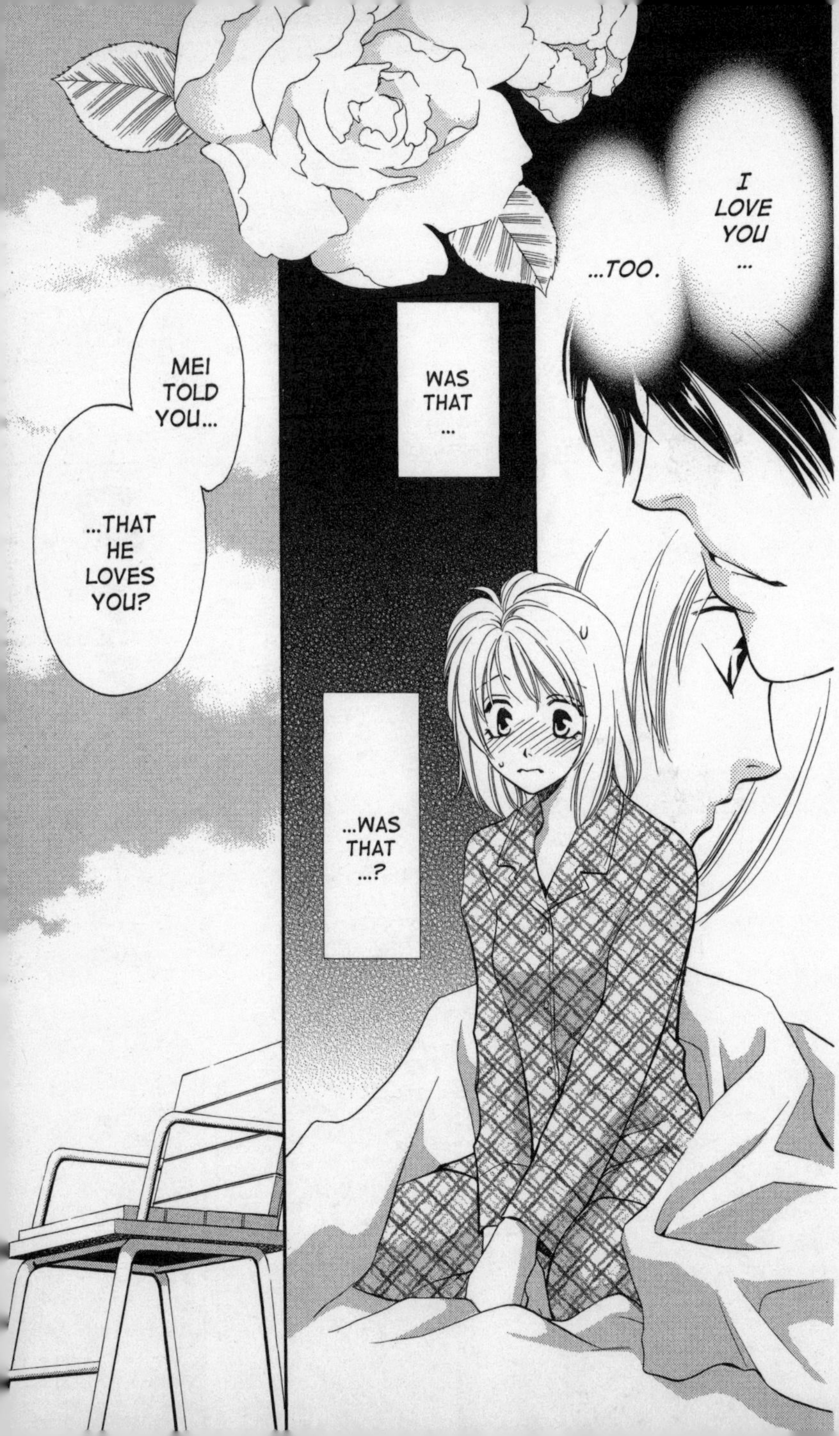
I LOVE YOU ...
...TOO.
WAS THAT ...
...WAS THAT ...?
MEI TOLD YOU...
...THAT HE LOVES YOU?

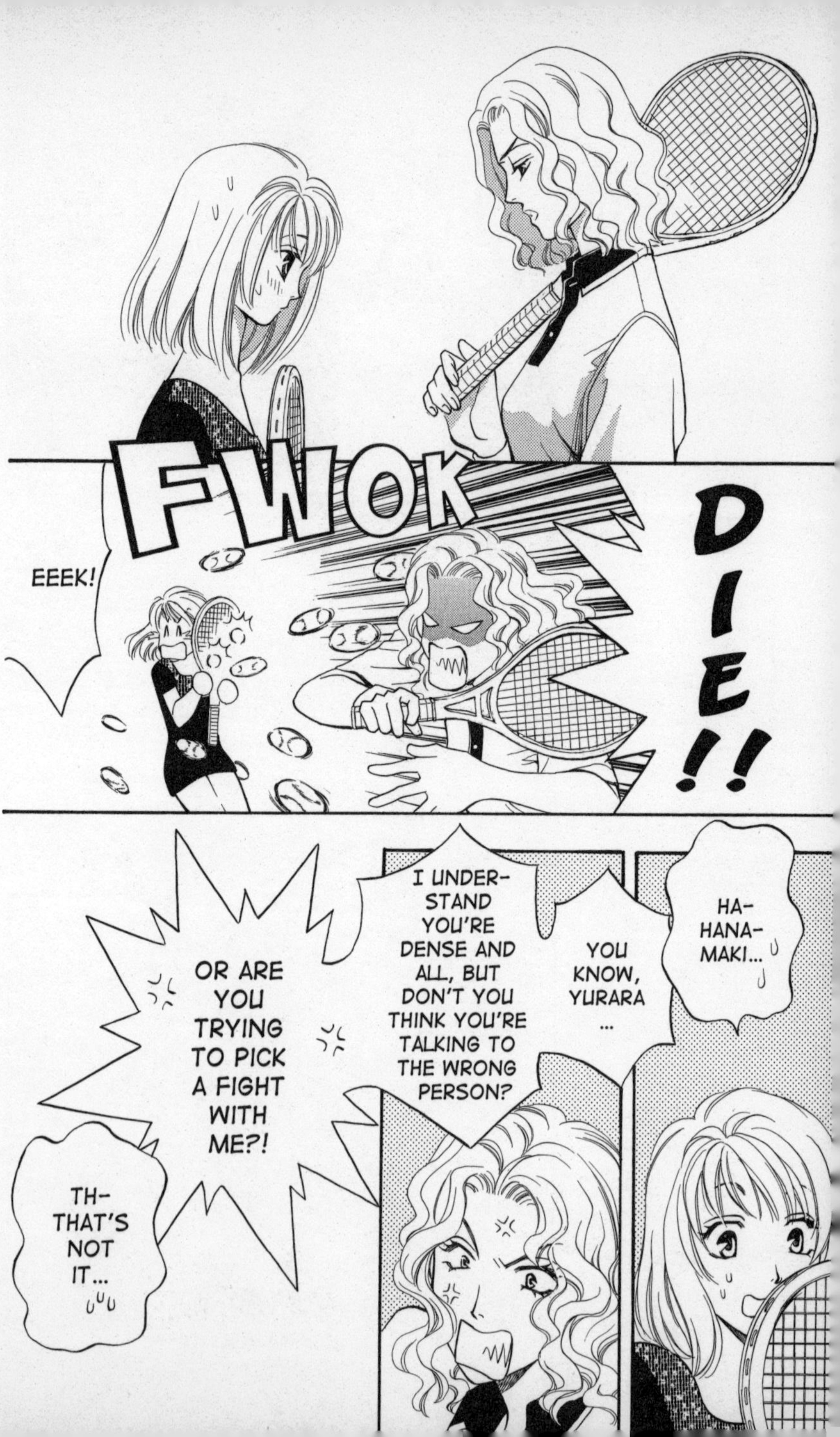
DIE!!
FWOK
EEEK!
HA-HANA-MAKI...
YOU KNOW, YURARA...
I UNDER-STAND YOU'RE DENSE AND ALL, BUT DON'T YOU THINK YOU'RE TALKING TO THE WRONG PERSON?
OR ARE YOU TRYING TO PICK A FIGHT WITH ME?!
TH-THAT'S NOT IT...

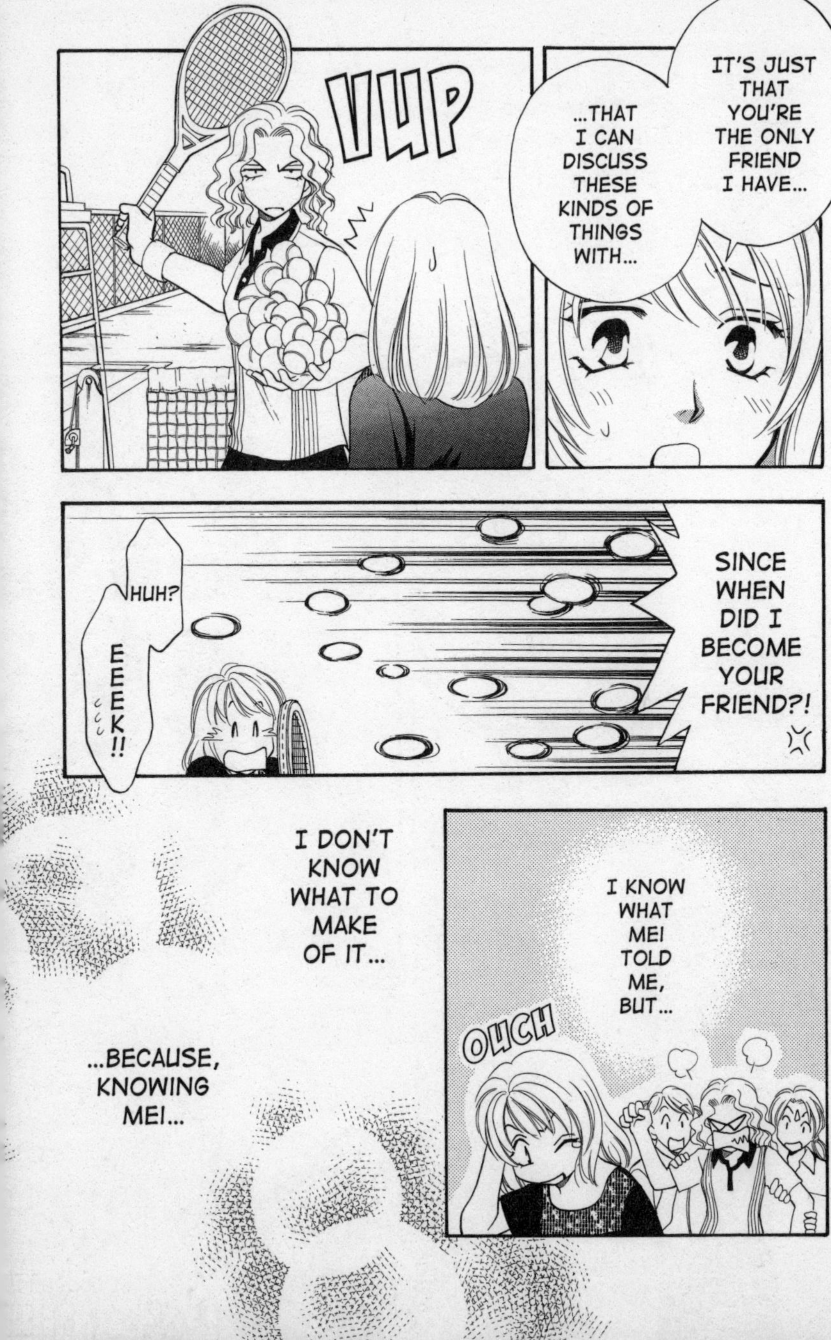
IT'S JUST THAT YOU'RE THE ONLY FRIEND I HAVE...
...THAT I CAN DISCUSS THESE KINDS OF THINGS WITH...
VUP
SINCE WHEN DID I BECOME YOUR FRIEND?!
HUH?
EEEEK!!
I KNOW WHAT MEI TOLD ME, BUT...
OUCH
I DON'T KNOW WHAT TO MAKE OF IT...
...BECAUSE, KNOWING MEI...

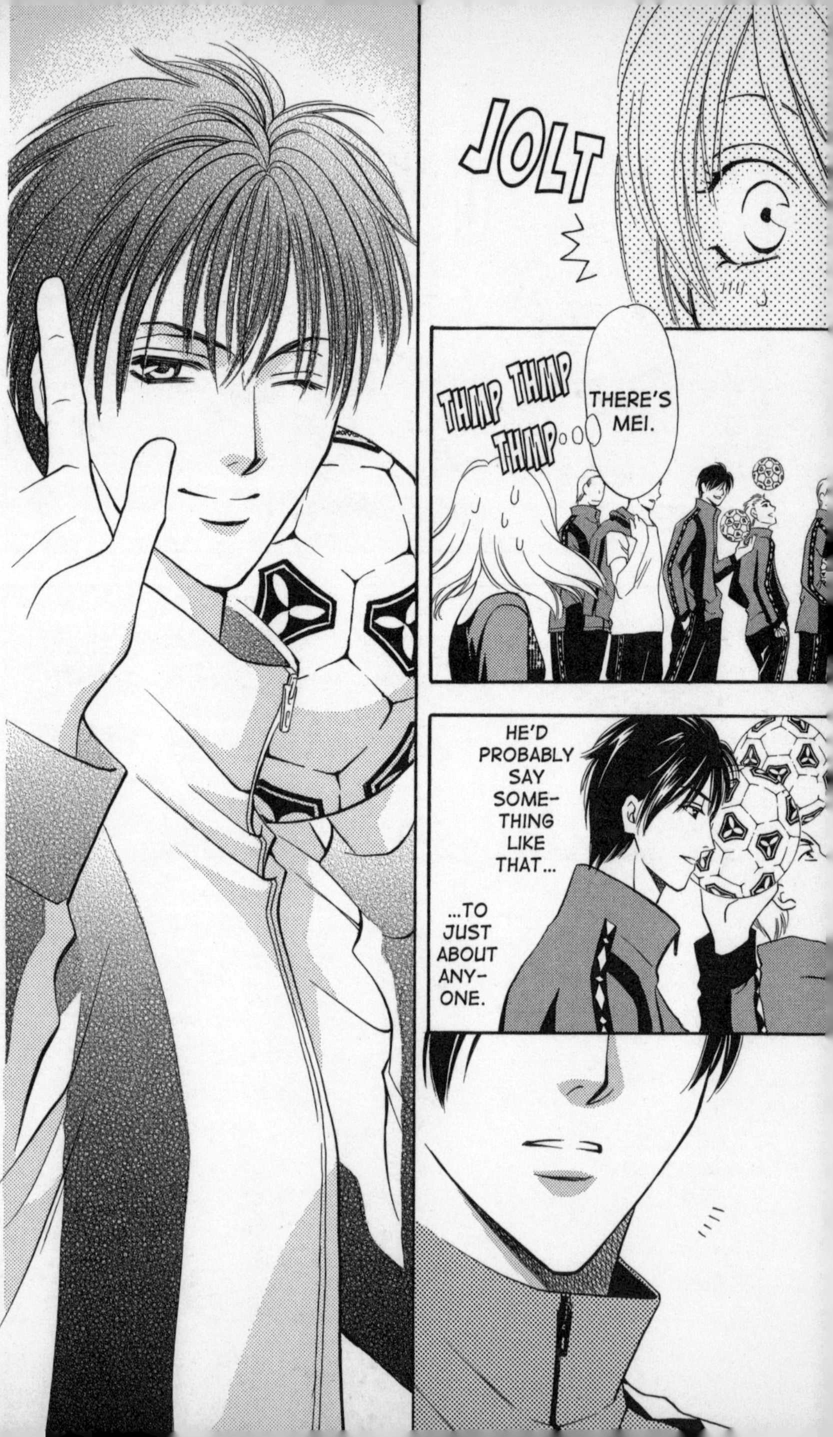
JOLT
THERE'S MEI.
THMP THMP THMP
HE'D PROBABLY SAY SOME-THING LIKE THAT...
...TO JUST ABOUT ANY-ONE.

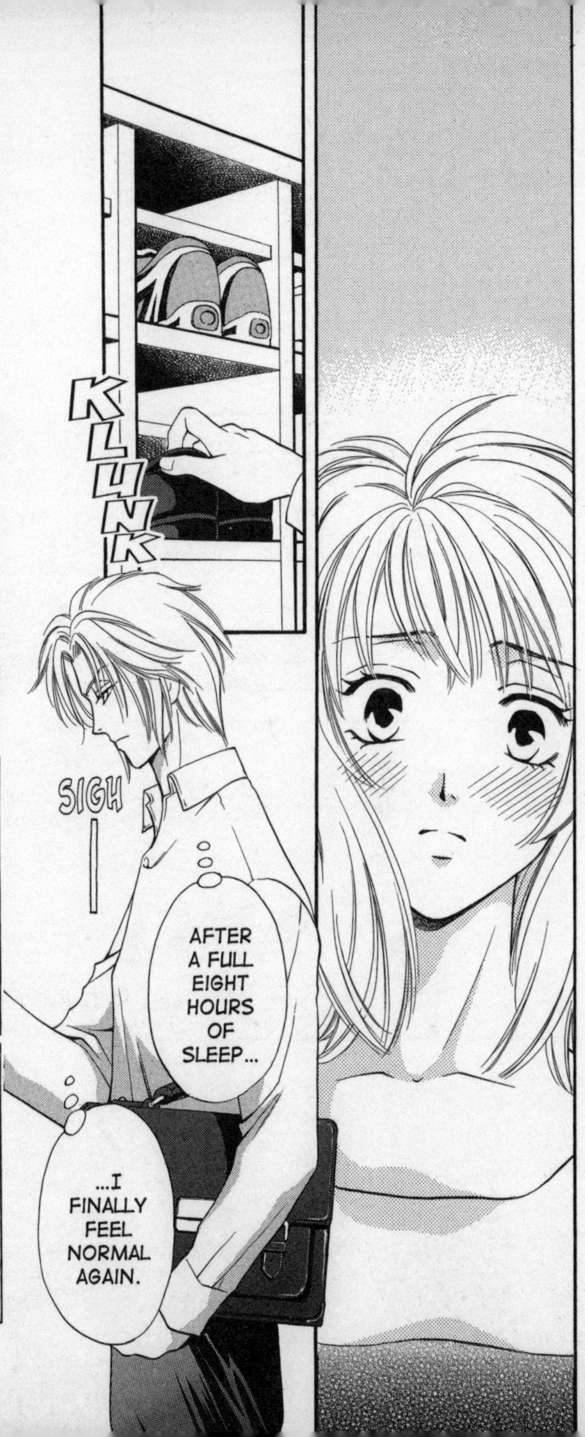
KLUNK
SIGH
AFTER A FULL EIGHT HOURS OF SLEEP...
...I FINALLY FEEL NORMAL AGAIN.

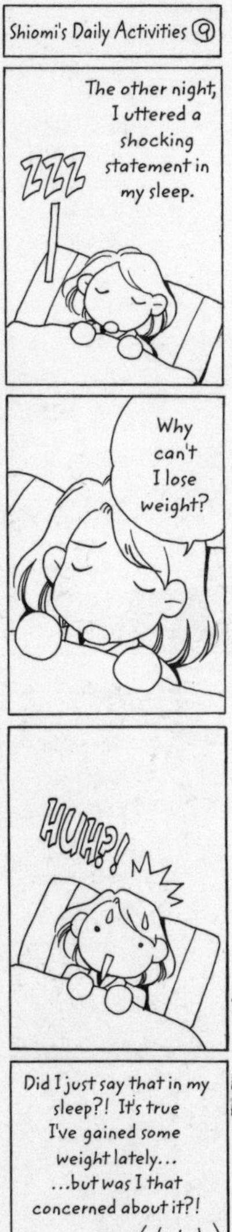
Shiomi's Daily Activities ⑨
The other night, I uttered a shocking statement in my sleep.
ZZZ
Why can't I lose weight?
HUH?!
Did I just say that in my sleep?! It's true I've gained some weight lately... ...but was I that concerned about it?!
GASP

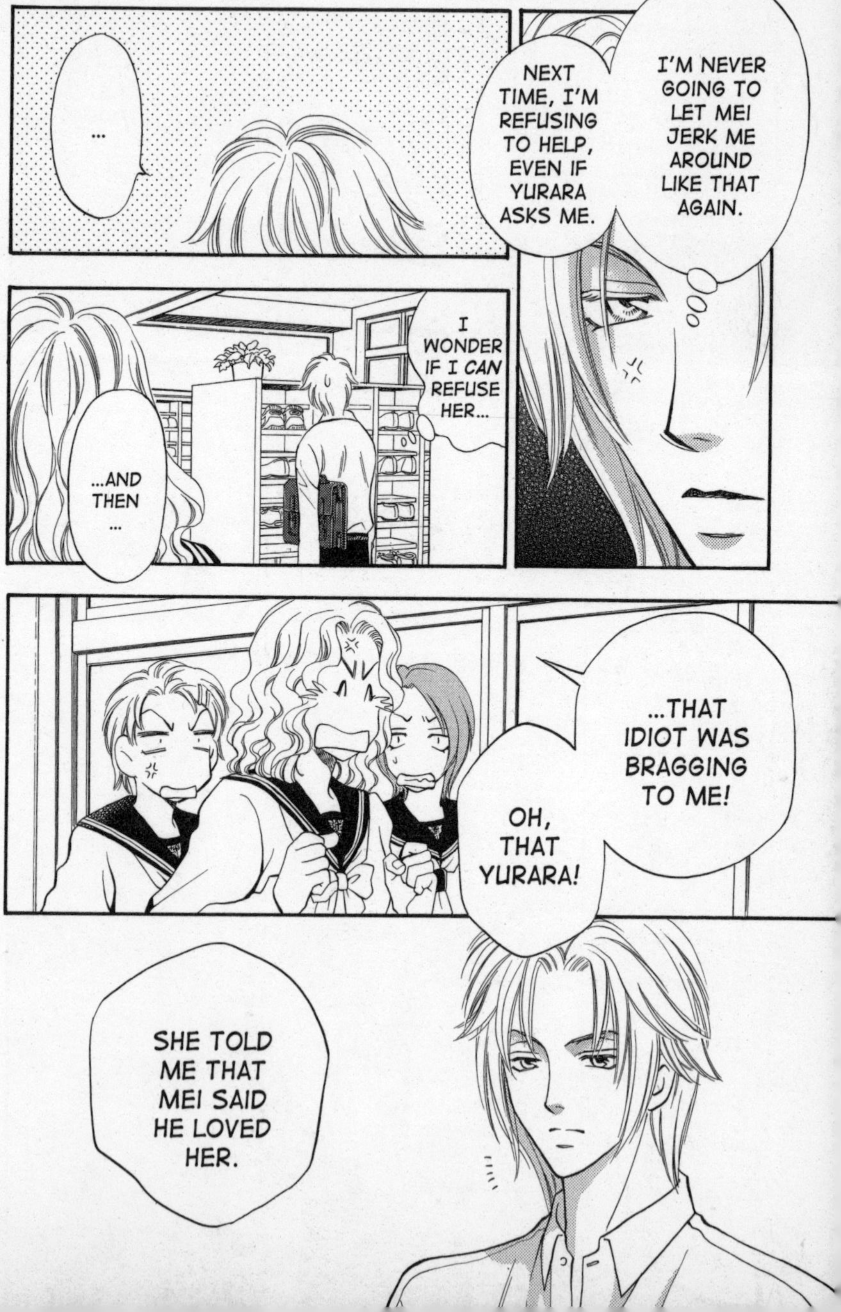
I'M NEVER GOING TO LET MEI JERK ME AROUND LIKE THAT AGAIN.
NEXT TIME, I'M REFUSING TO HELP, EVEN IF YURARA ASKS ME.
...
I WONDER IF I *CAN* REFUSE HER...
...AND THEN ...
...THAT IDIOT WAS BRAGGING TO ME!
OH, THAT YURARA!
SHE TOLD ME THAT MEI SAID HE LOVED HER.

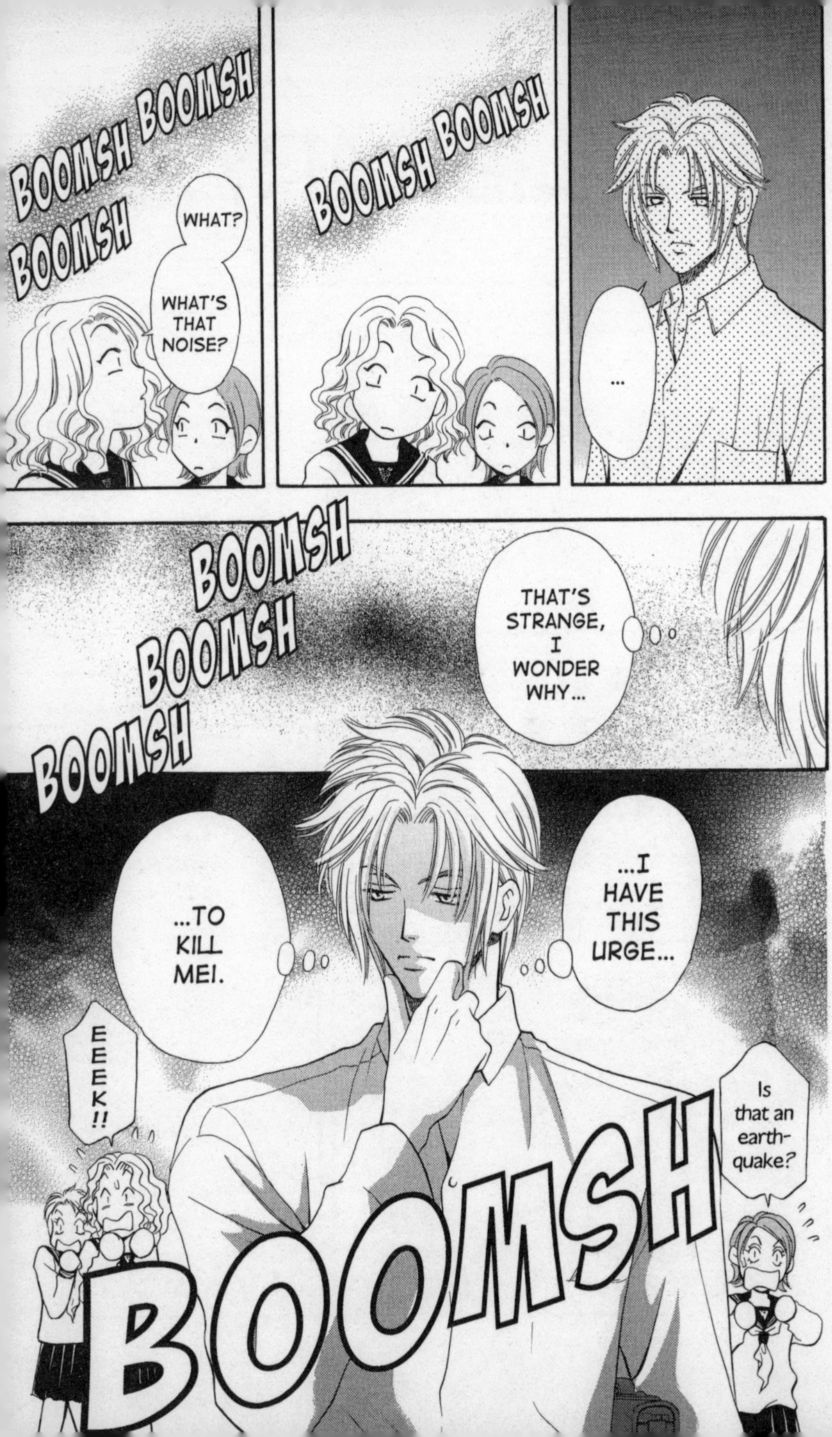
...
BOOMSH BOOMSH
BOOMSH BOOMSH BOOMSH
WHAT?
WHAT'S THAT NOISE?
THAT'S STRANGE, I WONDER WHY...
BOOMSH BOOMSH BOOMSH
...I HAVE THIS URGE...
...TO KILL MEI.
Is that an earth-quake?
BOOMSH
EEEK!!

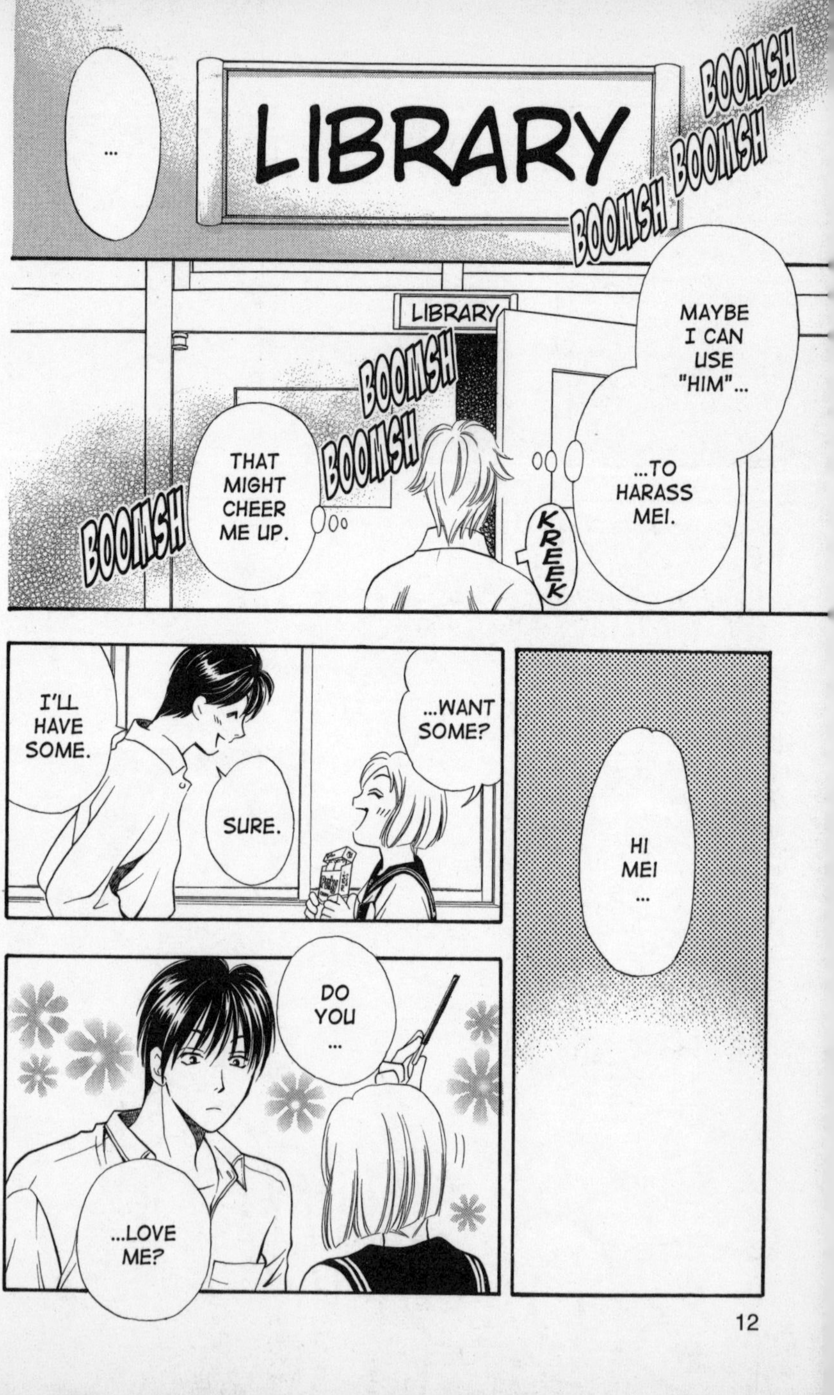
BOOMSH
BOOMSH
BOOMSH BOOMSH
LIBRARY
...
MAYBE I CAN USE "HIM"...
...TO HARASS MEI.
KREEK
LIBRARY
BOOMSH
BOOMSH
THAT MIGHT CHEER ME UP.
BOOMSH
HI MEI ...
...WANT SOME?
SURE.
I'LL HAVE SOME.
DO YOU ...
...LOVE ME?

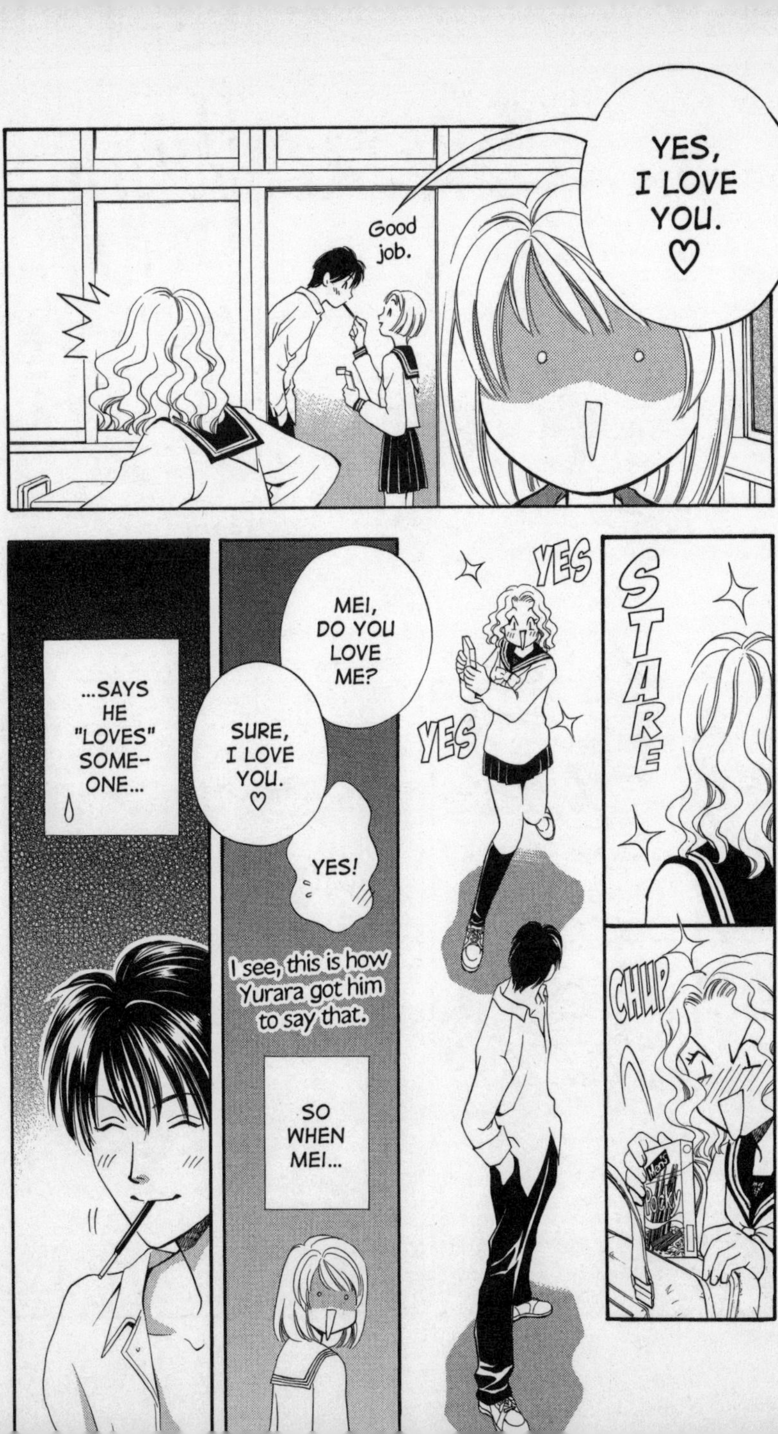
YES, I LOVE YOU. ♡
Good job.
STARE
CHUP
YES
YES
MEI, DO YOU LOVE ME?
SURE, I LOVE YOU. ♡
YES!
I see, this is how Yurara got him to say that.
SO WHEN MEI...
...SAYS HE "LOVES" SOME-ONE...

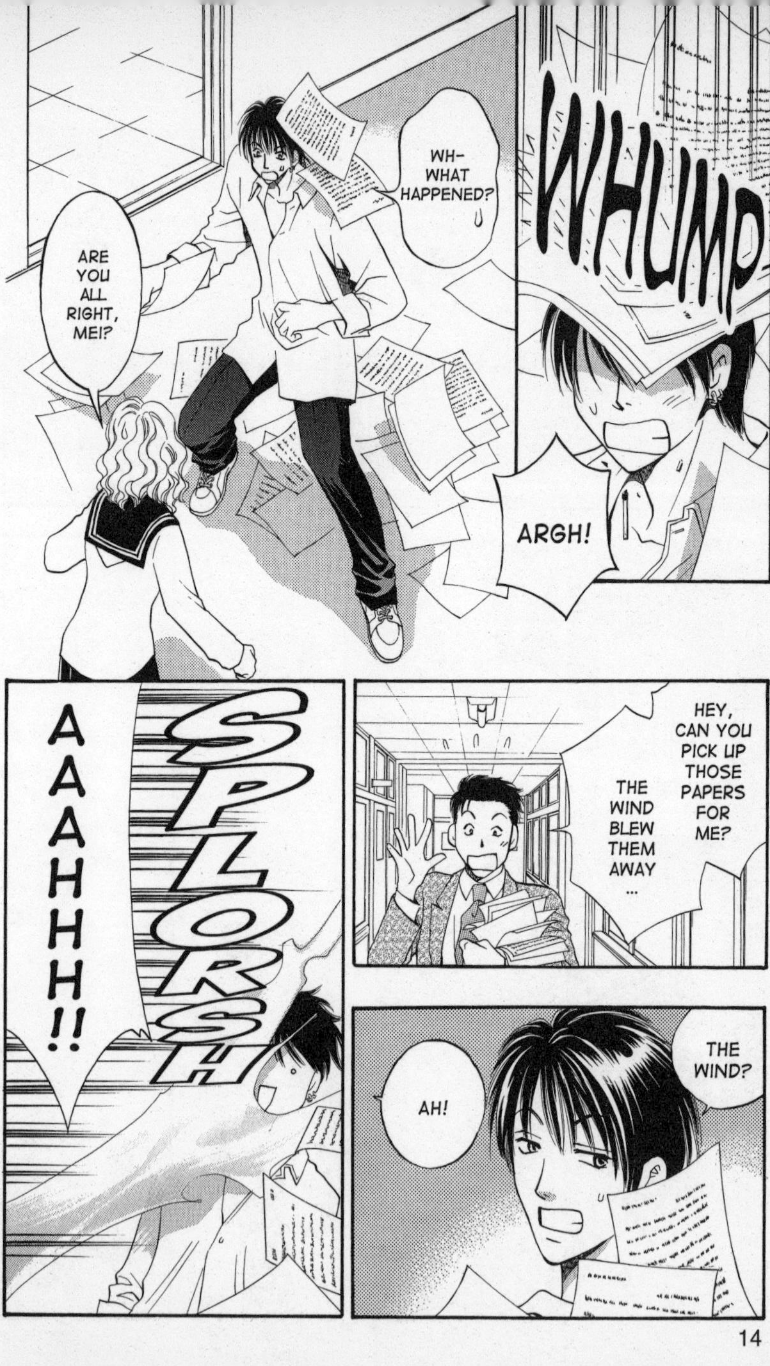
WHUMP
ARGH!
WH-WHAT HAPPENED?
ARE YOU ALL RIGHT, MEI?
HEY, CAN YOU PICK UP THOSE PAPERS FOR ME?
THE WIND BLEW THEM AWAY ...
THE WIND?
AH!
SPLORSH
AAAHHH!!

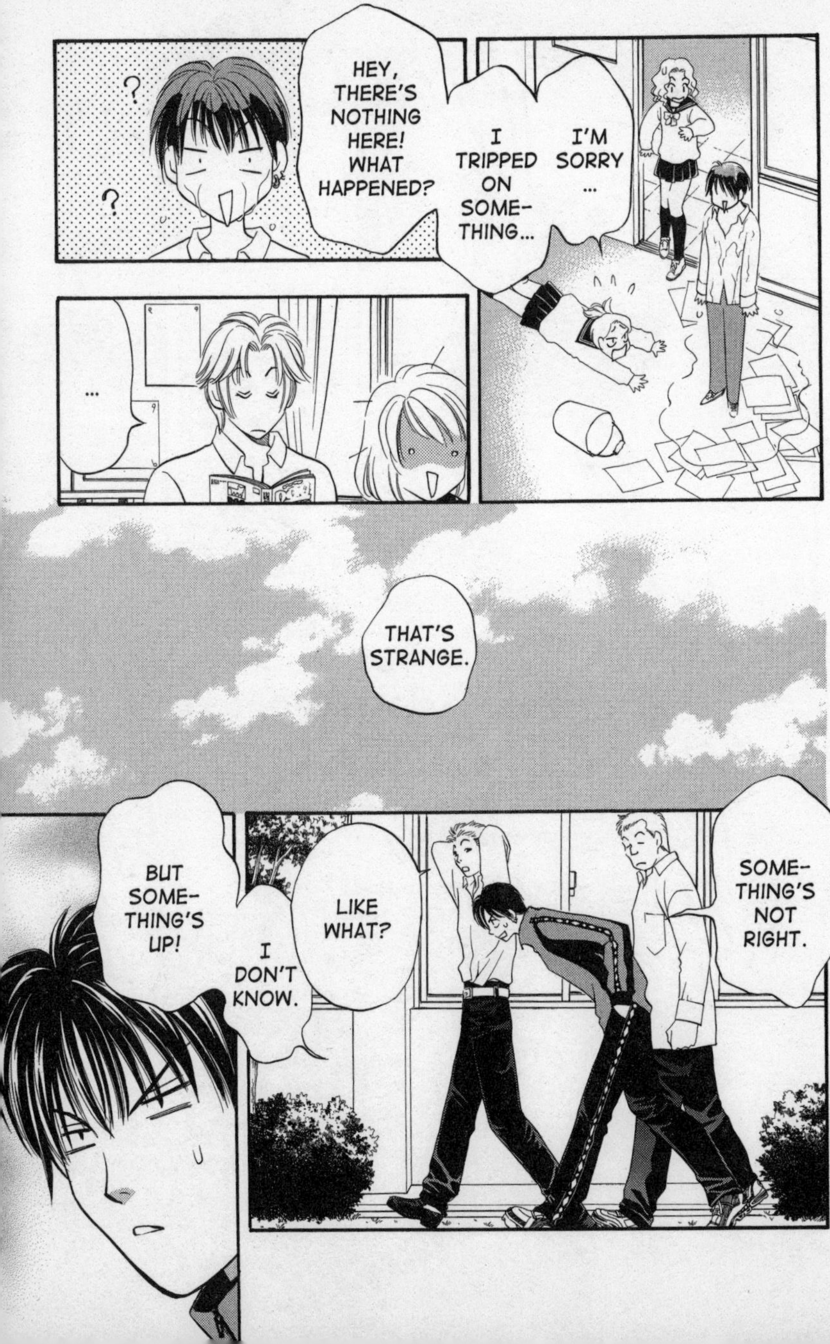
I'M SORRY ...
I TRIPPED ON SOME-THING...
HEY, THERE'S NOTHING HERE! WHAT HAPPENED?
...
THAT'S STRANGE.
SOME-THING'S NOT RIGHT.
LIKE WHAT?
BUT SOME-THING'S UP!
I DON'T KNOW.

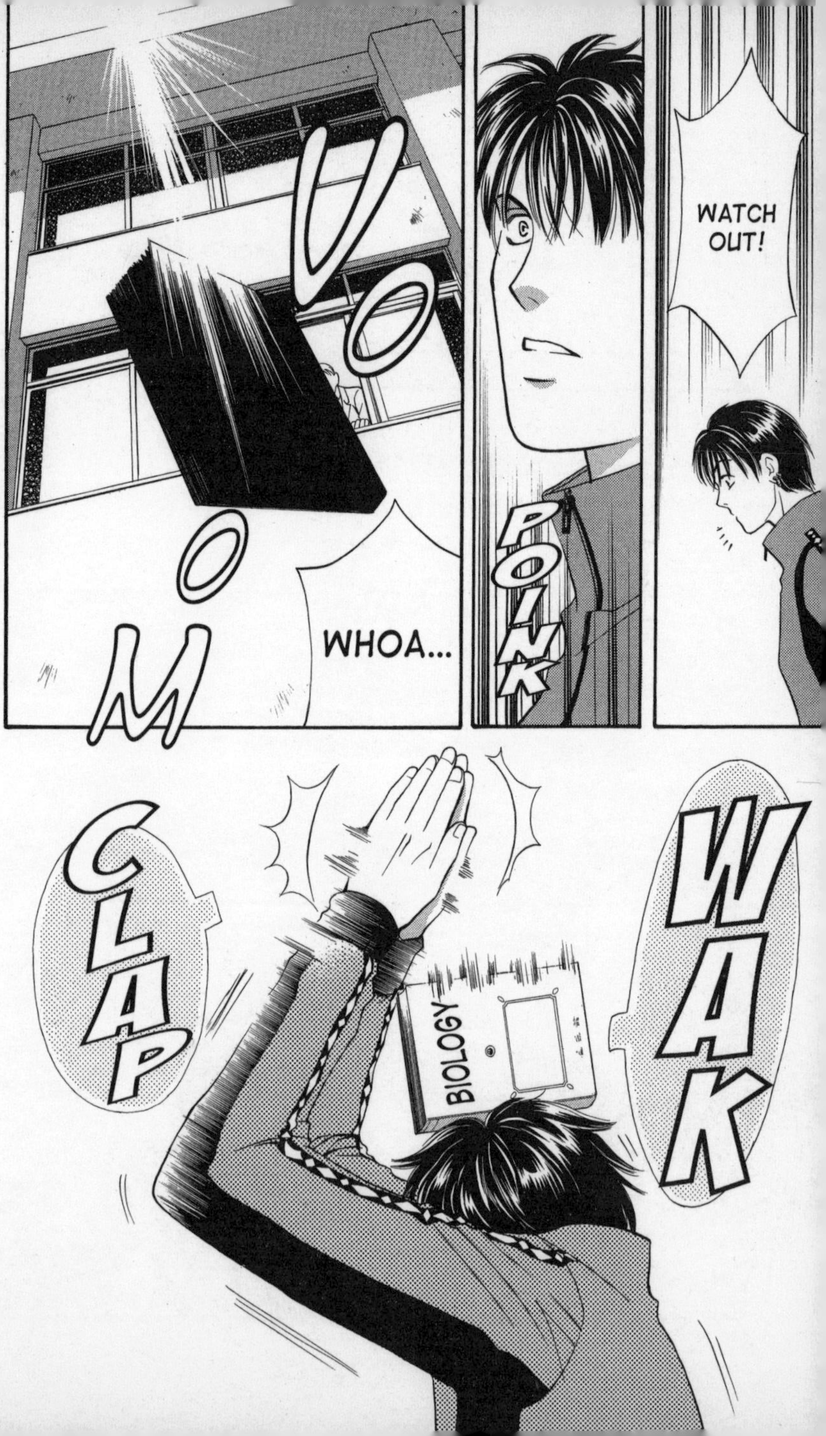
WATCH OUT!
POINK
VOOM
WHOA...
WAK
CLAP
BIOLOGY

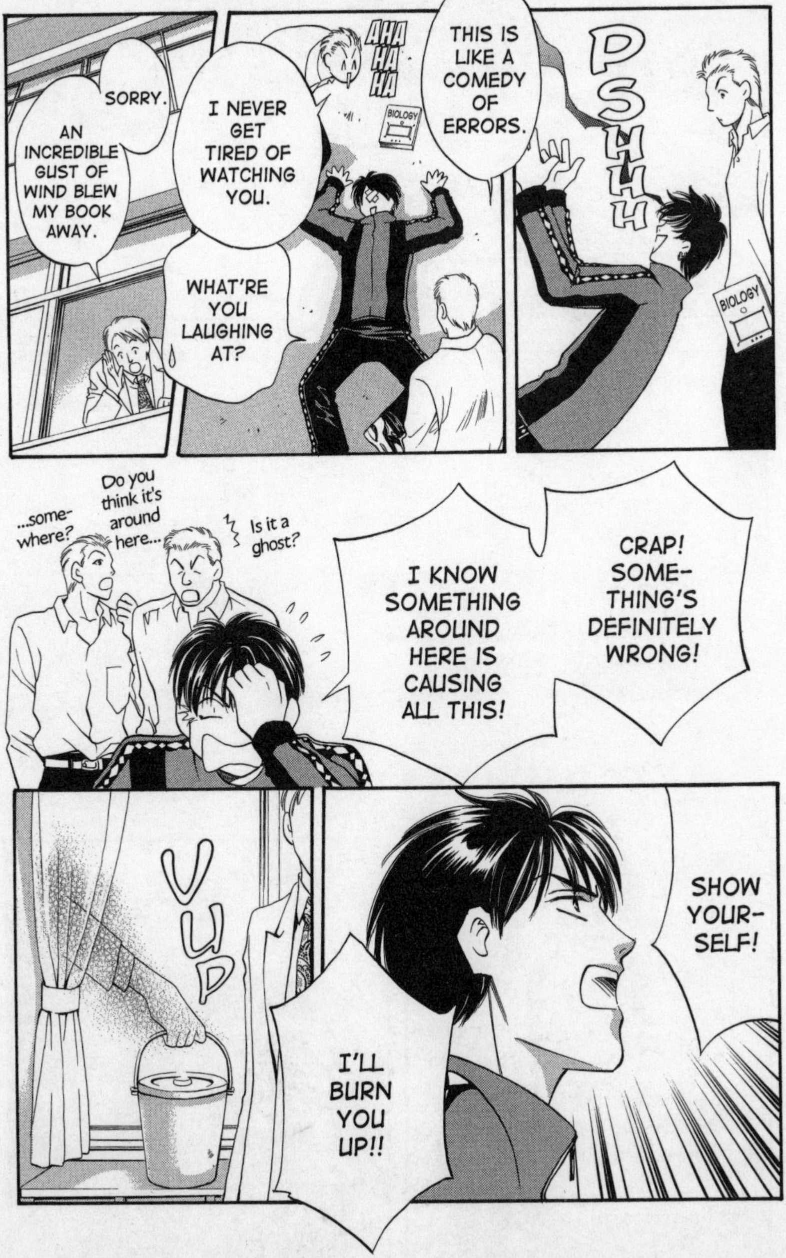
PSHHH
THIS IS LIKE A COMEDY OF ERRORS.
AHAHAHA
BIOLOGY
I NEVER GET TIRED OF WATCHING YOU.
WHAT'RE YOU LAUGHING AT?
SORRY.
AN INCREDIBLE GUST OF WIND BLEW MY BOOK AWAY.
CRAP! SOME-THING'S DEFINITELY WRONG!
I KNOW SOMETHING AROUND HERE IS CAUSING ALL THIS!
Is it a ghost?
Do you think it's around here...
...some-where?
SHOW YOUR-SELF!
I'LL BURN YOU UP!!
VUD

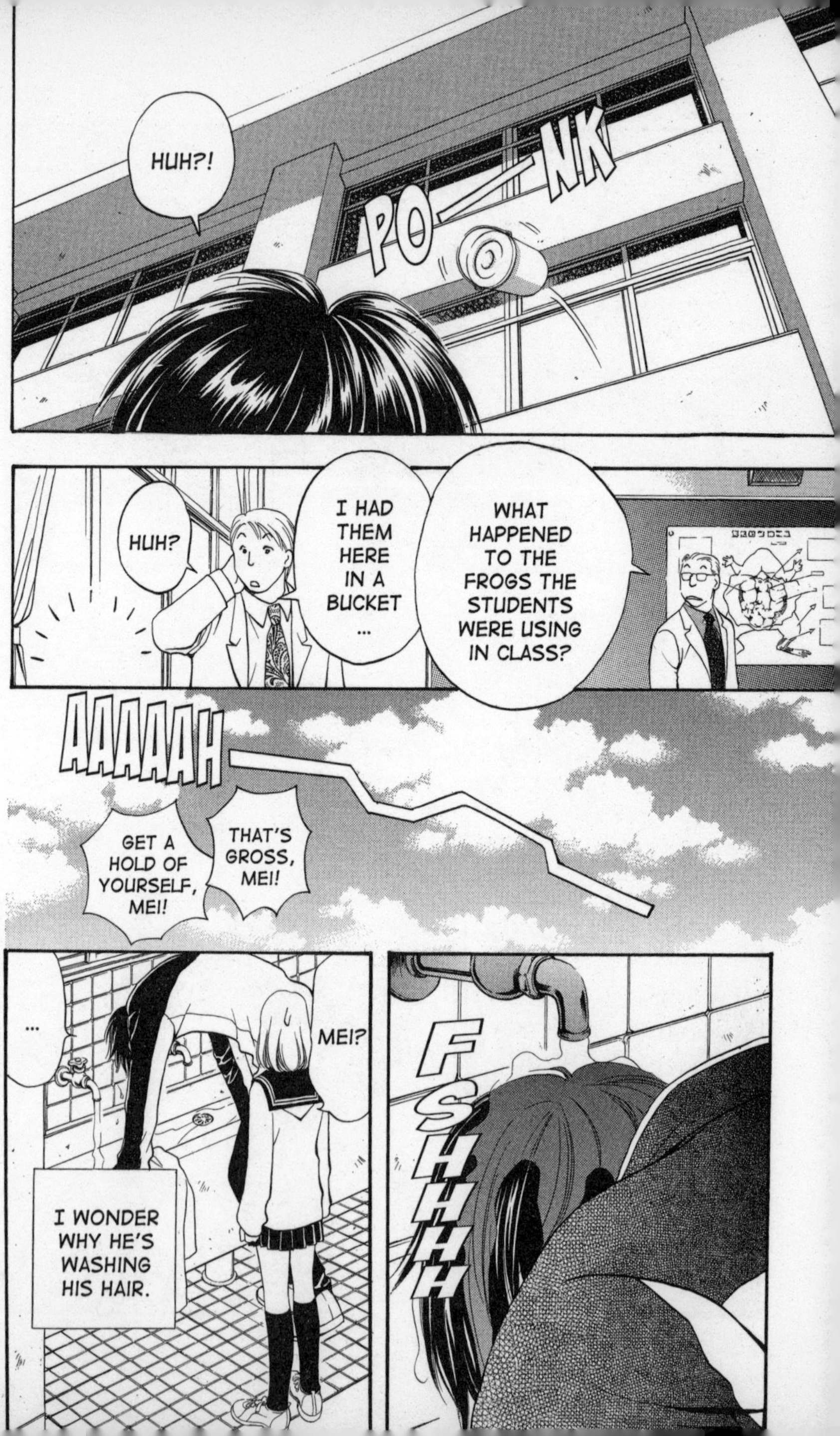
PO—NK
HUH?!
WHAT HAPPENED TO THE FROGS THE STUDENTS WERE USING IN CLASS?
I HAD THEM HERE IN A BUCKET ...
HUH?
AAAAAH
THAT'S GROSS, MEI!
GET A HOLD OF YOURSELF, MEI!
FSHHHHH
MEI?
...
I WONDER WHY HE'S WASHING HIS HAIR.

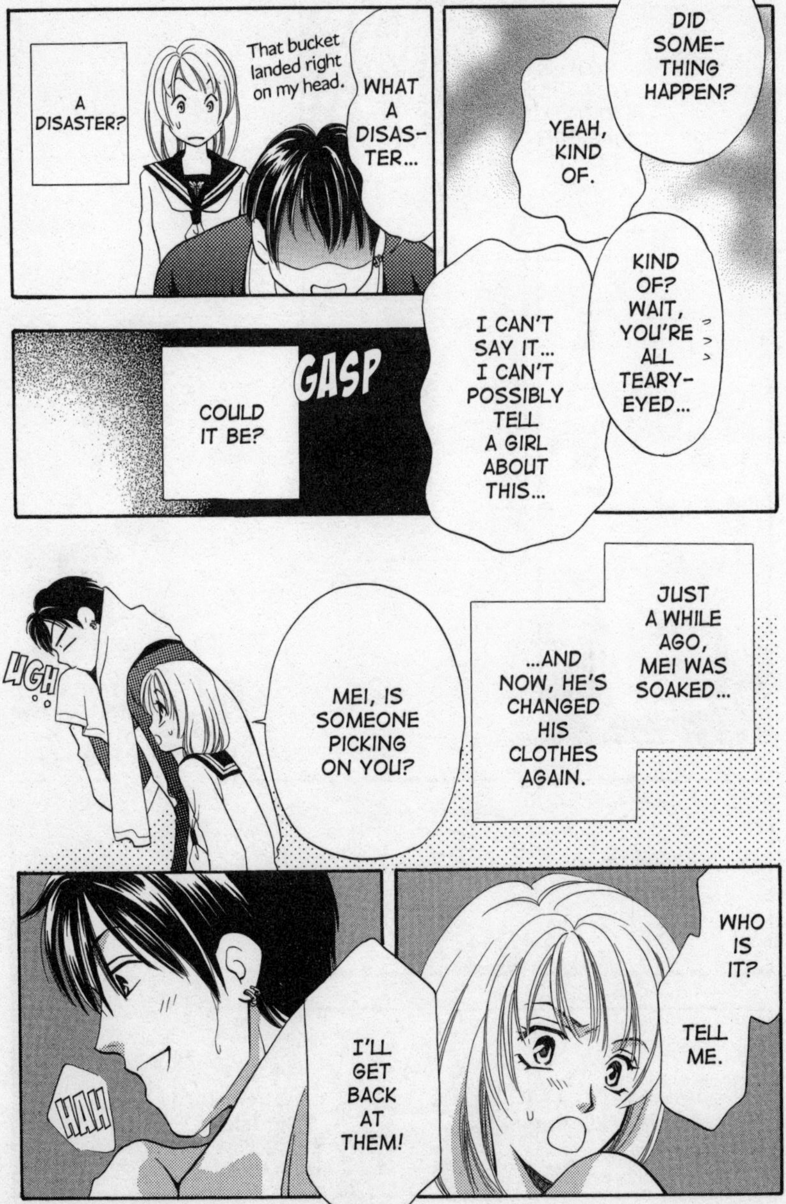

DID SOMETHING HAPPEN?
YEAH, KIND OF.
KIND OF? WAIT, YOU'RE ALL TEARY-EYED...
I CAN'T SAY IT... I CAN'T POSSIBLY TELL A GIRL ABOUT THIS...
WHAT A DISASTER...
That bucket landed right on my head.
A DISASTER?
GASP
COULD IT BE?
JUST A WHILE AGO, MEI WAS SOAKED...
...AND NOW, HE'S CHANGED HIS CLOTHES AGAIN.
MEI, IS SOMEONE PICKING ON YOU?
UGH
WHO IS IT?
TELL ME.
I'LL GET BACK AT THEM!
HAH

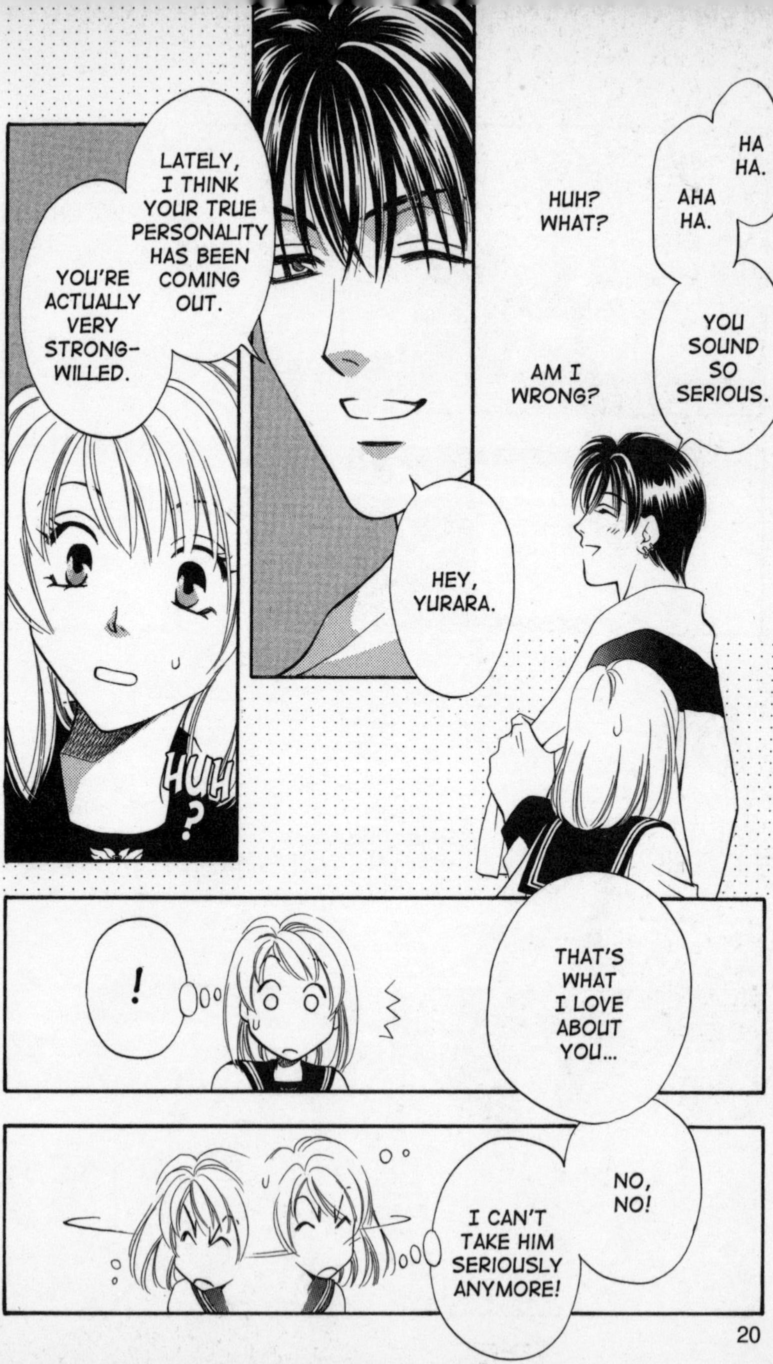

HA HA. AHA HA.
YOU SOUND SO SERIOUS.
HUH? WHAT?
AM I WRONG?
HEY, YURARA.
LATELY, I THINK YOUR TRUE PERSONALITY HAS BEEN COMING OUT.
YOU'RE ACTUALLY VERY STRONG-WILLED.
HUH?
THAT'S WHAT I LOVE ABOUT YOU...
!
NO, NO!
I CAN'T TAKE HIM SERIOUSLY ANYMORE!

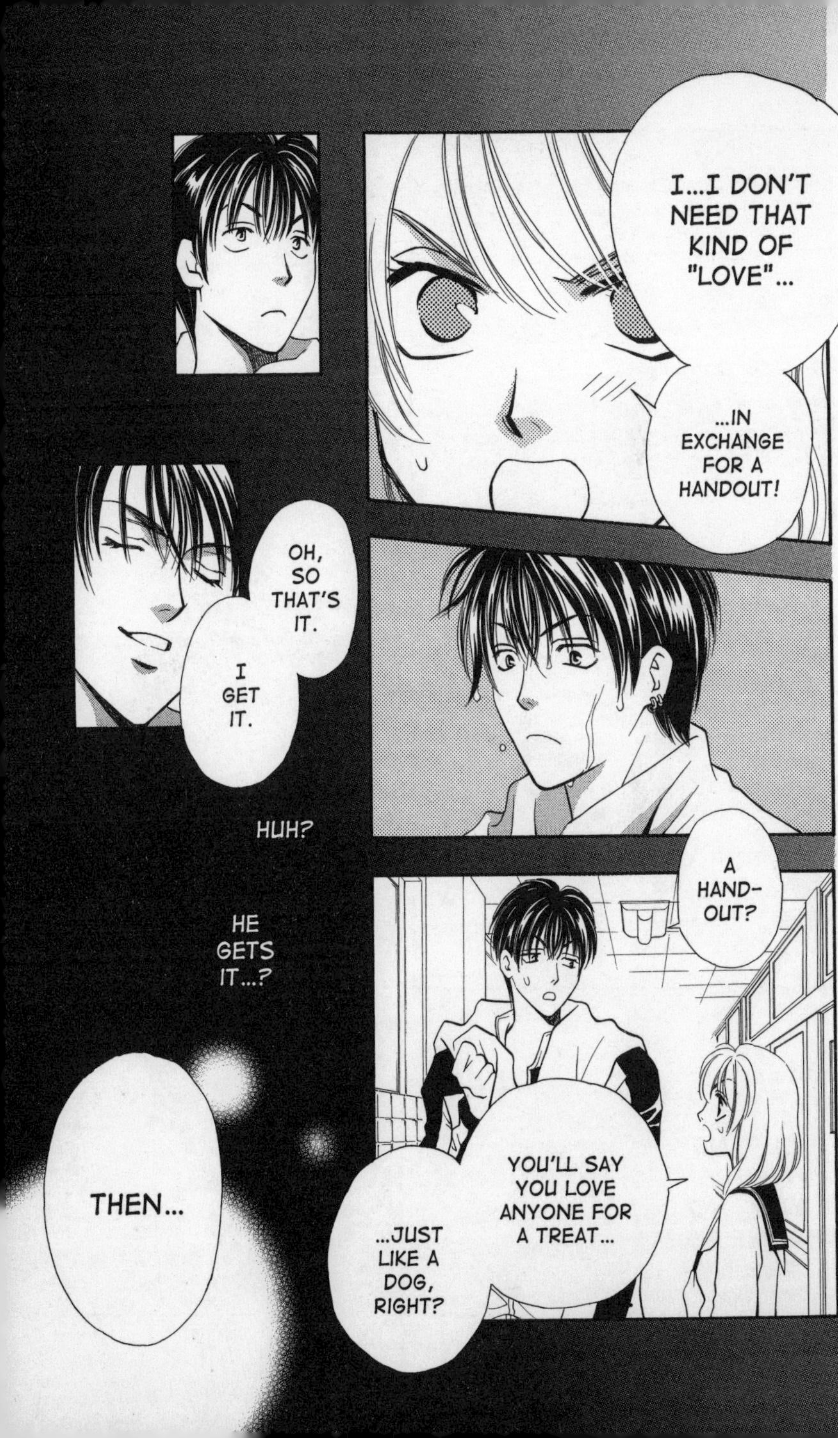
I...I DON'T NEED THAT KIND OF "LOVE"...
...IN EXCHANGE FOR A HANDOUT!
OH, SO THAT'S IT.
I GET IT.
HUH?
HE GETS IT...?
A HAND-OUT?
YOU'LL SAY YOU LOVE ANYONE FOR A TREAT...
...JUST LIKE A DOG, RIGHT?
THEN...

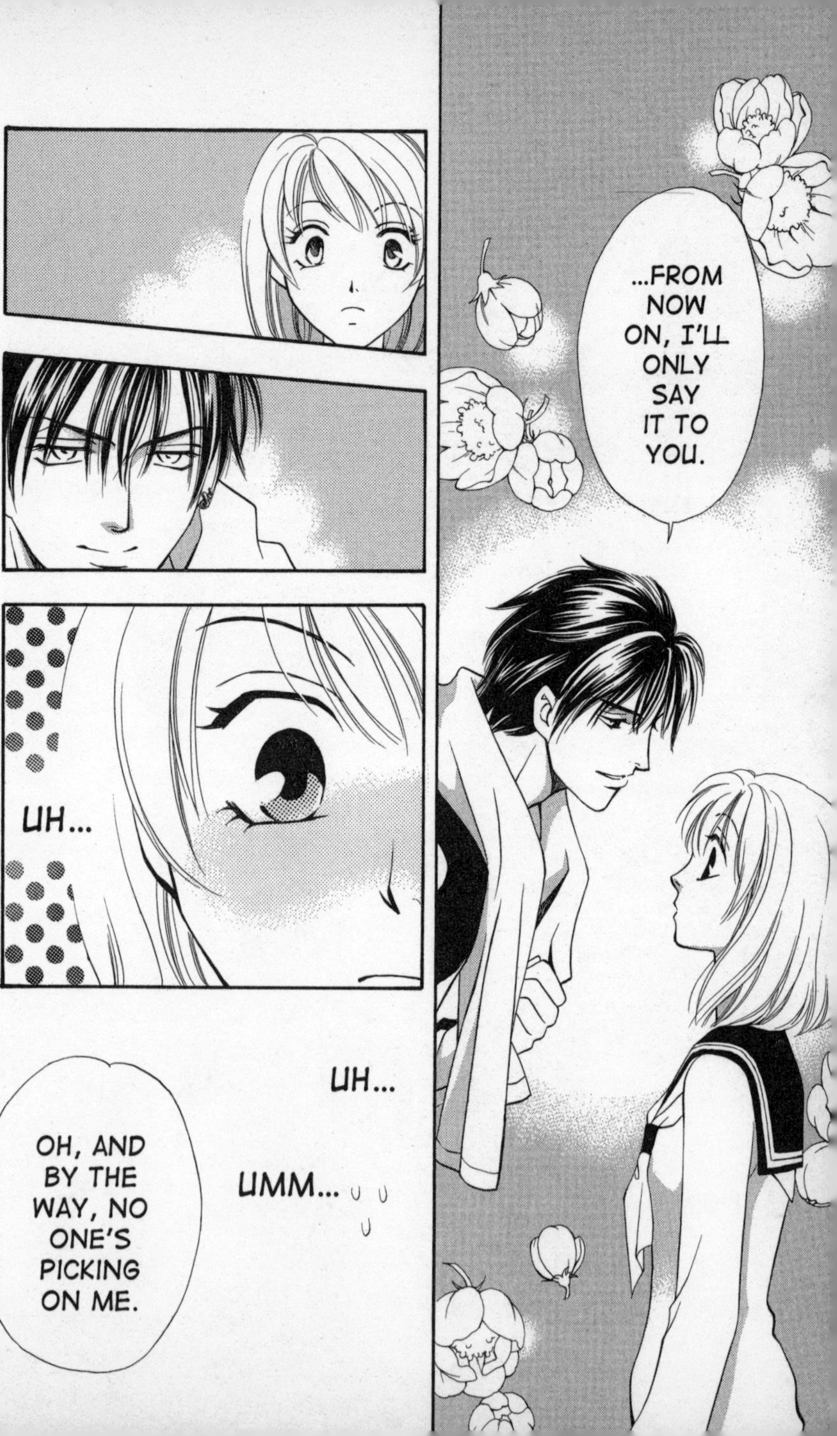
...FROM NOW ON, I'LL ONLY SAY IT TO YOU.
UH...
UH...
UMM...
OH, AND BY THE WAY, NO ONE'S PICKING ON ME.

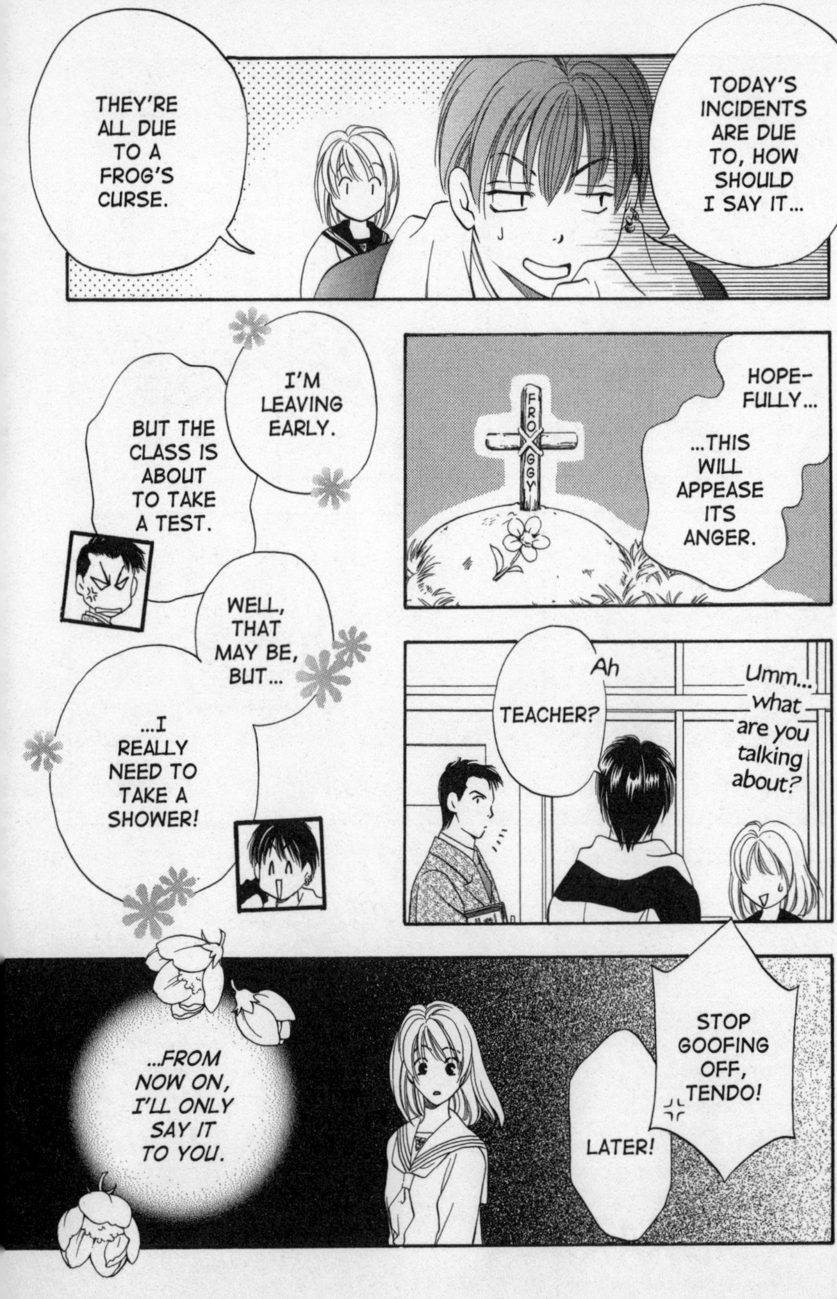
TODAY'S INCIDENTS ARE DUE TO, HOW SHOULD I SAY IT...
THEY'RE ALL DUE TO A FROG'S CURSE.
HOPE-FULLY...
...THIS WILL APPEASE ITS ANGER.
FROGGY
Umm... what are you talking about?
Ah
TEACHER?
I'M LEAVING EARLY.
BUT THE CLASS IS ABOUT TO TAKE A TEST.
WELL, THAT MAY BE, BUT...
...I REALLY NEED TO TAKE A SHOWER!
STOP GOOFING OFF, TENDO!
LATER!
...FROM NOW ON, I'LL ONLY SAY IT TO YOU.

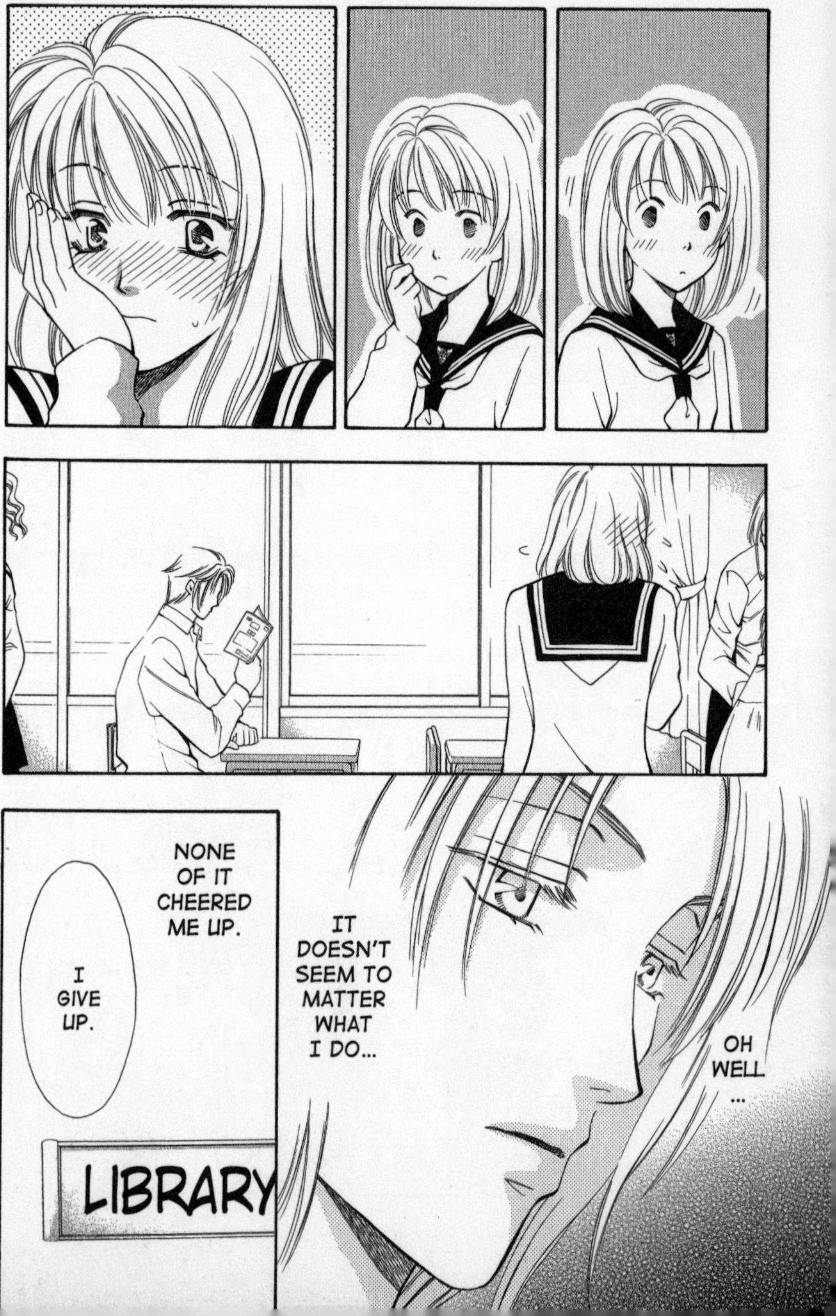
OH WELL ...
IT DOESN'T SEEM TO MATTER WHAT I DO...
NONE OF IT CHEERED ME UP.
I GIVE UP.
LIBRARY

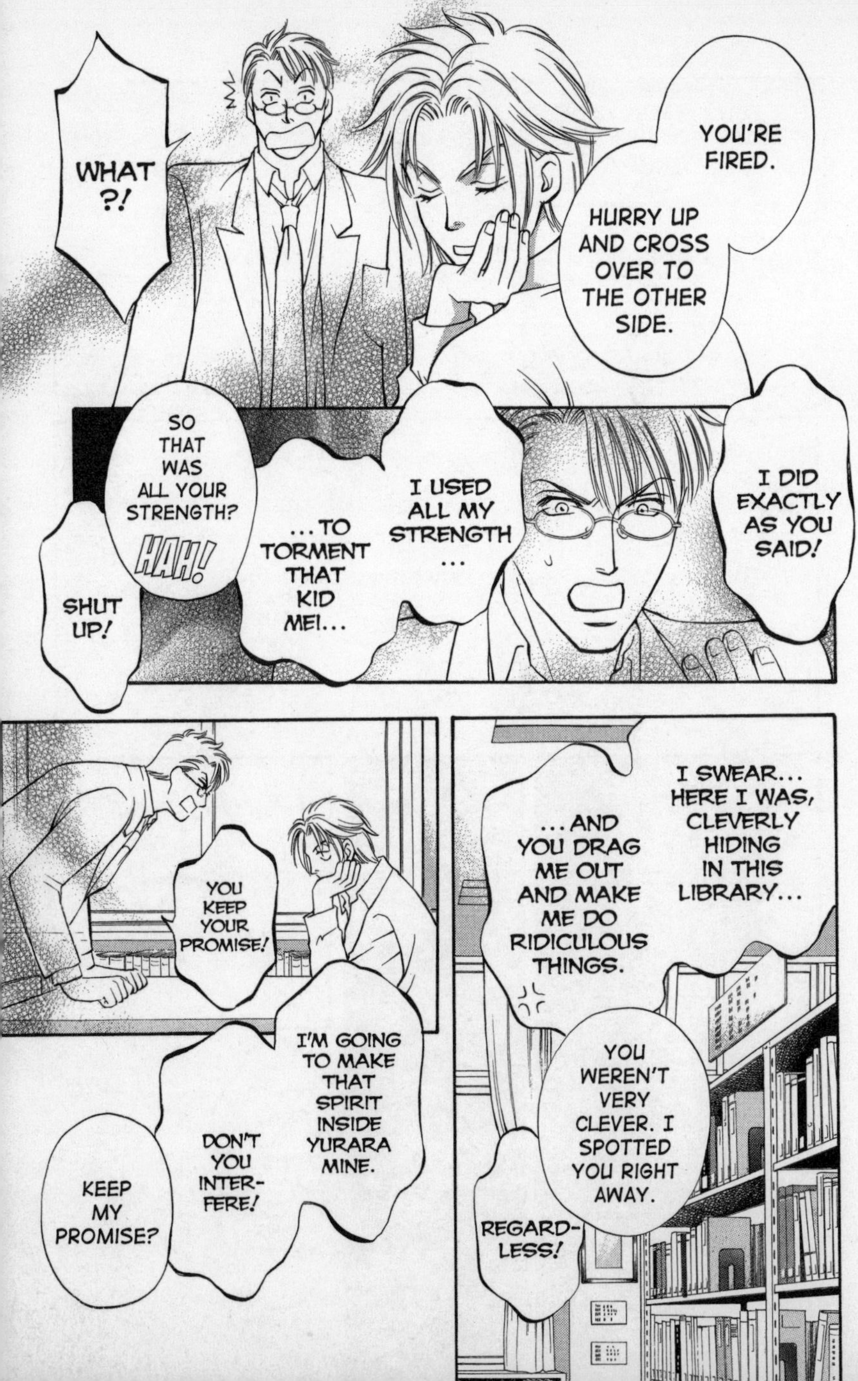
YOU'RE FIRED.
HURRY UP AND CROSS OVER TO THE OTHER SIDE.
WHAT?!
I DID EXACTLY AS YOU SAID!
I USED ALL MY STRENGTH ...
...TO TORMENT THAT KID MEI...
SO THAT WAS ALL YOUR STRENGTH?
HAH!
SHUT UP!
I SWEAR... HERE I WAS, CLEVERLY HIDING IN THIS LIBRARY...
...AND YOU DRAG ME OUT AND MAKE ME DO RIDICULOUS THINGS.
YOU WEREN'T VERY CLEVER. I SPOTTED YOU RIGHT AWAY.
REGARDLESS!
YOU KEEP YOUR PROMISE!
I'M GOING TO MAKE THAT SPIRIT INSIDE YURARA MINE.
DON'T YOU INTERFERE!
KEEP MY PROMISE?

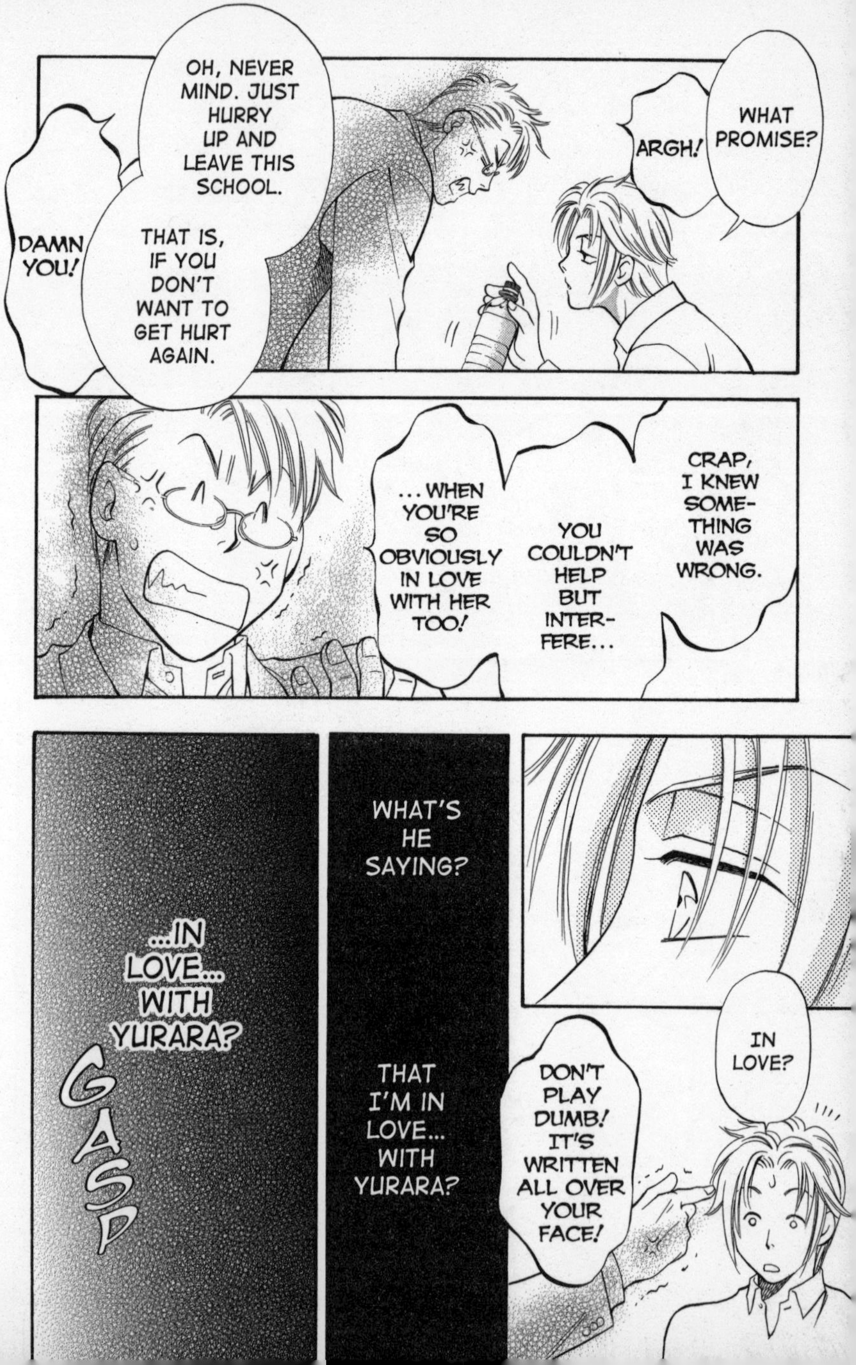
WHAT PROMISE?
ARGH!
DAMN YOU!
OH, NEVER MIND. JUST HURRY UP AND LEAVE THIS SCHOOL.
THAT IS, IF YOU DON'T WANT TO GET HURT AGAIN.
CRAP, I KNEW SOME-THING WAS WRONG.
YOU COULDN'T HELP BUT INTER-FERE...
...WHEN YOU'RE SO OBVIOUSLY IN LOVE WITH HER TOO!
IN LOVE?
DON'T PLAY DUMB! IT'S WRITTEN ALL OVER YOUR FACE!
WHAT'S HE SAYING?
THAT I'M IN LOVE... WITH YURARA?
...IN LOVE... WITH YURARA?
GASP

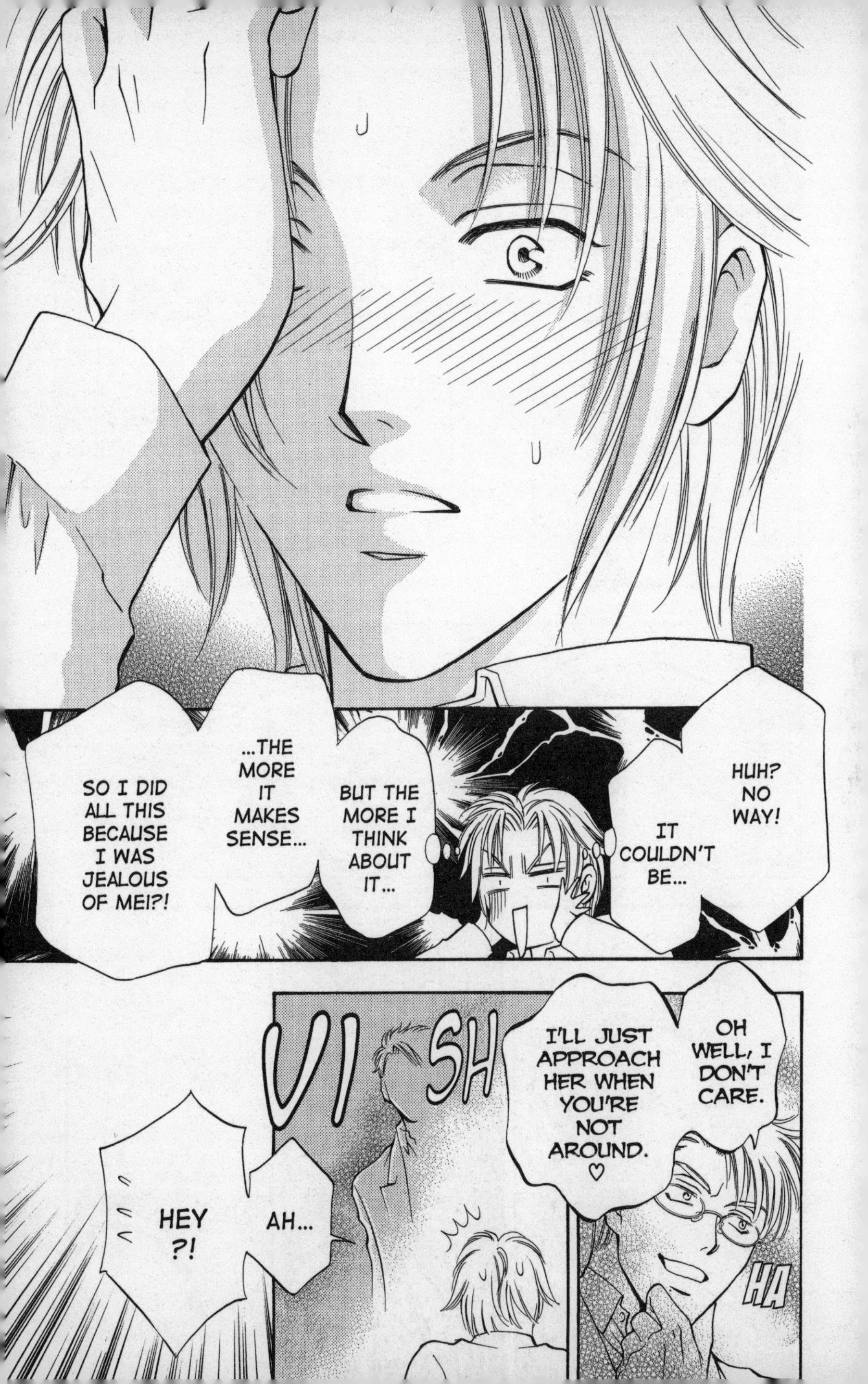
HUH? NO WAY!
IT COULDN'T BE...
BUT THE MORE I THINK ABOUT IT...
...THE MORE IT MAKES SENSE...
SO I DID ALL THIS BECAUSE I WAS JEALOUS OF MEI?!
OH WELL, I DON'T CARE.
I'LL JUST APPROACH HER WHEN YOU'RE NOT AROUND. ♡
HA
VISH
AH...
HEY?!

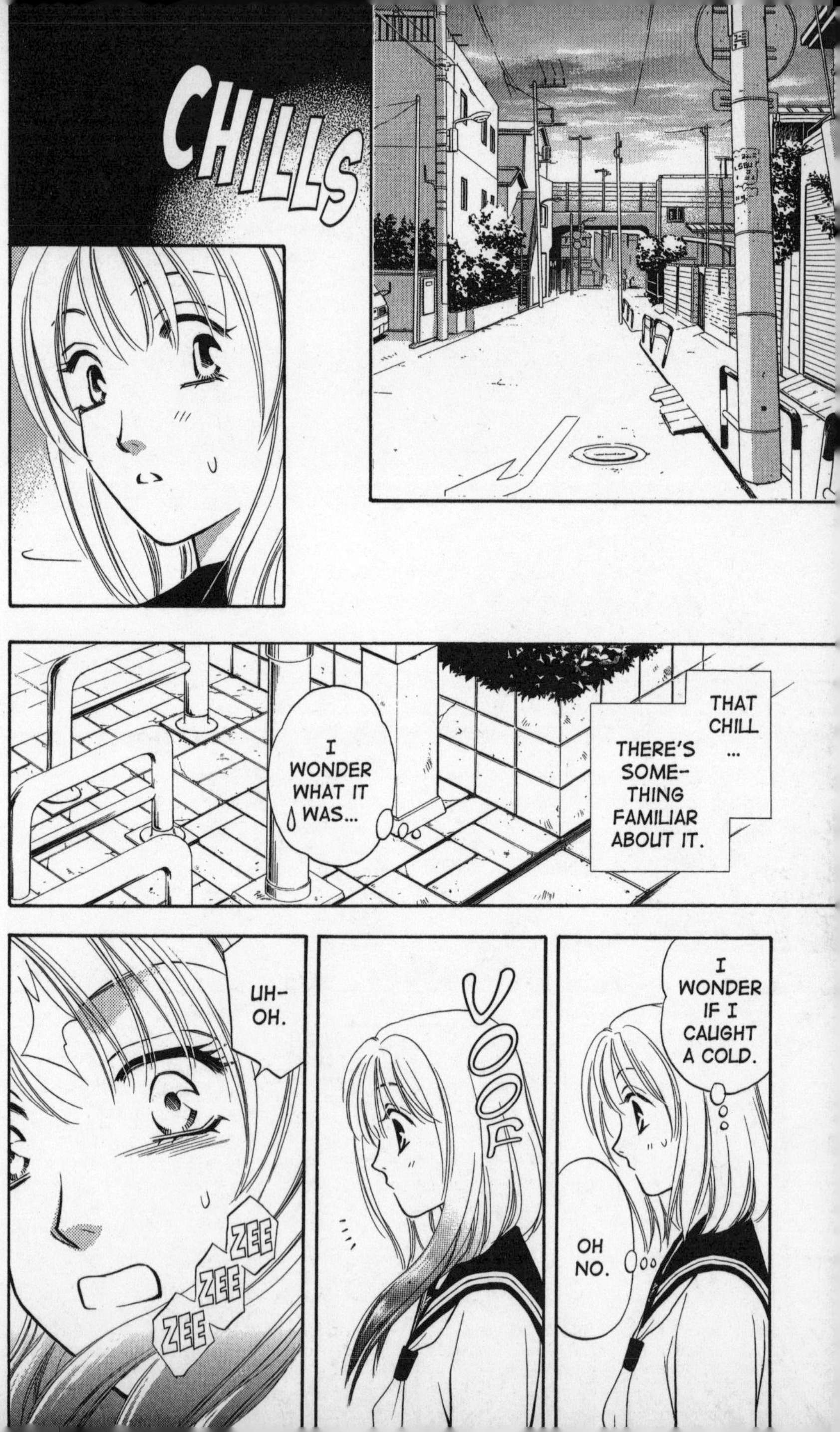
CHILLS
THAT CHILL ...
THERE'S SOMETHING FAMILIAR ABOUT IT.
I WONDER WHAT IT WAS...
I WONDER IF I CAUGHT A COLD.
OH NO.
VOOF
UH-OH.
ZEE
ZEE
ZEE

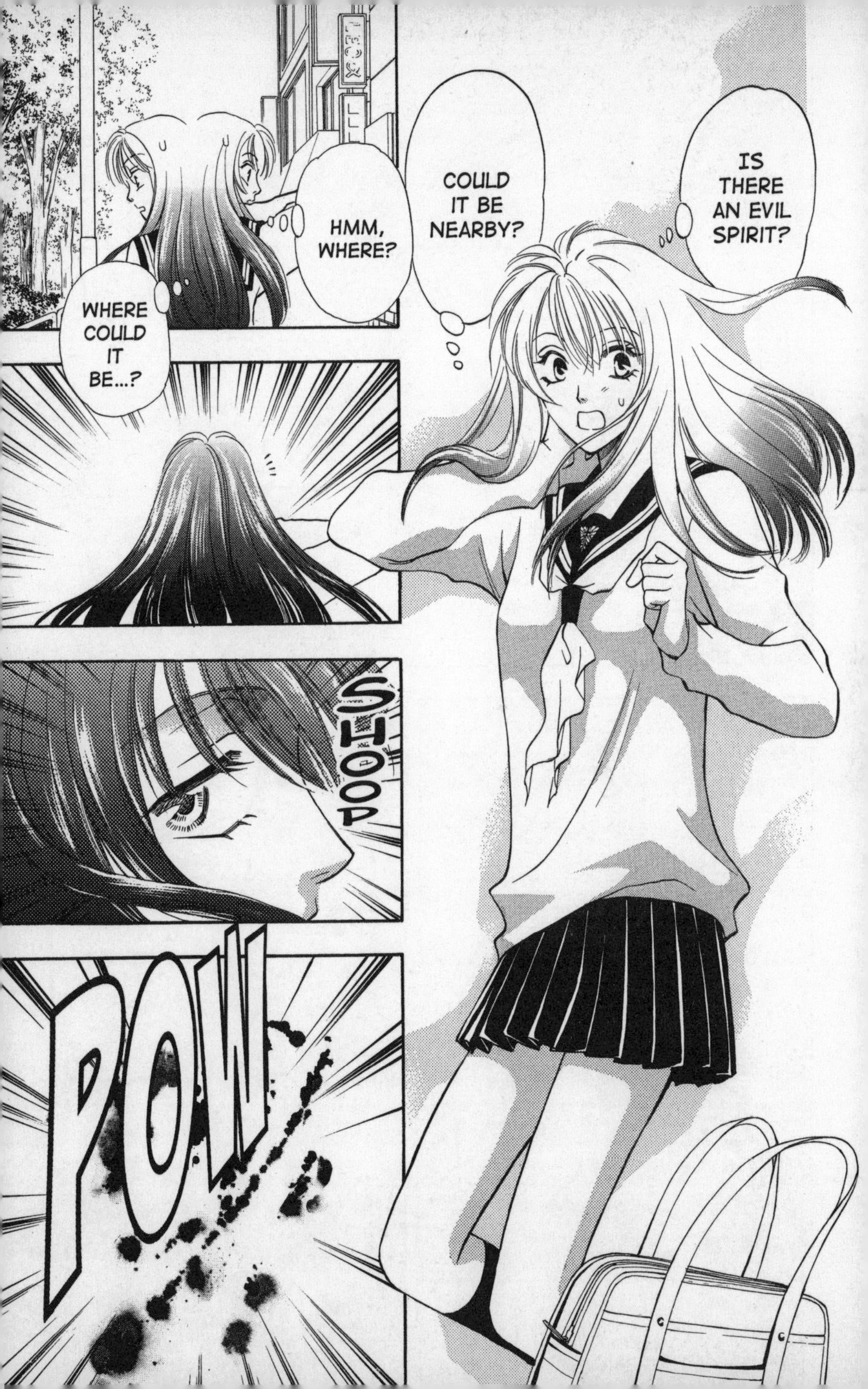
IS THERE AN EVIL SPIRIT?
COULD IT BE NEARBY?
HMM, WHERE?
WHERE COULD IT BE...?
SHOOP
POW

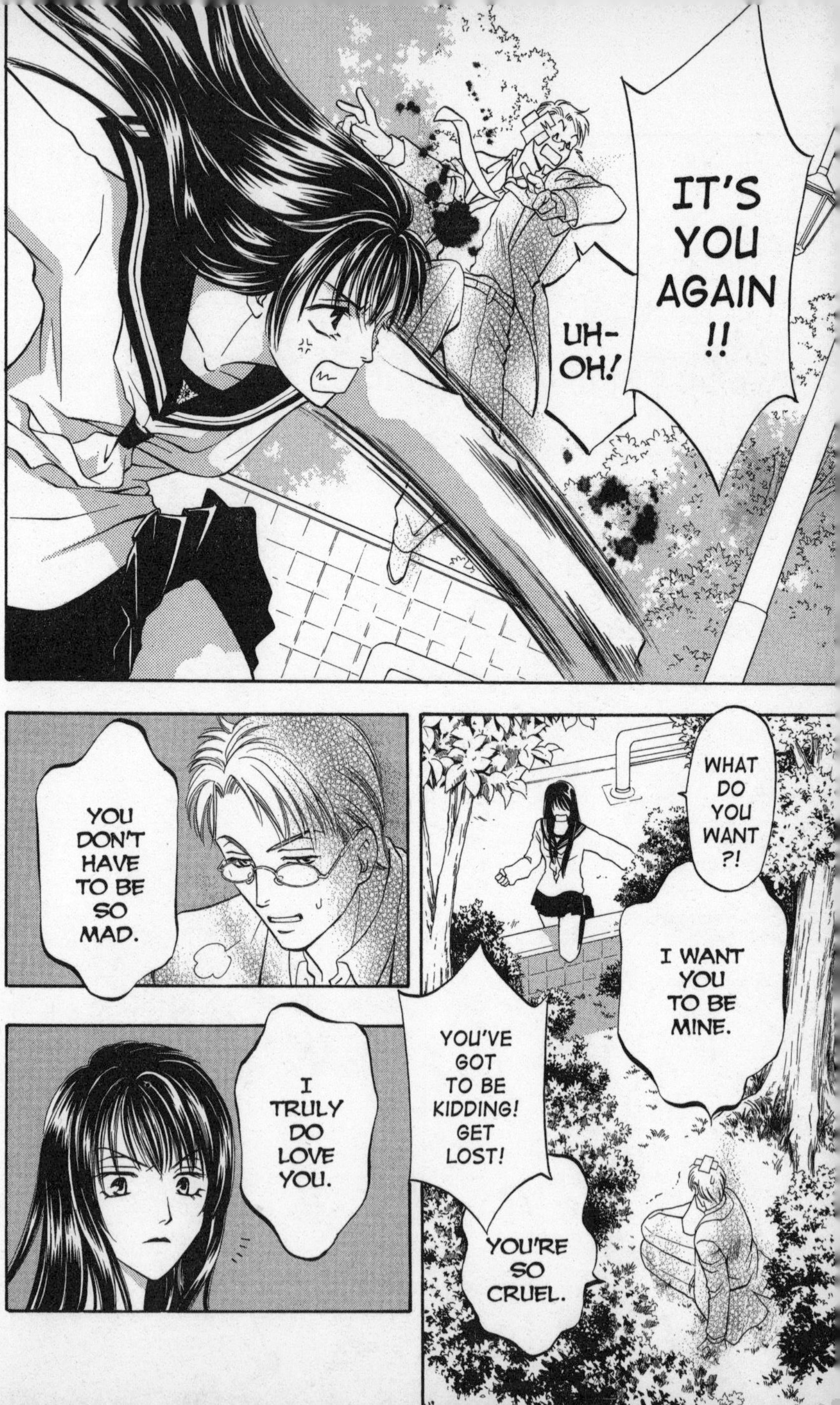
IT'S YOU AGAIN !!
UH-OH!
WHAT DO YOU WANT ?!
I WANT YOU TO BE MINE.
YOU'VE GOT TO BE KIDDING! GET LOST!
YOU'RE SO CRUEL.
YOU DON'T HAVE TO BE SO MAD.
I TRULY DO LOVE YOU.

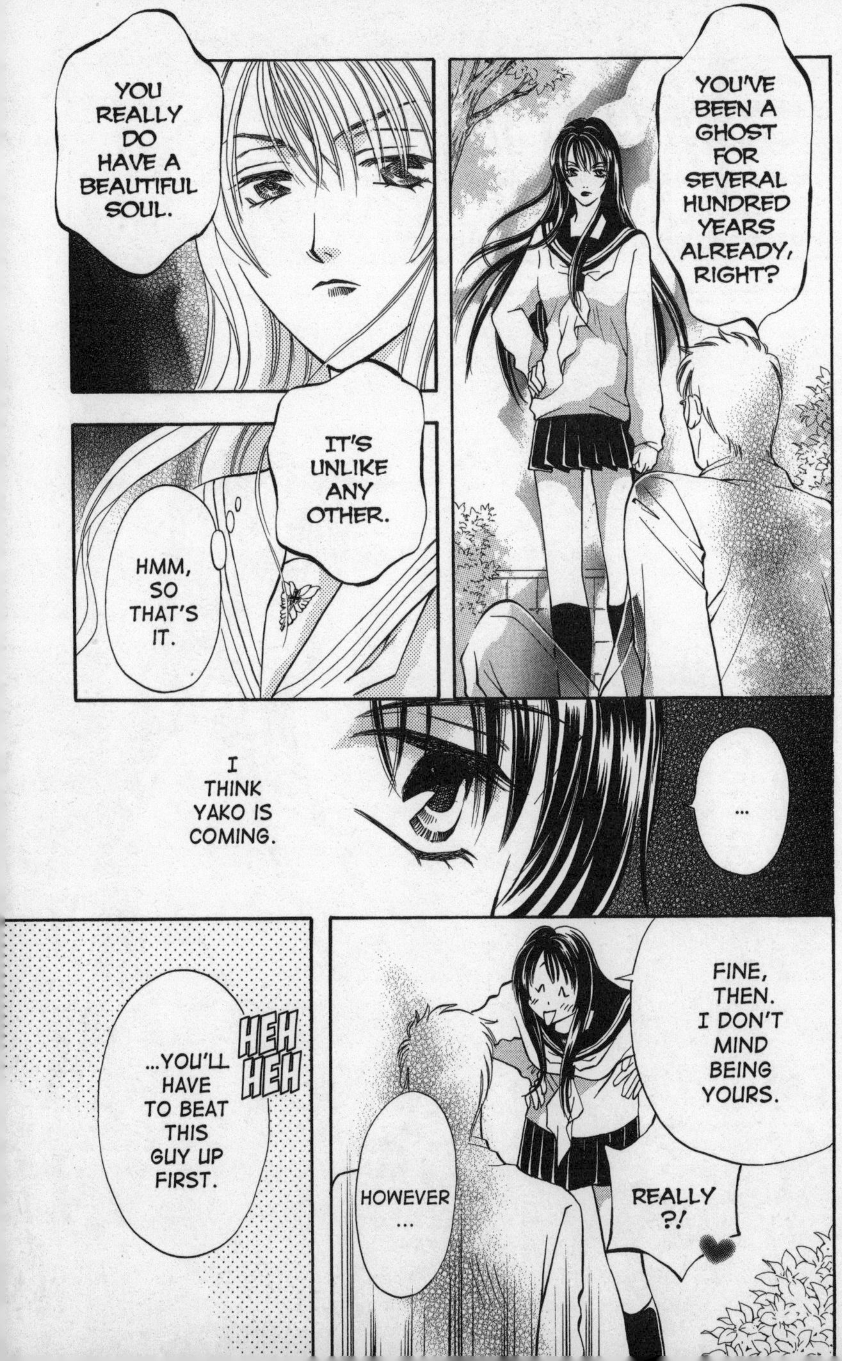
YOU'VE BEEN A GHOST FOR SEVERAL HUNDRED YEARS ALREADY, RIGHT?
YOU REALLY DO HAVE A BEAUTIFUL SOUL.
IT'S UNLIKE ANY OTHER.
HMM, SO THAT'S IT.
...
I THINK YAKO IS COMING.
FINE, THEN. I DON'T MIND BEING YOURS.
REALLY?!
HOWEVER...
HEH HEH
...YOU'LL HAVE TO BEAT THIS GUY UP FIRST.

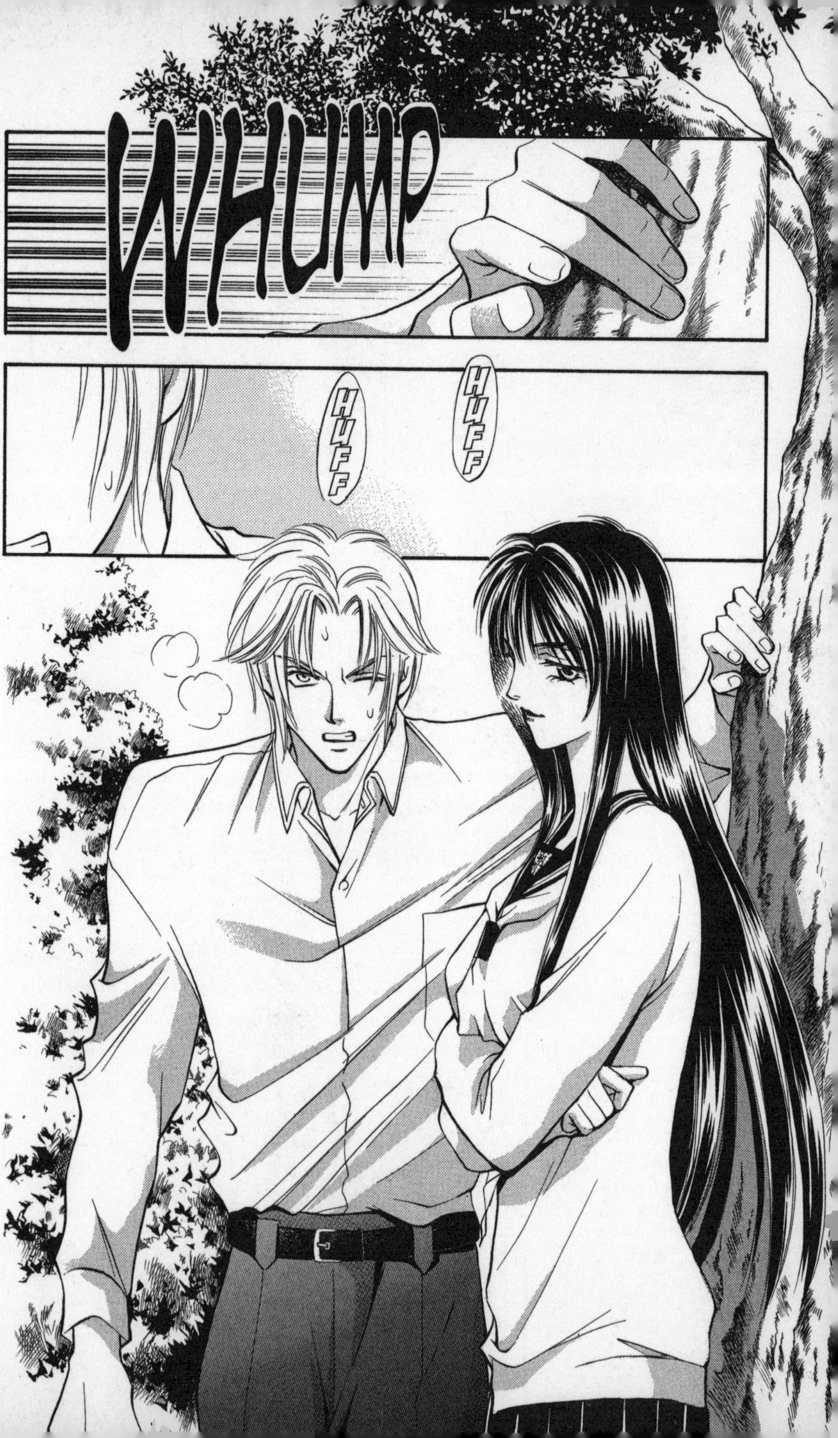
WHUMP
HUFF
HUFF

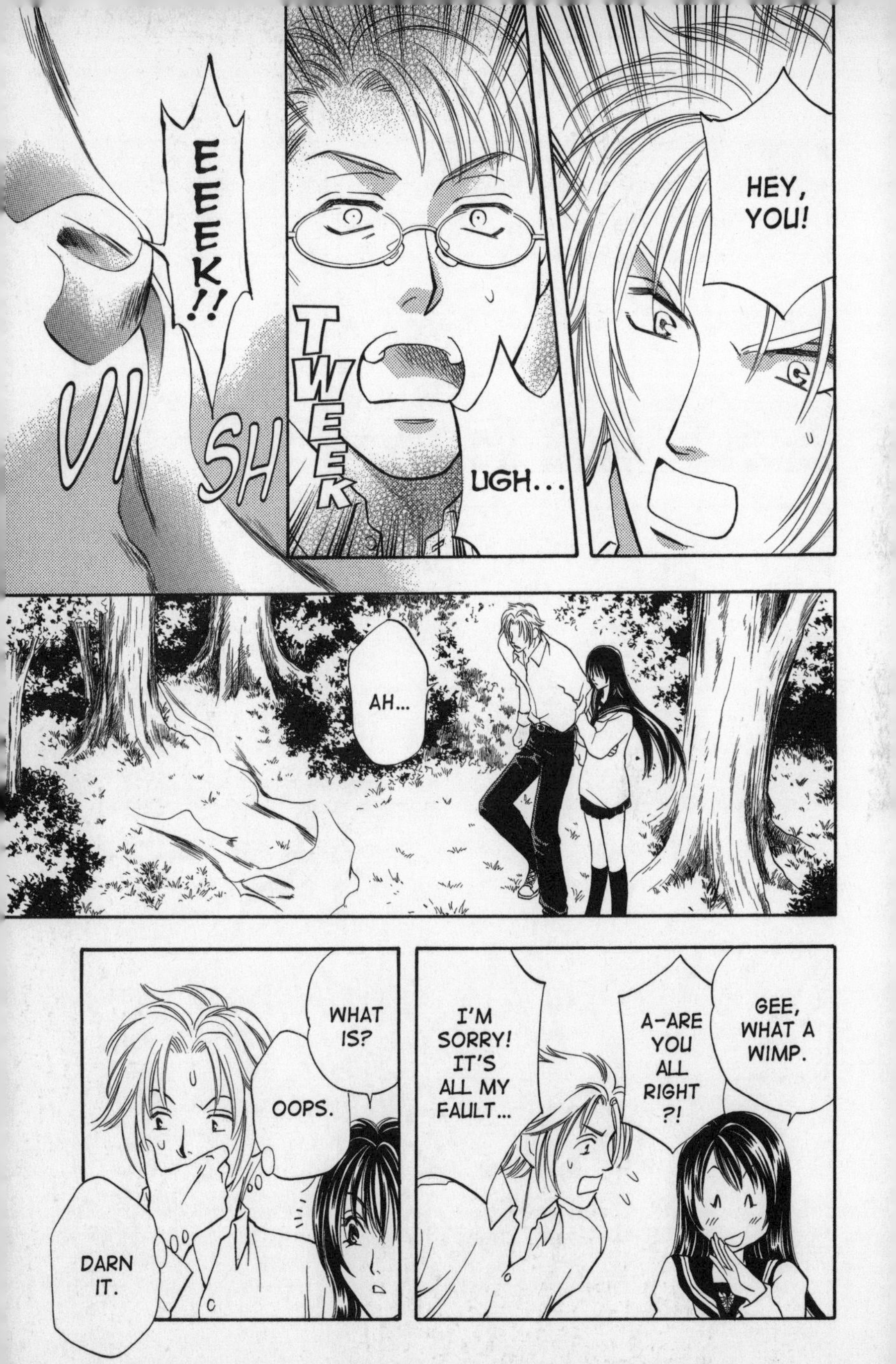
HEY, YOU!
UGH...
TWEEEK
EEEEK!!
VISH
AH...
GEE, WHAT A WIMP.
A-ARE YOU ALL RIGHT?!
I'M SORRY! IT'S ALL MY FAULT...
WHAT IS?
OOPS.
DARN IT.

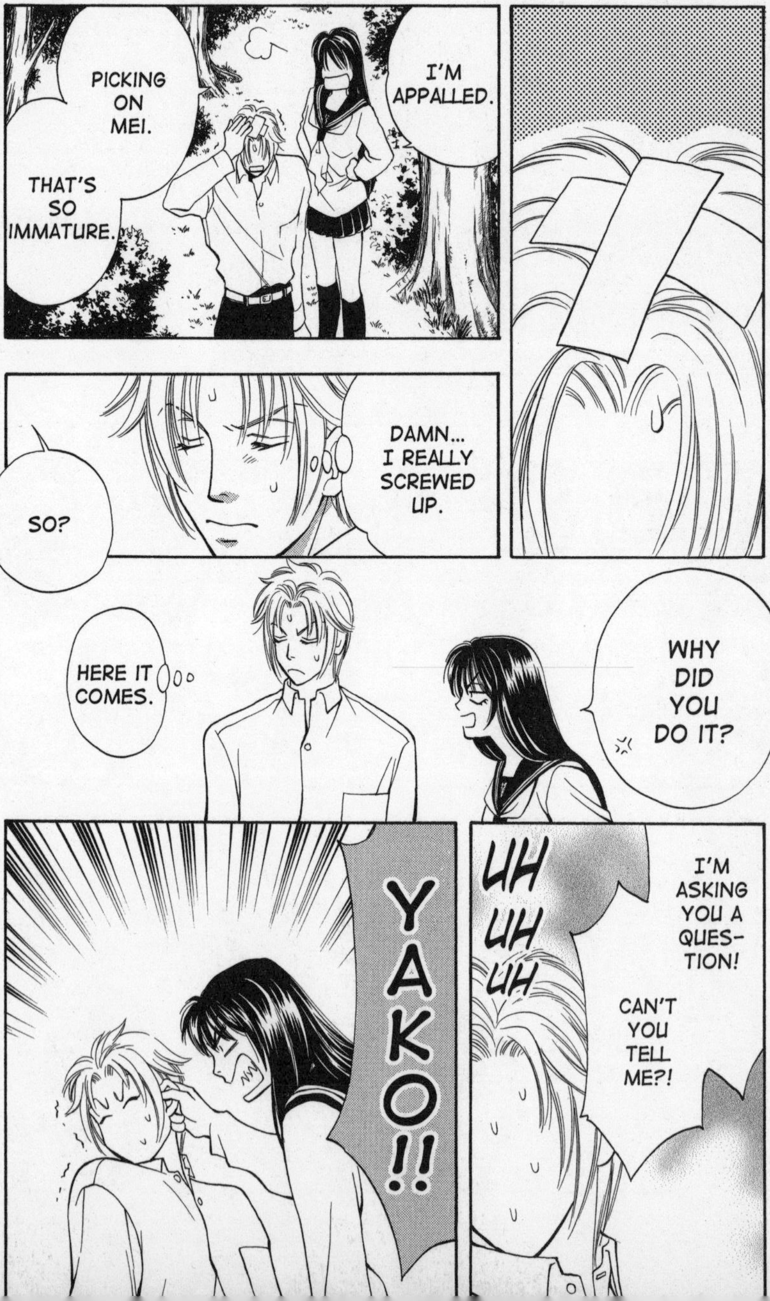
I'M APPALLED.
PICKING ON MEI.
THAT'S SO IMMATURE.
DAMN... I REALLY SCREWED UP.
SO?
WHY DID YOU DO IT?
HERE IT COMES.
UH UH UH
I'M ASKING YOU A QUES-TION!
CAN'T YOU TELL ME?!
YAKO!!

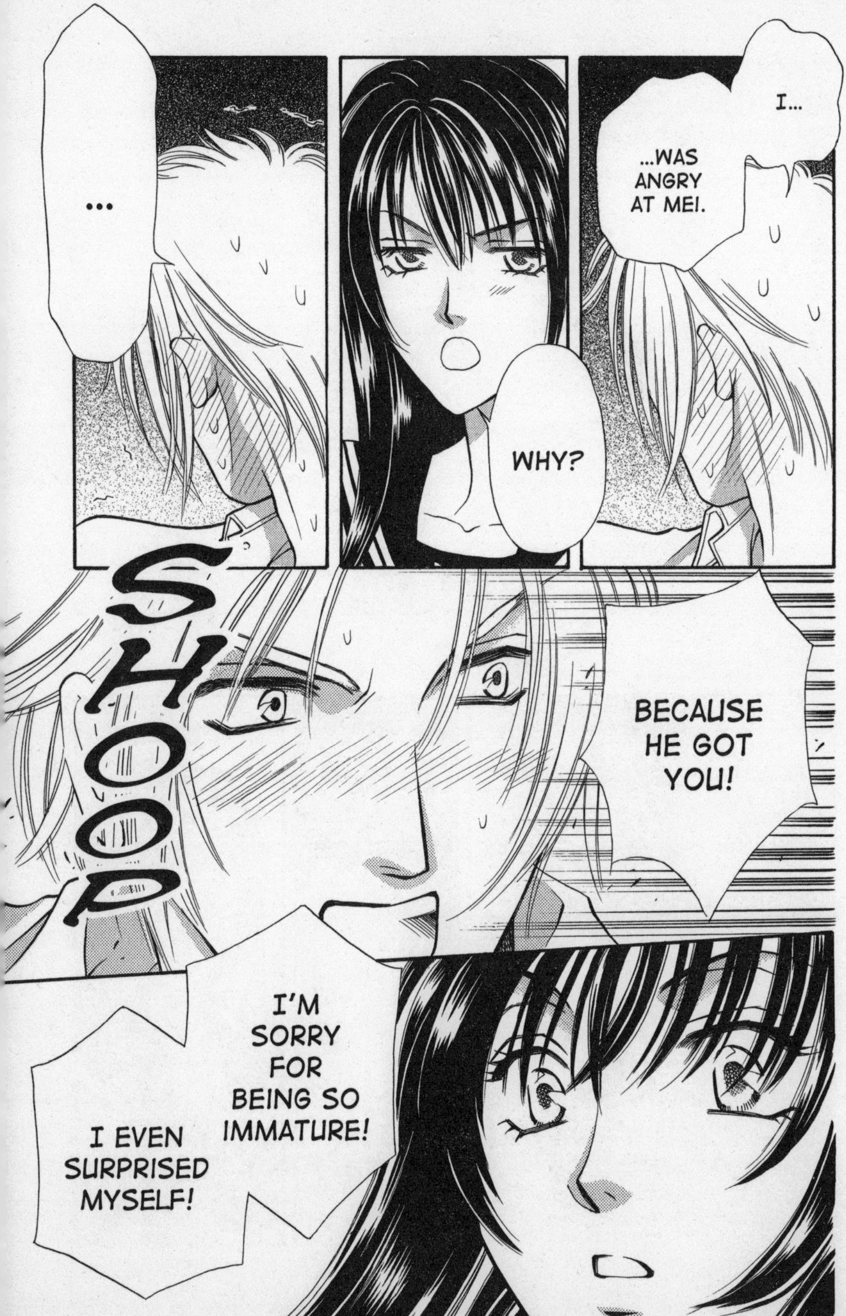
I...
...WAS ANGRY AT MEI.
WHY?
...
BECAUSE HE GOT YOU!
SHOOP
I'M SORRY FOR BEING SO IMMATURE!
I EVEN SURPRISED MYSELF!

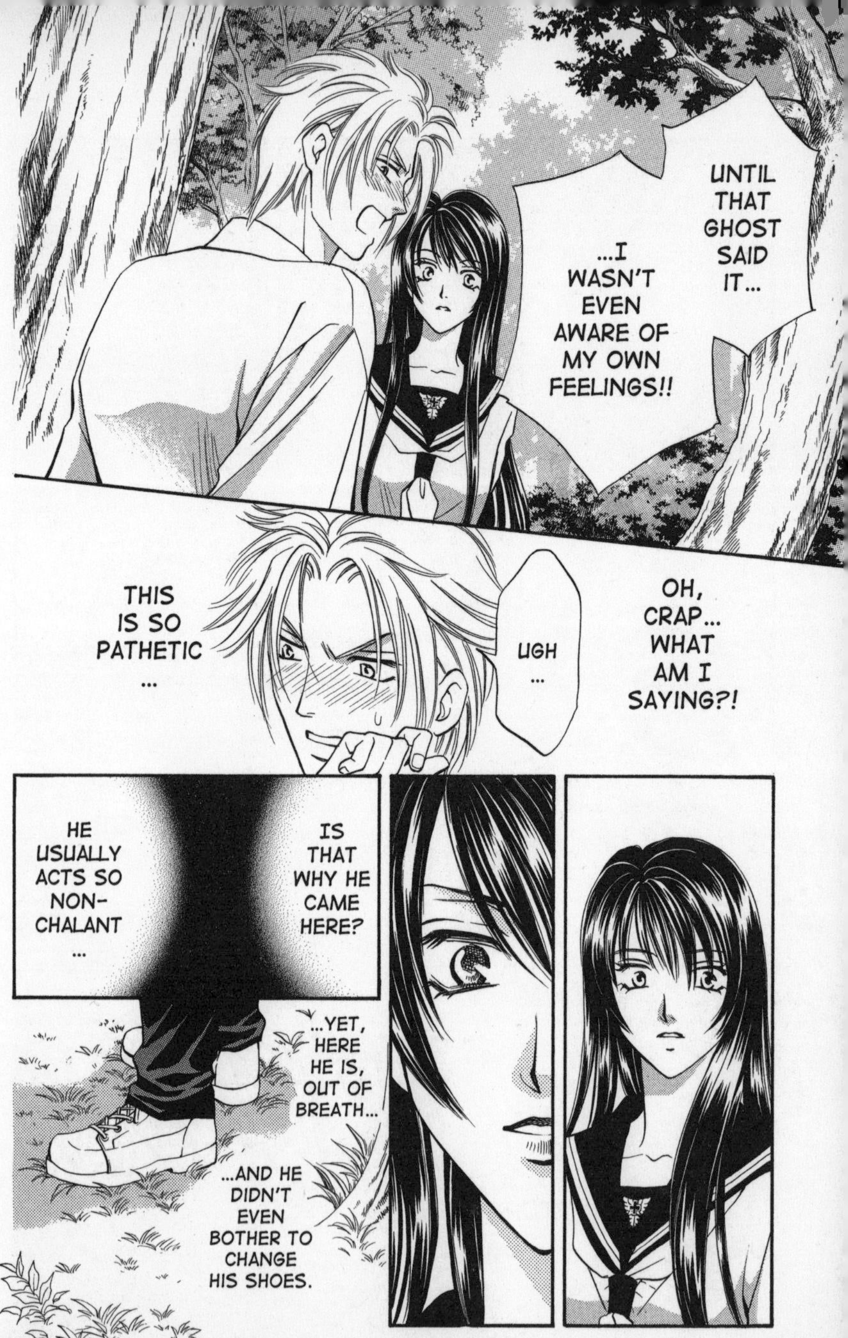
UNTIL THAT GHOST SAID IT...
...I WASN'T EVEN AWARE OF MY OWN FEELINGS!!
OH, CRAP... WHAT AM I SAYING?!
UGH ...
THIS IS SO PATHETIC ...
IS THAT WHY HE CAME HERE?
HE USUALLY ACTS SO NON-CHALANT ...
...YET, HERE HE IS, OUT OF BREATH...
...AND HE DIDN'T EVEN BOTHER TO CHANGE HIS SHOES.

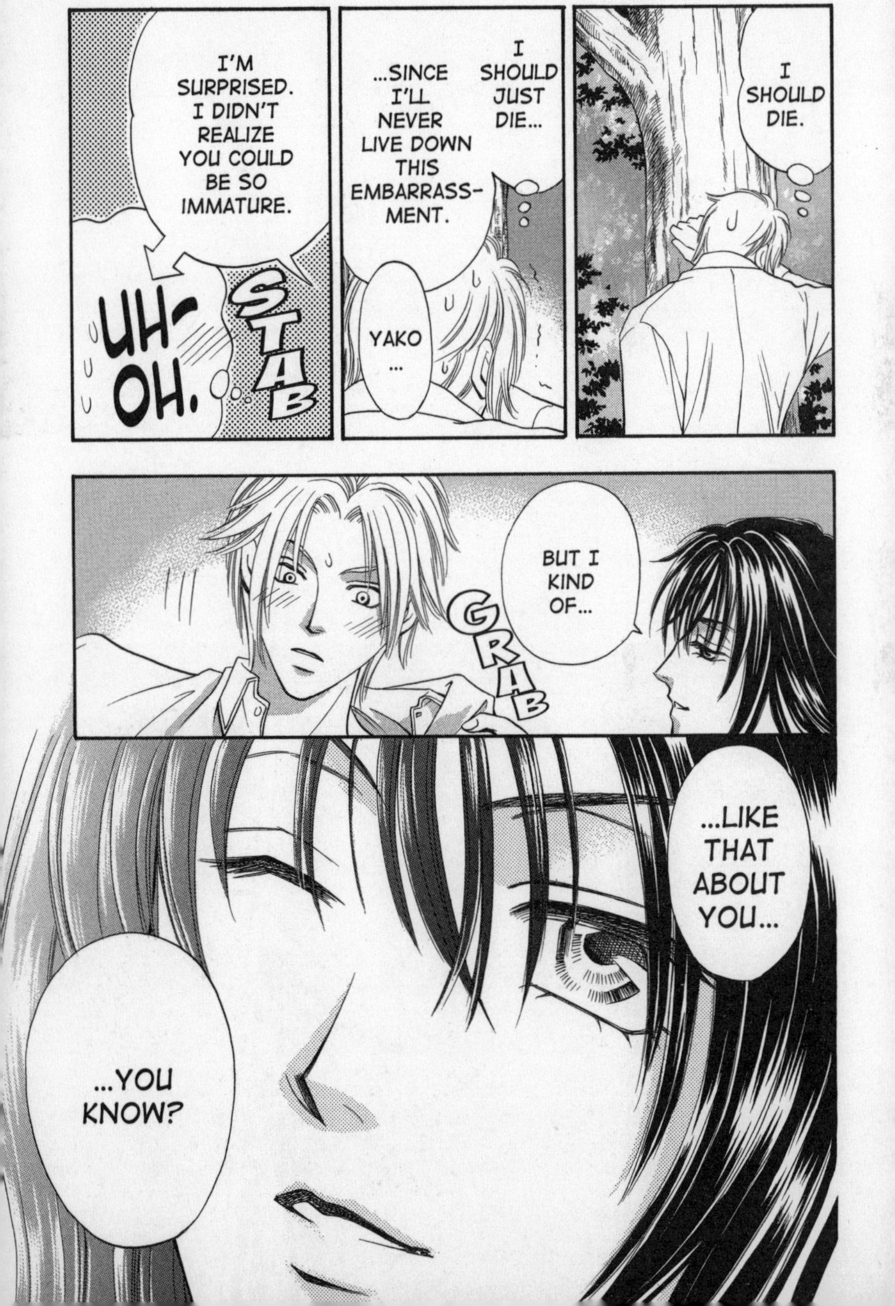
I SHOULD DIE.
I SHOULD JUST DIE...
...SINCE I'LL NEVER LIVE DOWN THIS EMBARRASSMENT.
YAKO ...
I'M SURPRISED. I DIDN'T REALIZE YOU COULD BE SO IMMATURE.
STAB
UH-OH.
BUT I KIND OF...
GRAB
...LIKE THAT ABOUT YOU...
...YOU KNOW?

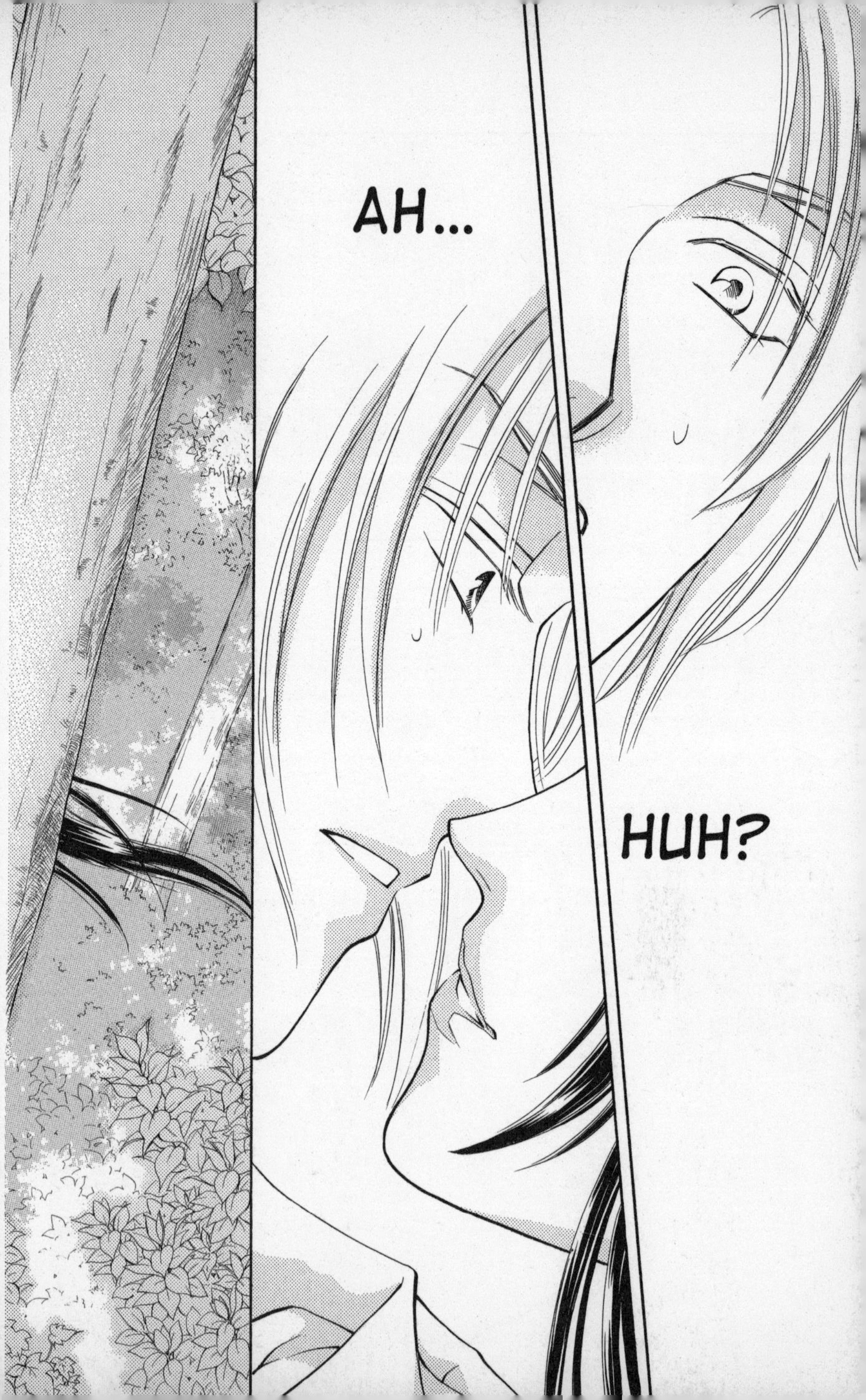
HUH?
AH...

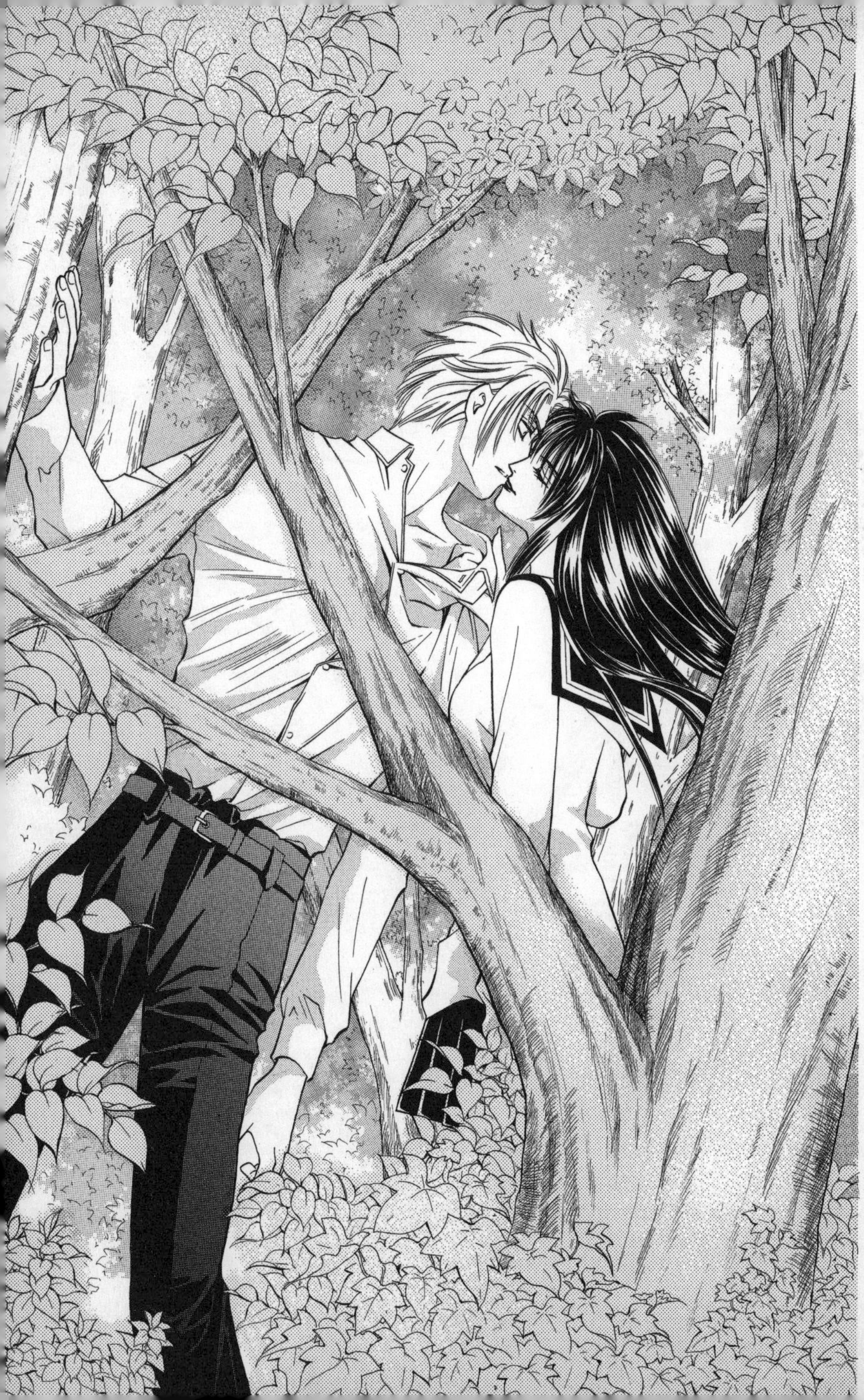

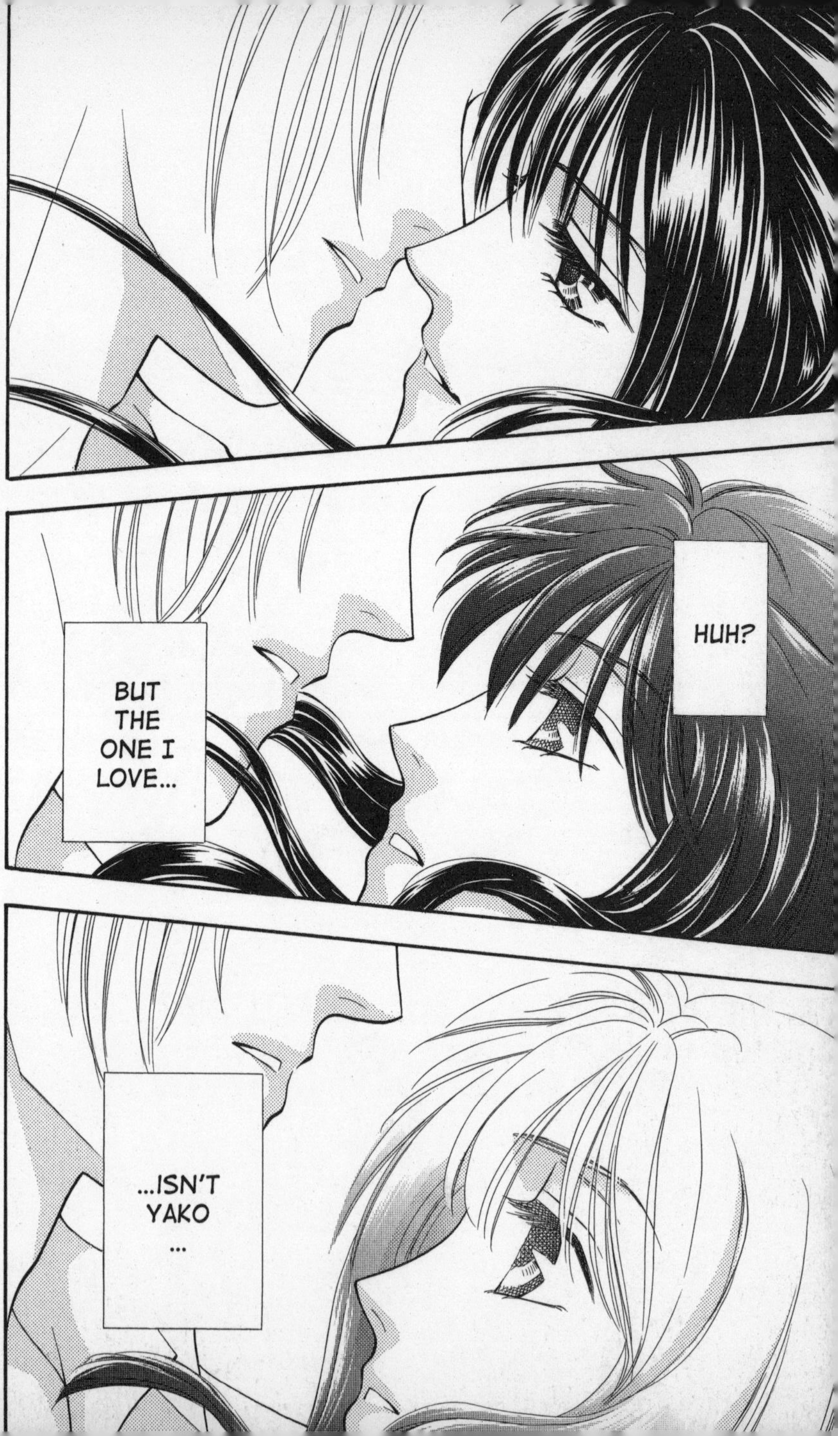
HUH?
BUT THE ONE I LOVE...
...ISN'T YAKO ...

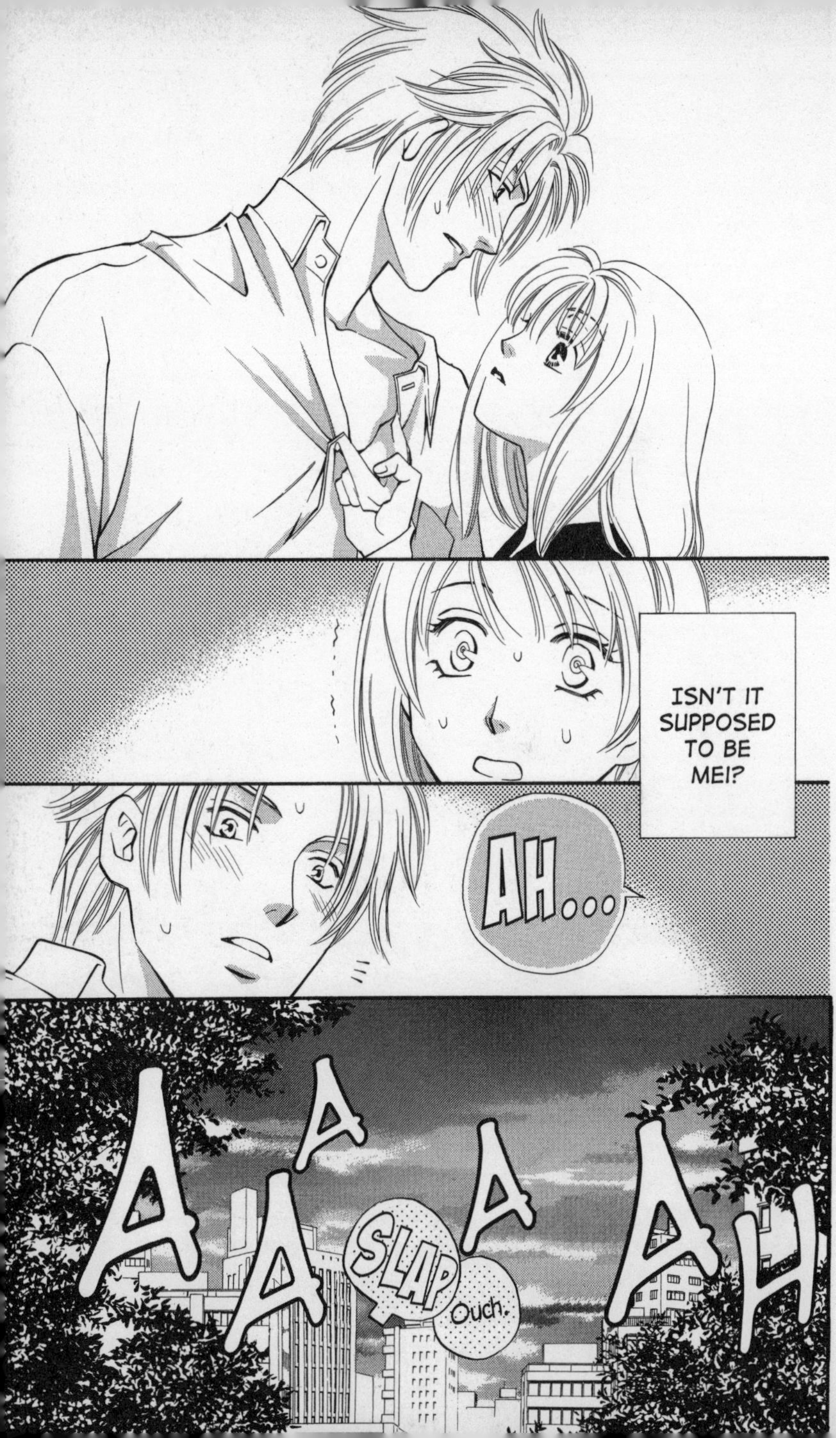
ISN'T IT SUPPOSED TO BE MEI?
AH...
AAAAAH
SLAP
Ouch.

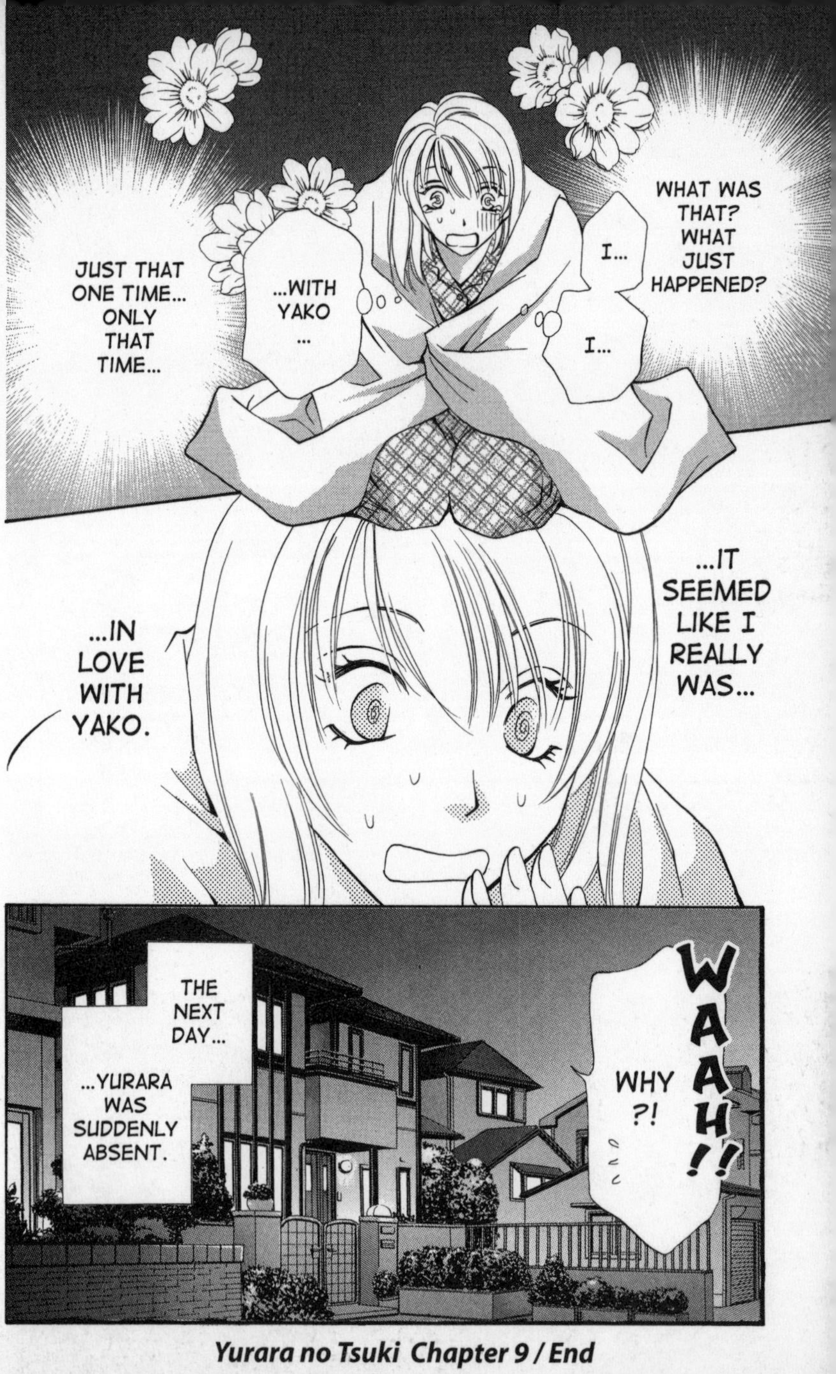
WHAT WAS THAT? WHAT JUST HAPPENED?
I...
I...
...WITH YAKO ...
JUST THAT ONE TIME... ONLY THAT TIME...
...IT SEEMED LIKE I REALLY WAS...
...IN LOVE WITH YAKO.
WAAH!!
WHY ?!
THE NEXT DAY...
...YURARA WAS SUDDENLY ABSENT.

Yurara no Tsuki Chapter 9 / End

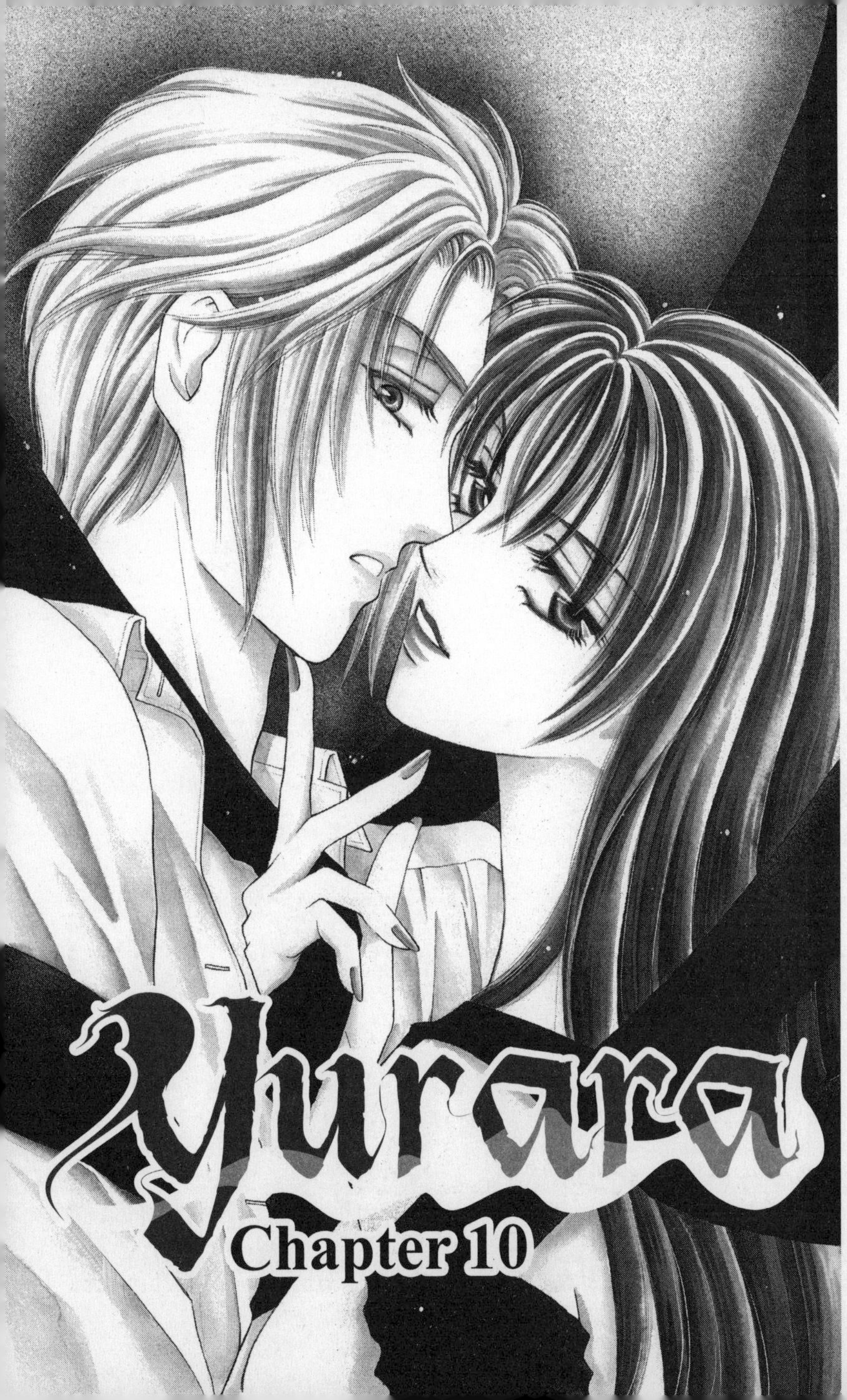
Yurara
Chapter 10

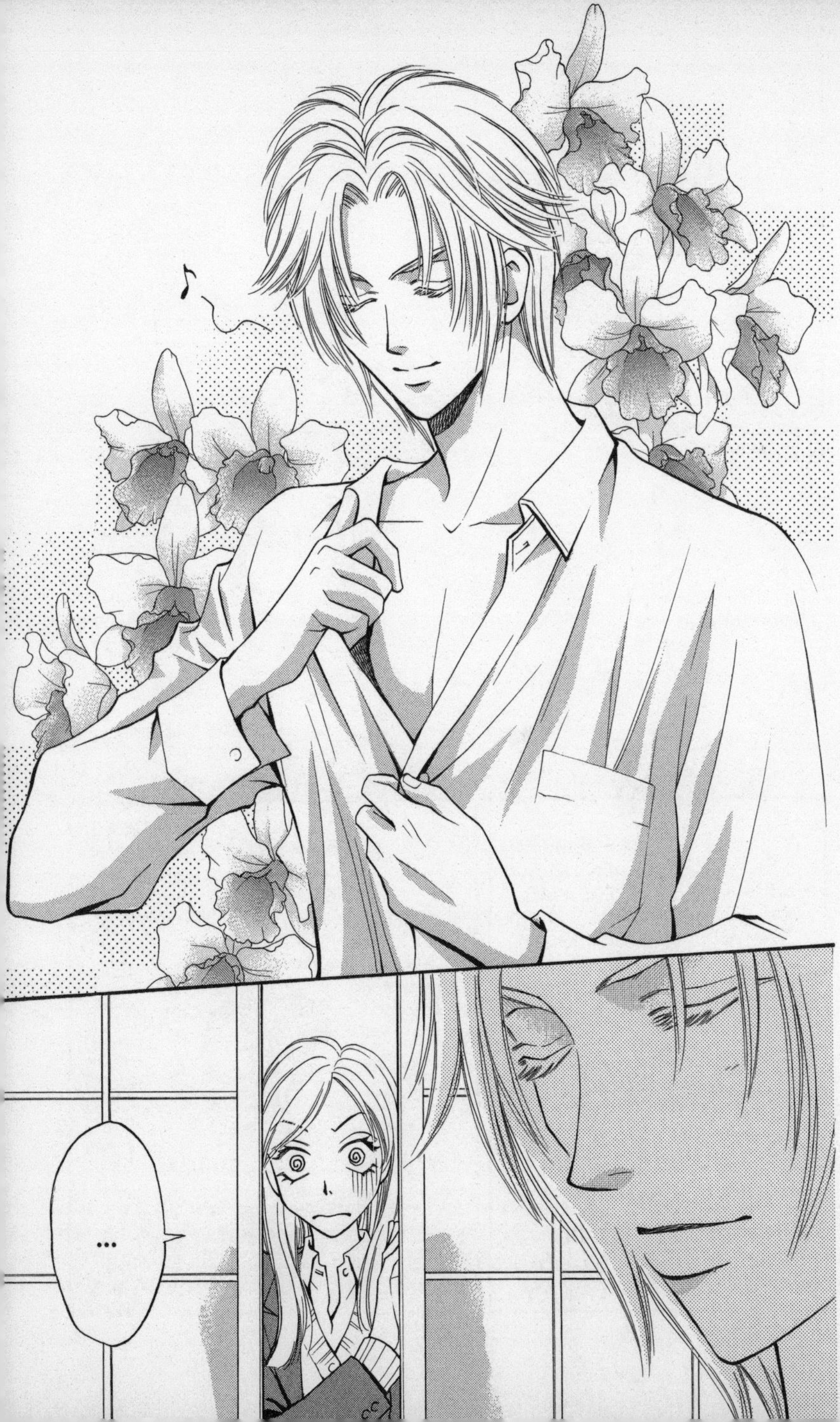
...

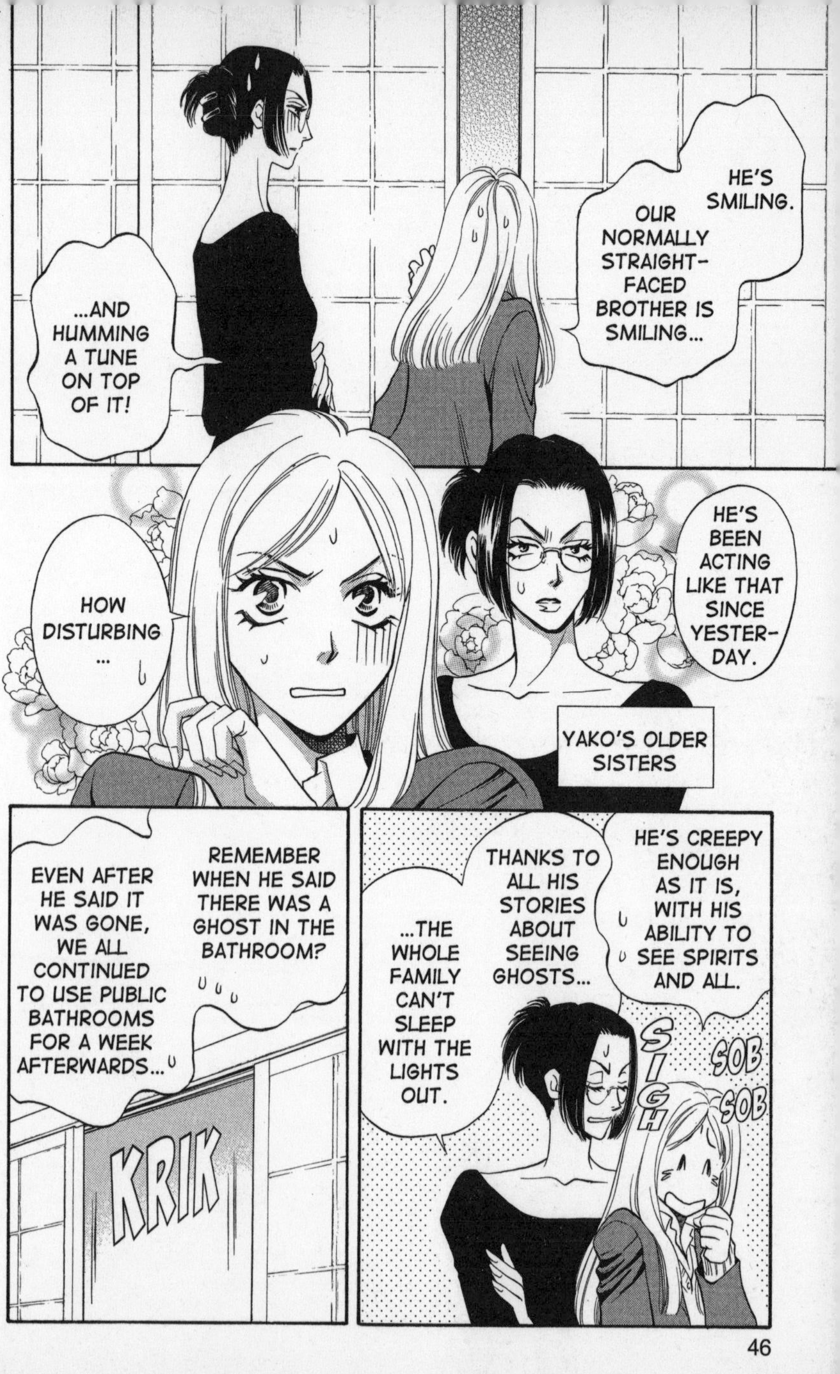
HE'S SMILING.
OUR NORMALLY STRAIGHT-FACED BROTHER IS SMILING...
...AND HUMMING A TUNE ON TOP OF IT!
HE'S BEEN ACTING LIKE THAT SINCE YESTER-DAY.
HOW DISTURBING ...
YAKO'S OLDER SISTERS
HE'S CREEPY ENOUGH AS IT IS, WITH HIS ABILITY TO SEE SPIRITS AND ALL.
THANKS TO ALL HIS STORIES ABOUT SEEING GHOSTS...
...THE WHOLE FAMILY CAN'T SLEEP WITH THE LIGHTS OUT.
SOB SOB
SIGH
REMEMBER WHEN HE SAID THERE WAS A GHOST IN THE BATHROOM?
EVEN AFTER HE SAID IT WAS GONE, WE ALL CONTINUED TO USE PUBLIC BATHROOMS FOR A WEEK AFTERWARDS...
KRIK

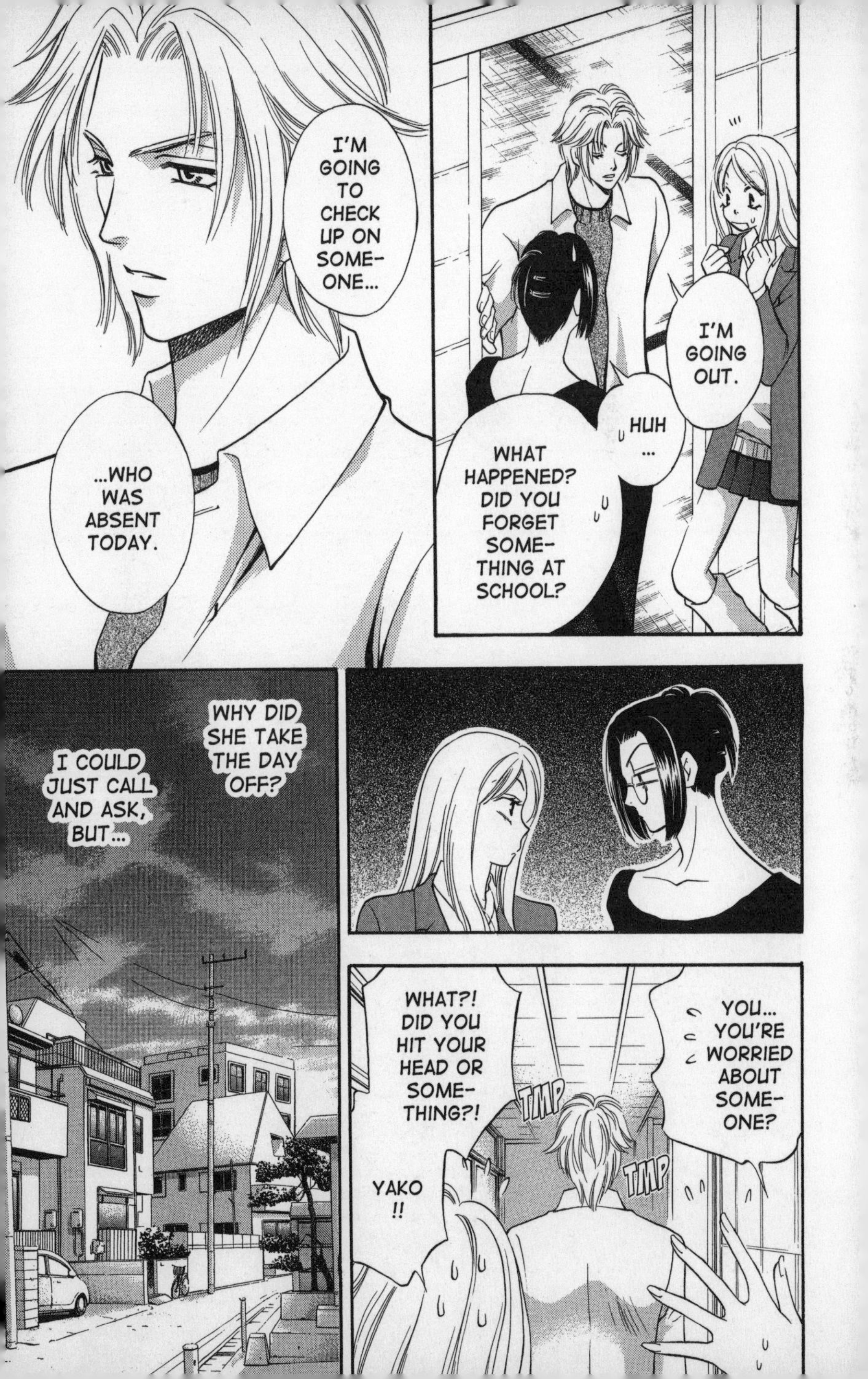
I'M GOING OUT.
HUH...
WHAT HAPPENED? DID YOU FORGET SOMETHING AT SCHOOL?
I'M GOING TO CHECK UP ON SOMEONE...
...WHO WAS ABSENT TODAY.
YOU... YOU'RE WORRIED ABOUT SOMEONE?
TMP
TMP
WHAT?! DID YOU HIT YOUR HEAD OR SOMETHING?!
YAKO !!
WHY DID SHE TAKE THE DAY OFF?
I COULD JUST CALL AND ASK, BUT...

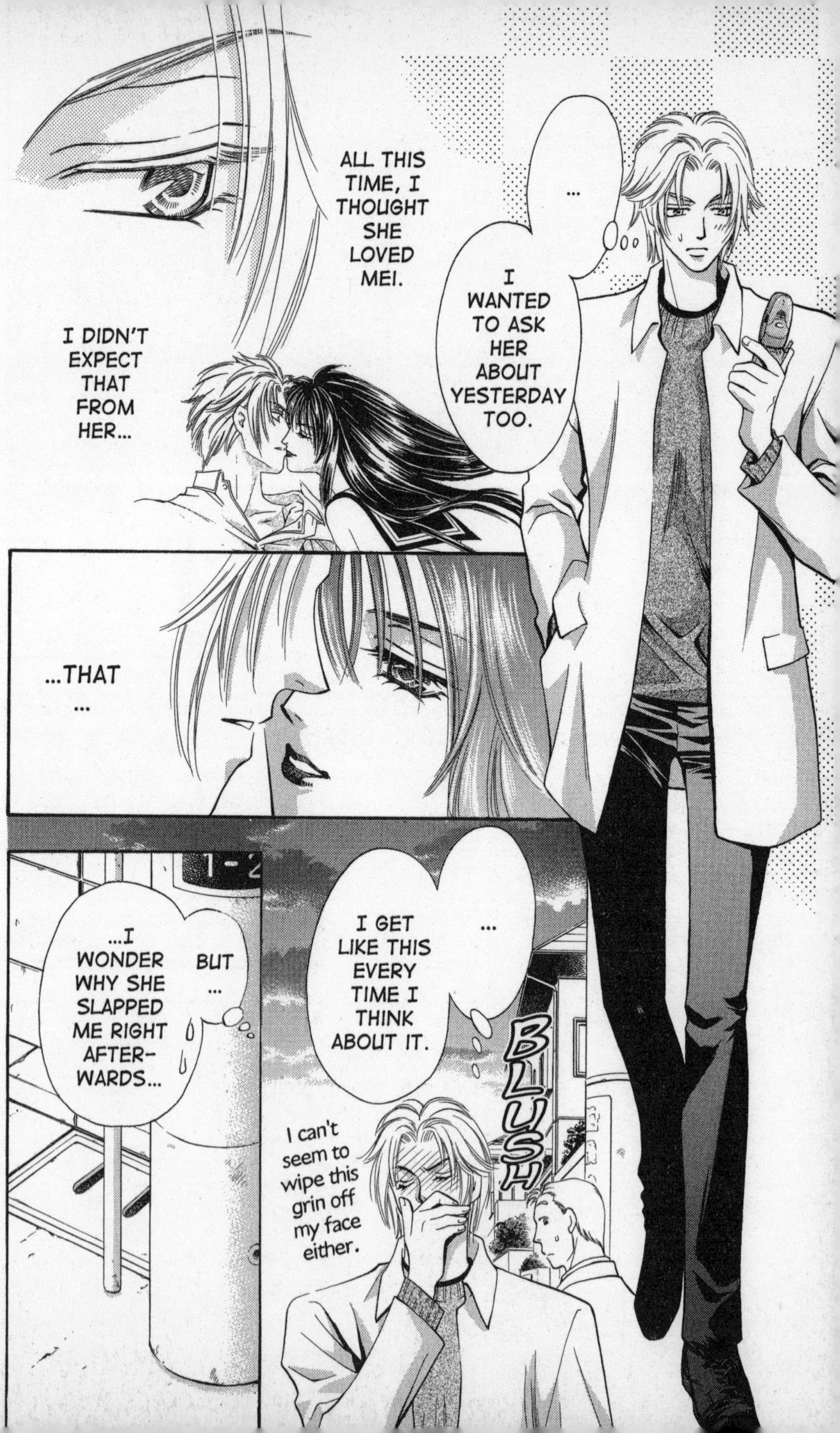
...
I WANTED TO ASK HER ABOUT YESTERDAY TOO.
ALL THIS TIME, I THOUGHT SHE LOVED MEI.
I DIDN'T EXPECT THAT FROM HER...
...THAT ...
...
I GET LIKE THIS EVERY TIME I THINK ABOUT IT.
BLUSH
I can't seem to wipe this grin off my face either.
BUT ...
...I WONDER WHY SHE SLAPPED ME RIGHT AFTER-WARDS...

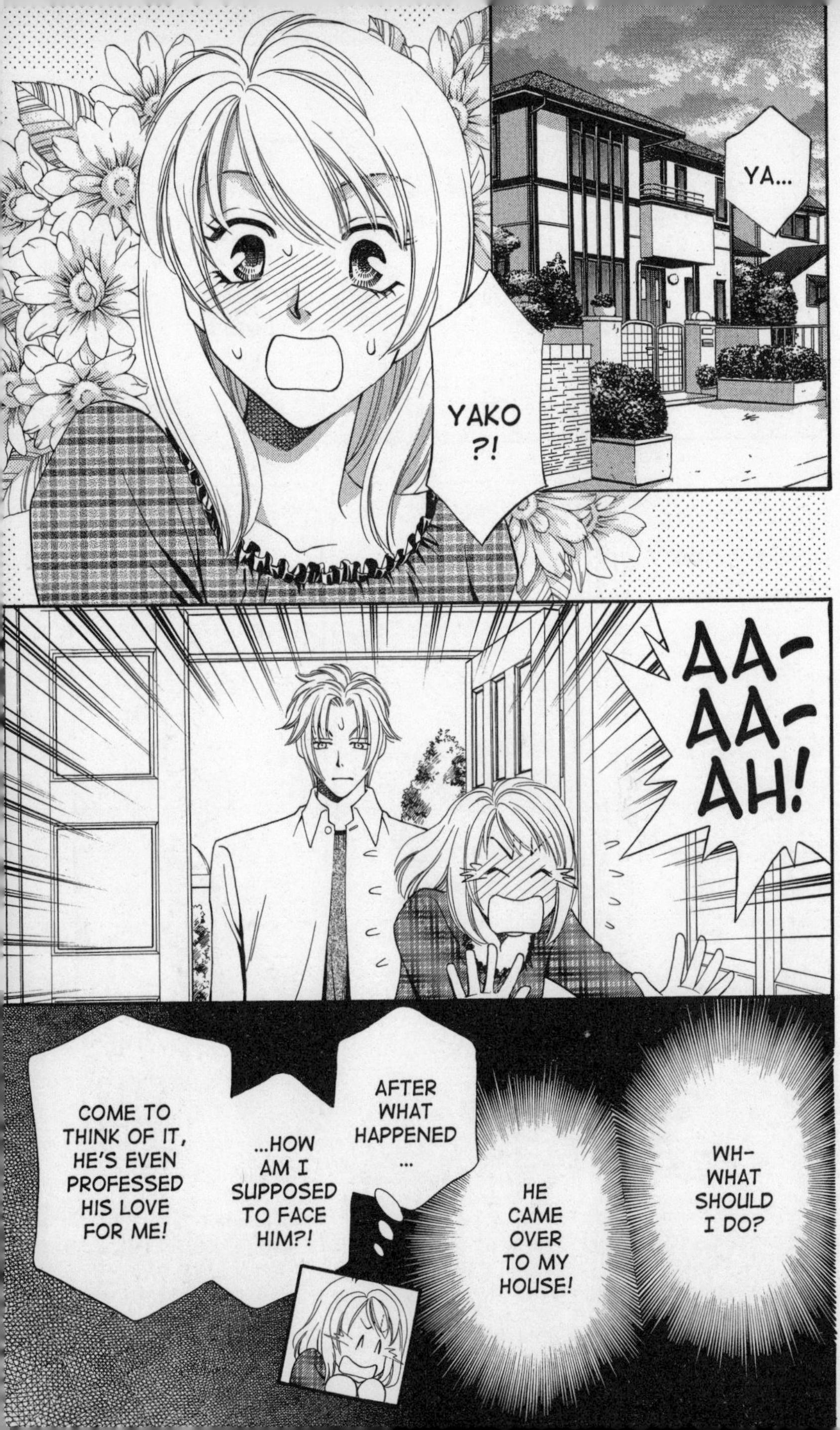
YA...
YAKO ?!
AA-AA-AH!
WH-WHAT SHOULD I DO?
HE CAME OVER TO MY HOUSE!
AFTER WHAT HAPPENED ...
...HOW AM I SUPPOSED TO FACE HIM?!
COME TO THINK OF IT, HE'S EVEN PROFESSED HIS LOVE FOR ME!

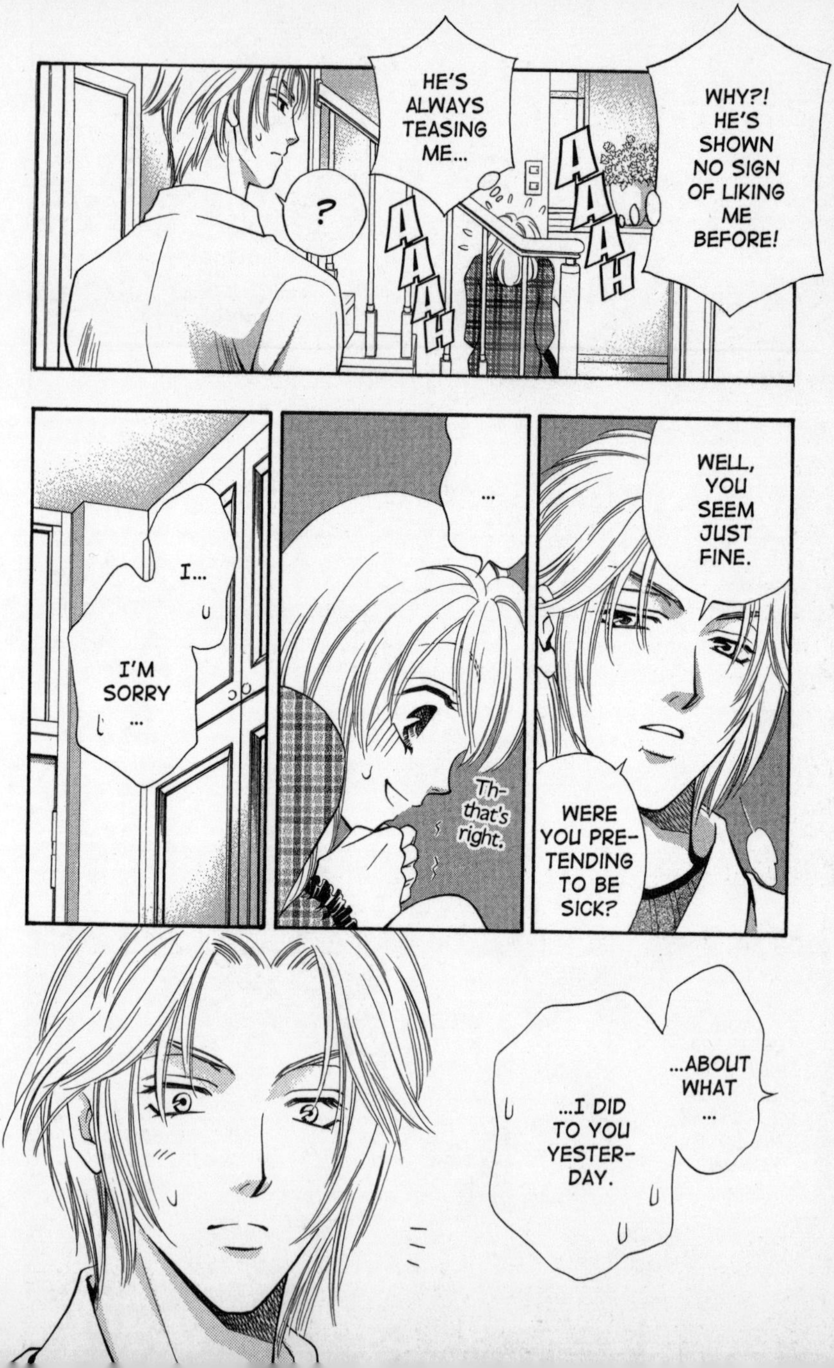
WHY?! HE'S SHOWN NO SIGN OF LIKING ME BEFORE!
AAAAH
HE'S ALWAYS TEASING ME...
AAAAH
?
WELL, YOU SEEM JUST FINE.
WERE YOU PRE-TENDING TO BE SICK?
...
Th-that's right.
I...
I'M SORRY...
...ABOUT WHAT...
...I DID TO YOU YESTER-DAY.

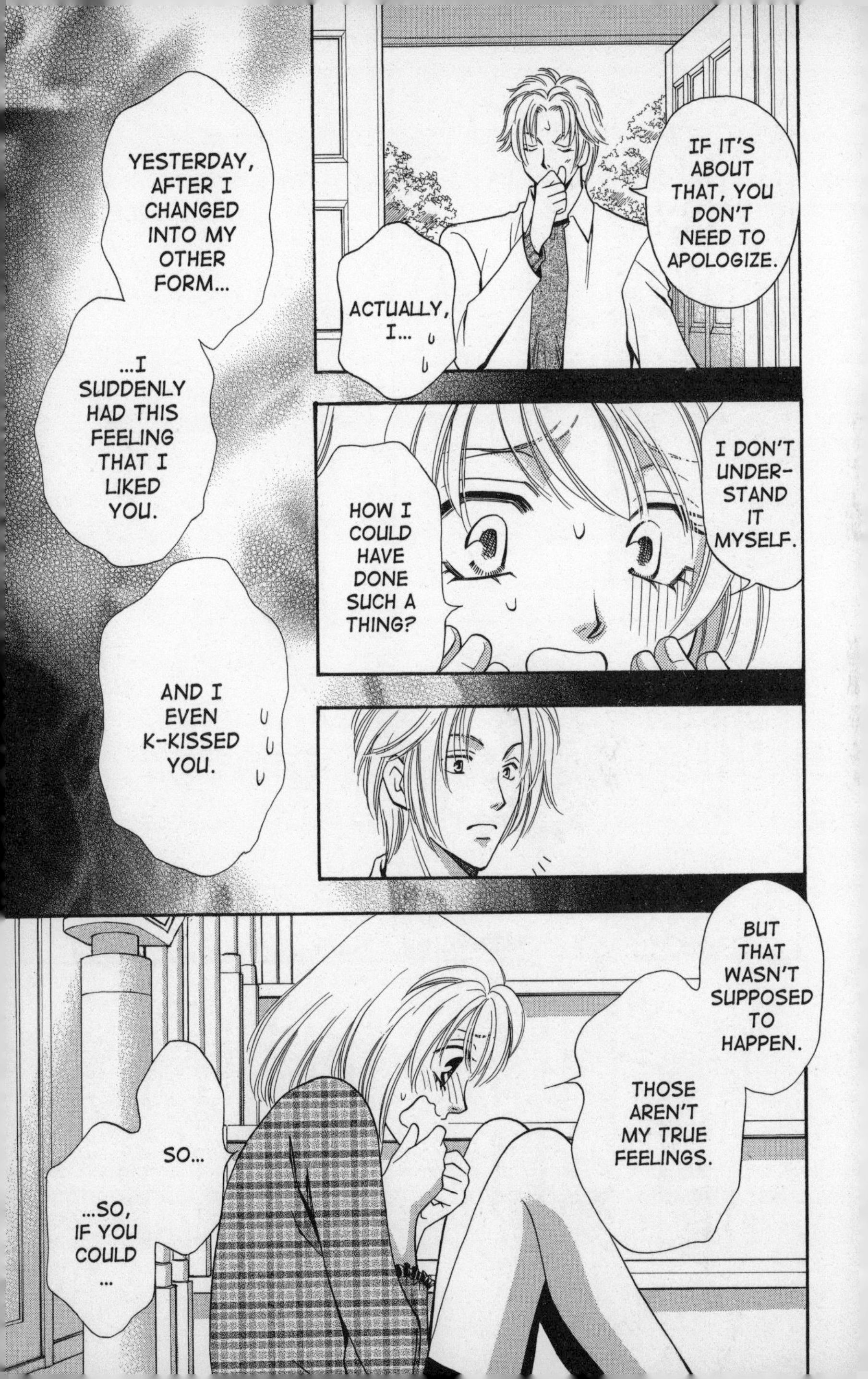
IF IT'S ABOUT THAT, YOU DON'T NEED TO APOLOGIZE.
ACTUALLY, I...
I DON'T UNDER-STAND IT MYSELF.
HOW I COULD HAVE DONE SUCH A THING?
YESTERDAY, AFTER I CHANGED INTO MY OTHER FORM...
...I SUDDENLY HAD THIS FEELING THAT I LIKED YOU.
AND I EVEN K-KISSED YOU.
BUT THAT WASN'T SUPPOSED TO HAPPEN.
THOSE AREN'T MY TRUE FEELINGS.
SO...
...SO, IF YOU COULD ...

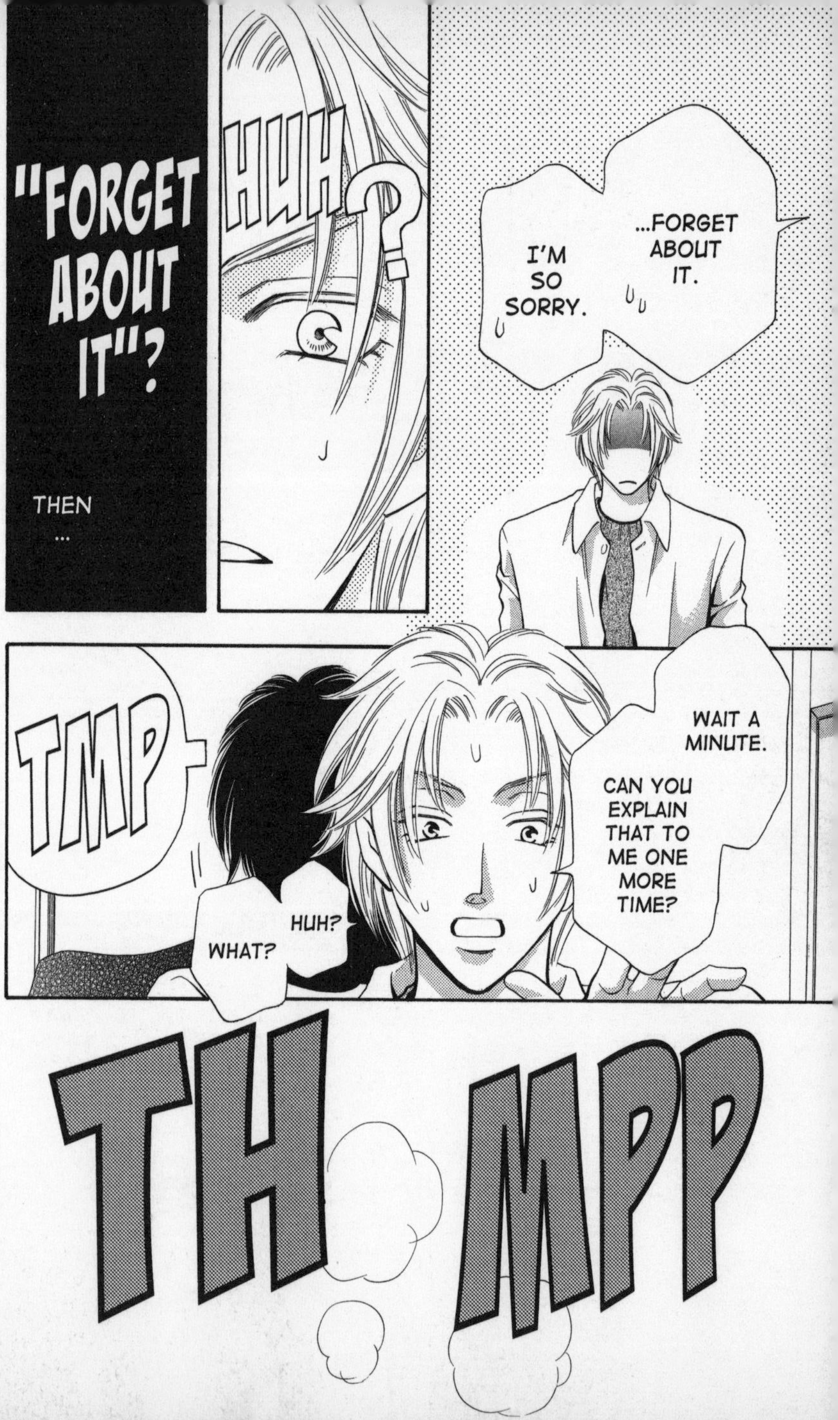

...FORGET ABOUT IT.
I'M SO SORRY.
HUH?
"FORGET ABOUT IT"?
THEN ...
WAIT A MINUTE.
CAN YOU EXPLAIN THAT TO ME ONE MORE TIME?
TMP
HUH?
WHAT?
TH MPP

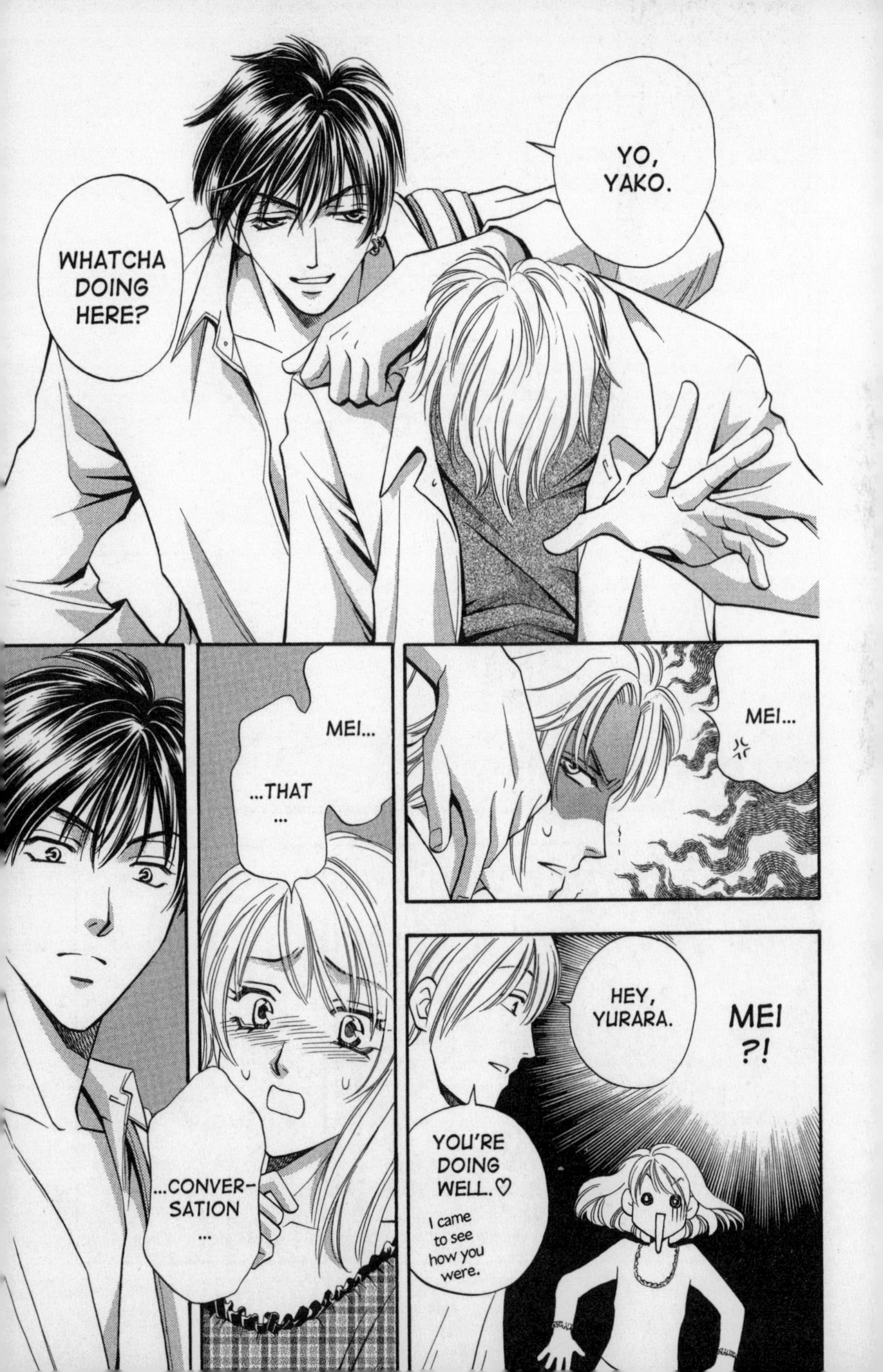
YO, YAKO.
WHATCHA DOING HERE?
MEI...
HEY, YURARA.
MEI ?!
YOU'RE DOING WELL.♡
I came to see how you were.
MEI...
...THAT ...
...CONVER-SATION ...

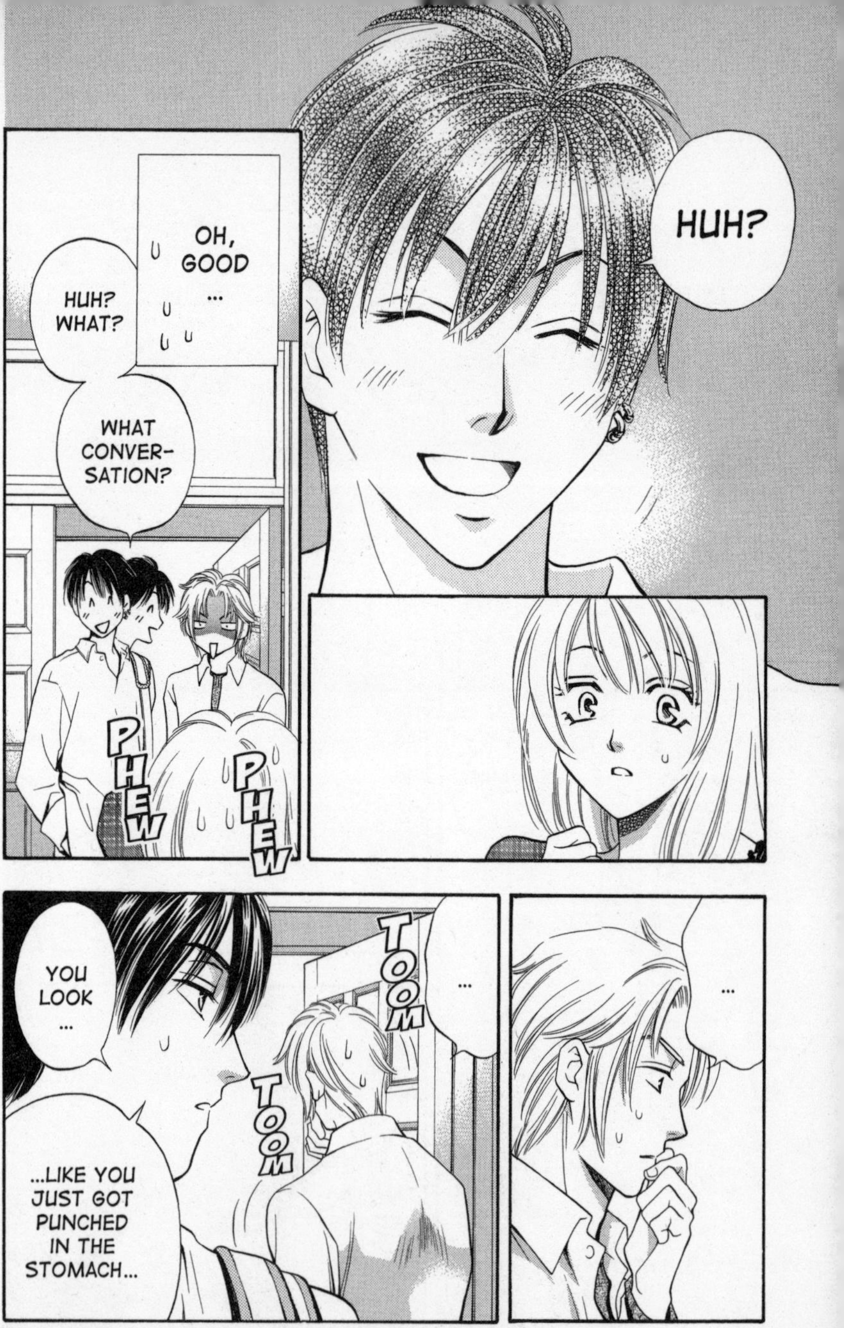
HUH?
OH, GOOD ...
HUH? WHAT?
WHAT CONVERSATION?
PHEW
PHEW
...
...
TOOM
TOOM
YOU LOOK ...
...LIKE YOU JUST GOT PUNCHED IN THE STOMACH...

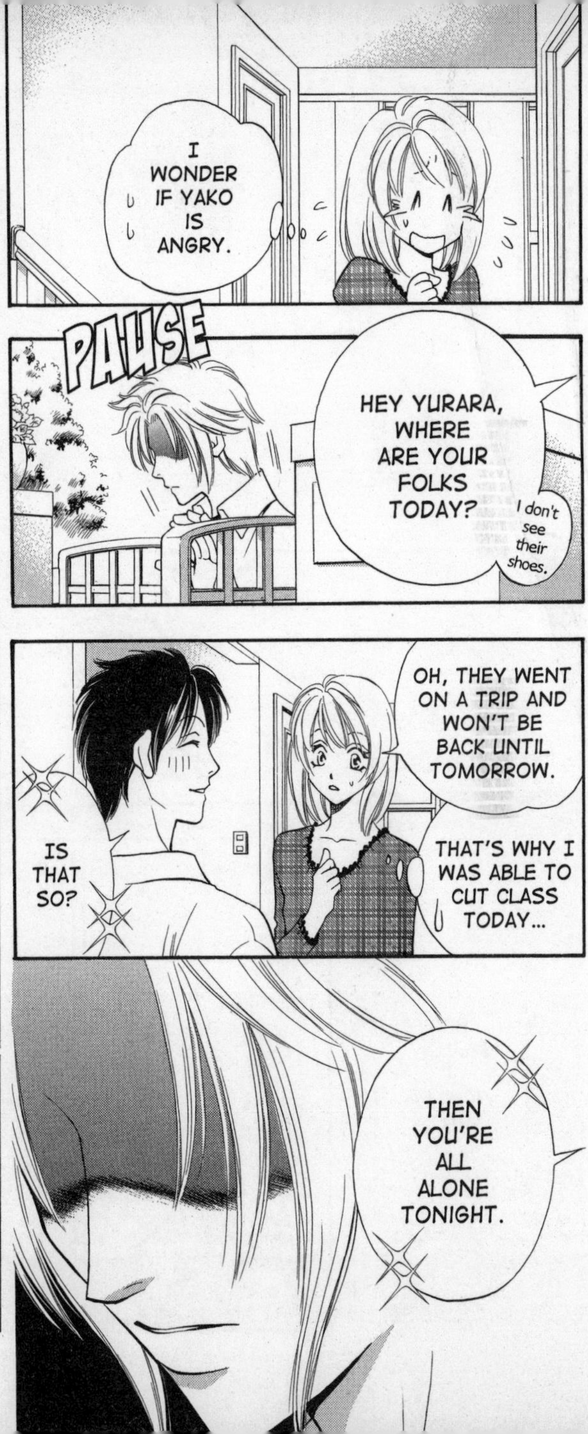
I WONDER IF YAKO IS ANGRY.
PAUSE
HEY YURARA, WHERE ARE YOUR FOLKS TODAY?
I don't see their shoes.
OH, THEY WENT ON A TRIP AND WON'T BE BACK UNTIL TOMORROW.
THAT'S WHY I WAS ABLE TO CUT CLASS TODAY...
IS THAT SO?
THEN YOU'RE ALL ALONE TONIGHT.

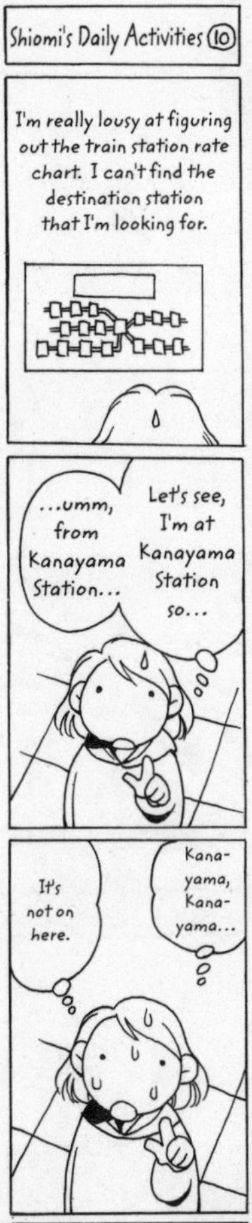
Shiomi's Daily Activities 10
I'm really lousy at figuring out the train station rate chart. I can't find the destination station that I'm looking for.
Let's see, I'm at Kanayama Station so...
...umm, from Kanayama Station...
Kana-yama, Kana-yama...
It's not on here.
HAH
"Present Station" ?!
当駅
My life may be difficult due to minor lapses such as this...

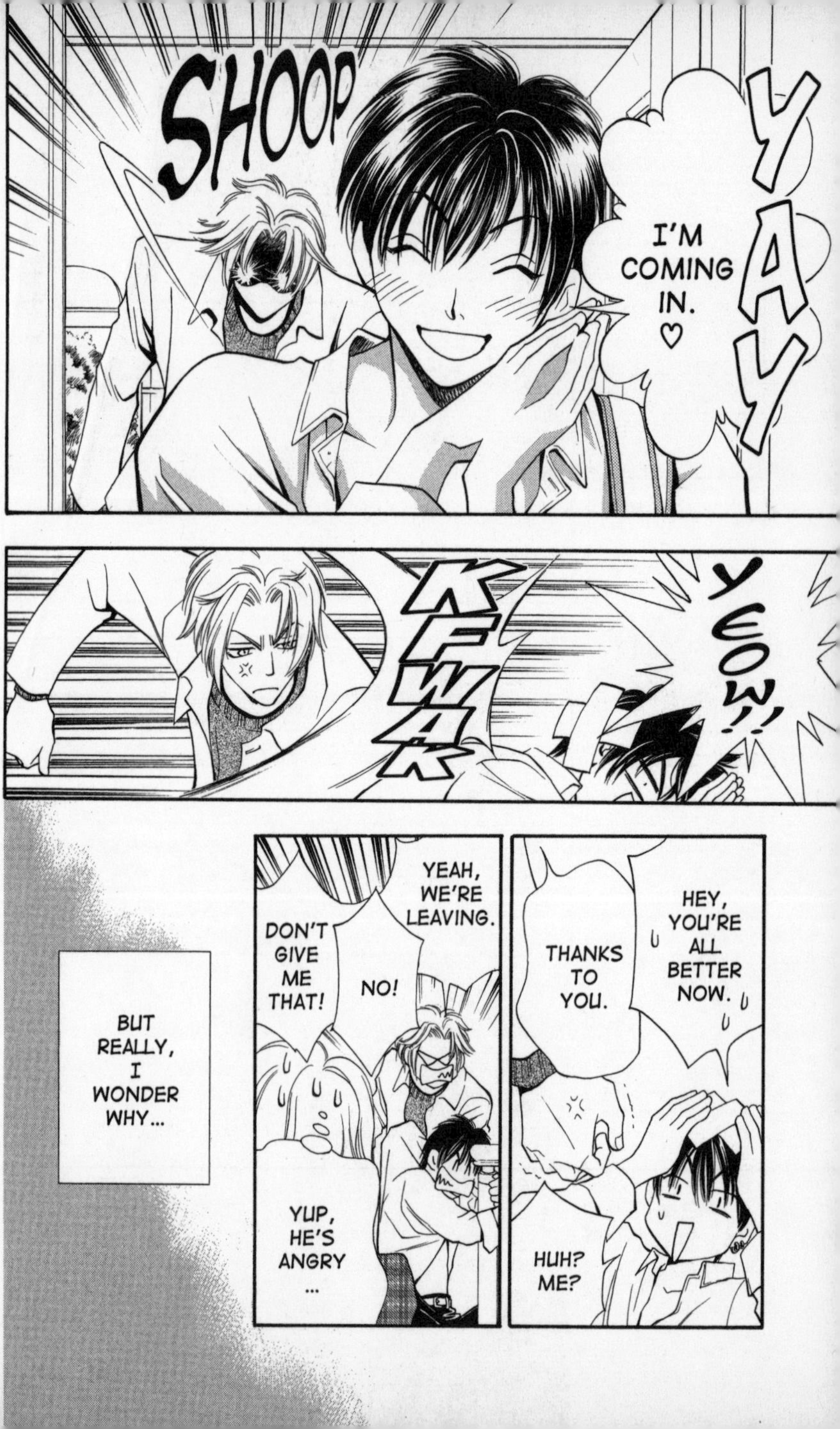
YAY
I'M COMING IN. ♡
SHOOP
YEOW!!
KFWAK
HEY, YOU'RE ALL BETTER NOW.
THANKS TO YOU.
HUH? ME?
YEAH, WE'RE LEAVING.
DON'T GIVE ME THAT!
NO!
YUP, HE'S ANGRY ...
BUT REALLY, I WONDER WHY...

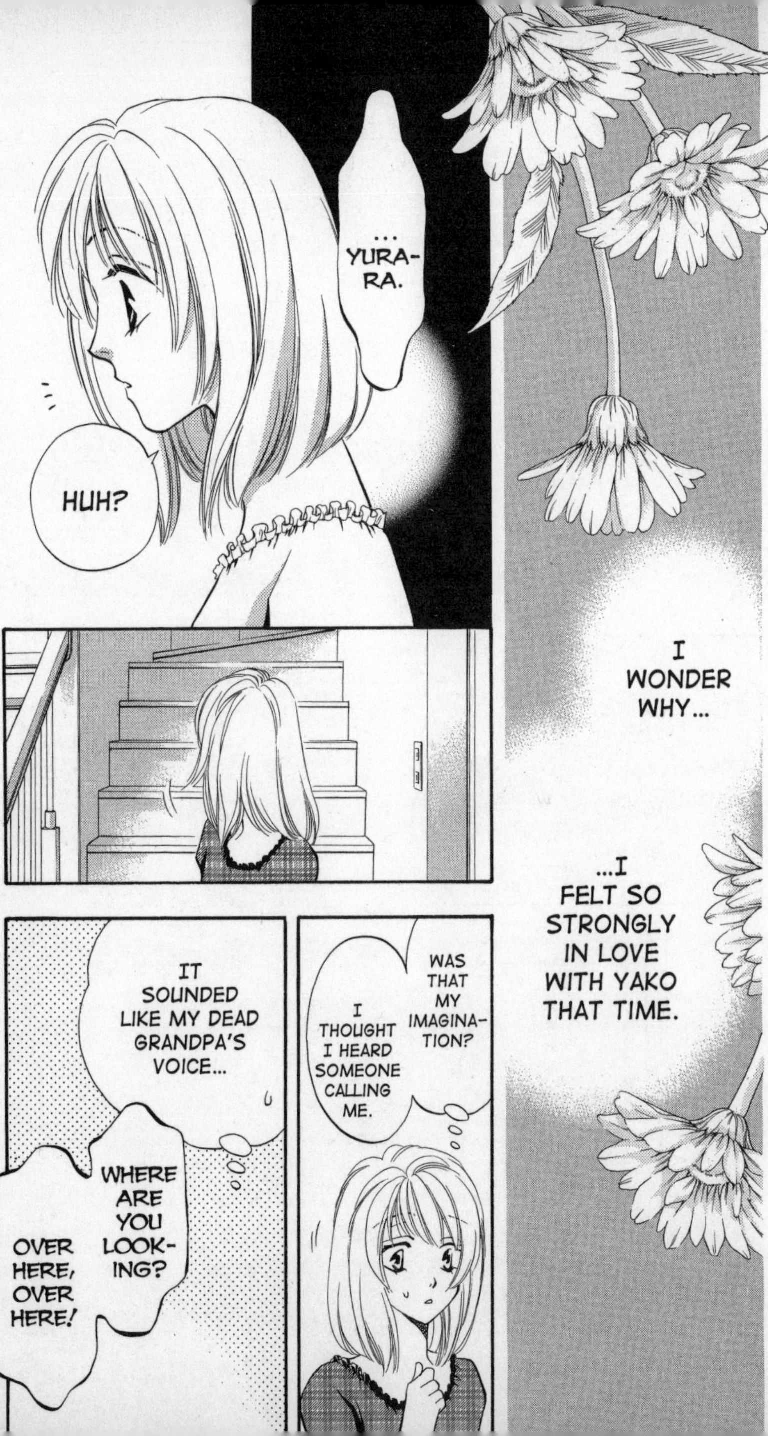
I WONDER WHY...
...I FELT SO STRONGLY IN LOVE WITH YAKO THAT TIME.
...YURA-RA.
HUH?
WAS THAT MY IMAGINATION?
I THOUGHT I HEARD SOMEONE CALLING ME.
IT SOUNDED LIKE MY DEAD GRANDPA'S VOICE...
WHERE ARE YOU LOOKING-ING?
OVER HERE, OVER HERE!

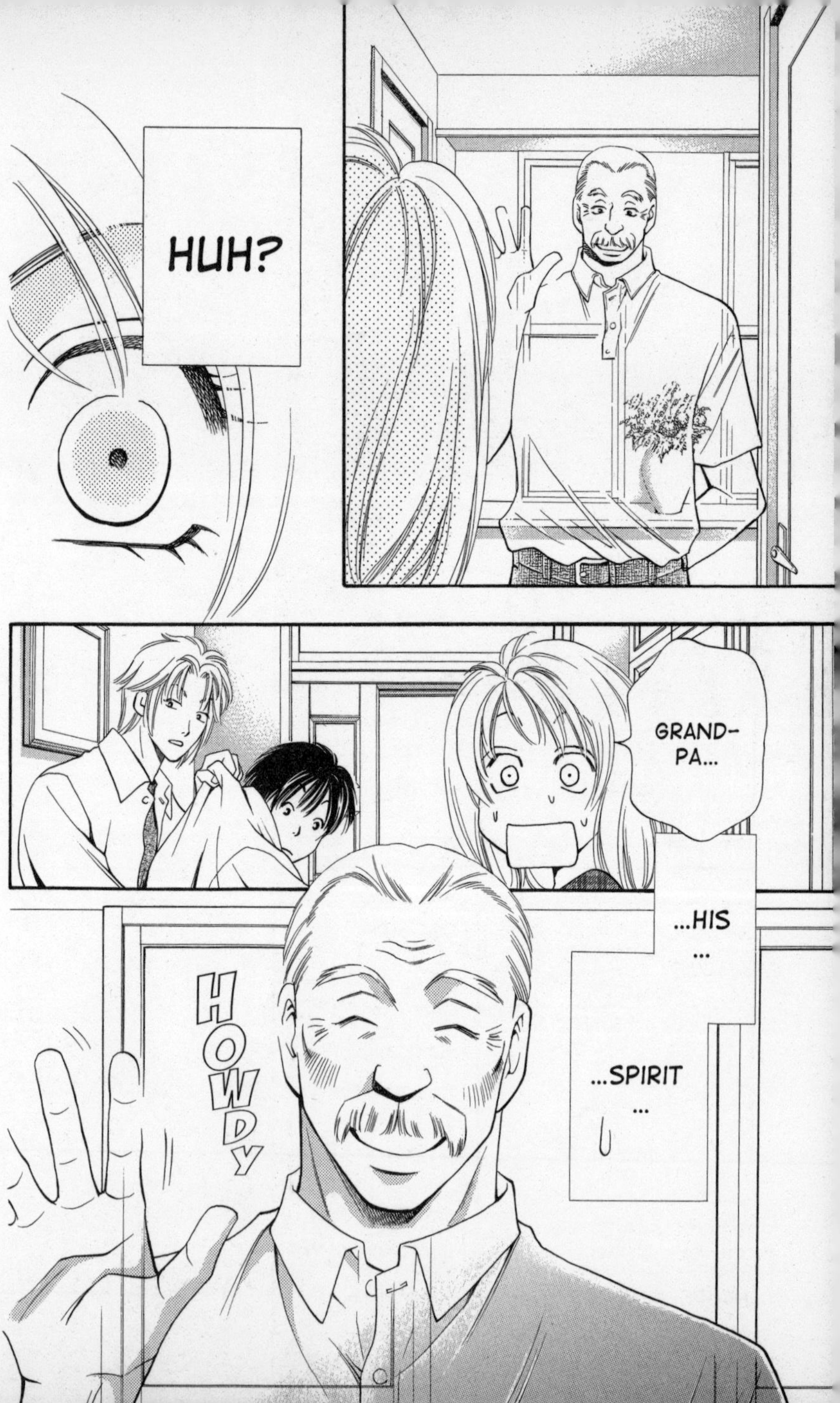
HUH?
GRAND-PA...
...HIS ...
...SPIRIT ...
HOWDY

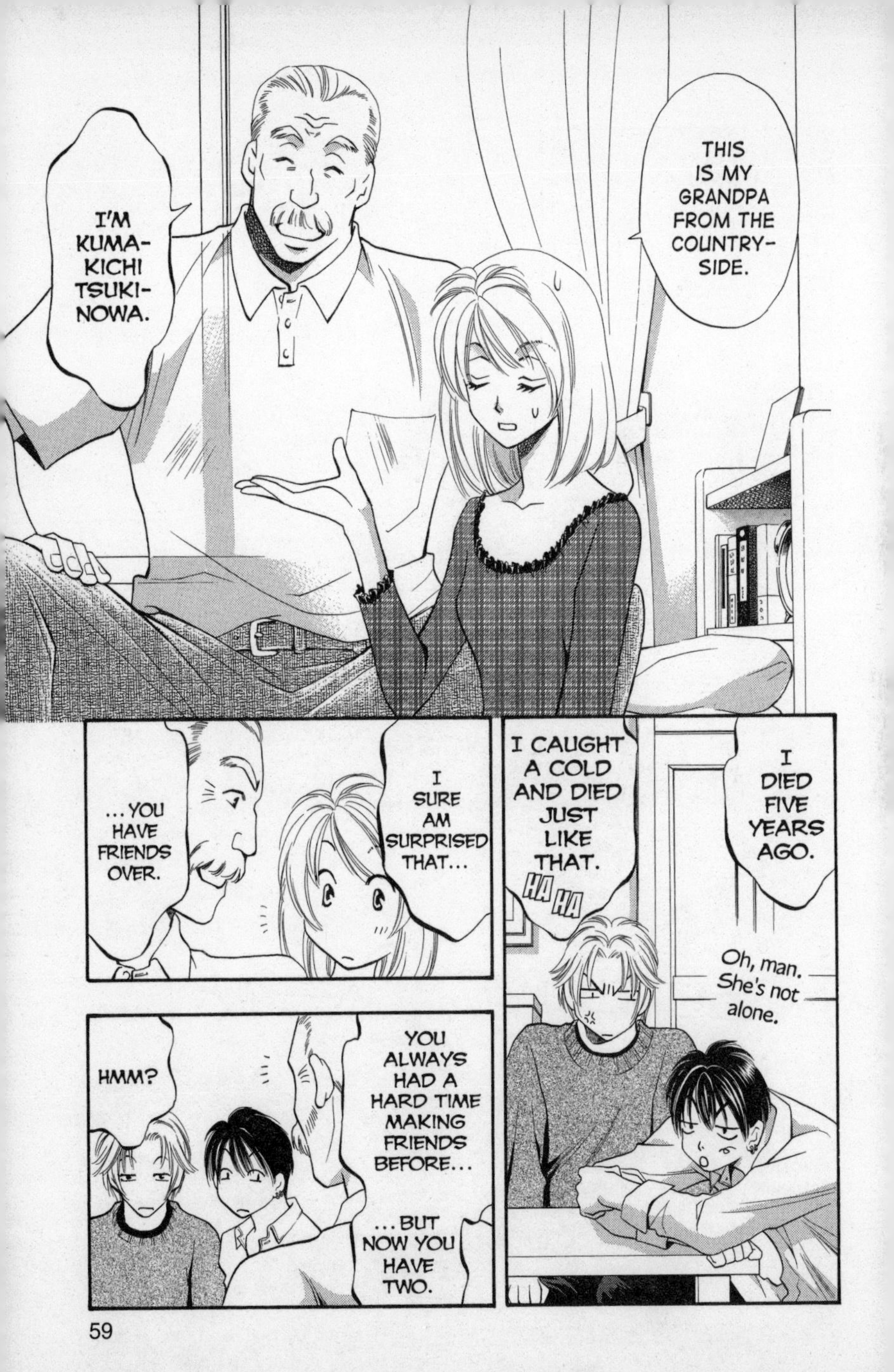
THIS IS MY GRANDPA FROM THE COUNTRYSIDE.
I'M KUMAKICHI TSUKINOWA.
I DIED FIVE YEARS AGO.
I CAUGHT A COLD AND DIED JUST LIKE THAT.
HA HA
Oh, man. She's not alone.
I SURE AM SURPRISED THAT...
...YOU HAVE FRIENDS OVER.
YOU ALWAYS HAD A HARD TIME MAKING FRIENDS BEFORE...
...BUT NOW YOU HAVE TWO.
HMM?

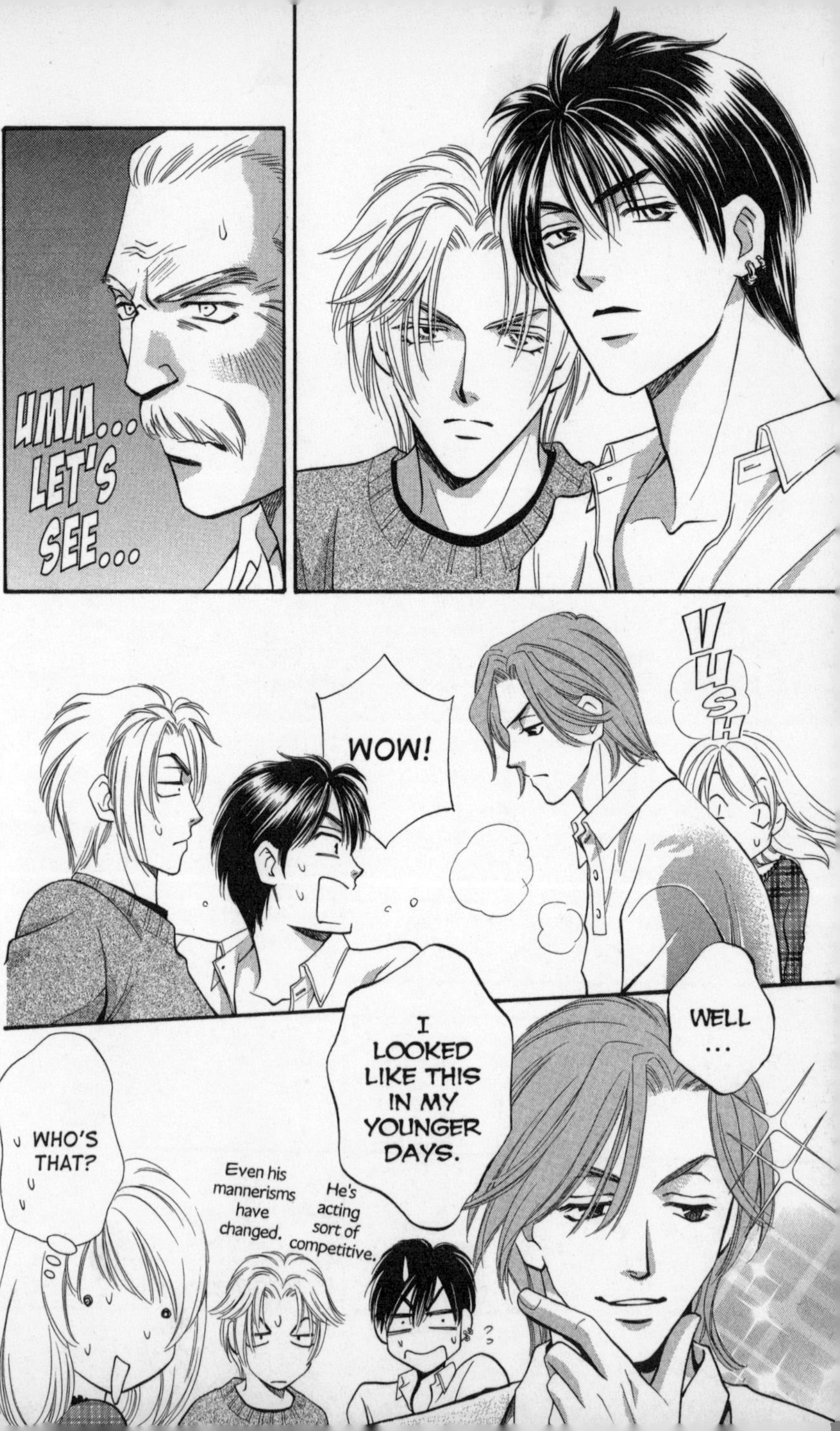
UMM... LET'S SEE...
VUSH
WOW!
WELL ...
I LOOKED LIKE THIS IN MY YOUNGER DAYS.
He's acting sort of competitive.
Even his mannerisms have changed.
WHO'S THAT?

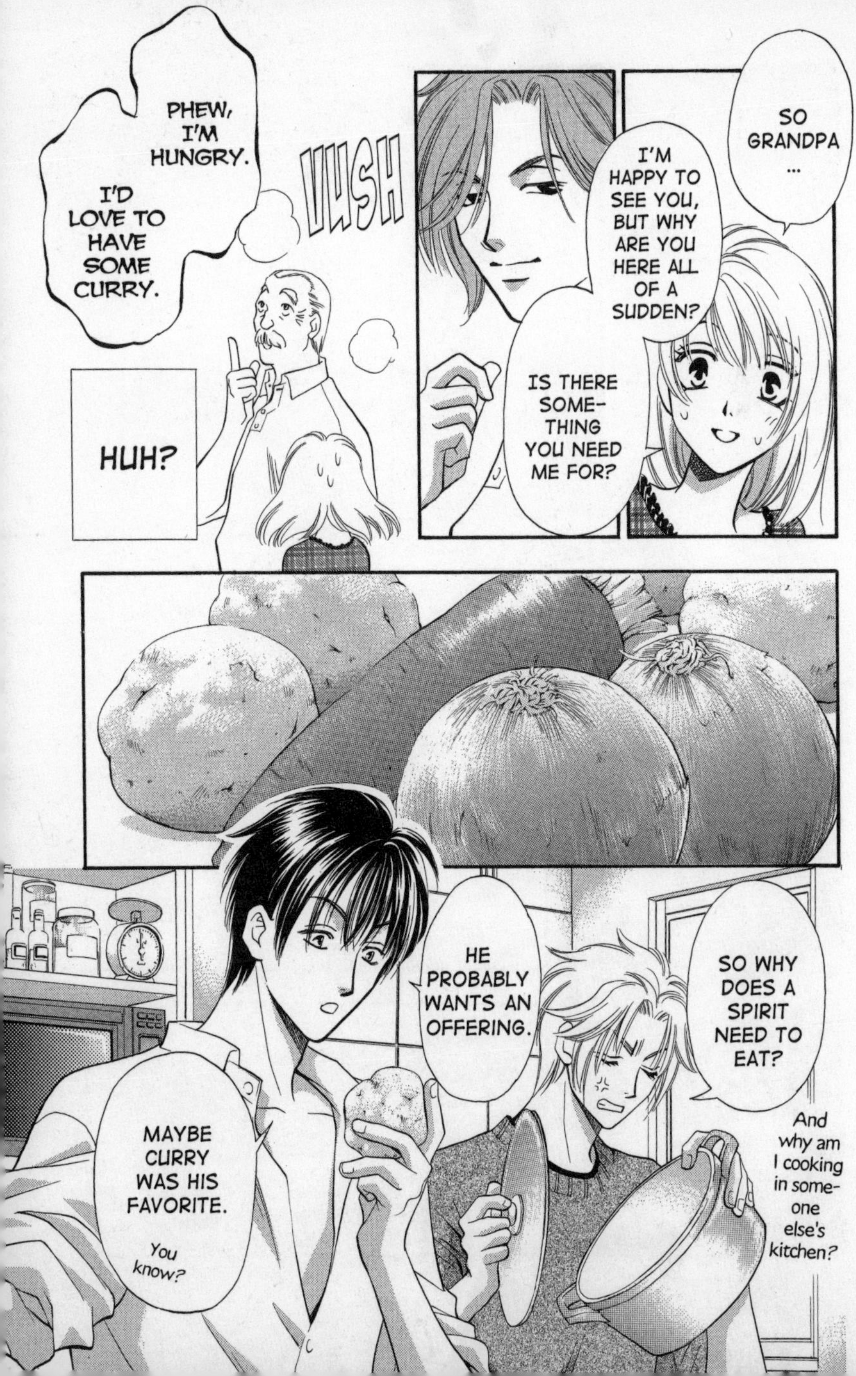
SO GRANDPA ...
I'M HAPPY TO SEE YOU, BUT WHY ARE YOU HERE ALL OF A SUDDEN?
IS THERE SOME-THING YOU NEED ME FOR?
PHEW, I'M HUNGRY.
I'D LOVE TO HAVE SOME CURRY.
VUSH
HUH?
SO WHY DOES A SPIRIT NEED TO EAT?
And why am I cooking in some-one else's kitchen?
HE PROBABLY WANTS AN OFFERING.
MAYBE CURRY WAS HIS FAVORITE.
You know?

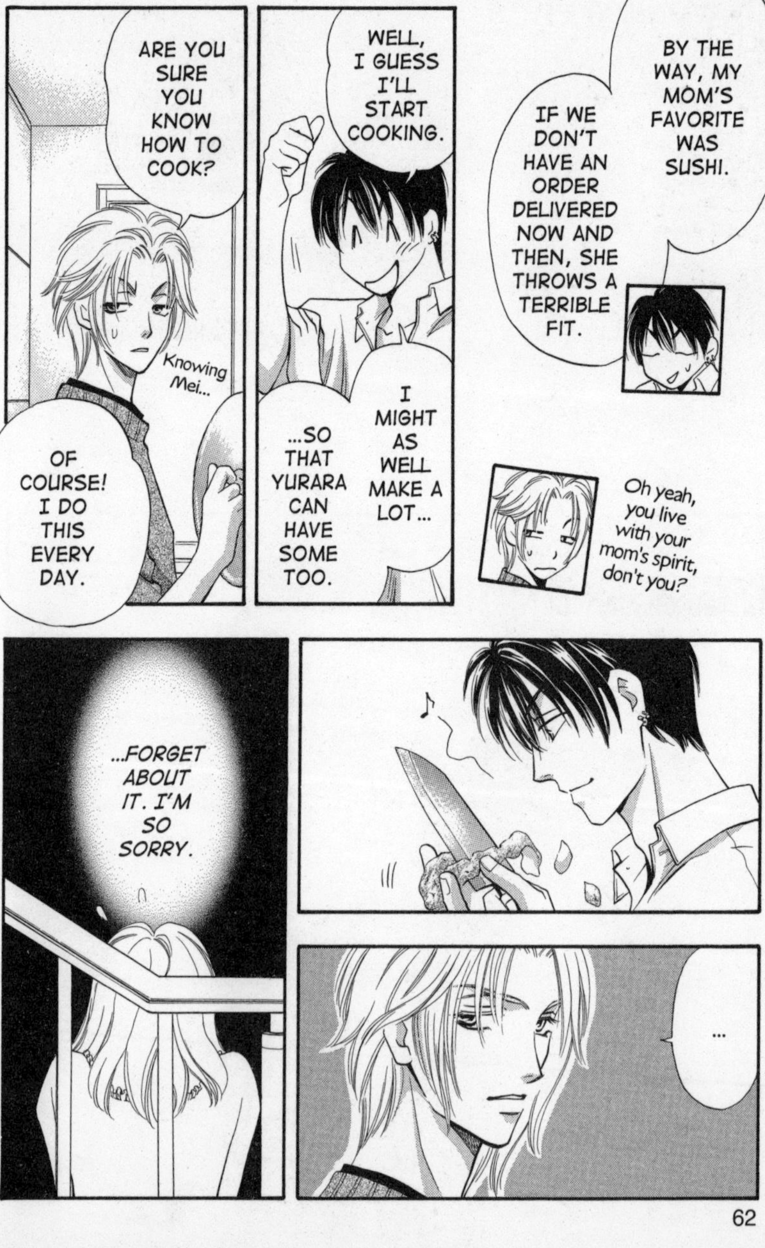
BY THE WAY, MY MOM'S FAVORITE WAS SUSHI.
IF WE DON'T HAVE AN ORDER DELIVERED NOW AND THEN, SHE THROWS A TERRIBLE FIT.
Oh yeah, you live with your mom's spirit, don't you?
WELL, I GUESS I'LL START COOKING.
I MIGHT AS WELL MAKE A LOT...
...SO THAT YURARA CAN HAVE SOME TOO.
ARE YOU SURE YOU KNOW HOW TO COOK?
Knowing Mei...
OF COURSE! I DO THIS EVERY DAY.
...
...FORGET ABOUT IT. I'M SO SORRY.

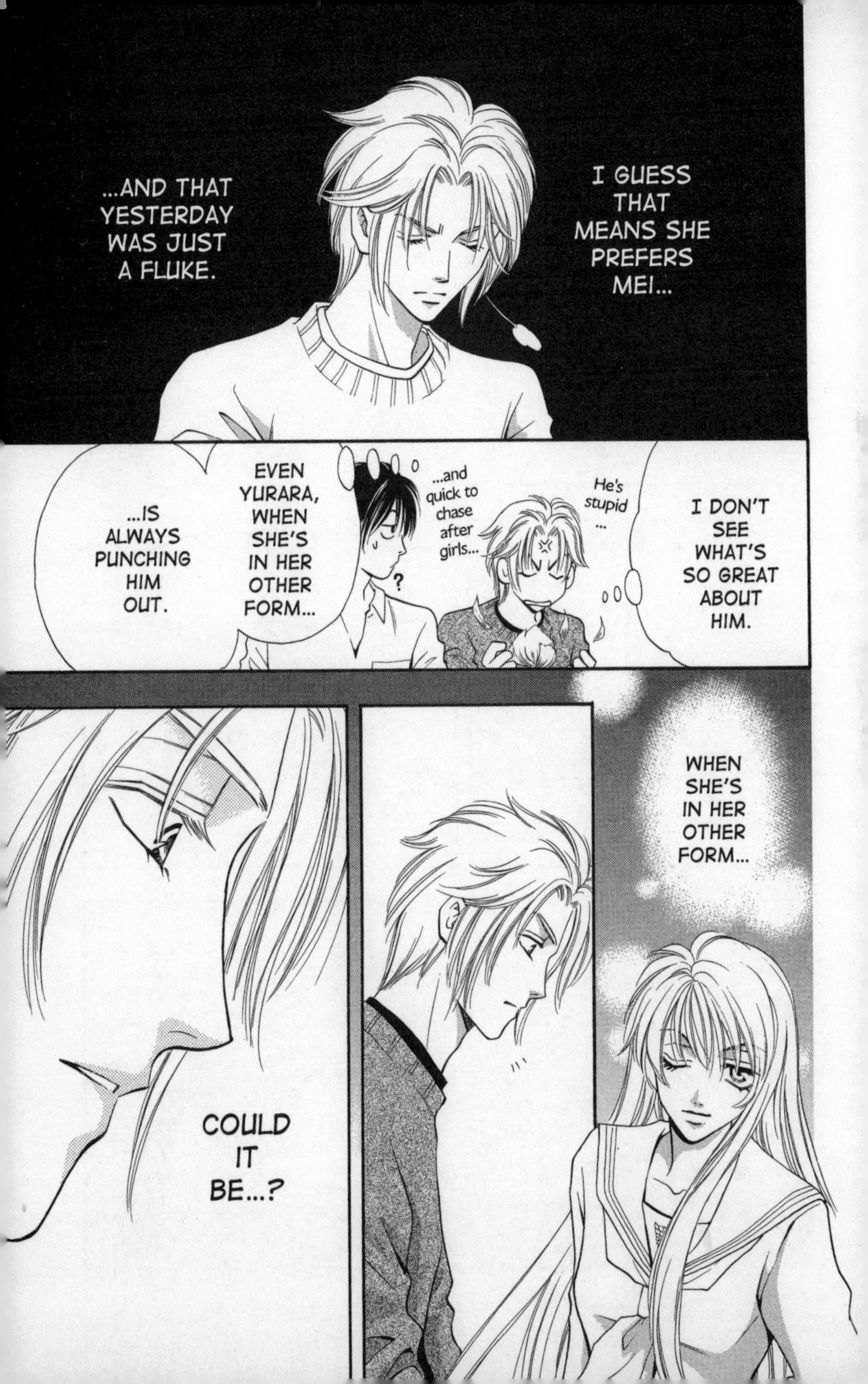
I GUESS THAT MEANS SHE PREFERS MEI...
...AND THAT YESTERDAY WAS JUST A FLUKE.
I DON'T SEE WHAT'S SO GREAT ABOUT HIM.
He's stupid ...
...and quick to chase after girls...
EVEN YURARA, WHEN SHE'S IN HER OTHER FORM...
...IS ALWAYS PUNCHING HIM OUT.
WHEN SHE'S IN HER OTHER FORM...
COULD IT BE...?

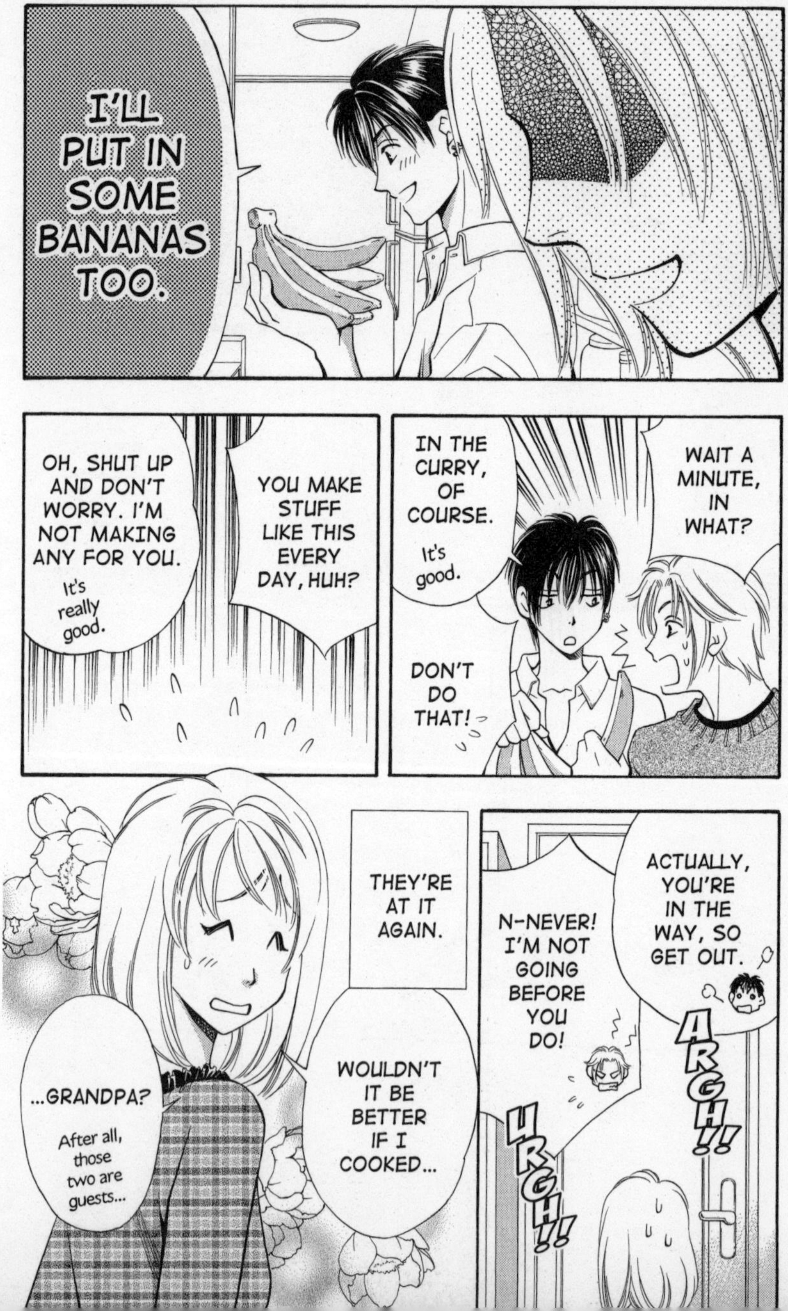
I'LL PUT IN SOME BANANAS TOO.
WAIT A MINUTE, IN WHAT?
IN THE CURRY, OF COURSE.
It's good.
DON'T DO THAT!
YOU MAKE STUFF LIKE THIS EVERY DAY, HUH?
OH, SHUT UP AND DON'T WORRY. I'M NOT MAKING ANY FOR YOU.
It's really good.
ACTUALLY, YOU'RE IN THE WAY, SO GET OUT.
ARGH!!
N-NEVER! I'M NOT GOING BEFORE YOU DO!
URGH!!
THEY'RE AT IT AGAIN.
WOULDN'T IT BE BETTER IF I COOKED...
...GRANDPA?
After all, those two are guests...

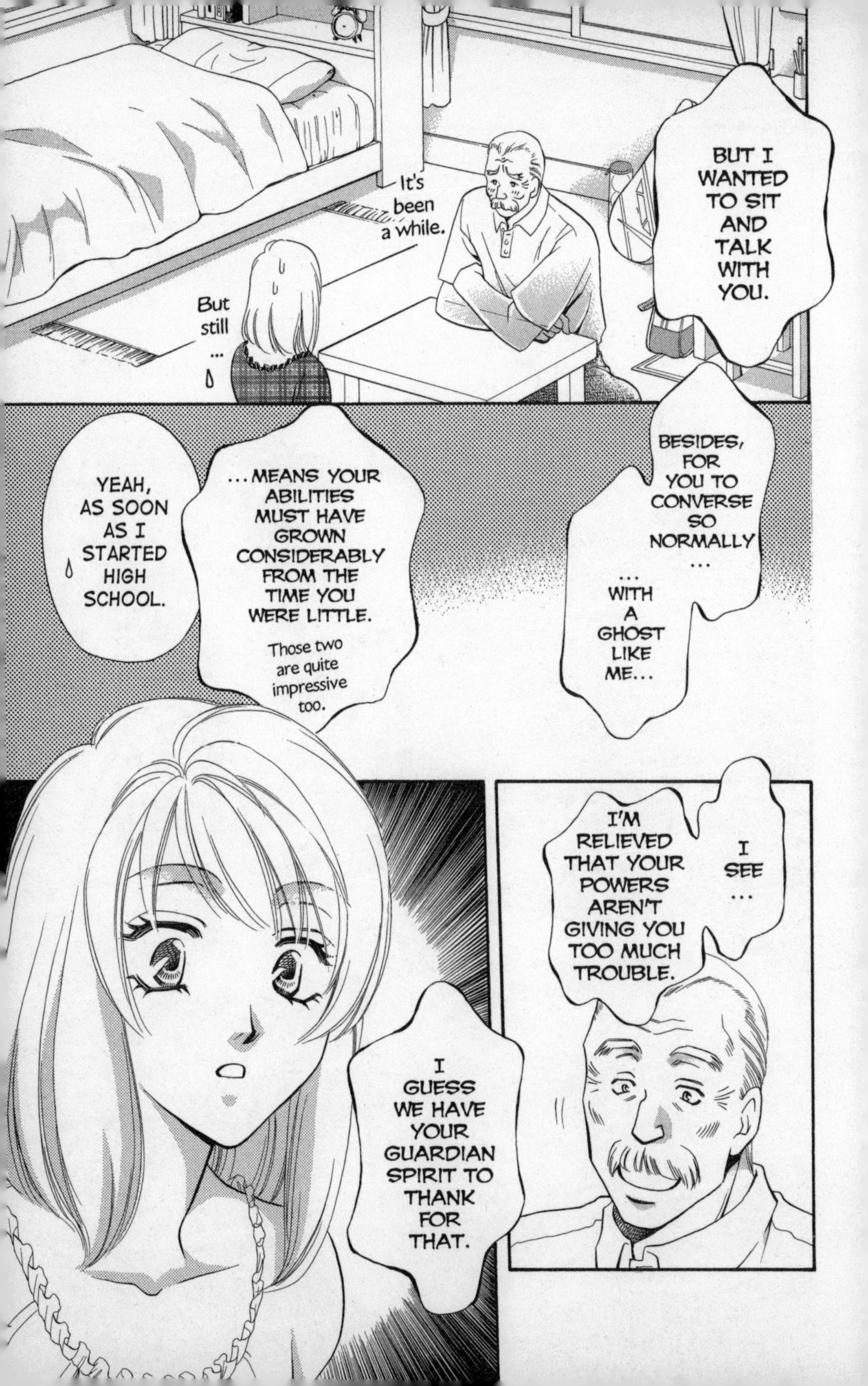
BUT I WANTED TO SIT AND TALK WITH YOU.
It's been a while.
But still ...
BESIDES, FOR YOU TO CONVERSE SO NORMALLY ...
... WITH A GHOST LIKE ME...
...MEANS YOUR ABILITIES MUST HAVE GROWN CONSIDERABLY FROM THE TIME YOU WERE LITTLE.
Those two are quite impressive too.
YEAH, AS SOON AS I STARTED HIGH SCHOOL.
I SEE ...
I'M RELIEVED THAT YOUR POWERS AREN'T GIVING YOU TOO MUCH TROUBLE.
I GUESS WE HAVE YOUR GUARDIAN SPIRIT TO THANK FOR THAT.

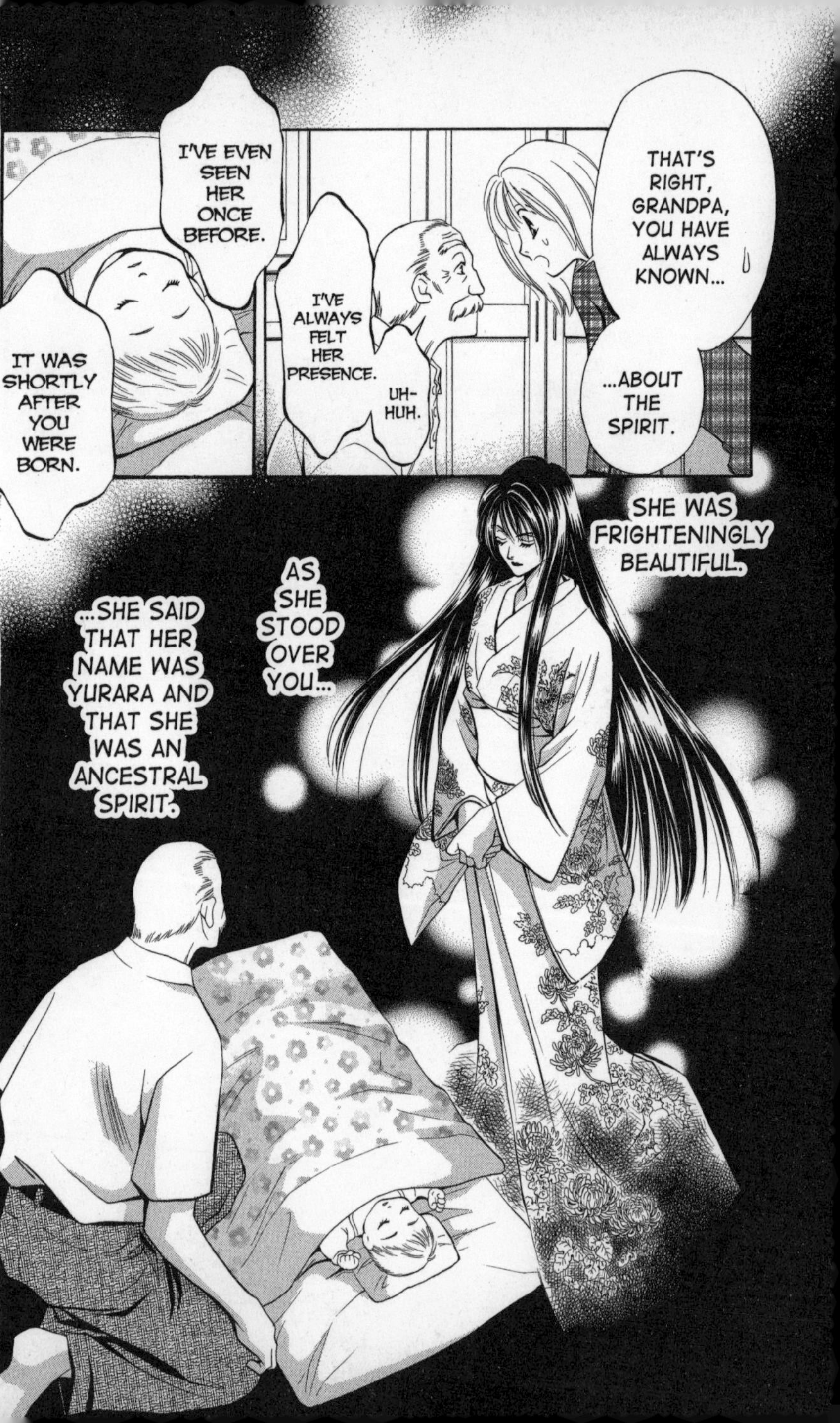
THAT'S RIGHT, GRANDPA, YOU HAVE ALWAYS KNOWN...
...ABOUT THE SPIRIT.
UH-HUH.
I'VE ALWAYS FELT HER PRESENCE.
I'VE EVEN SEEN HER ONCE BEFORE.
IT WAS SHORTLY AFTER YOU WERE BORN.
SHE WAS FRIGHTENINGLY BEAUTIFUL.
AS SHE STOOD OVER YOU...
...SHE SAID THAT HER NAME WAS YURARA AND THAT SHE WAS AN ANCESTRAL SPIRIT.

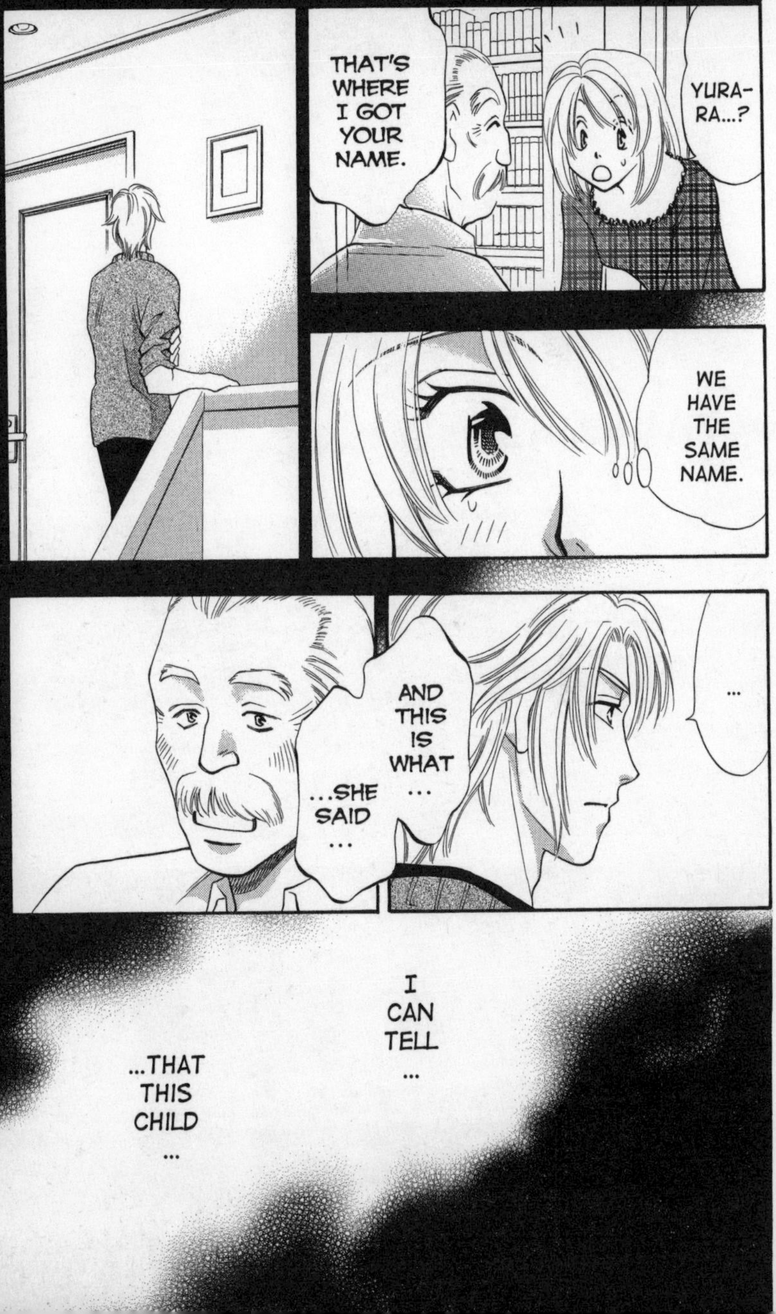
YURA-RA...?
THAT'S WHERE I GOT YOUR NAME.
WE HAVE THE SAME NAME.
...
AND THIS IS WHAT...
...SHE SAID...
I CAN TELL...
...THAT THIS CHILD...

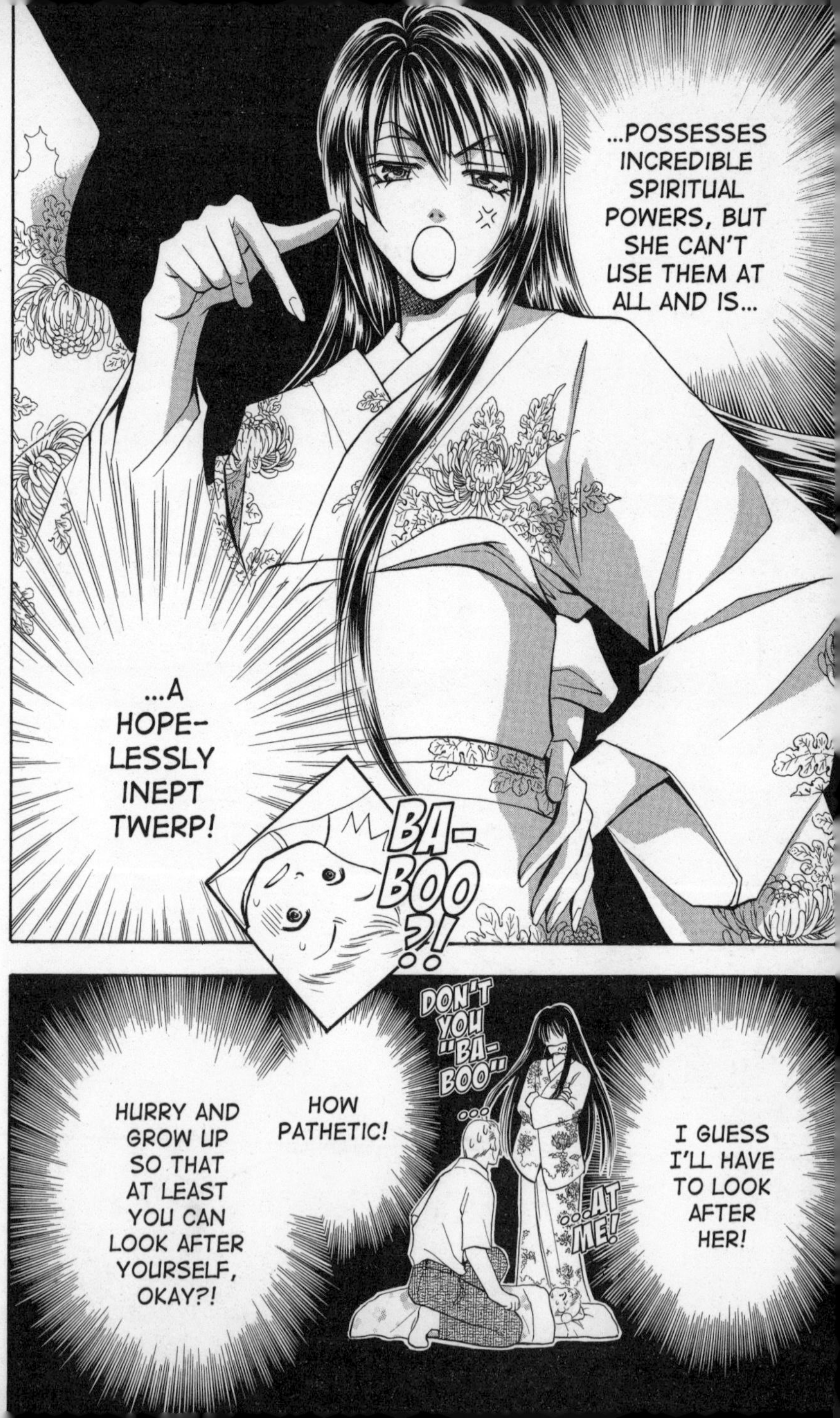
...POSSESSES INCREDIBLE SPIRITUAL POWERS, BUT SHE CAN'T USE THEM AT ALL AND IS...
...A HOPE-LESSLY INEPT TWERP!
BA-BOO?!
I GUESS I'LL HAVE TO LOOK AFTER HER!
DON'T YOU "BA-BOO"
...AT ME!
...
HOW PATHETIC!
HURRY AND GROW UP SO THAT AT LEAST YOU CAN LOOK AFTER YOURSELF, OKAY?!

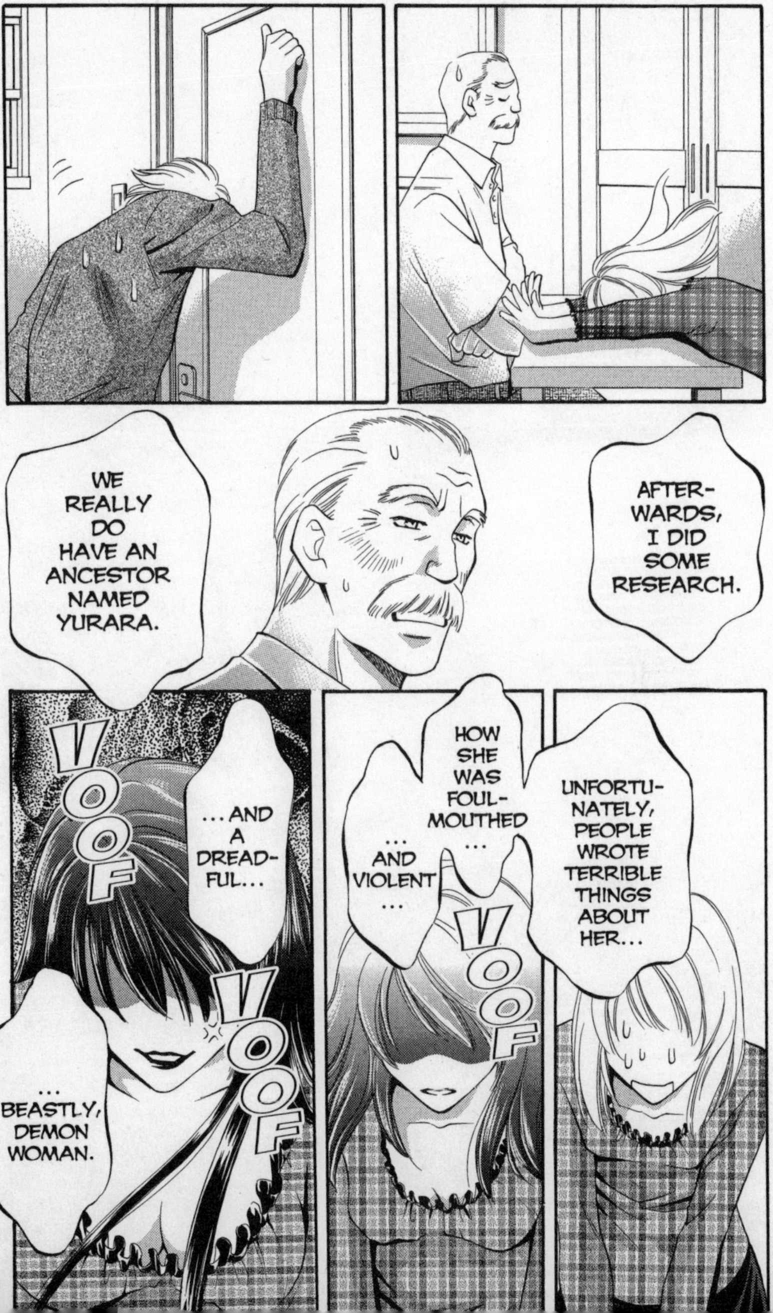
AFTER-
WARDS,
I DID
SOME
RESEARCH.
WE
REALLY
DO
HAVE AN
ANCESTOR
NAMED
YURARA.
UNFORTU-
NATELY,
PEOPLE
WROTE
TERRIBLE
THINGS
ABOUT
HER...
HOW
SHE
WAS
FOUL-
MOUTHED
...
...
AND
VIOLENT
...
VOOF
VOOF
...AND
A
DREAD-
FUL...
VOOF
...
BEASTLY,
DEMON
WOMAN.

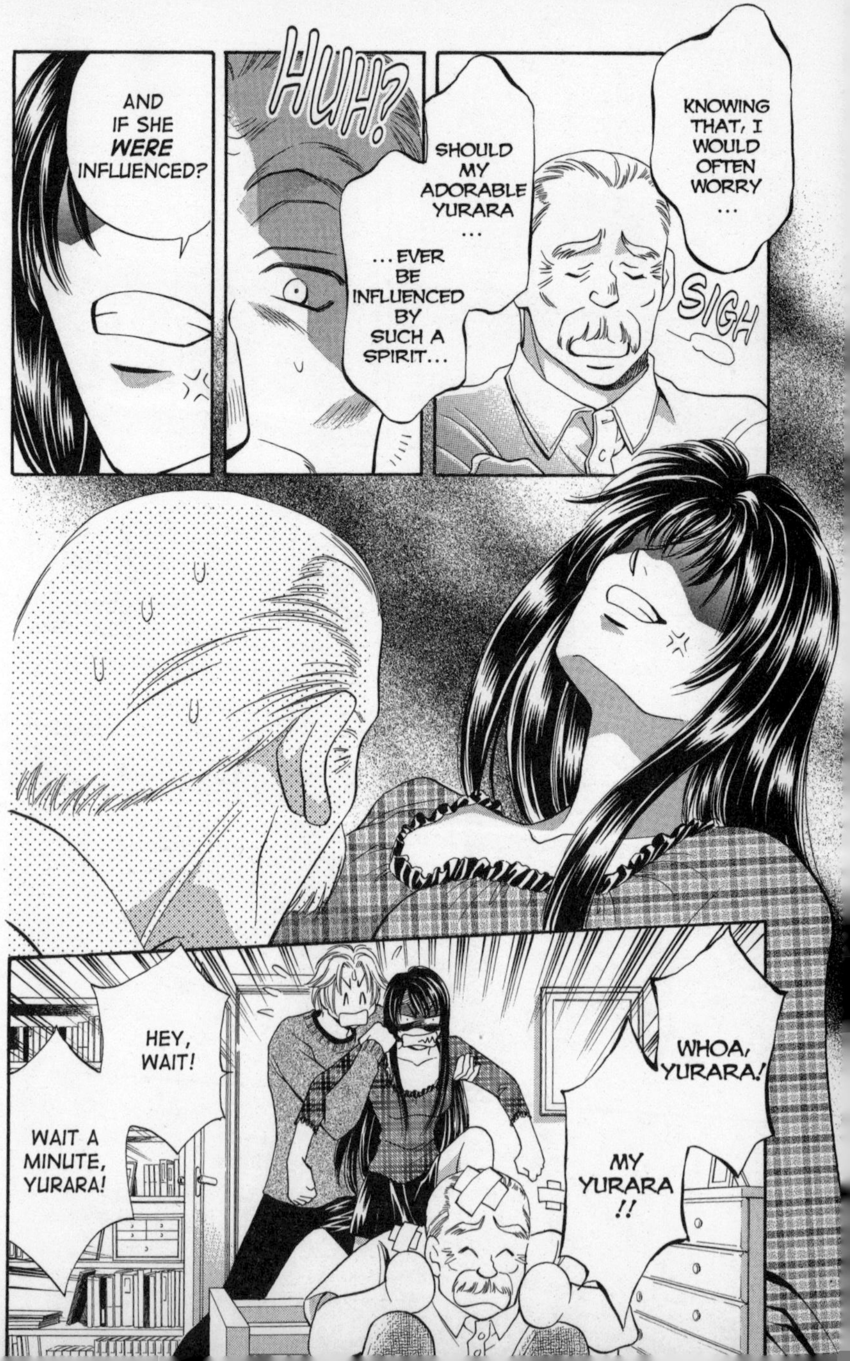
KNOWING THAT, I WOULD OFTEN WORRY ...
SIGH
SHOULD MY ADORABLE YURARA ...
...EVER BE INFLUENCED BY SUCH A SPIRIT...
HUH?
AND IF SHE WERE INFLUENCED?
WHOA, YURARA!
MY YURARA !!
HEY, WAIT!
WAIT A MINUTE, YURARA!

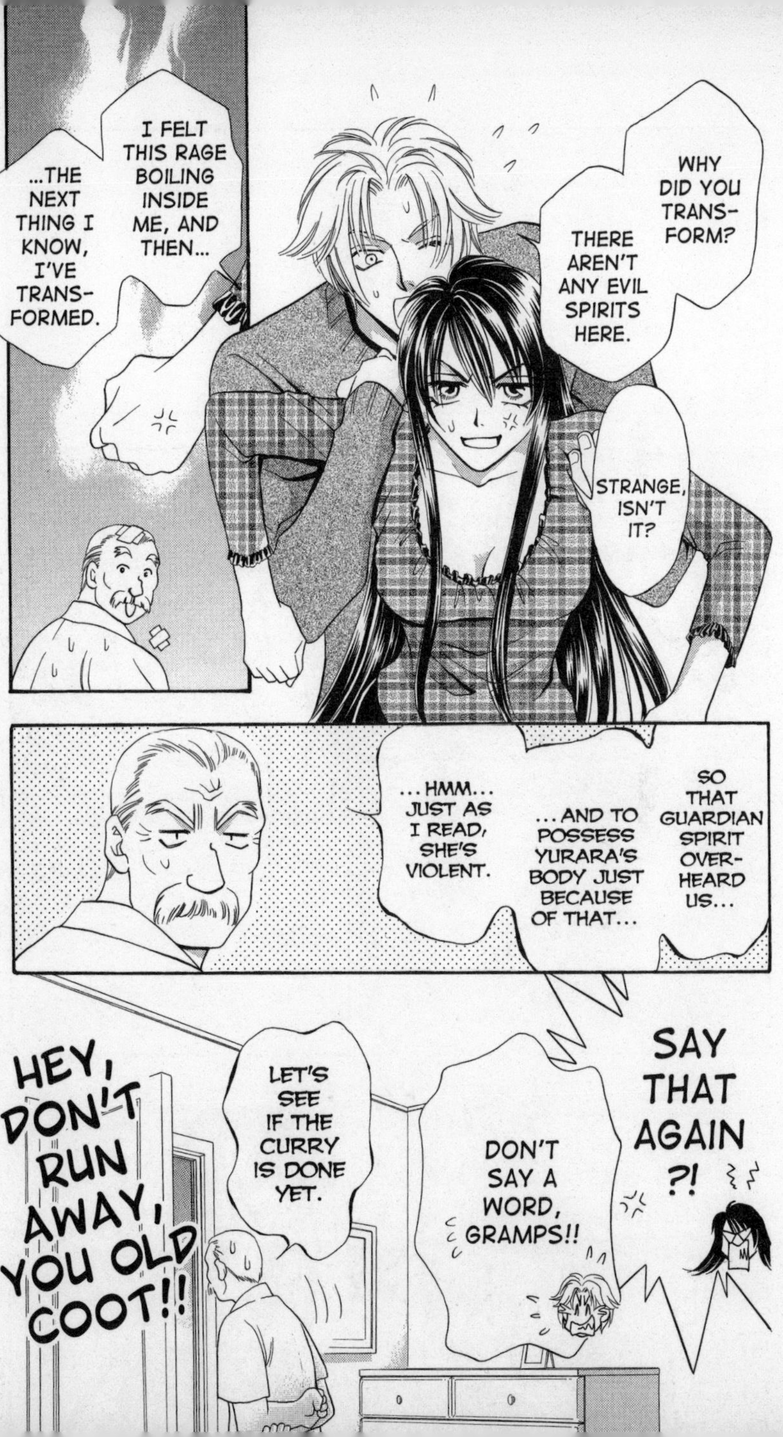
WHY DID YOU TRANS-FORM?
THERE AREN'T ANY EVIL SPIRITS HERE.
STRANGE, ISN'T IT?
I FELT THIS RAGE BOILING INSIDE ME, AND THEN...
...THE NEXT THING I KNOW, I'VE TRANS-FORMED.
SO THAT GUARDIAN SPIRIT OVER-HEARD US...
...AND TO POSSESS YURARA'S BODY JUST BECAUSE OF THAT...
...HMM... JUST AS I READ, SHE'S VIOLENT.
SAY THAT AGAIN?!
DON'T SAY A WORD, GRAMPS!!
LET'S SEE IF THE CURRY IS DONE YET.
HEY, DON'T RUN AWAY, YOU OLD COOT!!

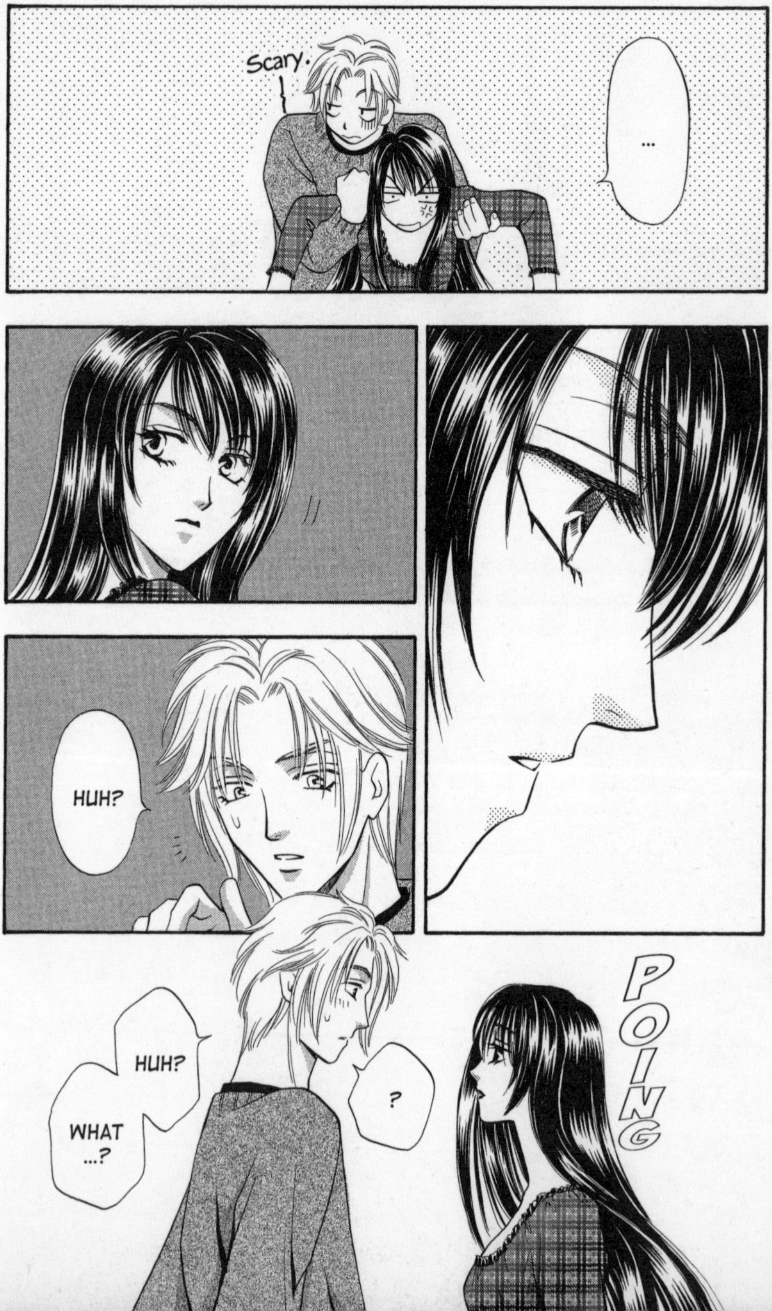
...
Scary.
HUH?
POING
?
HUH?
WHAT ...?

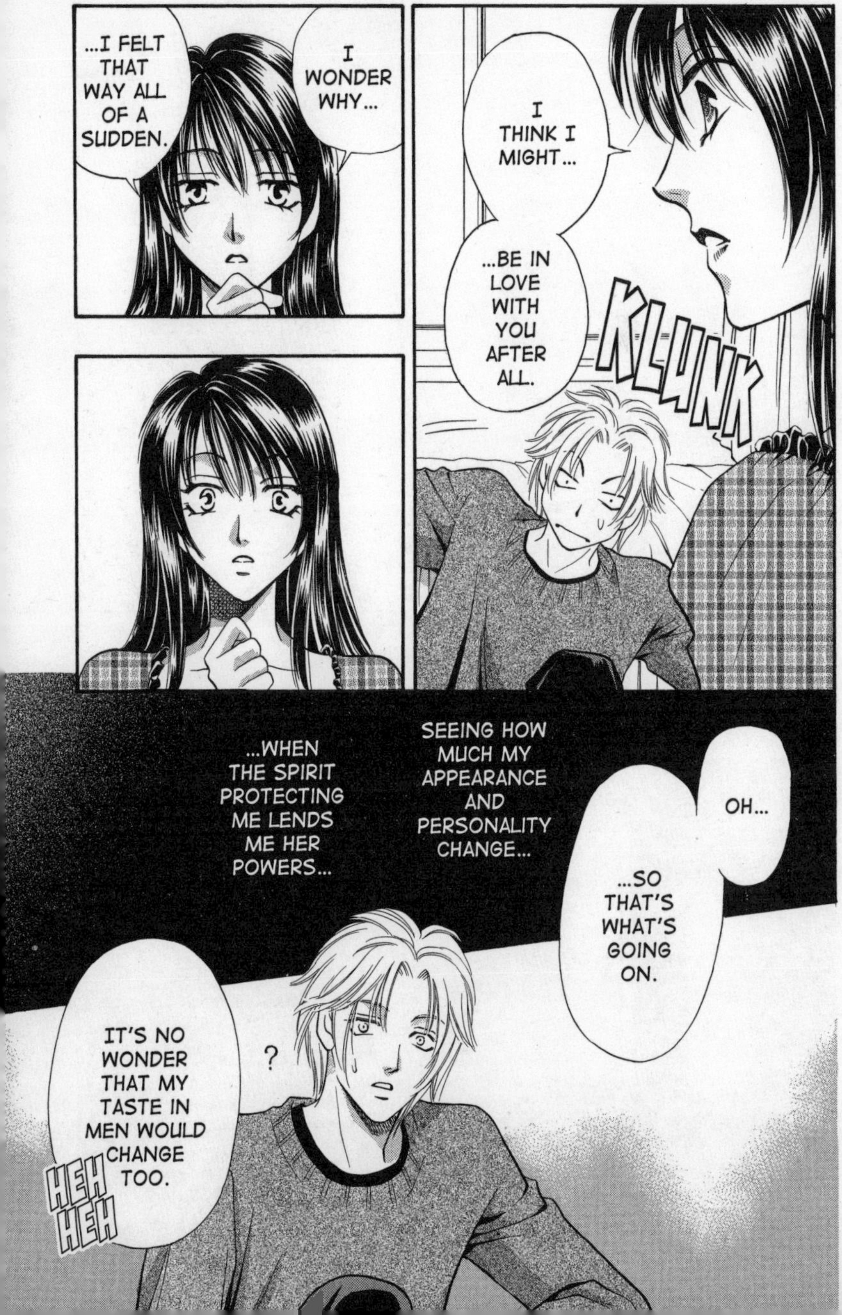
I THINK I MIGHT...
...BE IN LOVE WITH YOU AFTER ALL.
KLUNK
I WONDER WHY...
...I FELT THAT WAY ALL OF A SUDDEN.
OH...
...SO THAT'S WHAT'S GOING ON.
SEEING HOW MUCH MY APPEARANCE AND PERSONALITY CHANGE...
...WHEN THE SPIRIT PROTECTING ME LENDS ME HER POWERS...
?
IT'S NO WONDER THAT MY TASTE IN MEN WOULD CHANGE TOO.
HEH HEH

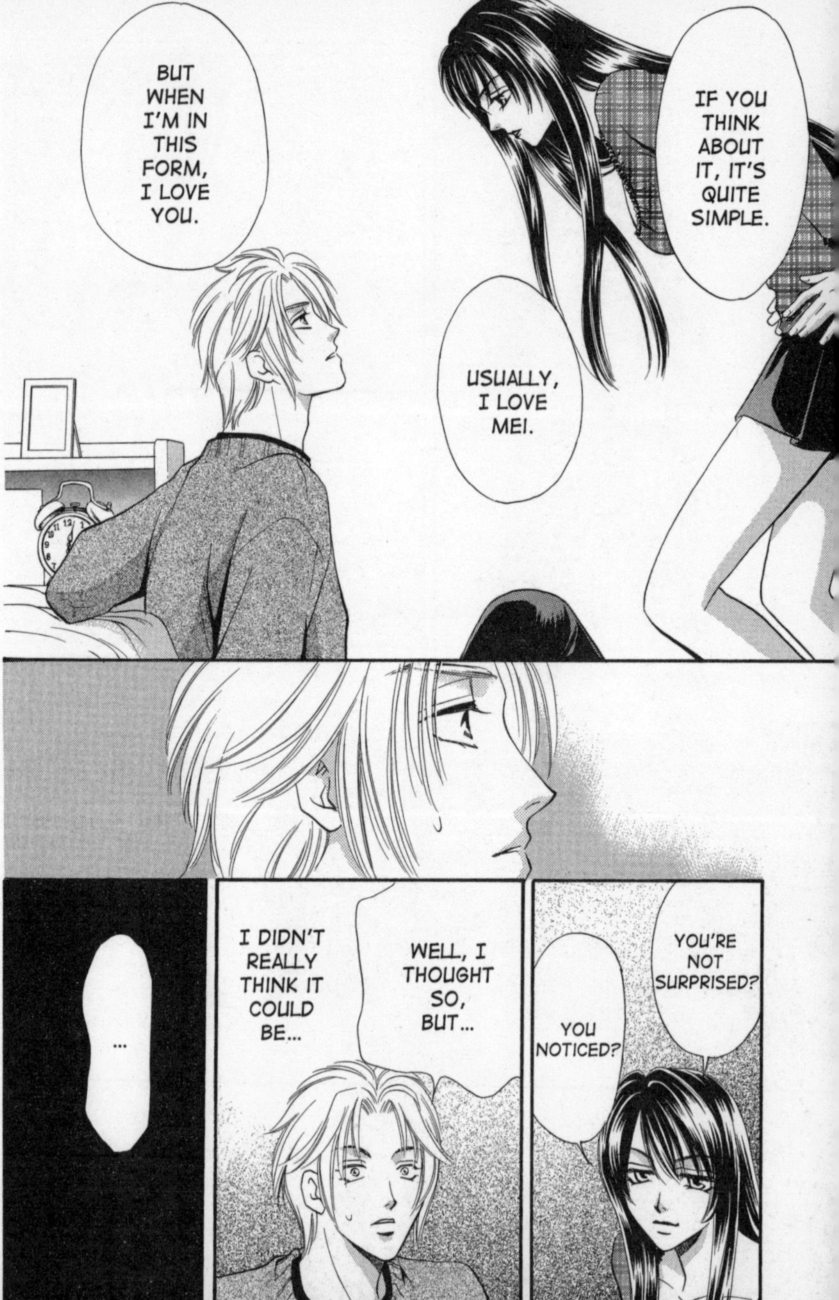
IF YOU THINK ABOUT IT, IT'S QUITE SIMPLE.
USUALLY, I LOVE MEI.
BUT WHEN I'M IN THIS FORM, I LOVE YOU.
YOU'RE NOT SURPRISED?
YOU NOTICED?
WELL, I THOUGHT SO, BUT...
I DIDN'T REALLY THINK IT COULD BE...
...

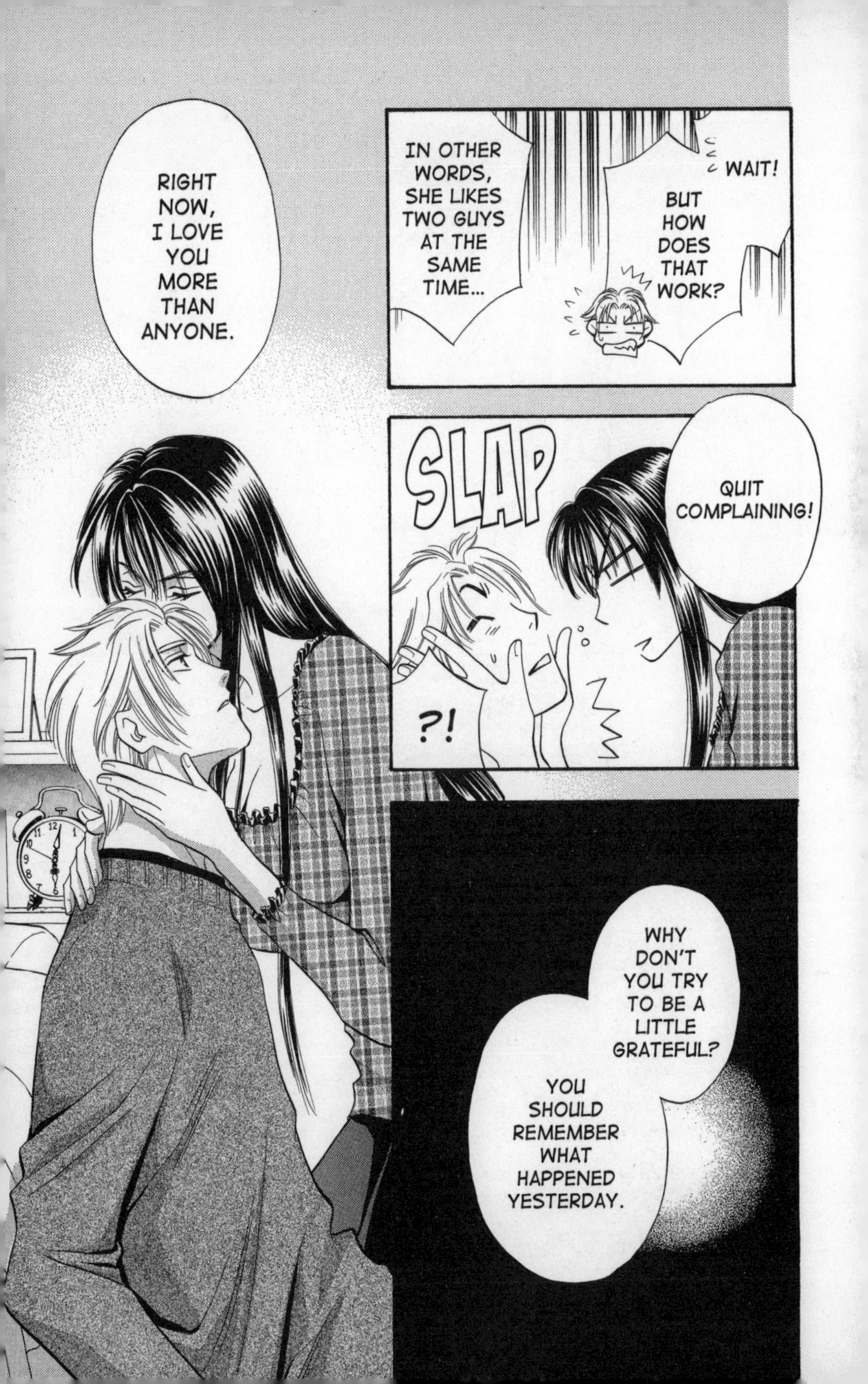
WAIT!
BUT HOW DOES THAT WORK?
IN OTHER WORDS, SHE LIKES TWO GUYS AT THE SAME TIME...
QUIT COMPLAINING!
SLAP
?!
WHY DON'T YOU TRY TO BE A LITTLE GRATEFUL?
YOU SHOULD REMEMBER WHAT HAPPENED YESTERDAY.
RIGHT NOW, I LOVE YOU MORE THAN ANYONE.

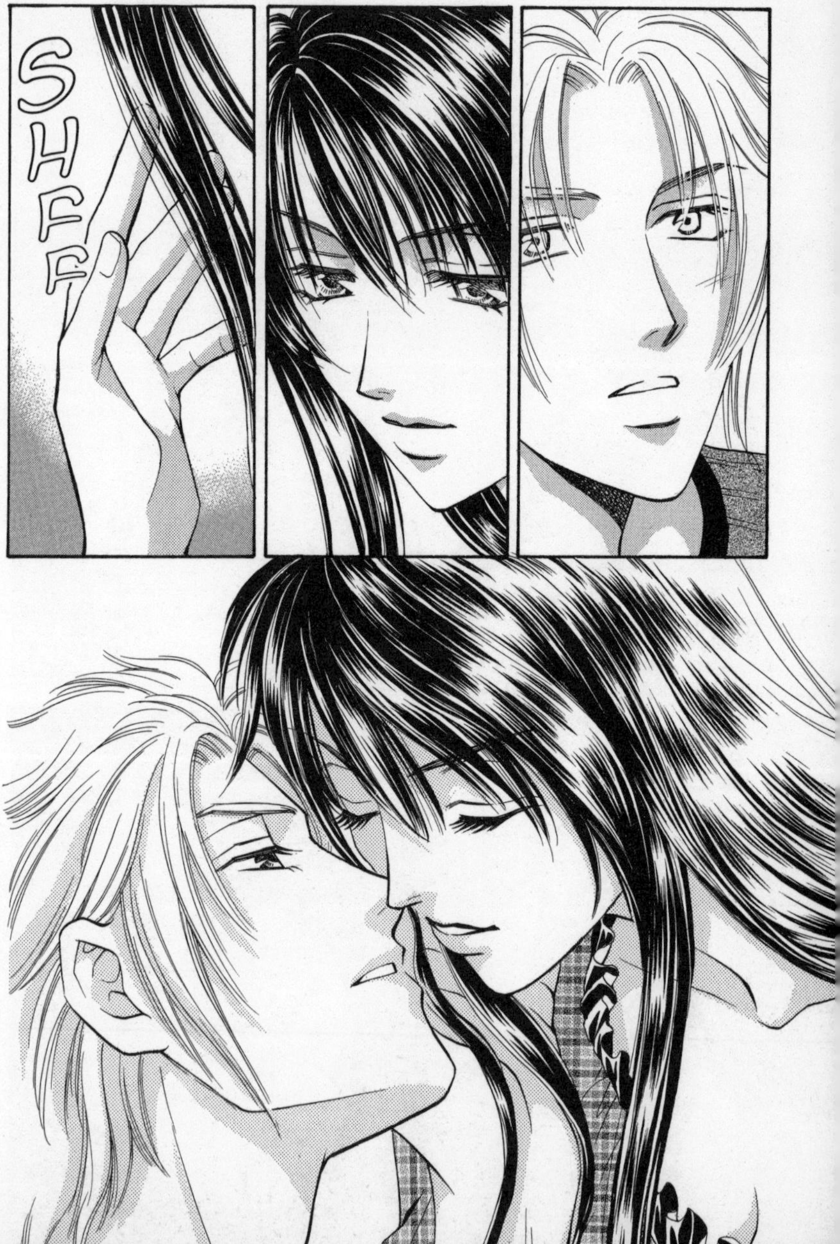
SHFF

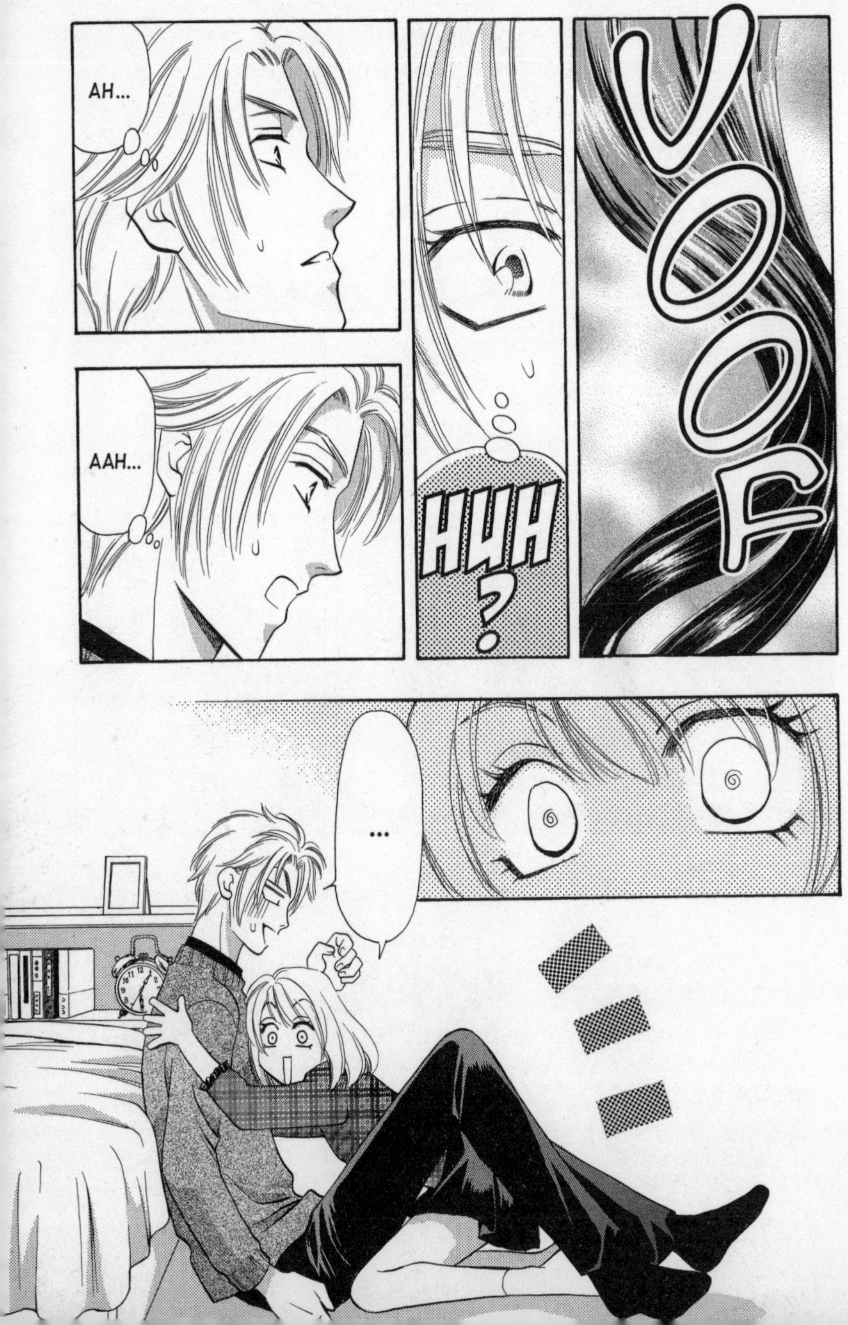
VOOF
HUH?
AH...
AAH...
...

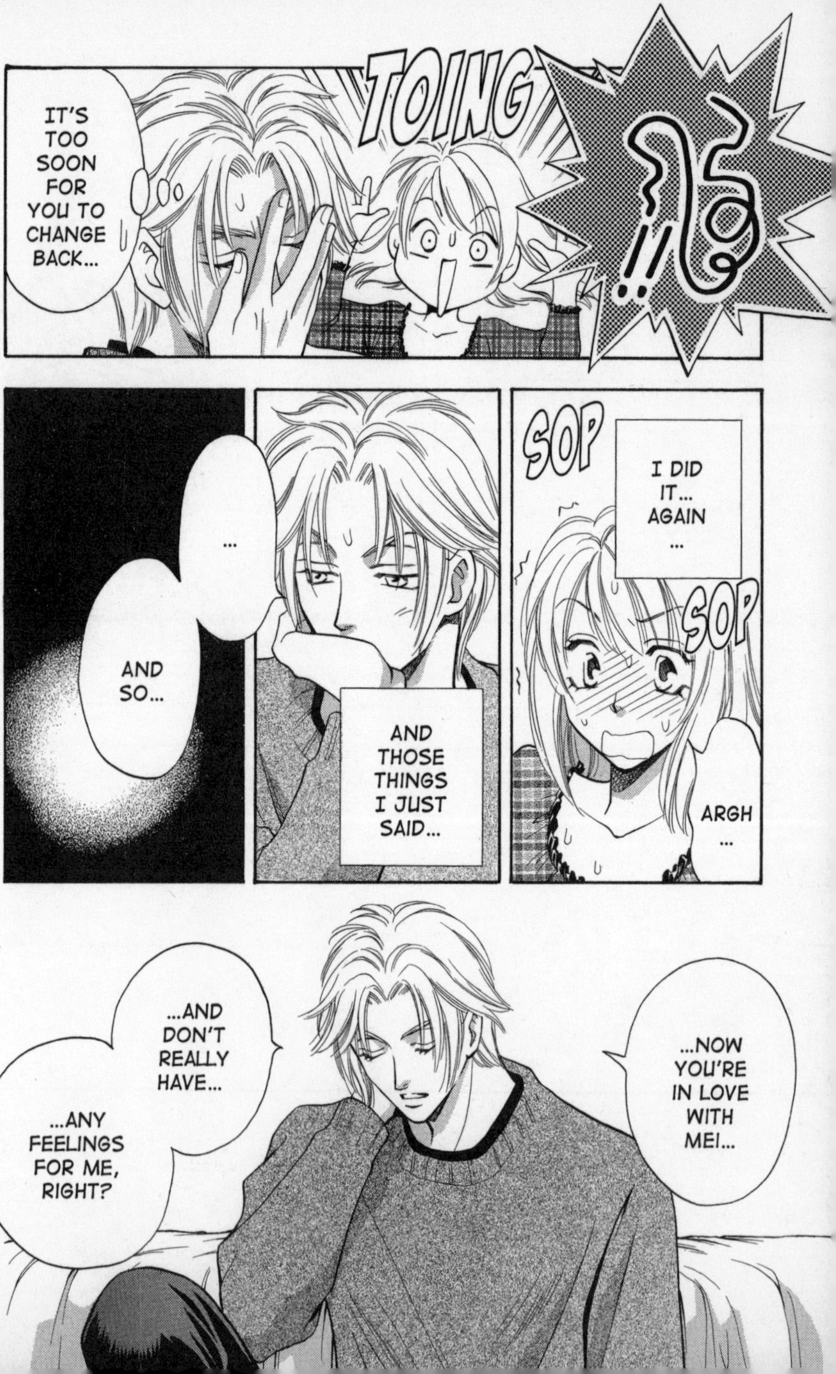
?!
TOING
IT'S TOO SOON FOR YOU TO CHANGE BACK...
SOP
I DID IT... AGAIN...
SOP
ARGH...
AND THOSE THINGS I JUST SAID...
...
AND SO...
...NOW YOU'RE IN LOVE WITH MEI...
...AND DON'T REALLY HAVE...
...ANY FEELINGS FOR ME, RIGHT?

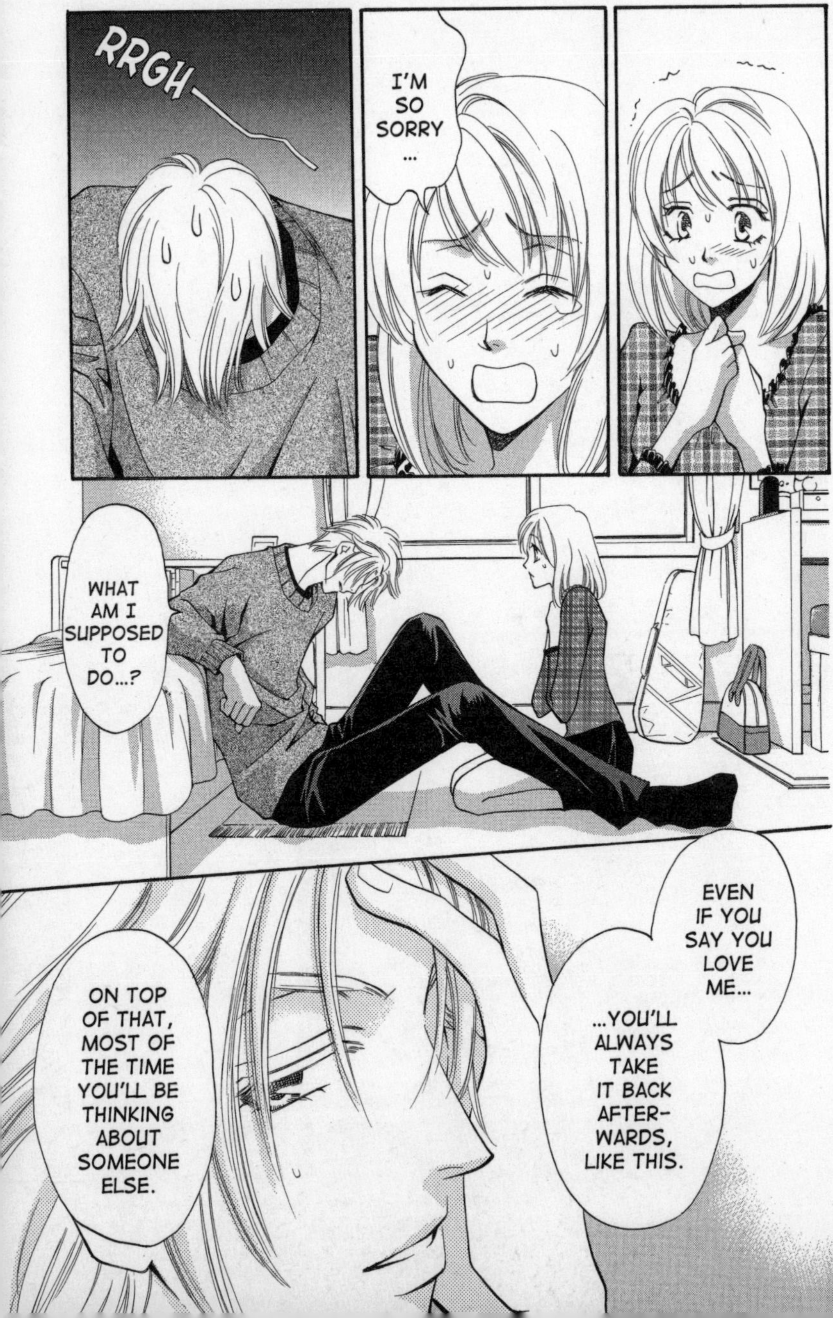
I'M SO SORRY ...
RRGH
WHAT AM I SUPPOSED TO DO...?
EVEN IF YOU SAY YOU LOVE ME...
...YOU'LL ALWAYS TAKE IT BACK AFTERWARDS, LIKE THIS.
ON TOP OF THAT, MOST OF THE TIME YOU'LL BE THINKING ABOUT SOMEONE ELSE.

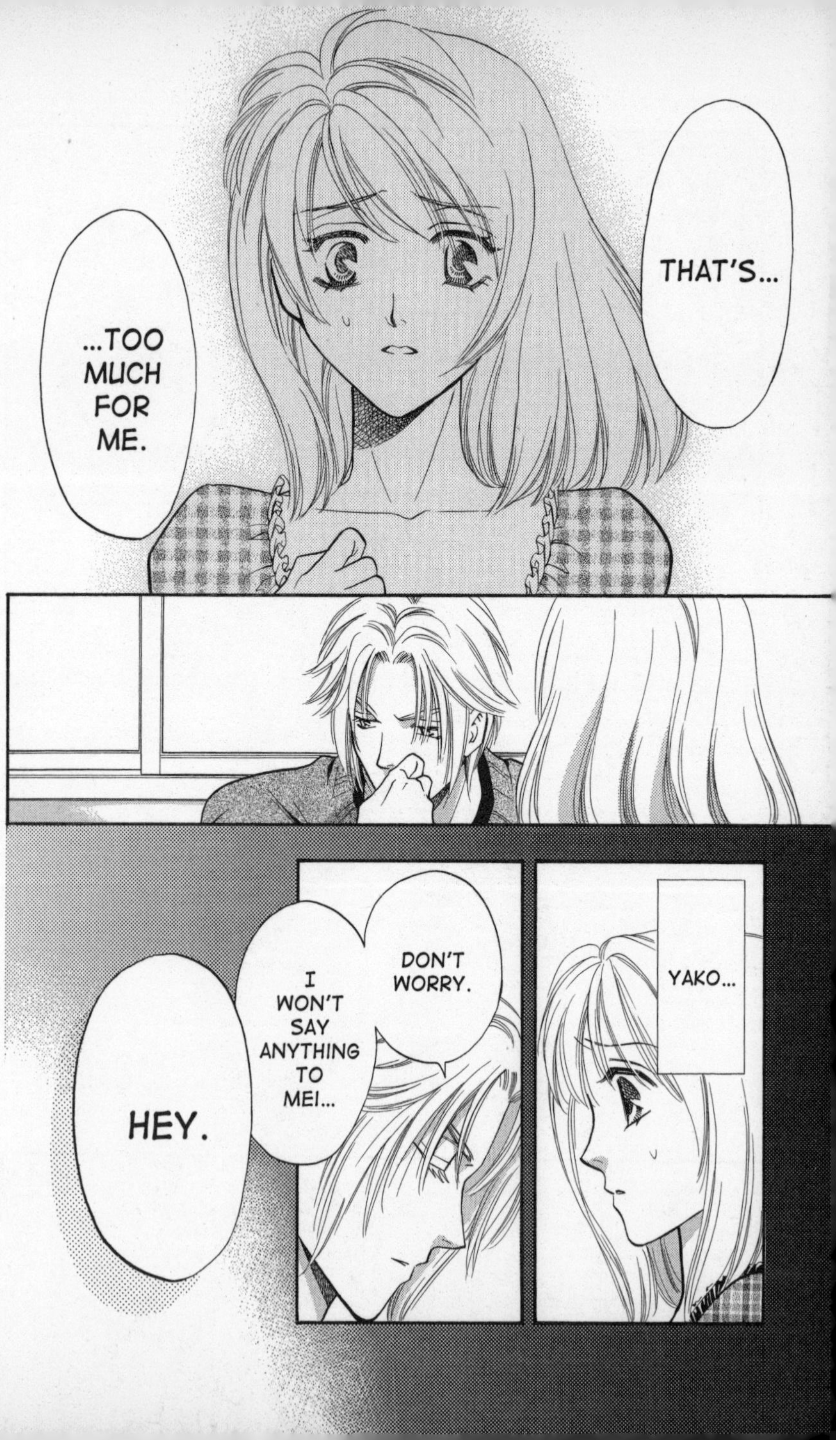
THAT'S...
...TOO MUCH FOR ME.
YAKO...
DON'T WORRY.
I WON'T SAY ANYTHING TO MEI...
HEY.

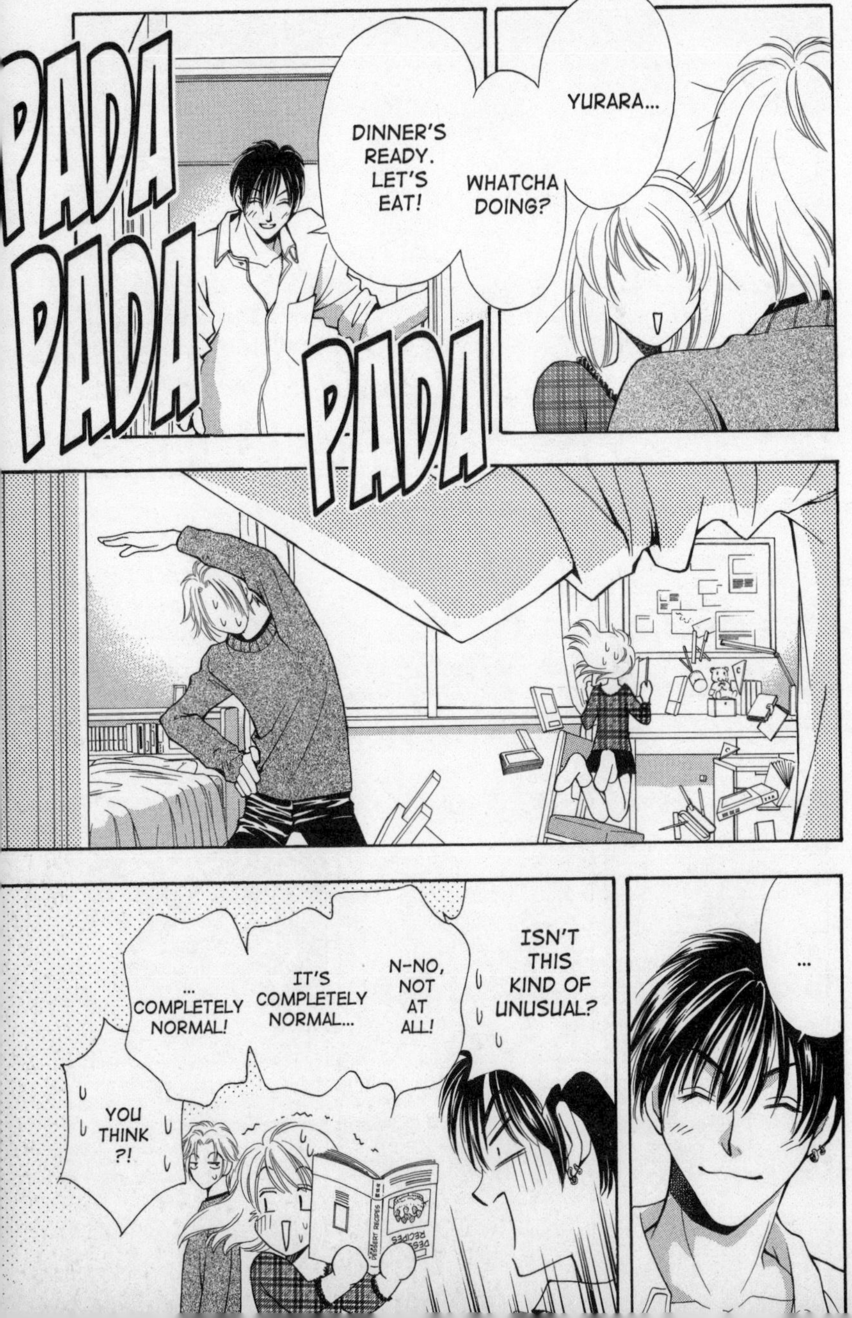
YURARA...
WHATCHA DOING?
DINNER'S READY. LET'S EAT!
PADA
PADA
PADA
...
ISN'T THIS KIND OF UNUSUAL?
N-NO, NOT AT ALL!
IT'S COMPLETELY NORMAL...
...COMPLETELY NORMAL!
YOU THINK?!
DESSERT RECIPES

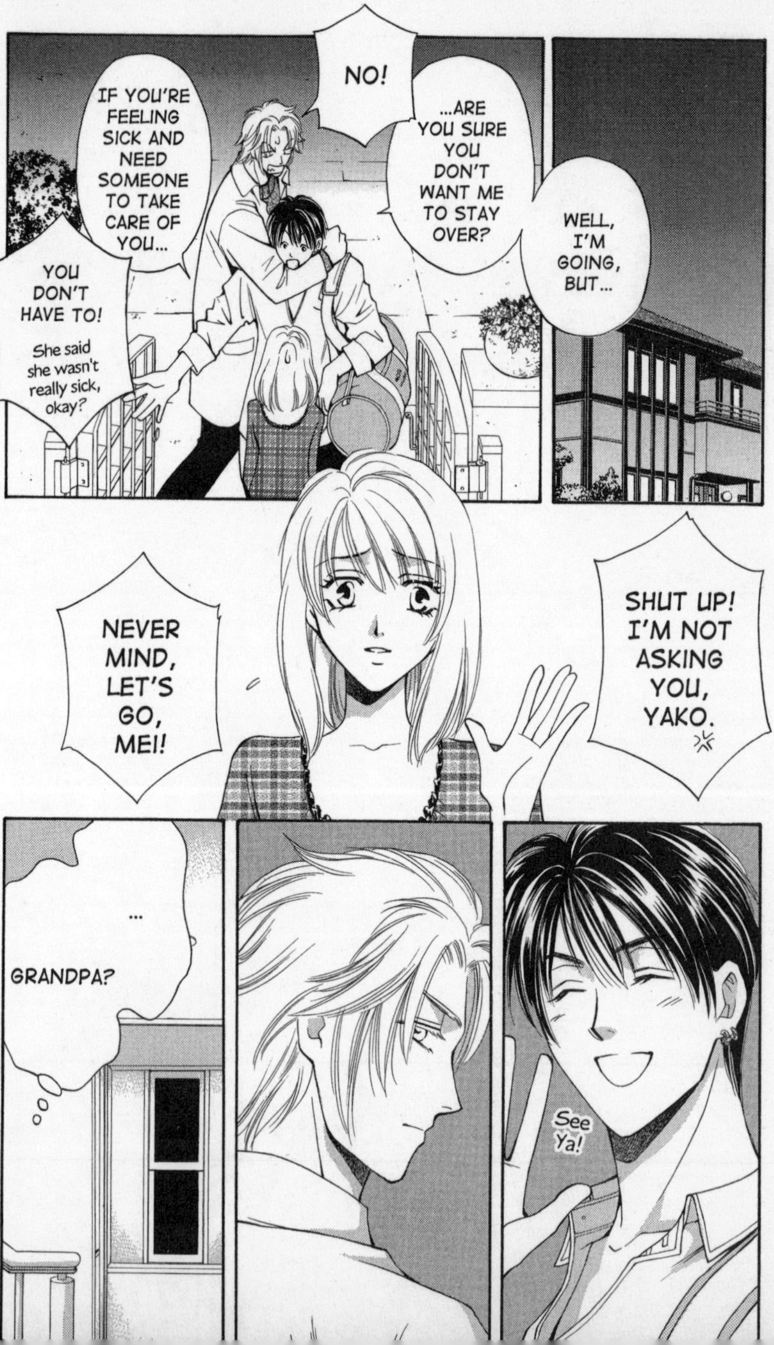
WELL, I'M GOING, BUT...
...ARE YOU SURE YOU DON'T WANT ME TO STAY OVER?
NO!
IF YOU'RE FEELING SICK AND NEED SOMEONE TO TAKE CARE OF YOU...
YOU DON'T HAVE TO!
She said she wasn't really sick, okay?
SHUT UP! I'M NOT ASKING YOU, YAKO.
NEVER MIND, LET'S GO, MEI!
See Ya!
...
GRANDPA?

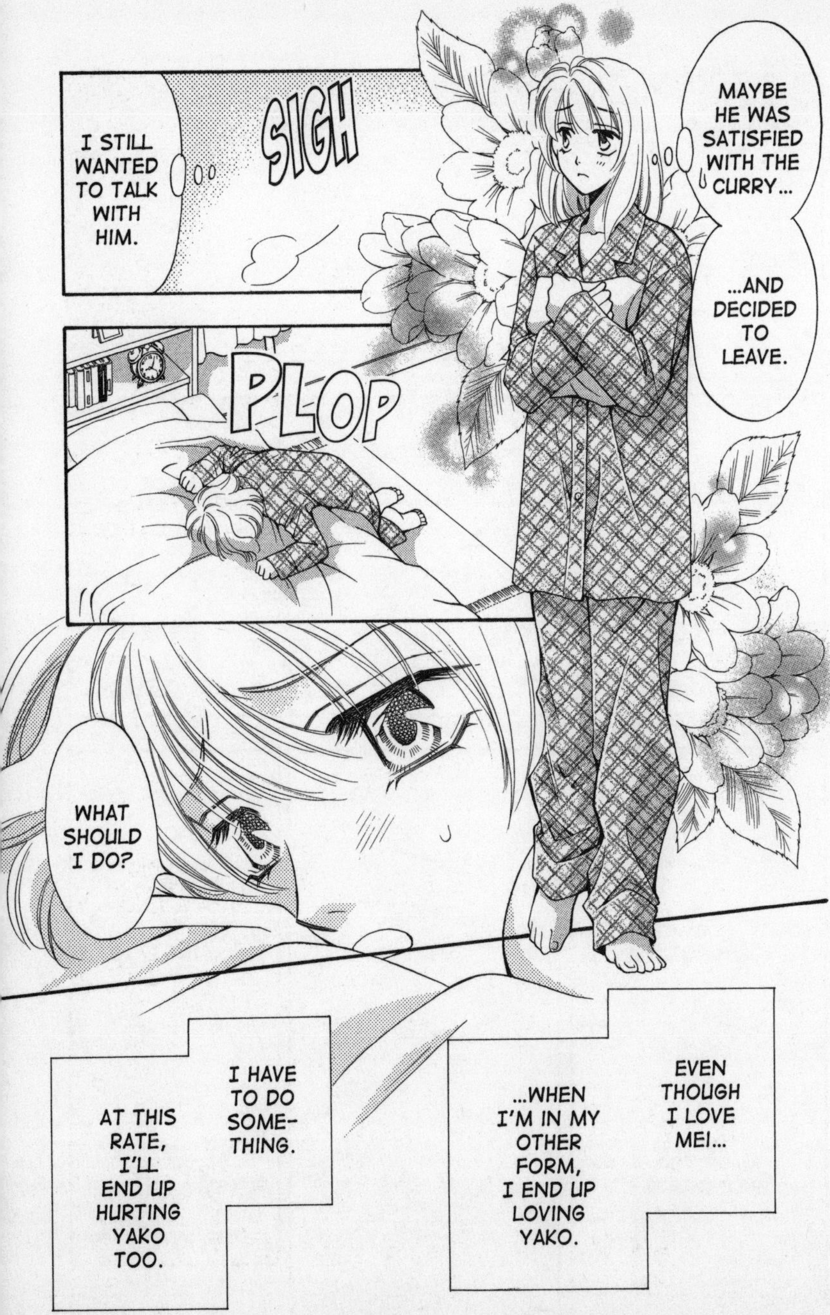
MAYBE HE WAS SATISFIED WITH THE CURRY...
...AND DECIDED TO LEAVE.
SIGH
I STILL WANTED TO TALK WITH HIM.
PLOP
WHAT SHOULD I DO?
EVEN THOUGH I LOVE MEI...
...WHEN I'M IN MY OTHER FORM, I END UP LOVING YAKO.
I HAVE TO DO SOME-THING.
AT THIS RATE, I'LL END UP HURTING YAKO TOO.

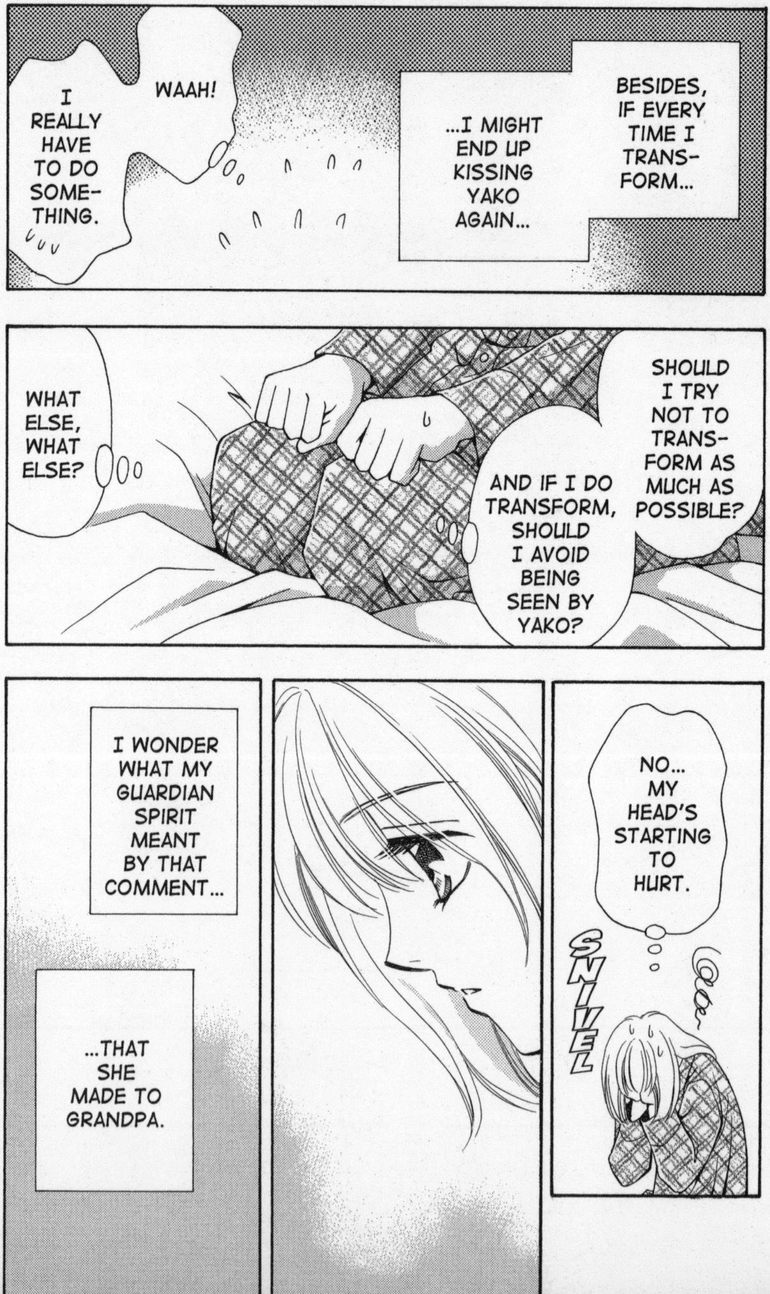
BESIDES, IF EVERY TIME I TRANSFORM...
...I MIGHT END UP KISSING YAKO AGAIN...
WAAH!
I REALLY HAVE TO DO SOMETHING.
SHOULD I TRY NOT TO TRANSFORM AS MUCH AS POSSIBLE?
AND IF I DO TRANSFORM, SHOULD I AVOID BEING SEEN BY YAKO?
WHAT ELSE, WHAT ELSE?
NO... MY HEAD'S STARTING TO HURT.
SNIVEL
I WONDER WHAT MY GUARDIAN SPIRIT MEANT BY THAT COMMENT...
...THAT SHE MADE TO GRANDPA.

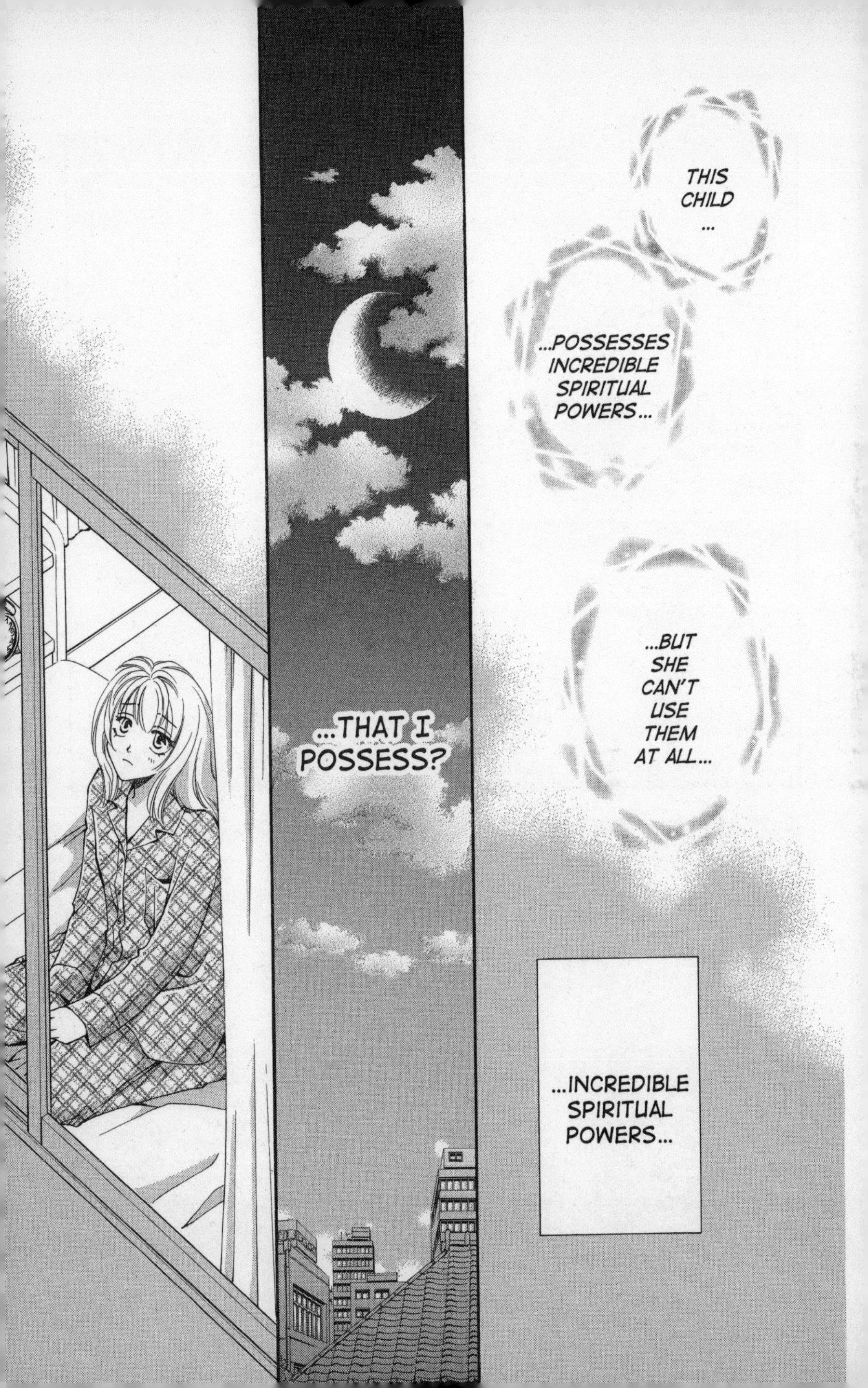
THIS CHILD ...
...POSSESSES INCREDIBLE SPIRITUAL POWERS...
...BUT SHE CAN'T USE THEM AT ALL...
...INCREDIBLE SPIRITUAL POWERS...
...THAT I POSSESS?

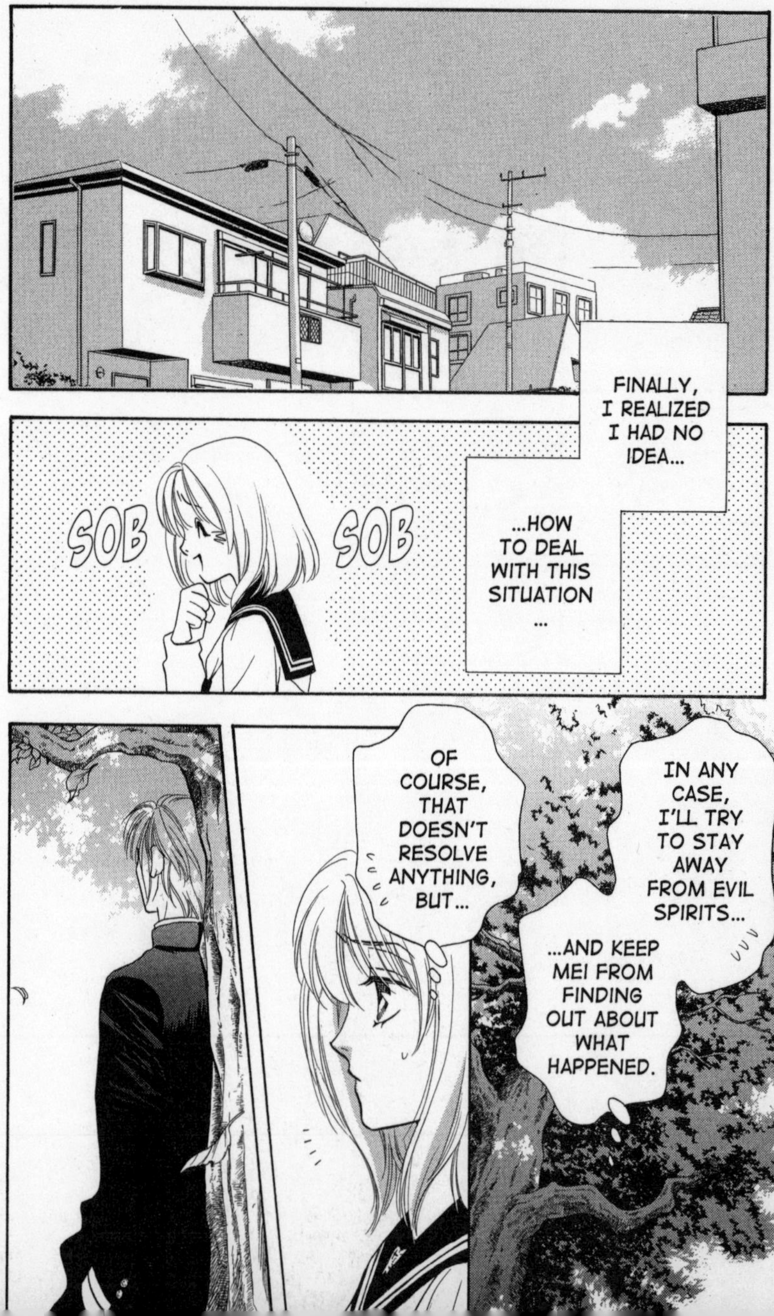
FINALLY, I REALIZED I HAD NO IDEA...
...HOW TO DEAL WITH THIS SITUATION ...
SOB SOB
OF COURSE, THAT DOESN'T RESOLVE ANYTHING, BUT...
IN ANY CASE, I'LL TRY TO STAY AWAY FROM EVIL SPIRITS...
...AND KEEP MEI FROM FINDING OUT ABOUT WHAT HAPPENED.

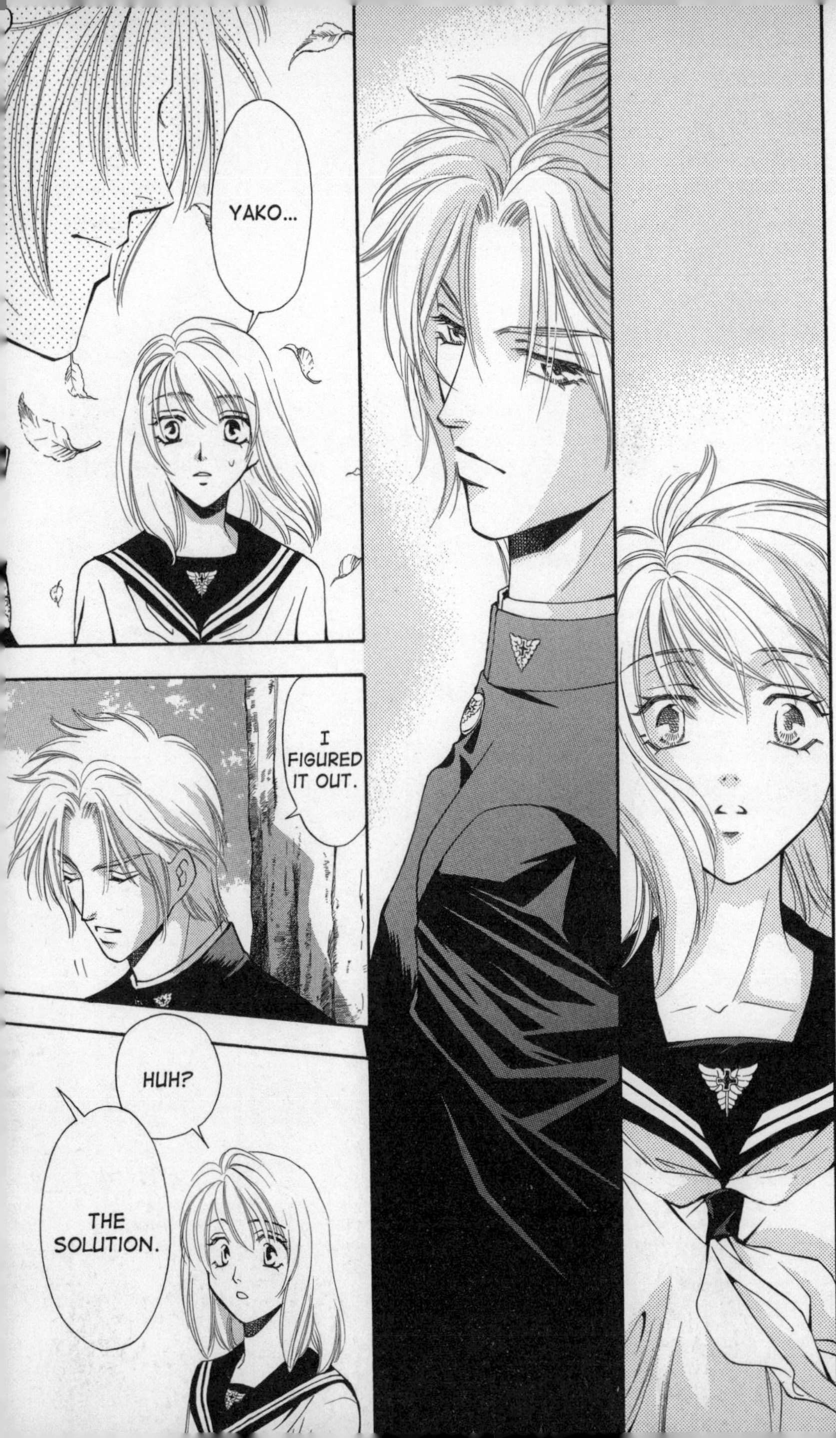
YAKO...
I FIGURED IT OUT.
HUH?
THE SOLUTION.

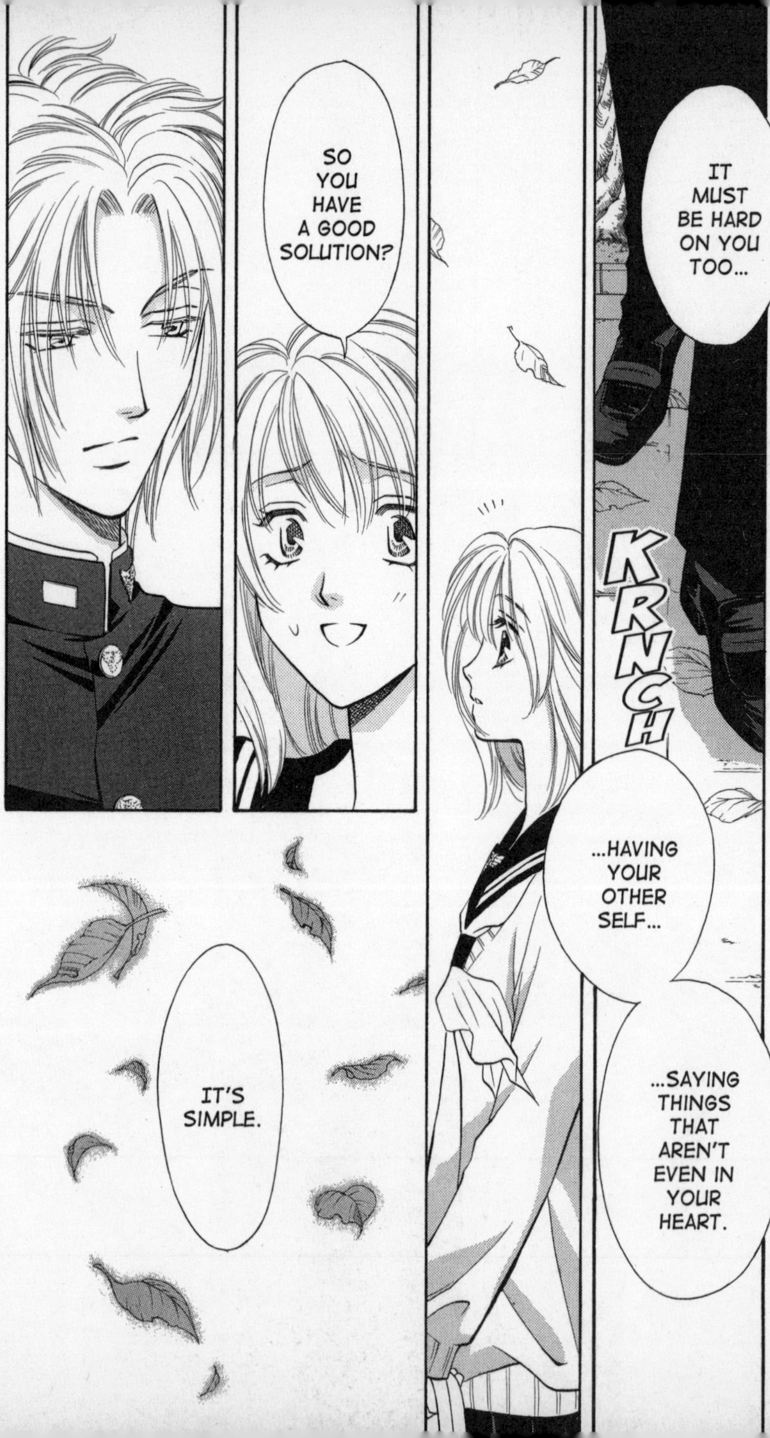

IT MUST BE HARD ON YOU TOO...
KRNCH
...HAVING YOUR OTHER SELF...
...SAYING THINGS THAT AREN'T EVEN IN YOUR HEART.
SO YOU HAVE A GOOD SOLUTION?
IT'S SIMPLE.

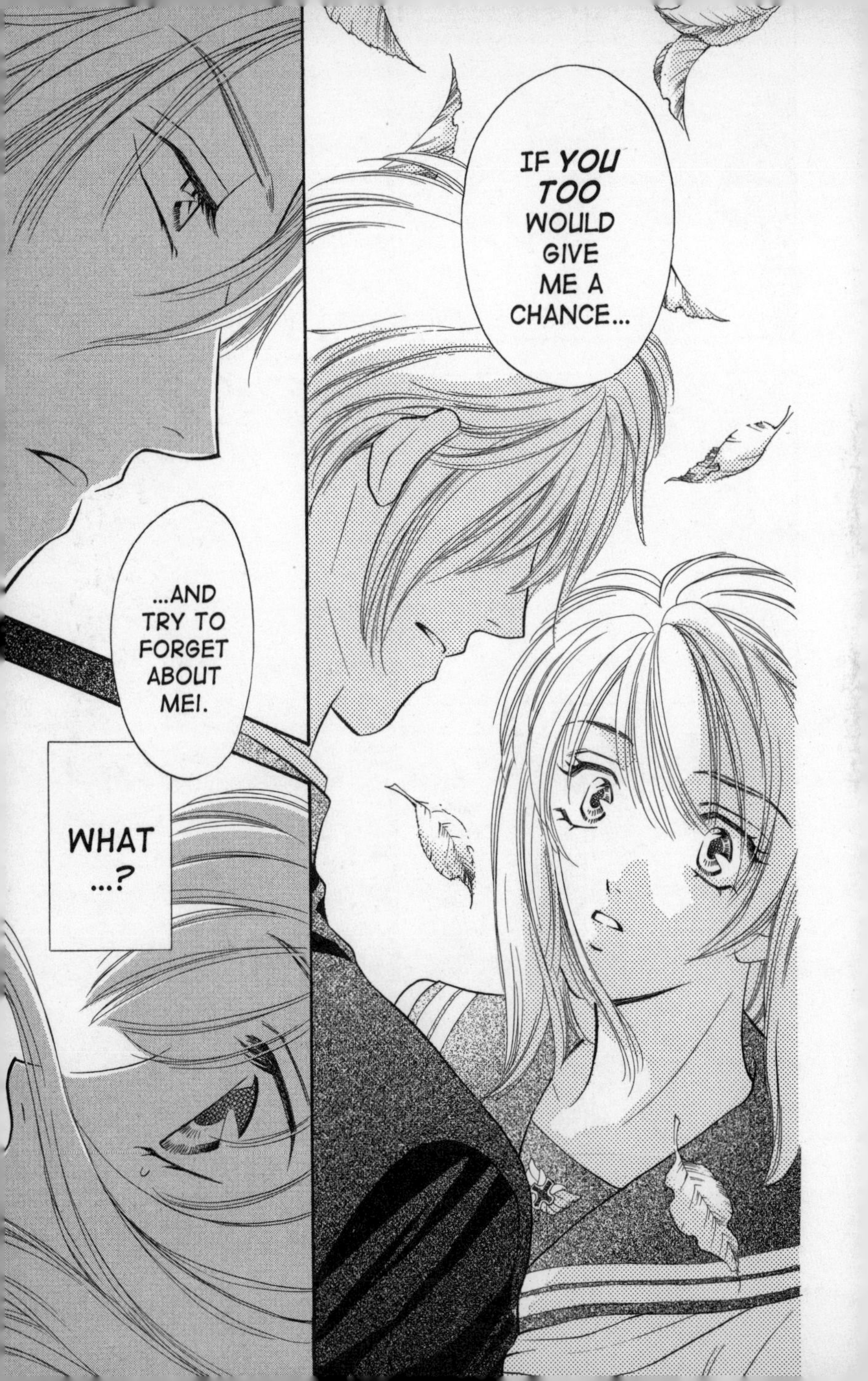
IF *YOU TOO* WOULD GIVE ME A CHANCE...
...AND TRY TO FORGET ABOUT MEI.
WHAT ...?

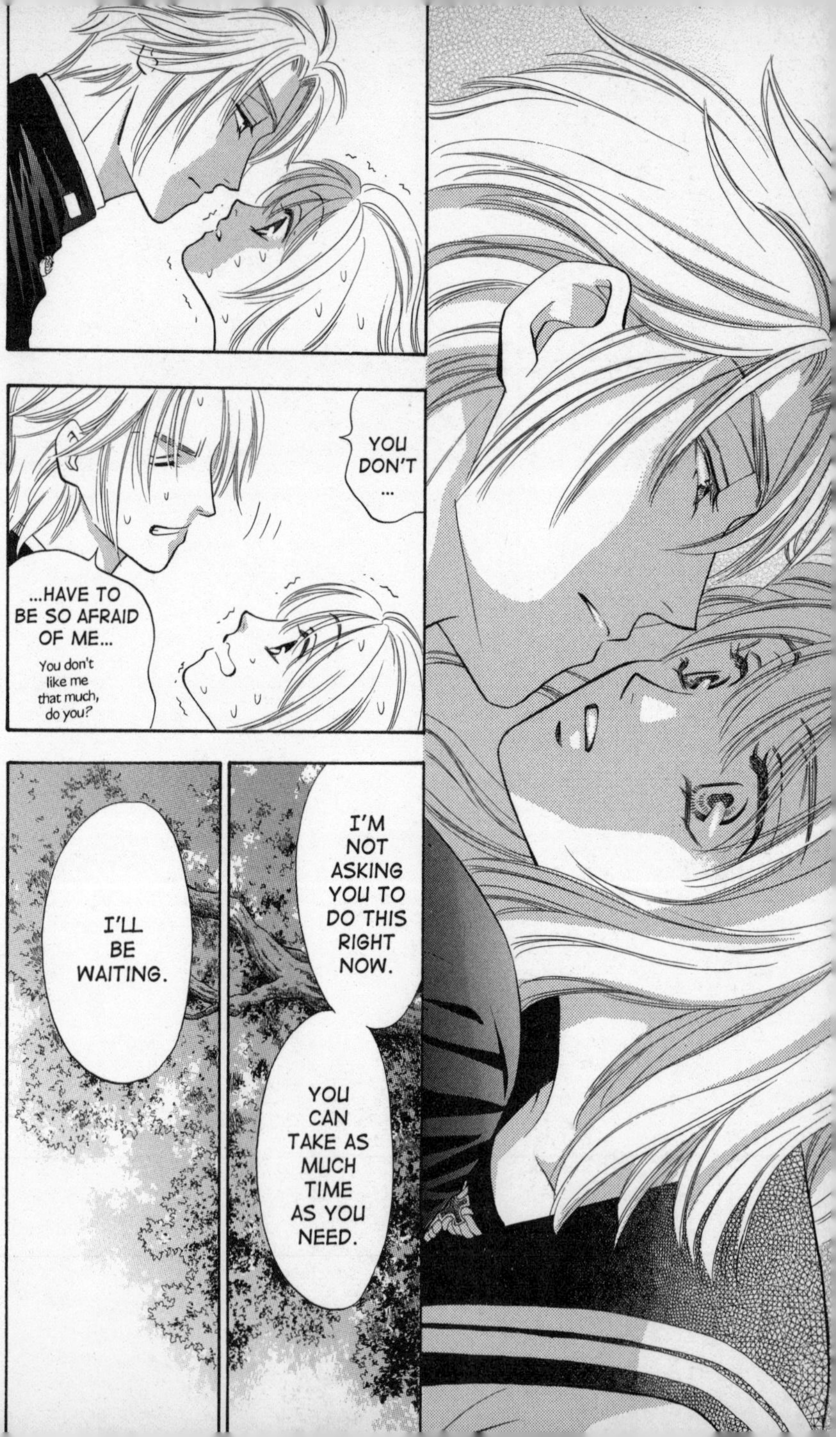
YOU DON'T ...
...HAVE TO BE SO AFRAID OF ME...
You don't like me that much, do you?
I'M NOT ASKING YOU TO DO THIS RIGHT NOW.
YOU CAN TAKE AS MUCH TIME AS YOU NEED.
I'LL BE WAITING.

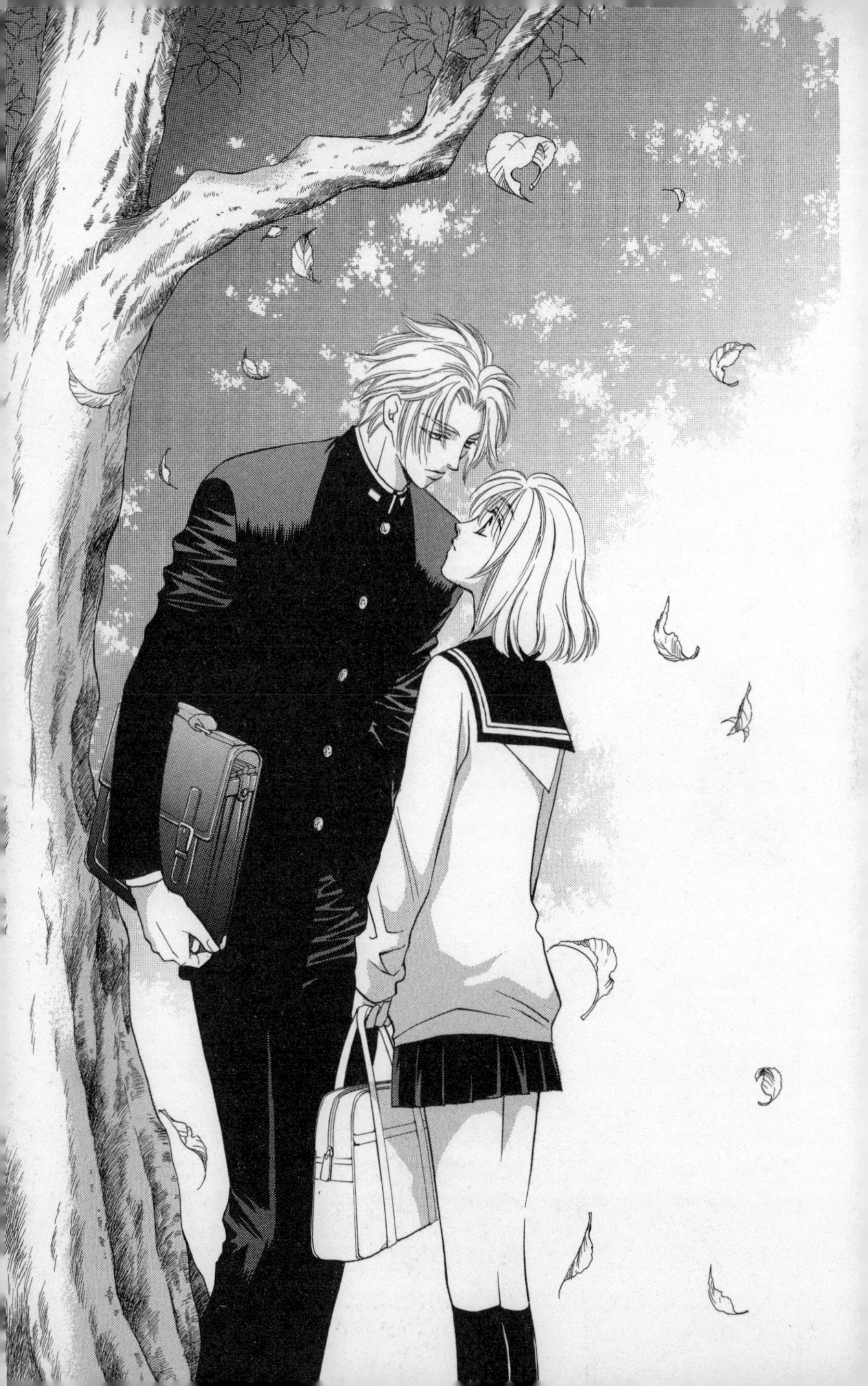

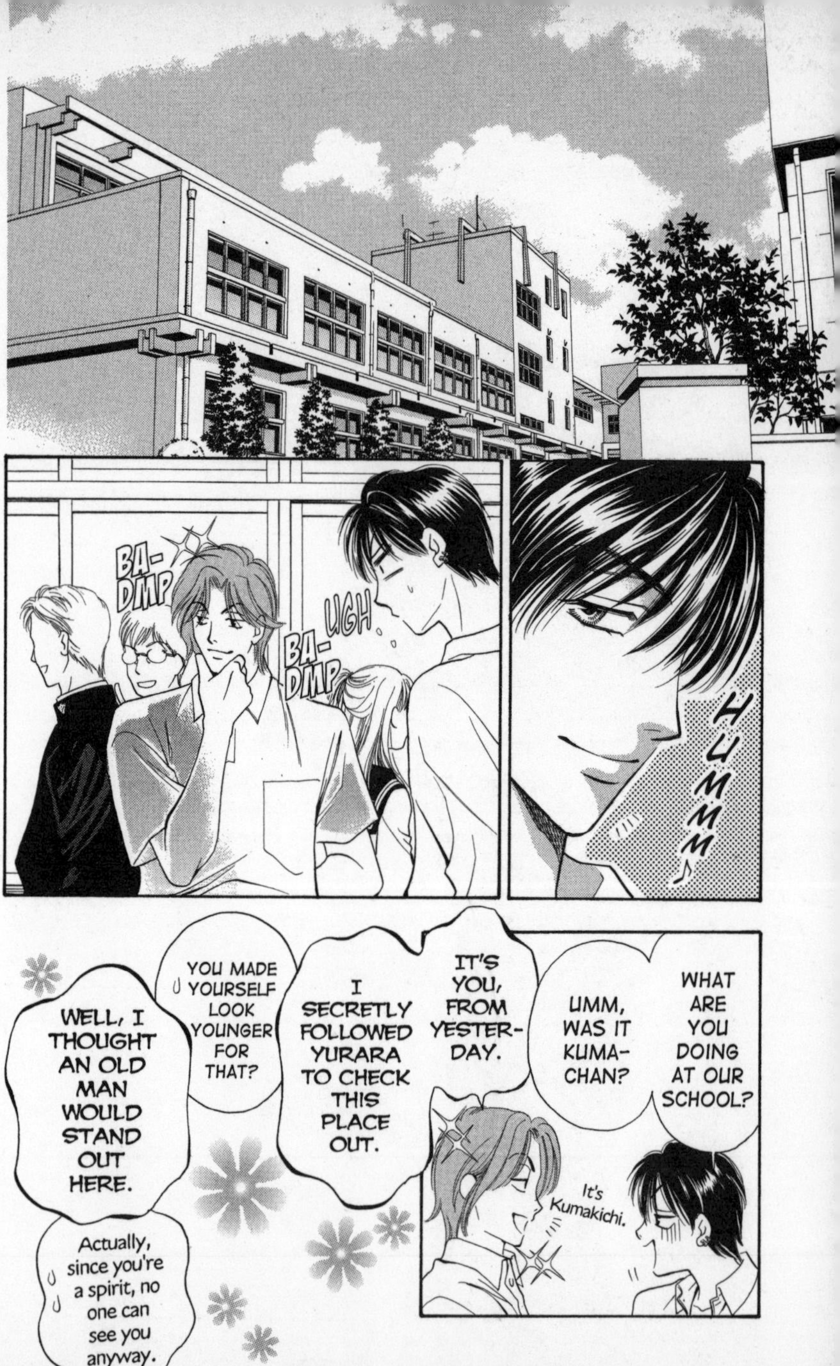
HUMMMM♪
BA-DMP
UGH
BA-DMP
WHAT ARE YOU DOING AT OUR SCHOOL?
UMM, WAS IT KUMA-CHAN?
It's Kumakichi.
IT'S YOU, FROM YESTER-DAY.
I SECRETLY FOLLOWED YURARA TO CHECK THIS PLACE OUT.
YOU MADE YOURSELF LOOK YOUNGER FOR THAT?
WELL, I THOUGHT AN OLD MAN WOULD STAND OUT HERE.
Actually, since you're a spirit, no one can see you anyway.

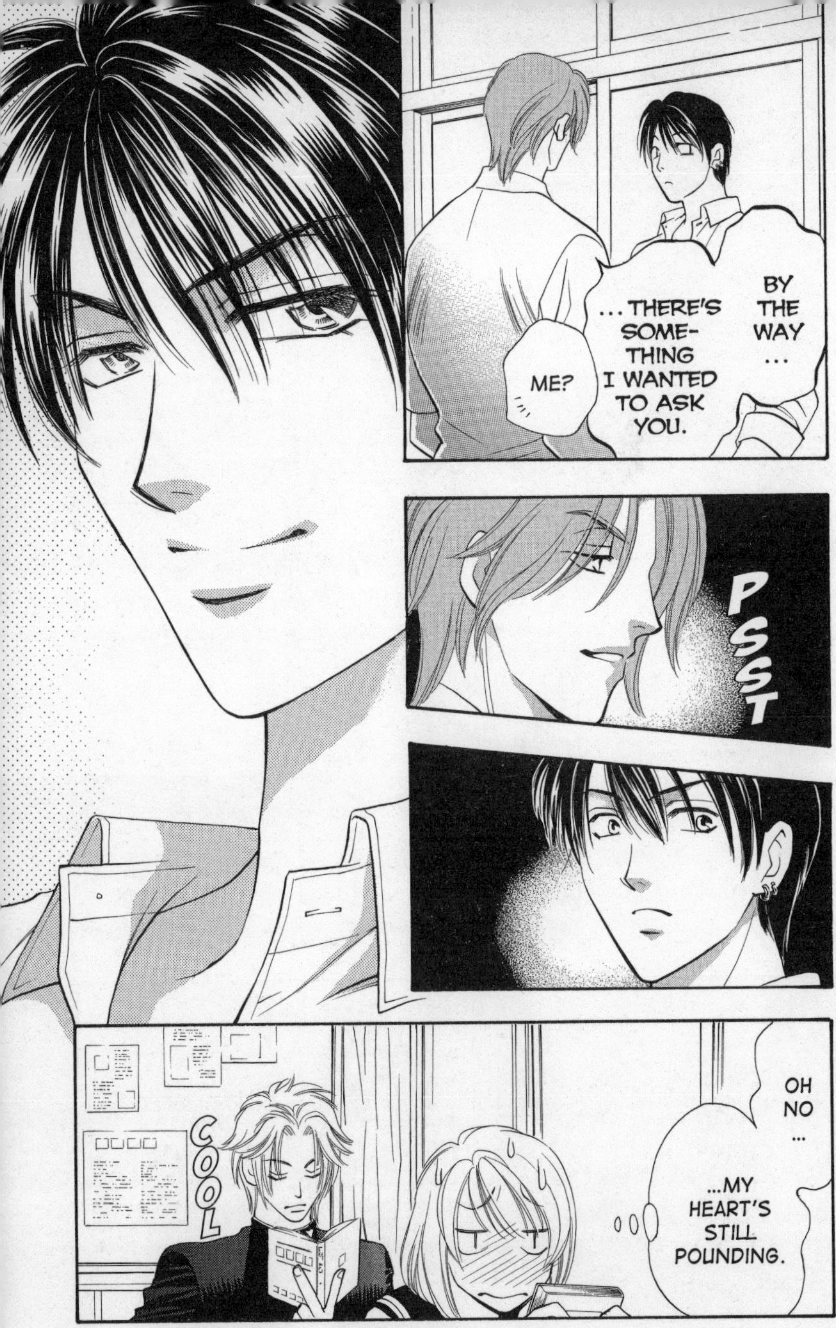
BY THE WAY ...
... THERE'S SOME-THING I WANTED TO ASK YOU.
ME?
PSST
OH NO ...
...MY HEART'S STILL POUNDING.
COOL

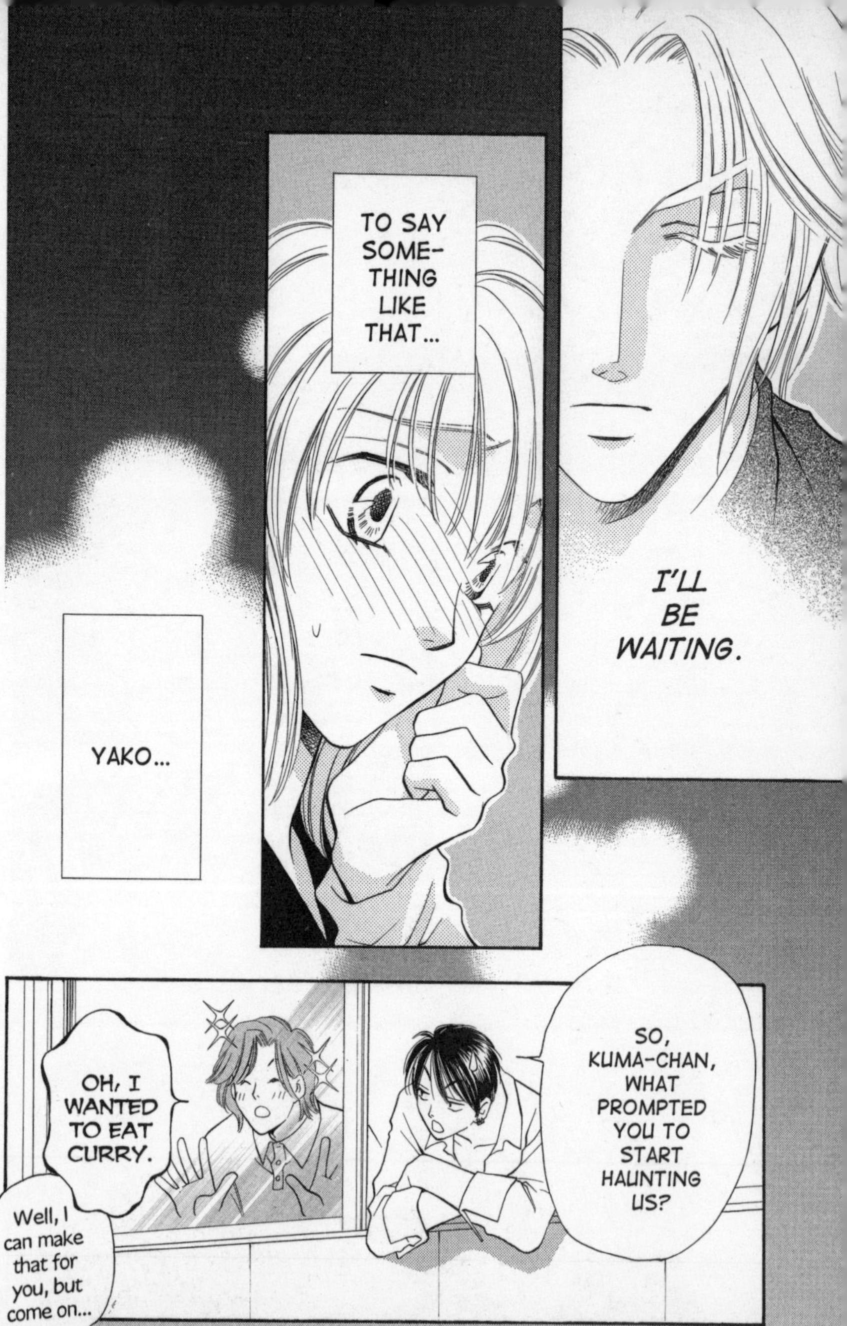
I'LL BE WAITING.
TO SAY SOMETHING LIKE THAT...
YAKO...
SO, KUMA-CHAN, WHAT PROMPTED YOU TO START HAUNTING US?
OH, I WANTED TO EAT CURRY.
Well, I can make that for you, but come on...

Yurara no Tsuki Chapter 10 / End

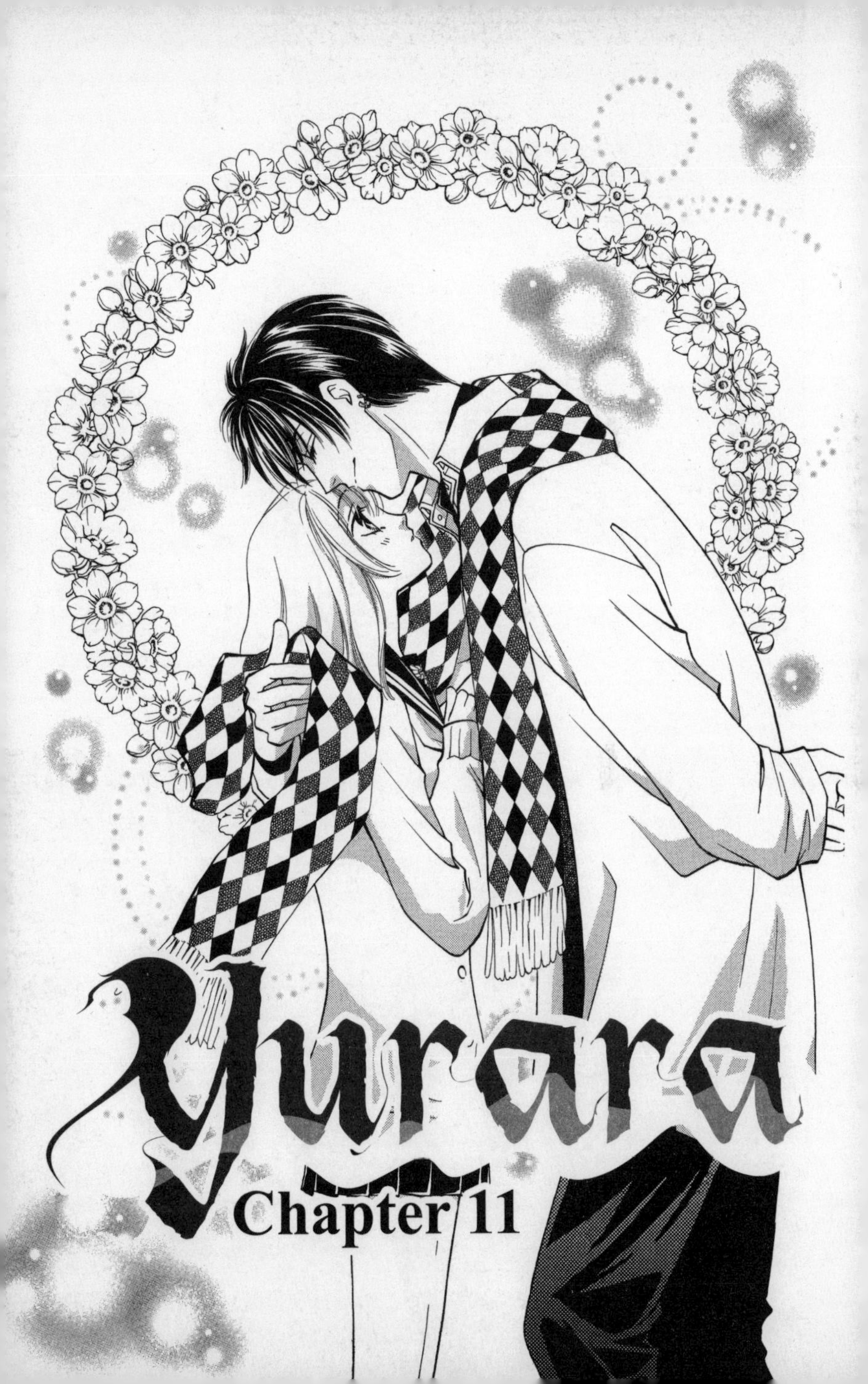
Yurara
Chapter 11

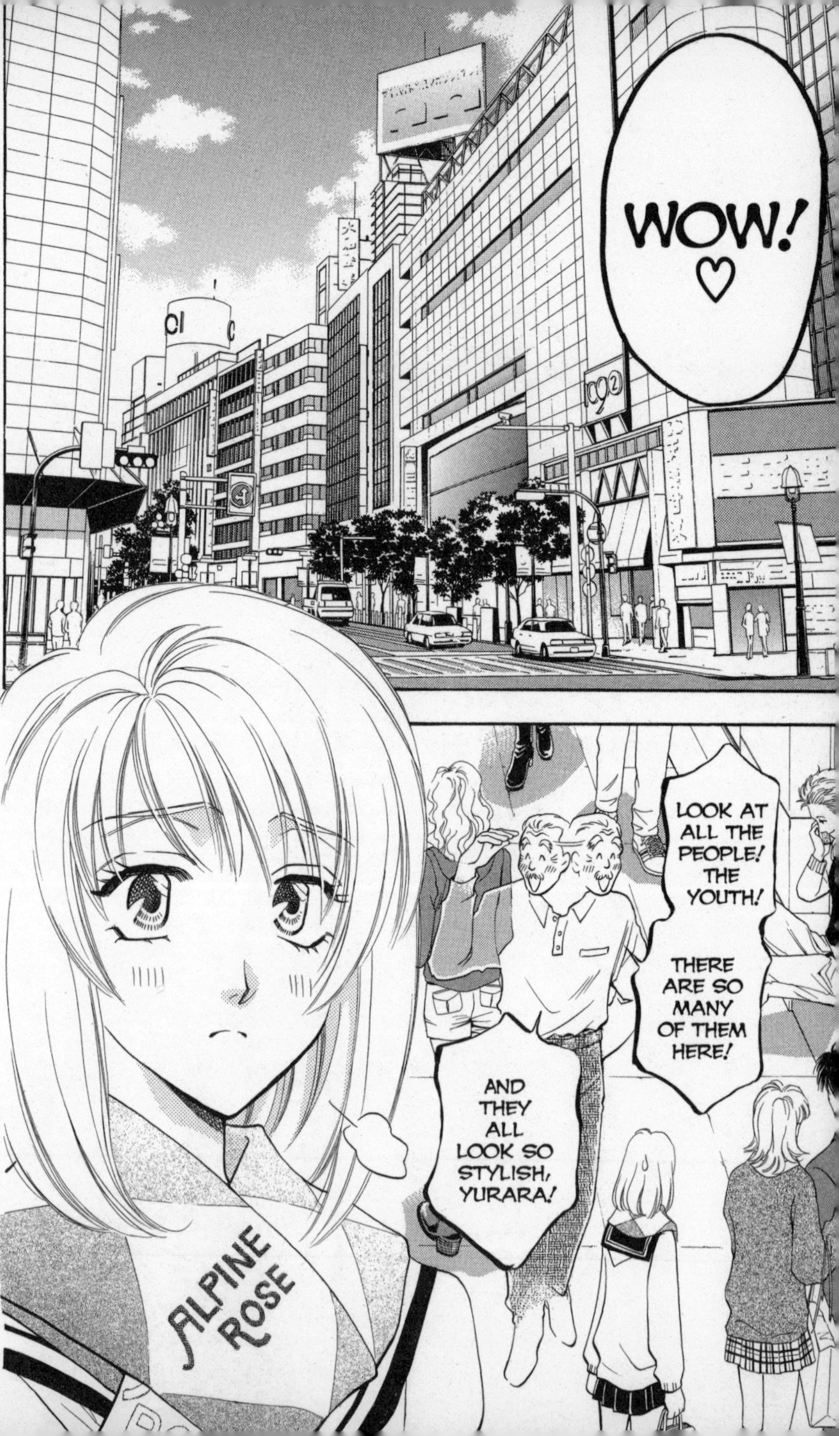
WOW! ♡
LOOK AT ALL THE PEOPLE! THE YOUTH!
THERE ARE SO MANY OF THEM HERE!
AND THEY ALL LOOK SO STYLISH, YURARA!
ALPINE ROSE

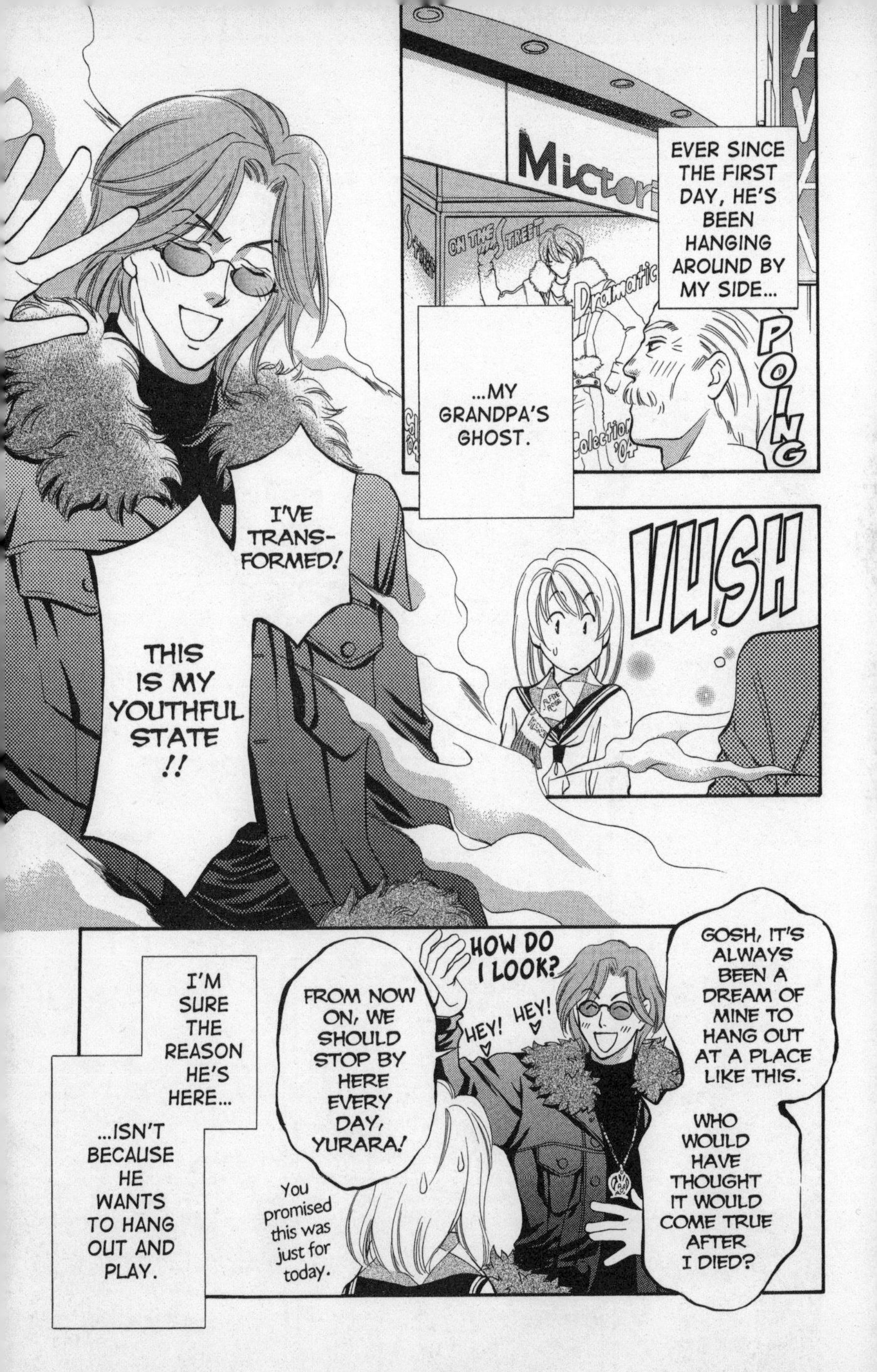
Mictori
ON TIME STREET
Dramatic
Collection '04
EVER SINCE THE FIRST DAY, HE'S BEEN HANGING AROUND BY MY SIDE...
POING
...MY GRANDPA'S GHOST.
VUSH
I'VE TRANS-FORMED!
THIS IS MY YOUTHFUL STATE !!
GOSH, IT'S ALWAYS BEEN A DREAM OF MINE TO HANG OUT AT A PLACE LIKE THIS.
WHO WOULD HAVE THOUGHT IT WOULD COME TRUE AFTER I DIED?
HOW DO I LOOK?
HEY! HEY!
FROM NOW ON, WE SHOULD STOP BY HERE EVERY DAY, YURARA!
You promised this was just for today.
I'M SURE THE REASON HE'S HERE...
...ISN'T BECAUSE HE WANTS TO HANG OUT AND PLAY.

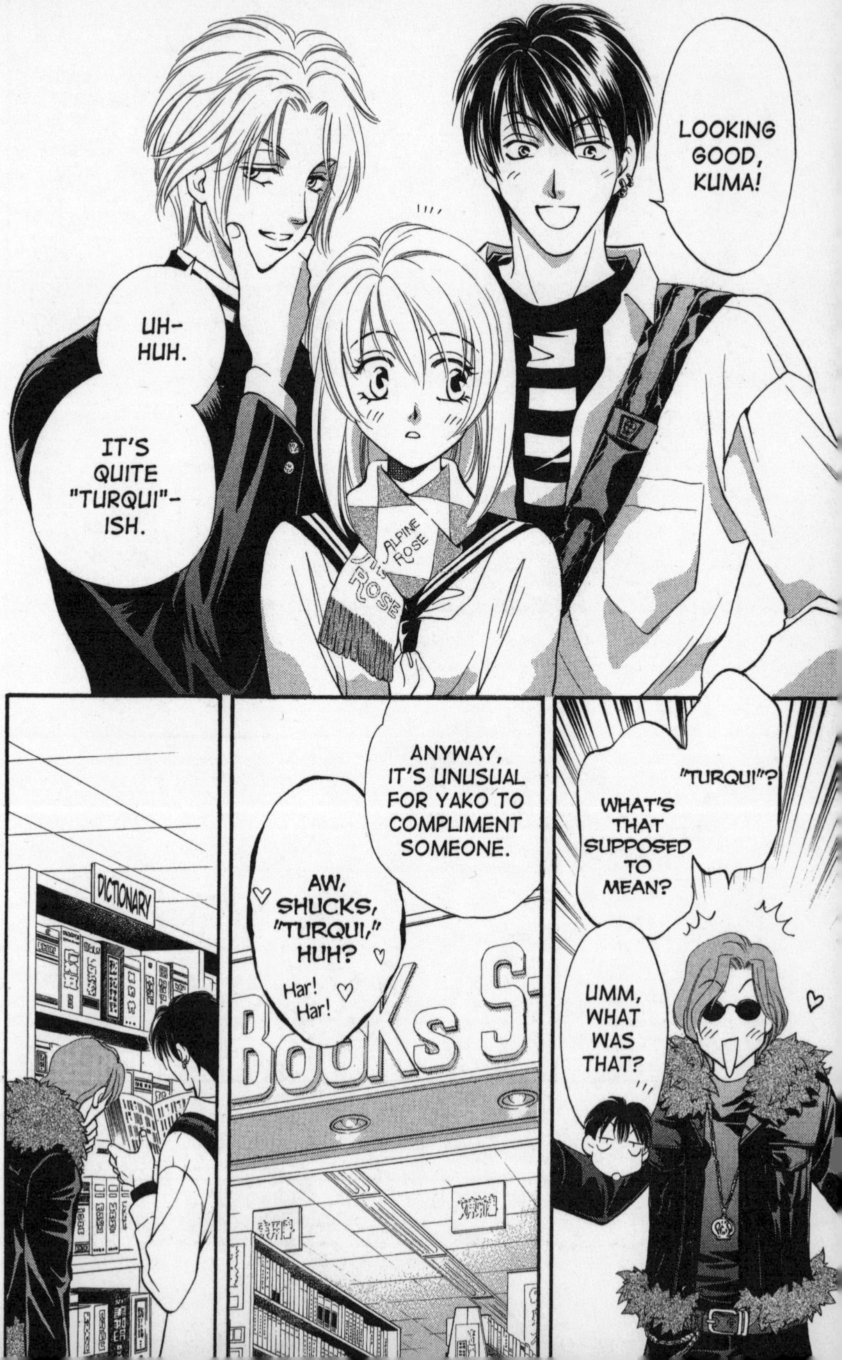
LOOKING GOOD, KUMA!
UH-HUH.
IT'S QUITE "TURQUI"-ISH.
"TURQUI"?
WHAT'S THAT SUPPOSED TO MEAN?
UMM, WHAT WAS THAT?
ANYWAY, IT'S UNUSUAL FOR YAKO TO COMPLIMENT SOMEONE.
AW, SHUCKS, "TURQUI," HUH?
Har! Har!
DICTIONARY

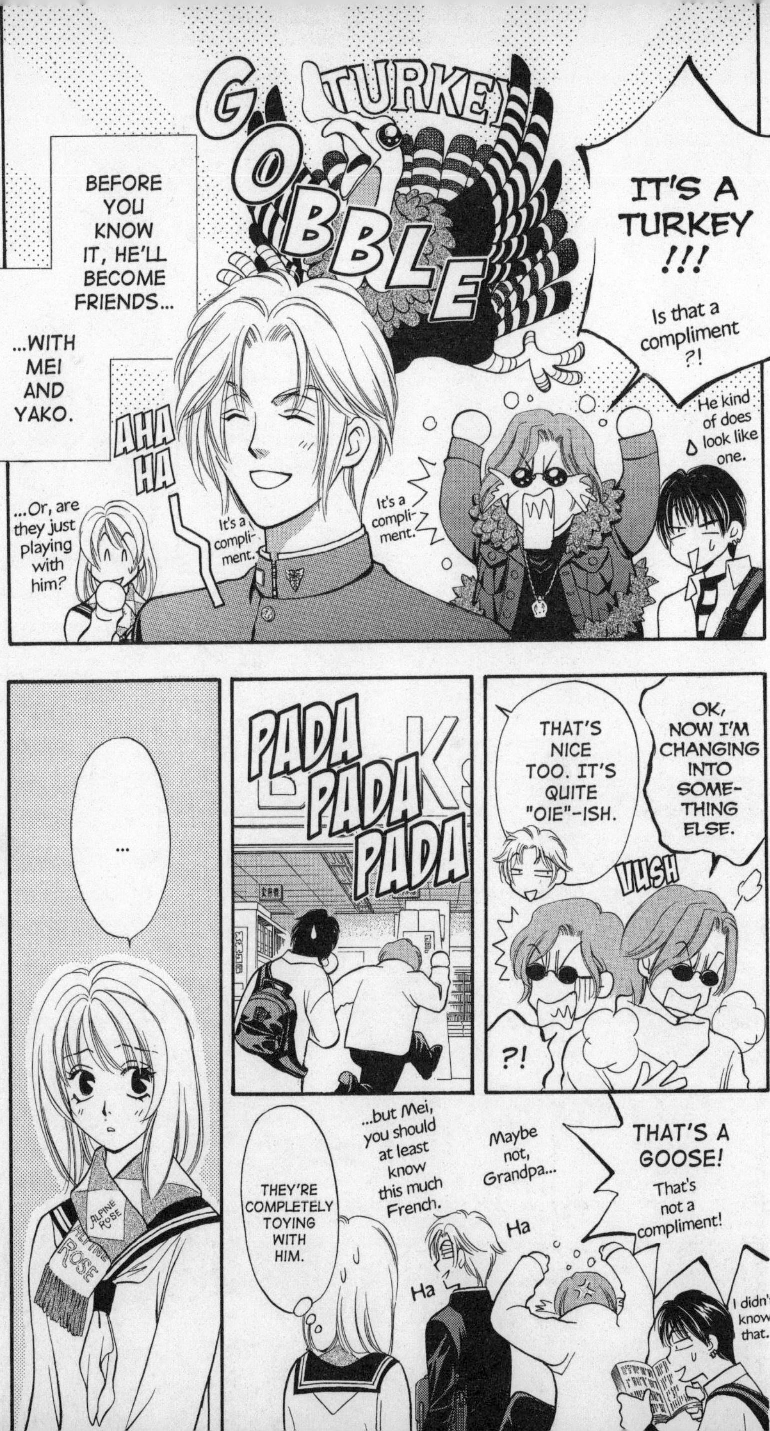
TURKEY
GOBBLE
IT'S A TURKEY!!!
Is that a compliment?!
BEFORE YOU KNOW IT, HE'LL BECOME FRIENDS...
...WITH MEI AND YAKO.
He kind of does look like one.
AHAHA HA
It's a compliment.
It's a compliment.
...Or, are they just playing with him?
OK, NOW I'M CHANGING INTO SOME-THING ELSE.
THAT'S NICE TOO. IT'S QUITE "OIE"-ISH.
VUSH
?!
PADA PADA PADA
THAT'S A GOOSE!
That's not a compliment!
Maybe not, Grandpa...
...but Mei, you should at least know this much French.
I didn't know that.
Ha
Ha
THEY'RE COMPLETELY TOYING WITH HIM.
...
ALPINE ROSE

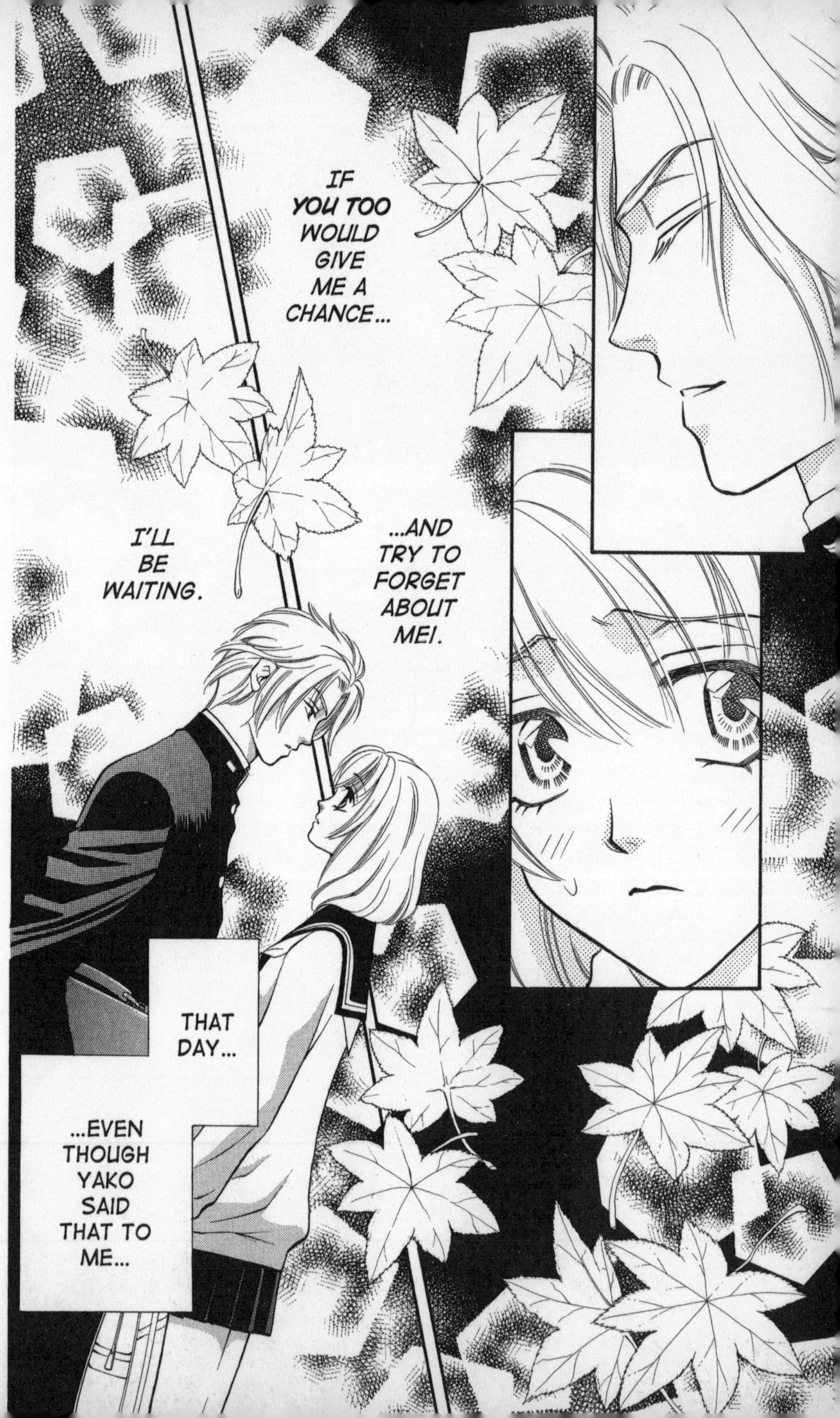
IF YOU TOO WOULD GIVE ME A CHANCE...
...AND TRY TO FORGET ABOUT MEI.
I'LL BE WAITING.
THAT DAY...
...EVEN THOUGH YAKO SAID THAT TO ME...

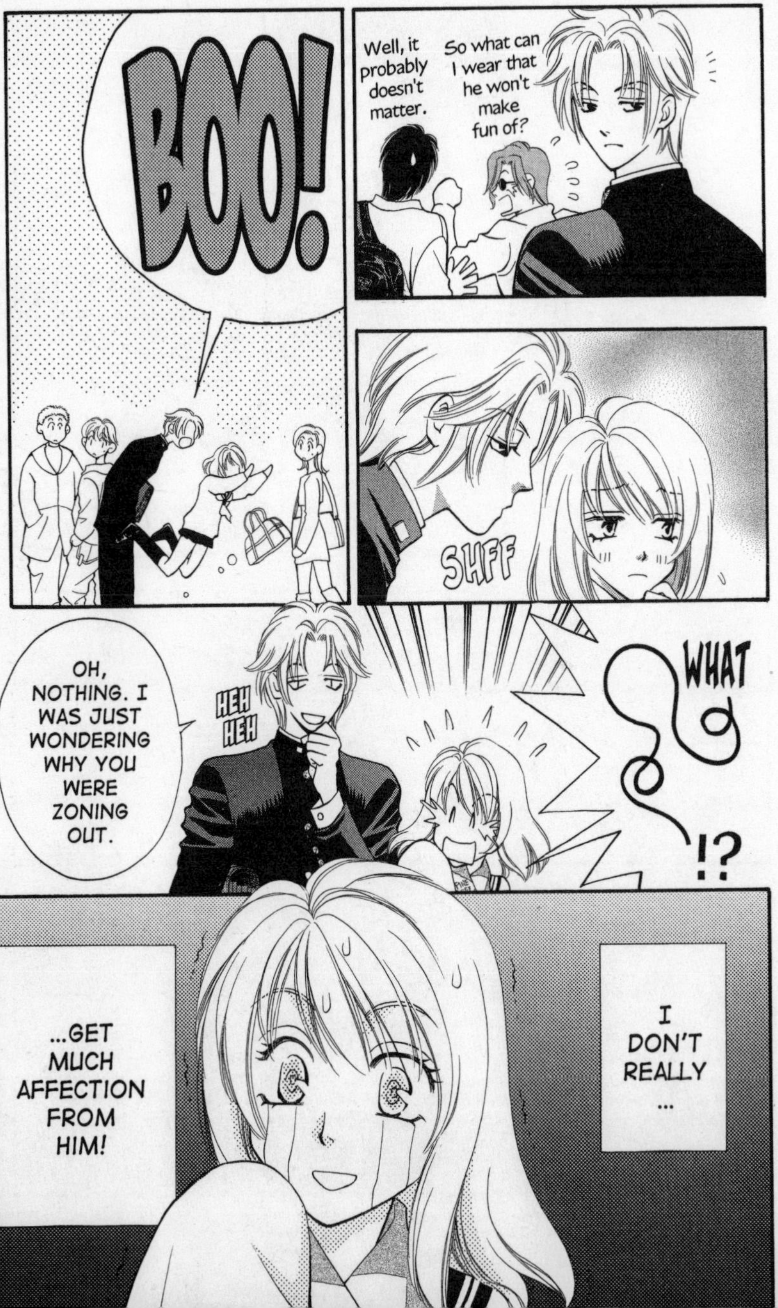
So what can I wear that he won't make fun of?
Well, it probably doesn't matter.
SHFF
BOO!
WHAT !?
HEH HEH
OH, NOTHING. I WAS JUST WONDERING WHY YOU WERE ZONING OUT.
I DON'T REALLY ...
...GET MUCH AFFECTION FROM HIM!

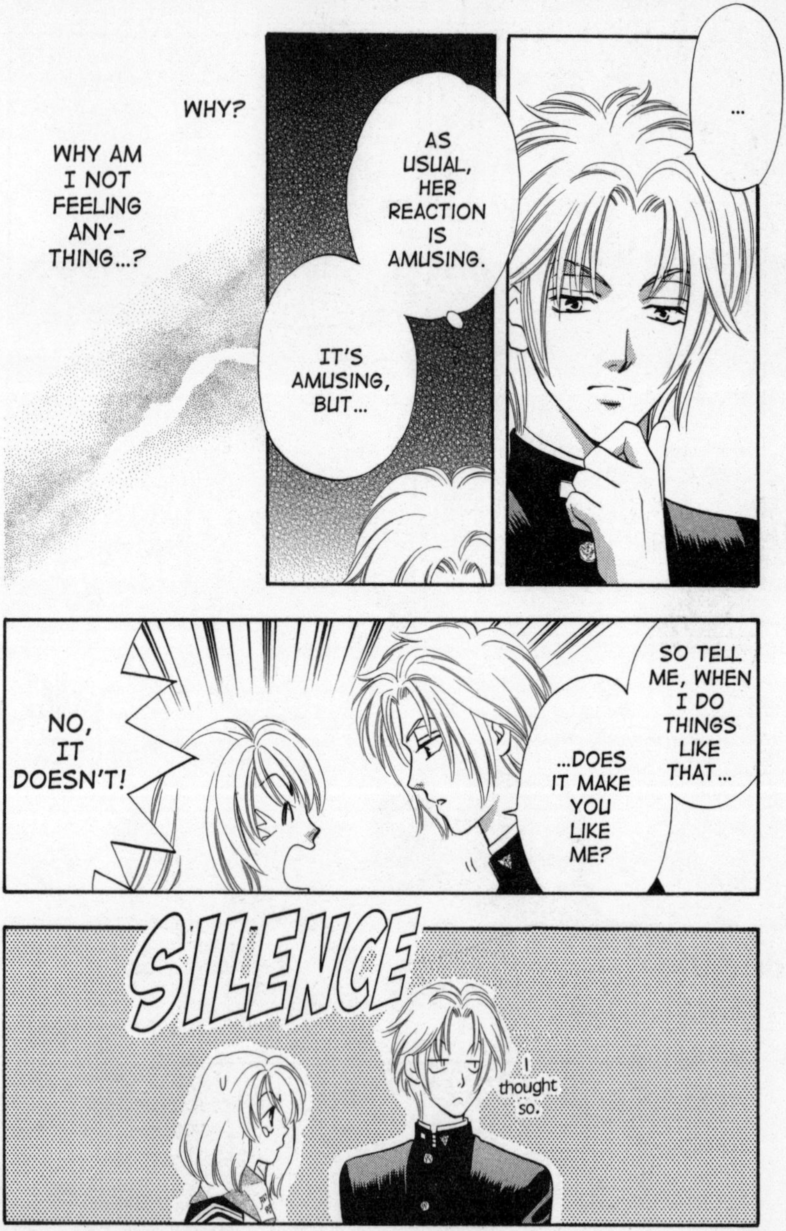
...
AS USUAL, HER REACTION IS AMUSING.
IT'S AMUSING, BUT...
WHY?
WHY AM I NOT FEELING ANY-THING...?
SO TELL ME, WHEN I DO THINGS LIKE THAT...
...DOES IT MAKE YOU LIKE ME?
NO, IT DOESN'T!
SILENCE
I thought so.

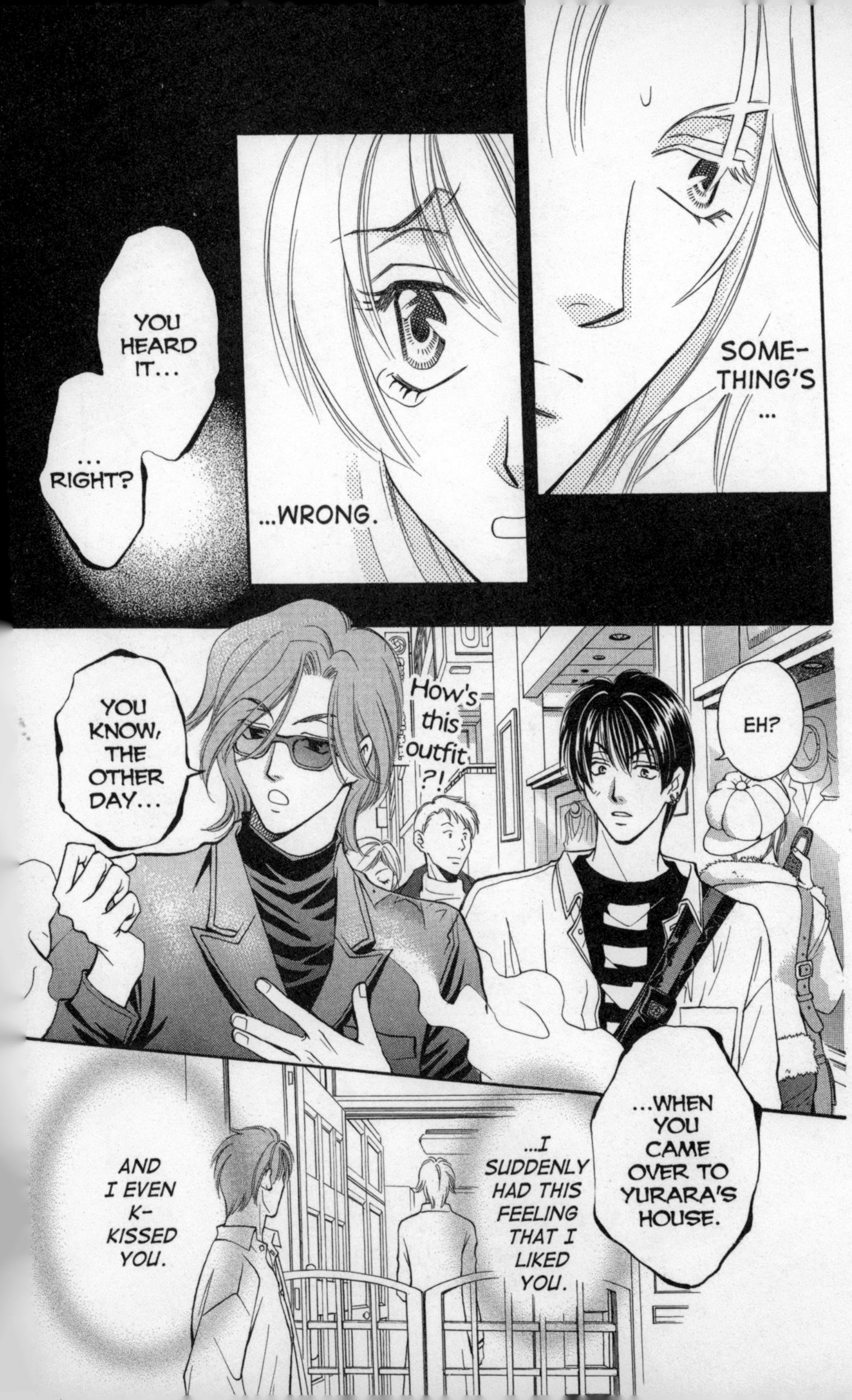
SOME-THING'S ...
...WRONG.
YOU HEARD IT... ...RIGHT?
EH?
How's this outfit?!
YOU KNOW, THE OTHER DAY...
...WHEN YOU CAME OVER TO YURARA'S HOUSE.
...I SUDDENLY HAD THIS FEELING THAT I LIKED YOU.
AND I EVEN K-KISSED YOU.

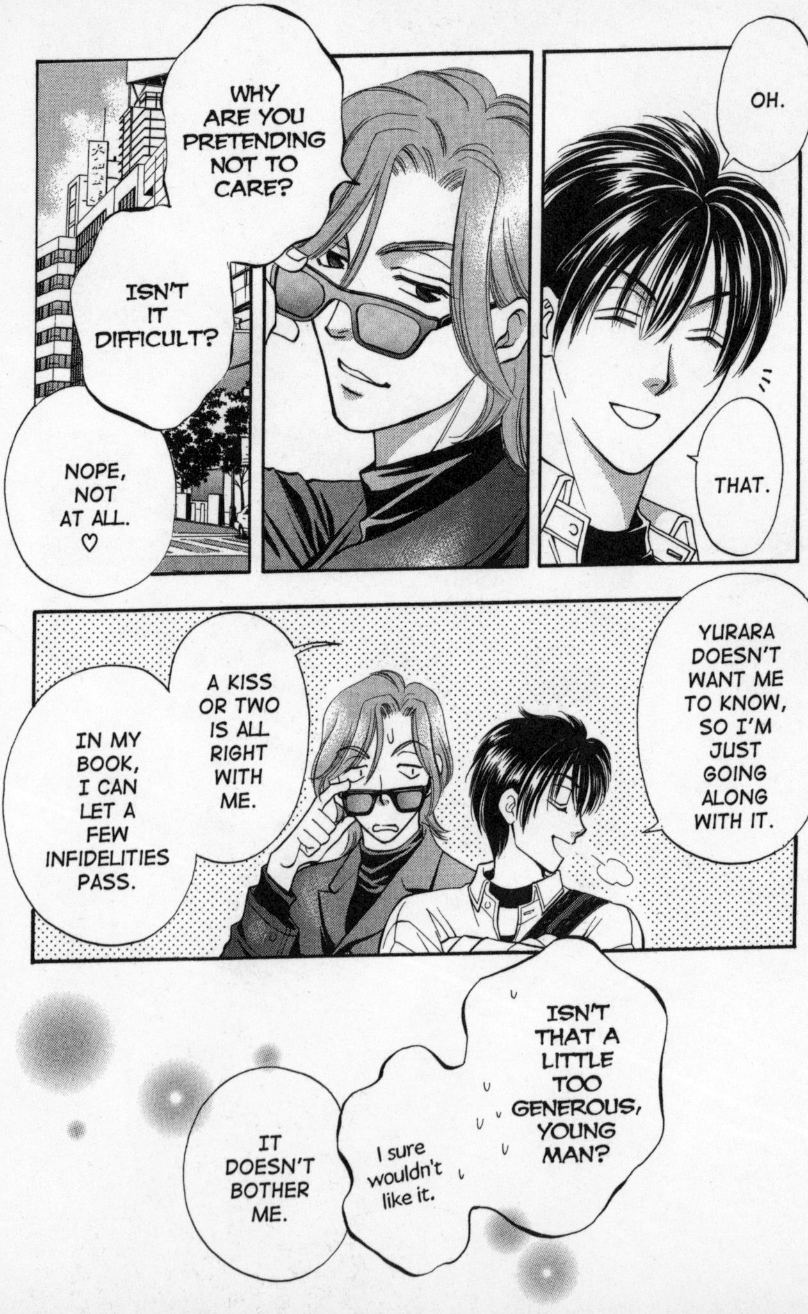
OH.
THAT.
WHY ARE YOU PRETENDING NOT TO CARE?
ISN'T IT DIFFICULT?
NOPE, NOT AT ALL. ♡
YURARA DOESN'T WANT ME TO KNOW, SO I'M JUST GOING ALONG WITH IT.
A KISS OR TWO IS ALL RIGHT WITH ME.
IN MY BOOK, I CAN LET A FEW INFIDELITIES PASS.
ISN'T THAT A LITTLE TOO GENEROUS, YOUNG MAN?
I sure wouldn't like it.
IT DOESN'T BOTHER ME.

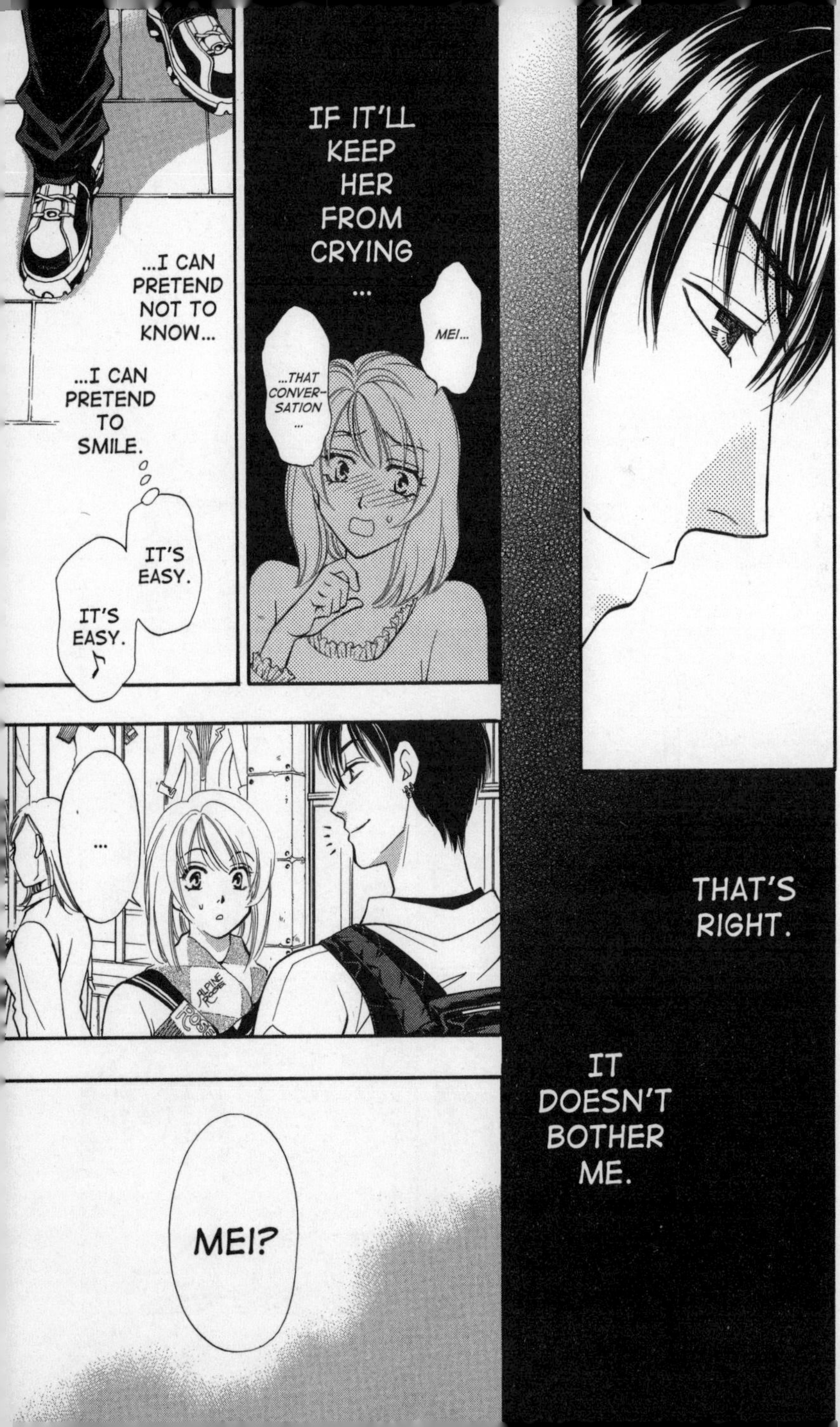
THAT'S RIGHT.
IT DOESN'T BOTHER ME.
IF IT'LL KEEP HER FROM CRYING...
MEI...
...THAT CONVERSATION...
...I CAN PRETEND NOT TO KNOW...
...I CAN PRETEND TO SMILE.
IT'S EASY.
IT'S EASY. ♪
...
MEI?

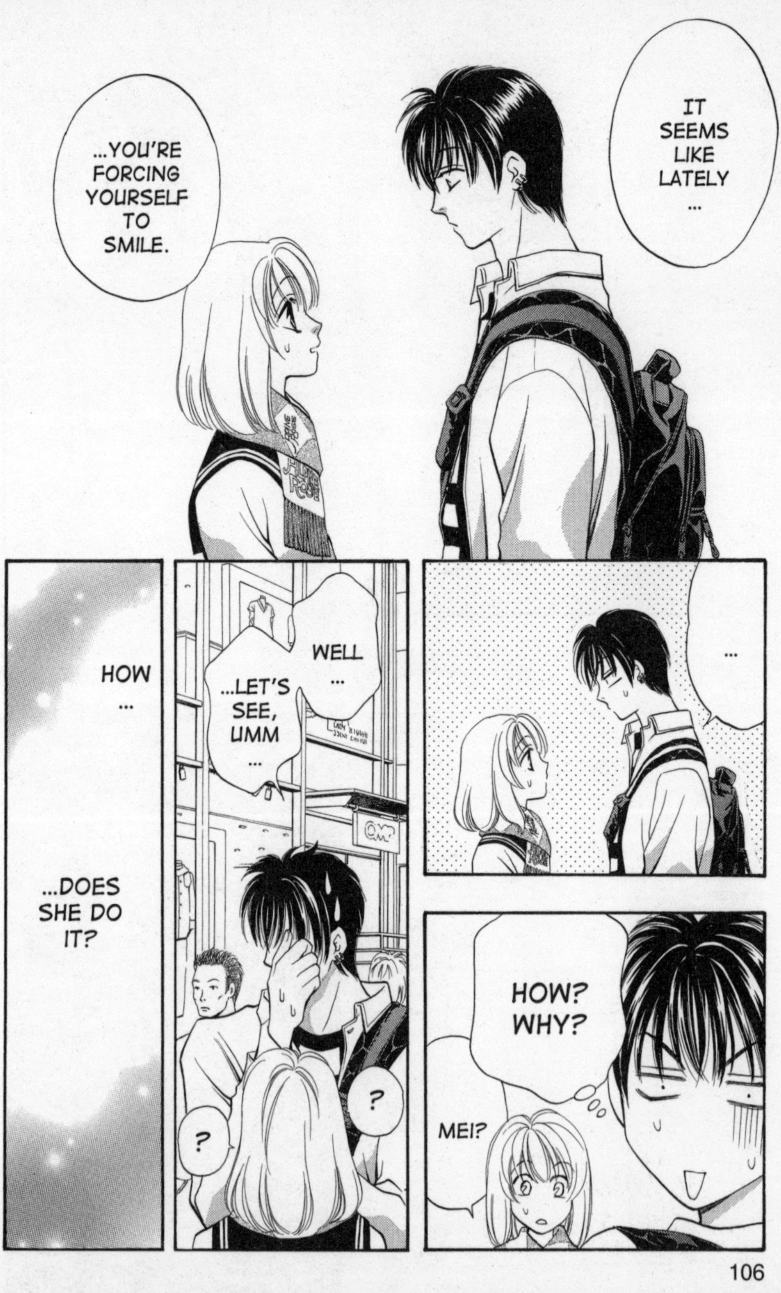
IT SEEMS LIKE LATELY ...
...YOU'RE FORCING YOURSELF TO SMILE.
...
HOW? WHY?
MEI?
WELL ...
...LET'S SEE, UMM ...
?
?
HOW ...
...DOES SHE DO IT?

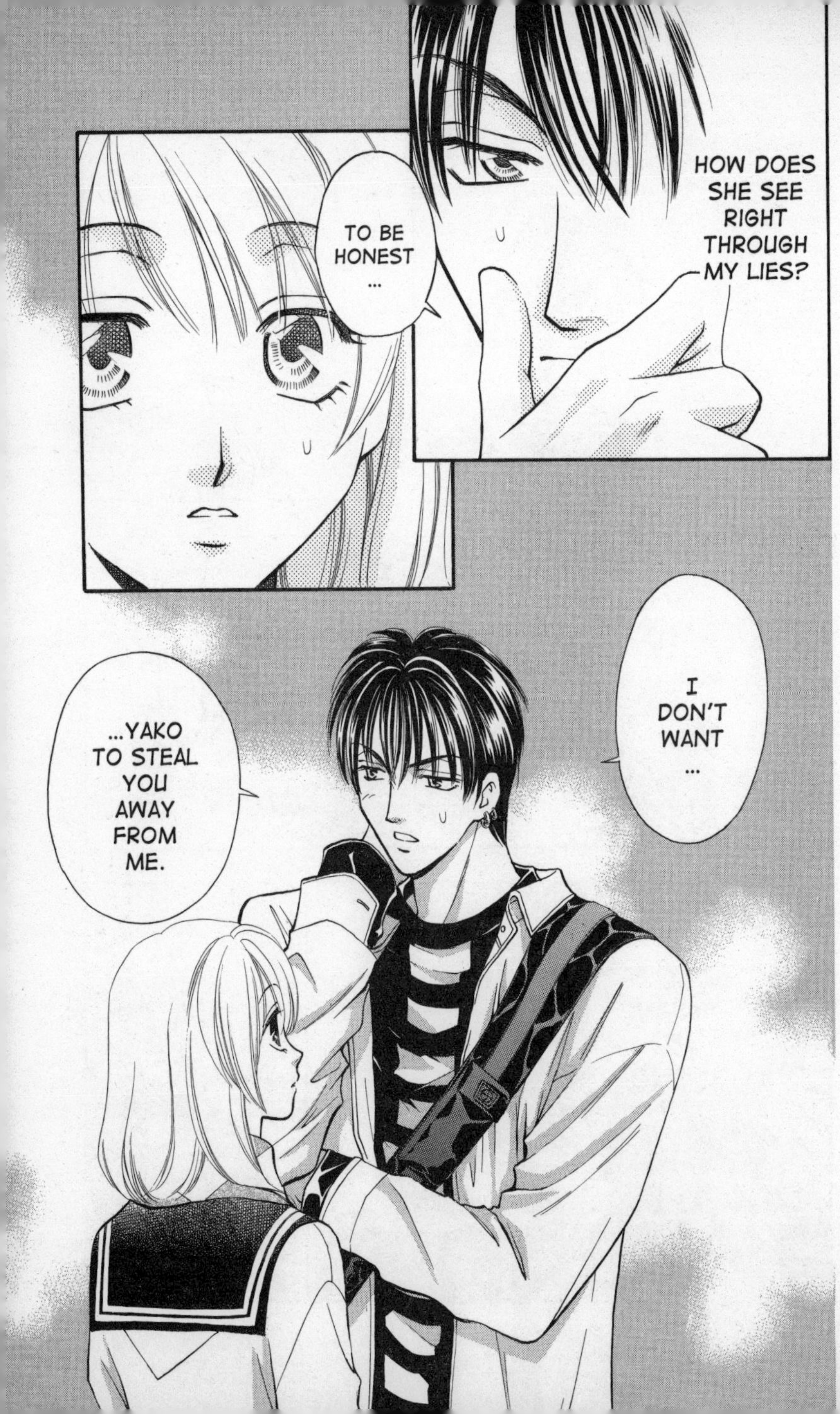
HOW DOES SHE SEE RIGHT THROUGH MY LIES?
TO BE HONEST ...
I DON'T WANT ...
...YAKO TO STEAL YOU AWAY FROM ME.

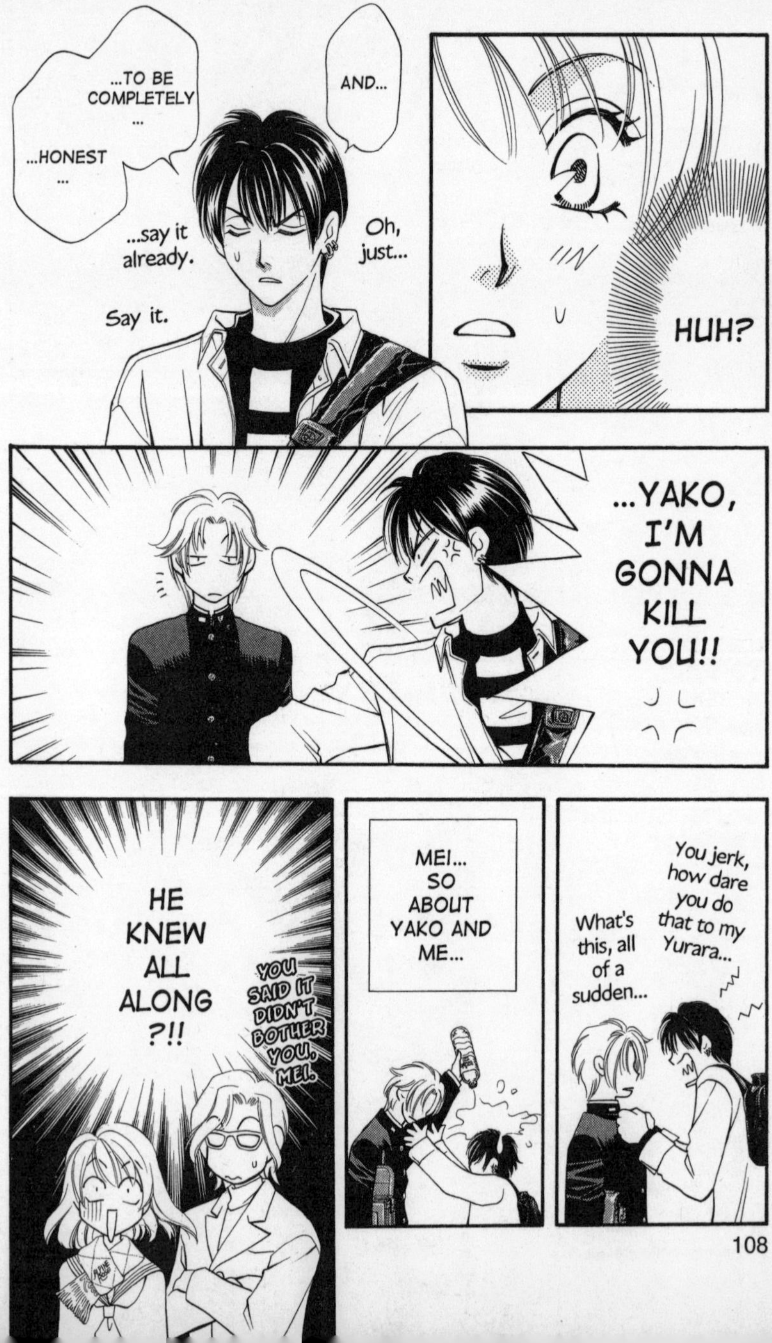
HUH?
AND...
...TO BE COMPLETELY ... ...HONEST ...
Oh, just...
...say it already.
Say it.
...YAKO, I'M GONNA KILL YOU!!
You jerk, how dare you do that to my Yurara...
What's this, all of a sudden...
MEI... SO ABOUT YAKO AND ME...
HE KNEW ALL ALONG?!!
YOU SAID IT DIDN'T BOTHER YOU, MEI.

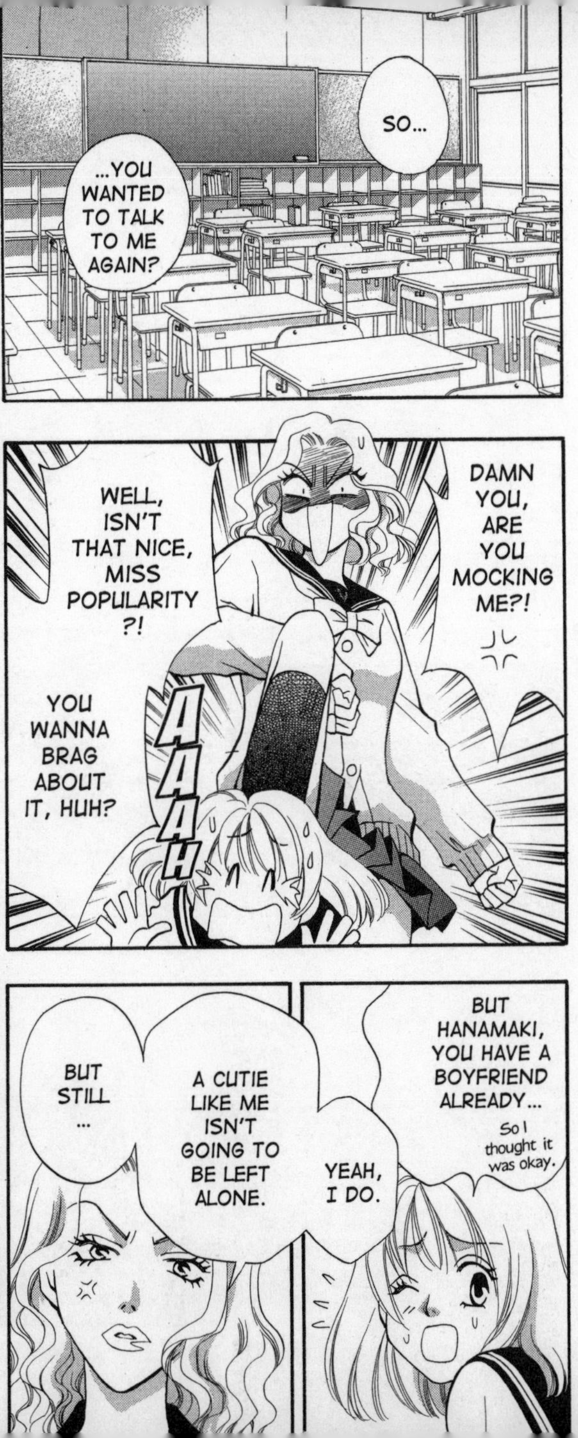
SO...
...YOU WANTED TO TALK TO ME AGAIN?
DAMN YOU, ARE YOU MOCKING ME?!
WELL, ISN'T THAT NICE, MISS POPULARITY?!
AAAAH
YOU WANNA BRAG ABOUT IT, HUH?
BUT HANAMAKI, YOU HAVE A BOYFRIEND ALREADY...
So I thought it was okay.
YEAH, I DO.
A CUTIE LIKE ME ISN'T GOING TO BE LEFT ALONE.
BUT STILL ...

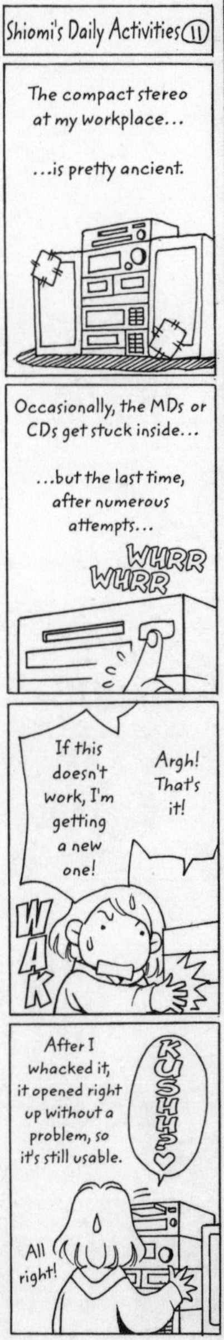
Shiomi's Daily Activities 11
The compact stereo at my workplace...
...is pretty ancient.
Occasionally, the MDs or CDs get stuck inside...
...but the last time, after numerous attempts...
WHRR WHRR
Argh! That's it!
If this doesn't work, I'm getting a new one!
WAK
After I whacked it, it opened right up without a problem, so it's still usable.
KUSHH♥
All right!

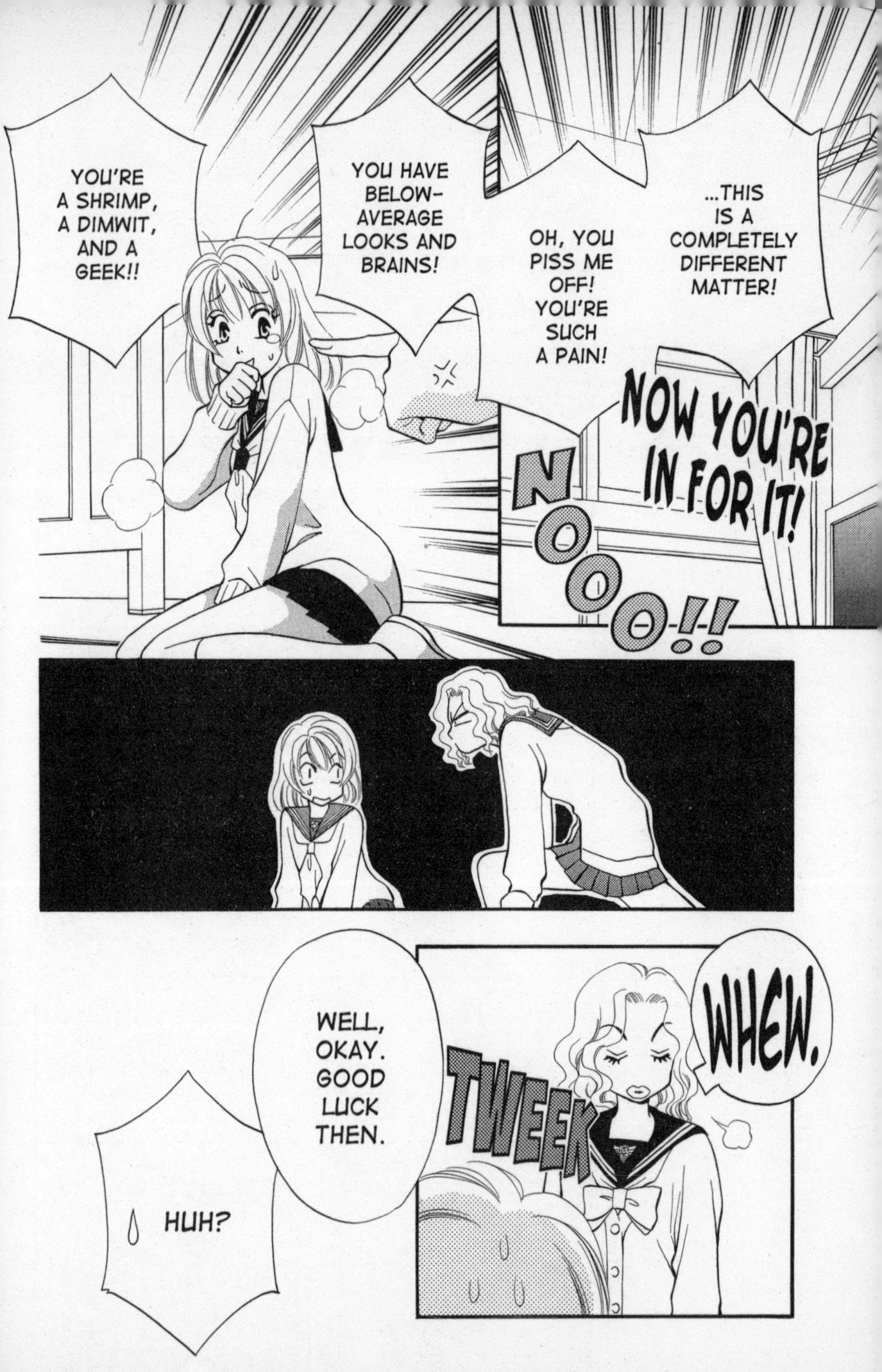
...THIS IS A COMPLETELY DIFFERENT MATTER!
OH, YOU PISS ME OFF! YOU'RE SUCH A PAIN!
NOW YOU'RE IN FOR IT!
YOU HAVE BELOW-AVERAGE LOOKS AND BRAINS!
YOU'RE A SHRIMP, A DIMWIT, AND A GEEK!!
NOOOO!!
WHEW.
TWEEK
WELL, OKAY. GOOD LUCK THEN.
HUH?

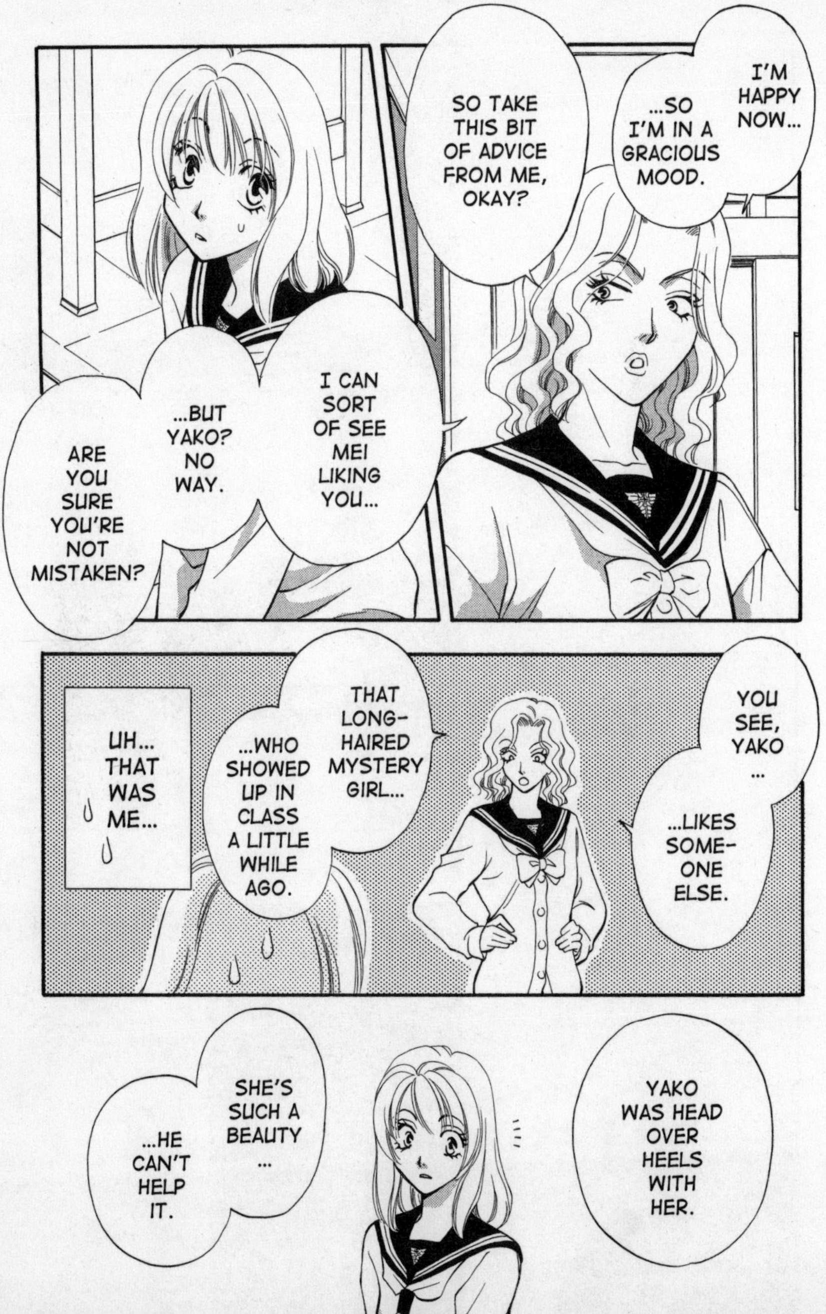
I'M HAPPY NOW...
...SO I'M IN A GRACIOUS MOOD.
SO TAKE THIS BIT OF ADVICE FROM ME, OKAY?
I CAN SORT OF SEE MEI LIKING YOU...
...BUT YAKO? NO WAY.
ARE YOU SURE YOU'RE NOT MISTAKEN?
YOU SEE, YAKO ...
...LIKES SOME-ONE ELSE.
THAT LONG-HAIRED MYSTERY GIRL...
...WHO SHOWED UP IN CLASS A LITTLE WHILE AGO.
UH... THAT WAS ME...
YAKO WAS HEAD OVER HEELS WITH HER.
SHE'S SUCH A BEAUTY ...
...HE CAN'T HELP IT.

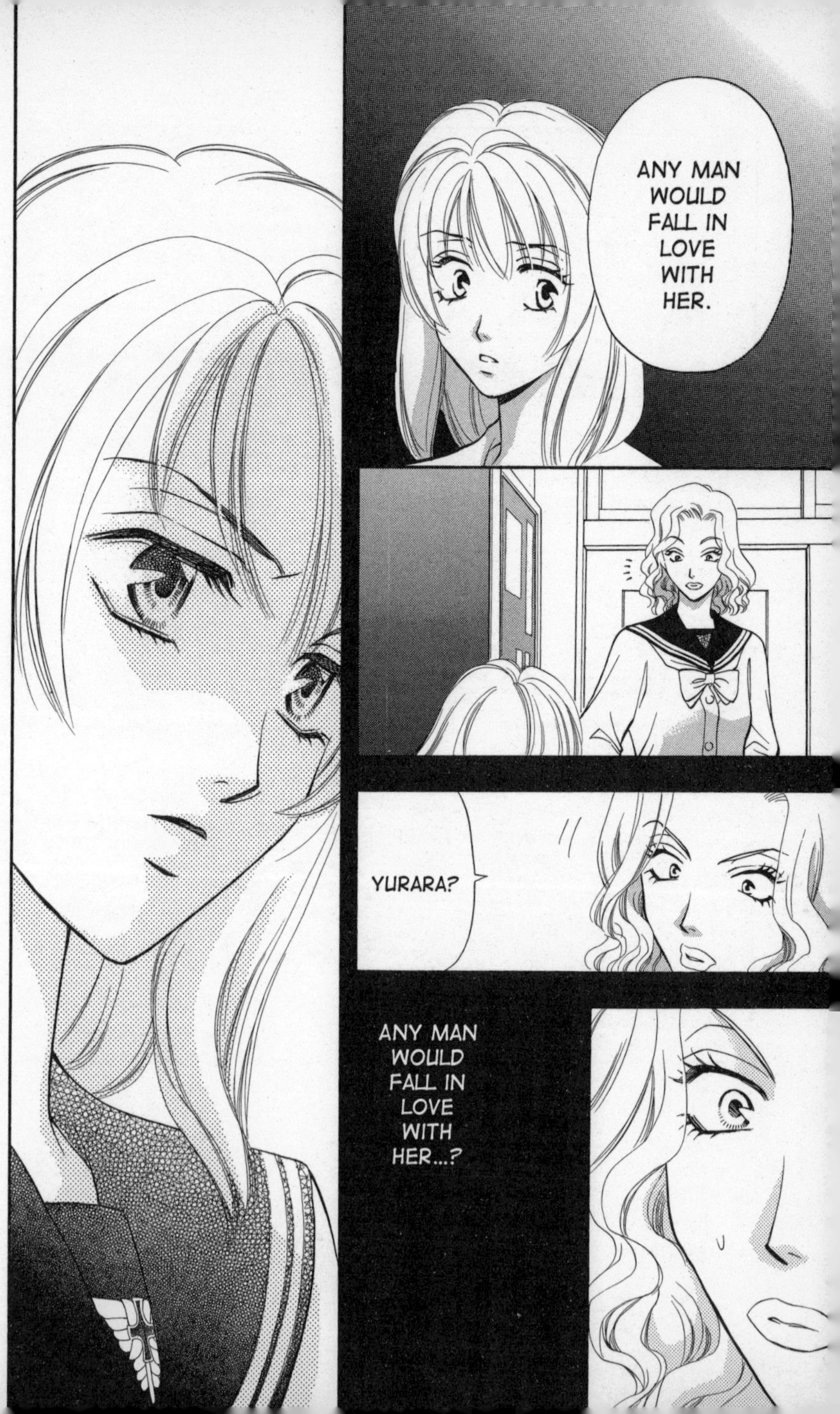
ANY MAN WOULD FALL IN LOVE WITH HER.
YURARA?
ANY MAN WOULD FALL IN LOVE WITH HER...?

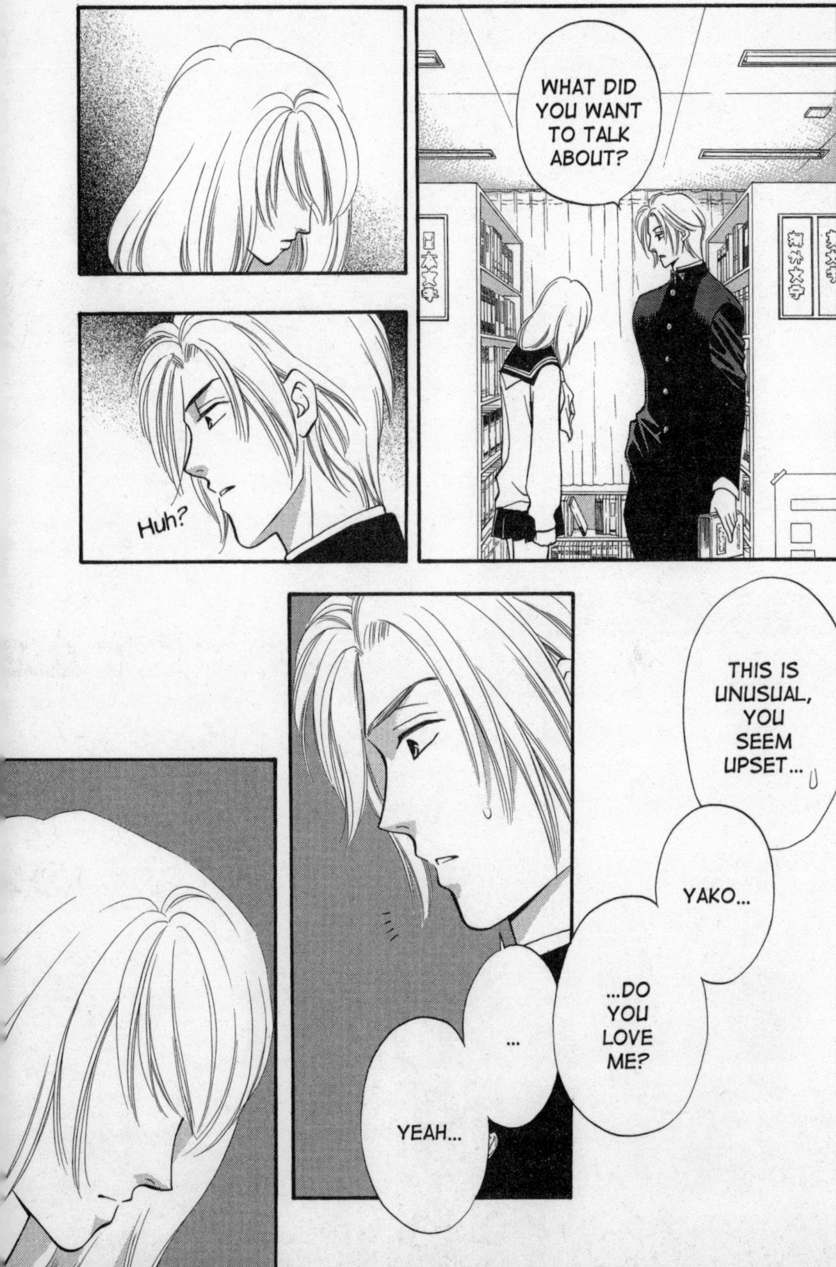
WHAT DID YOU WANT TO TALK ABOUT?
Huh?
THIS IS UNUSUAL, YOU SEEM UPSET...
YAKO...
...DO YOU LOVE ME?
...
YEAH...

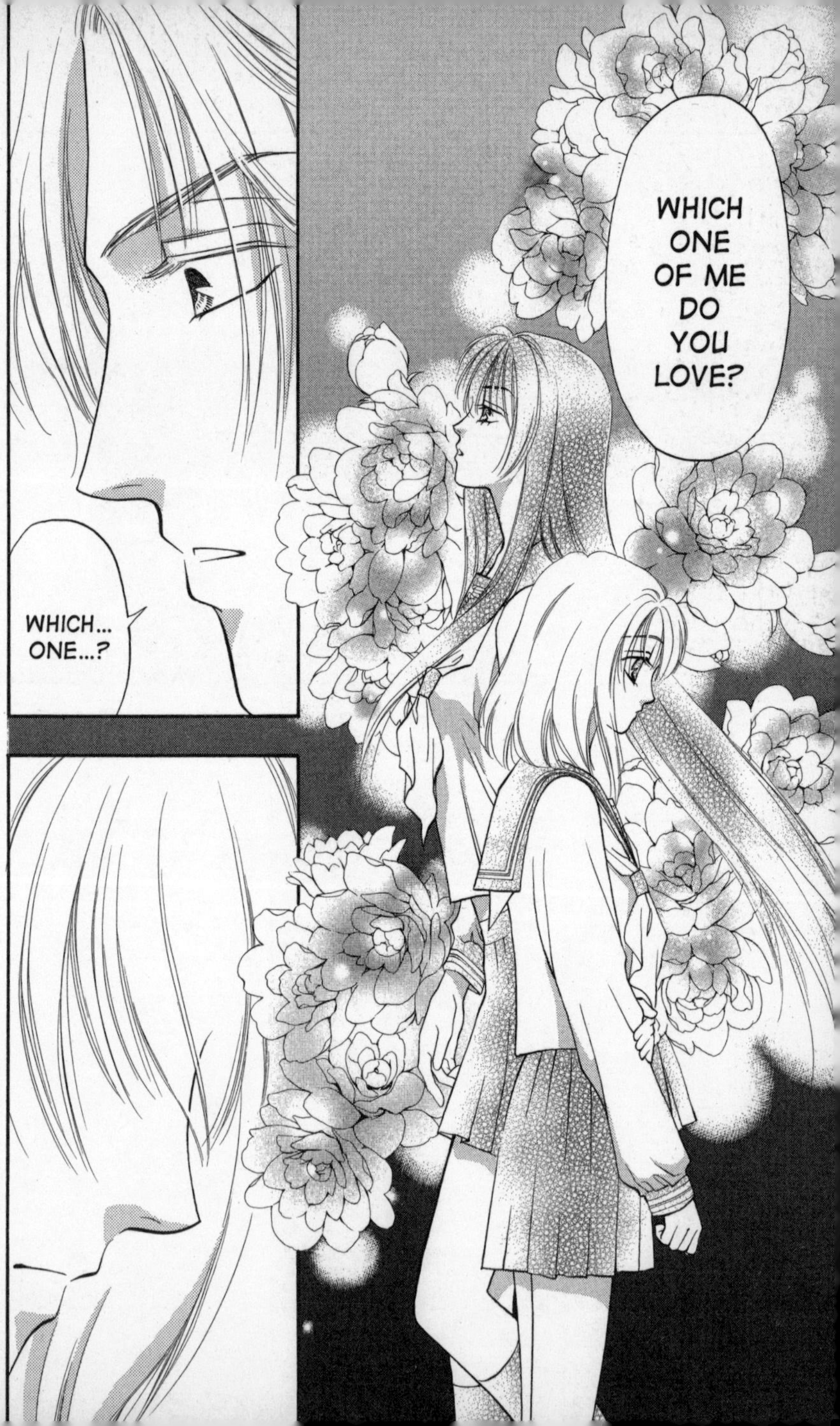
WHICH ONE OF ME DO YOU LOVE?
WHICH... ONE...?

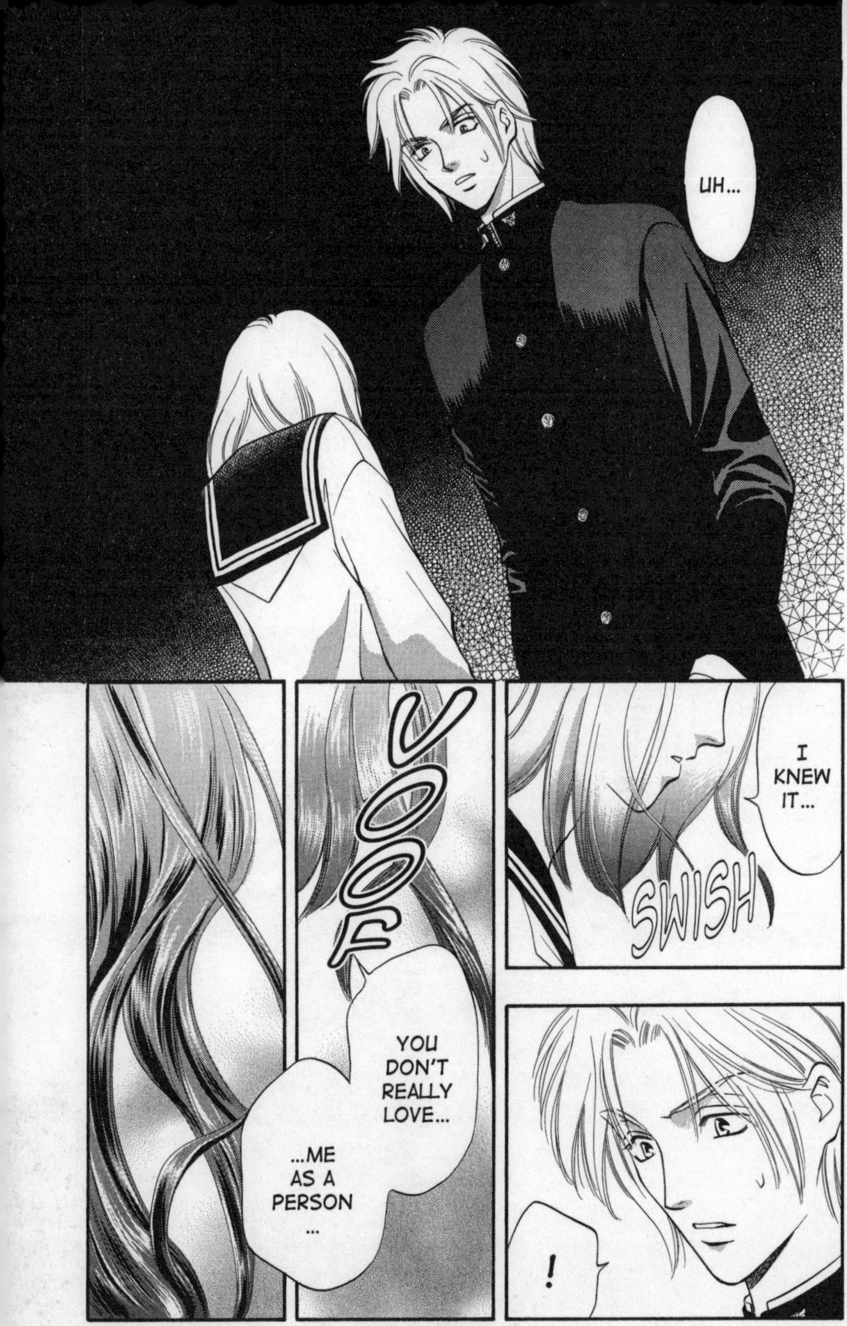
UH...
I KNEW IT...
SWISH
!
VOOOF
YOU DON'T REALLY LOVE...
...ME AS A PERSON ...

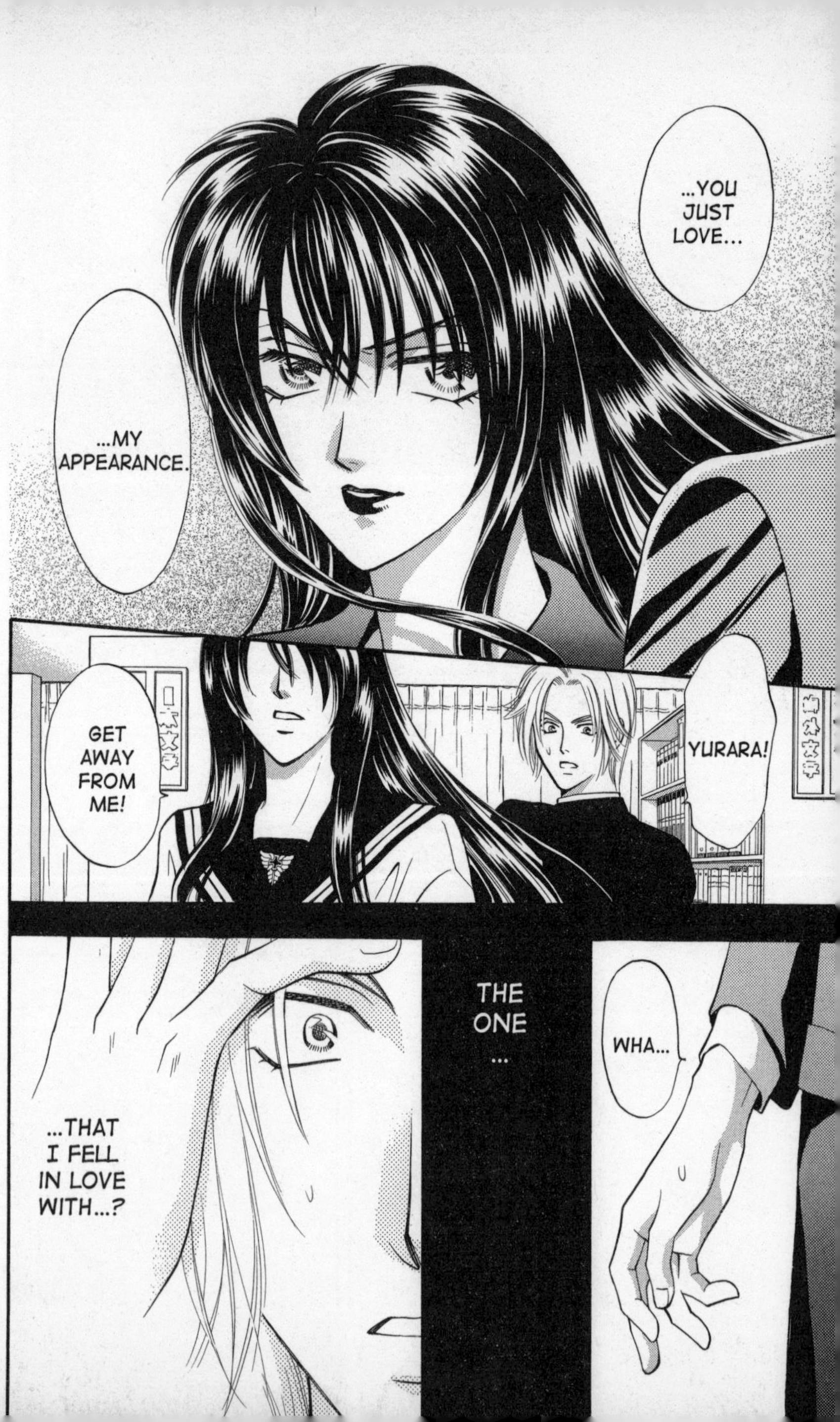
...YOU JUST LOVE...
...MY APPEARANCE.
YURARA!
GET AWAY FROM ME!
WHA...
THE ONE ...
...THAT I FELL IN LOVE WITH...?

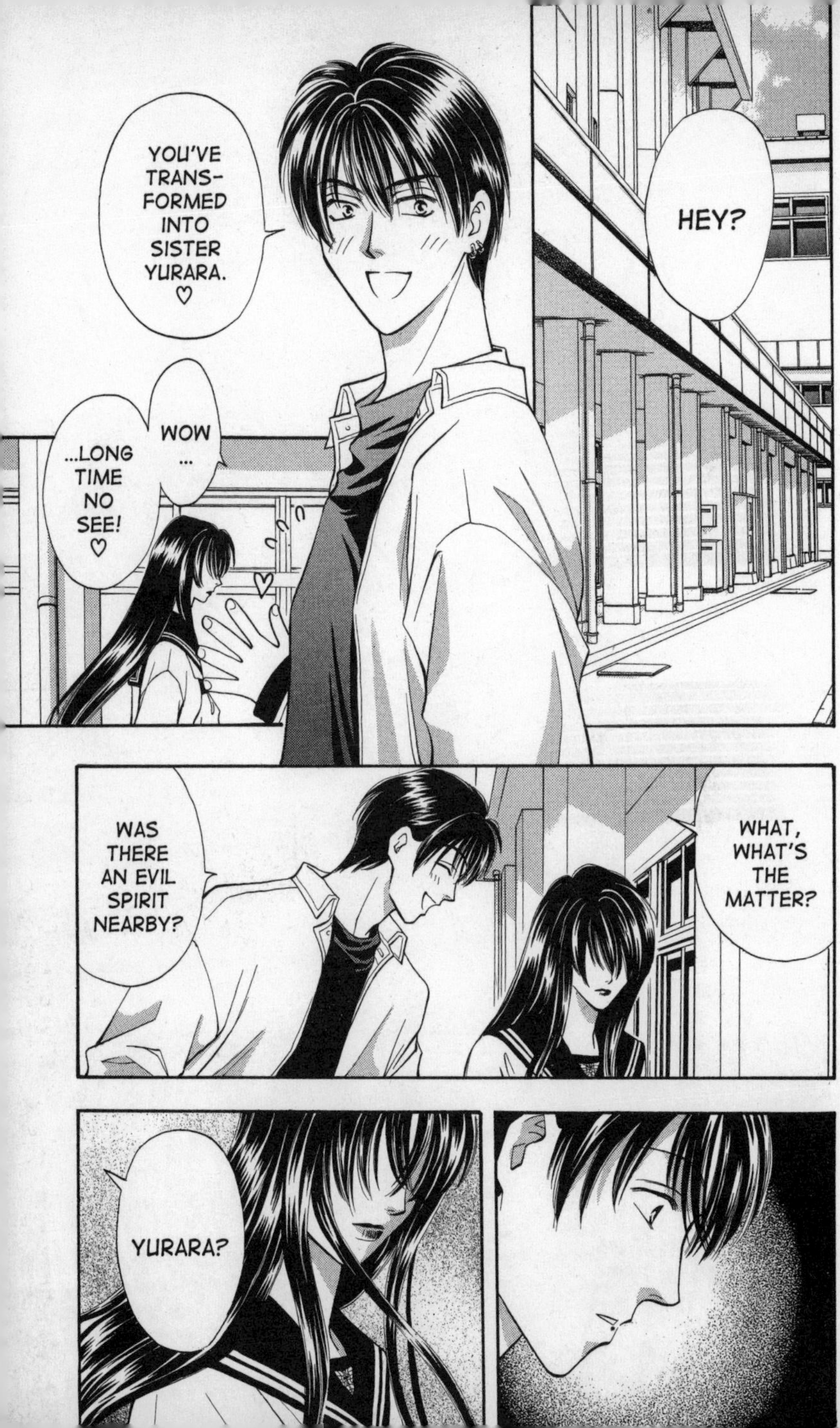
HEY?
YOU'VE TRANSFORMED INTO SISTER YURARA. ♡
WOW...
...LONG TIME NO SEE! ♡
WHAT, WHAT'S THE MATTER?
WAS THERE AN EVIL SPIRIT NEARBY?
YURARA?

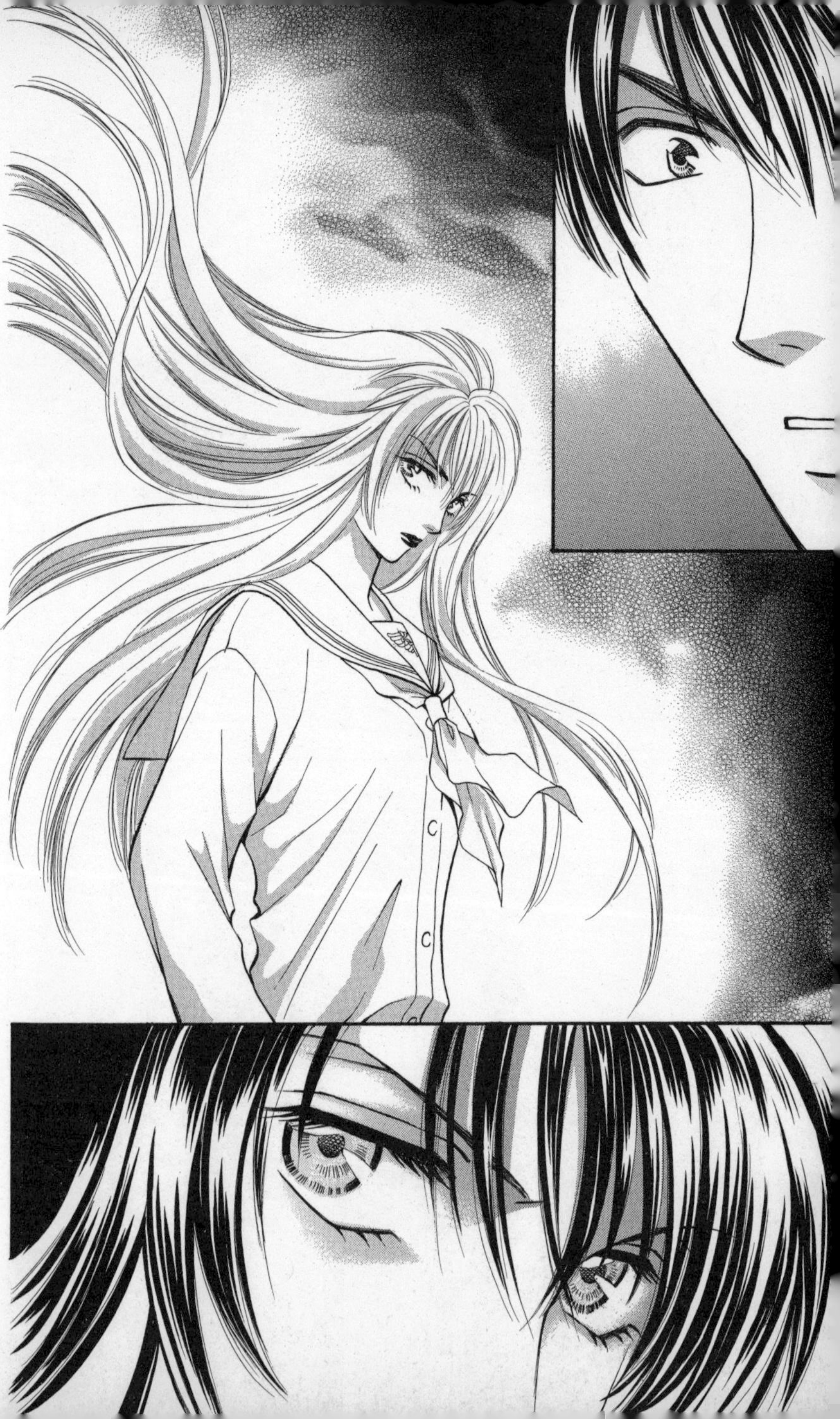

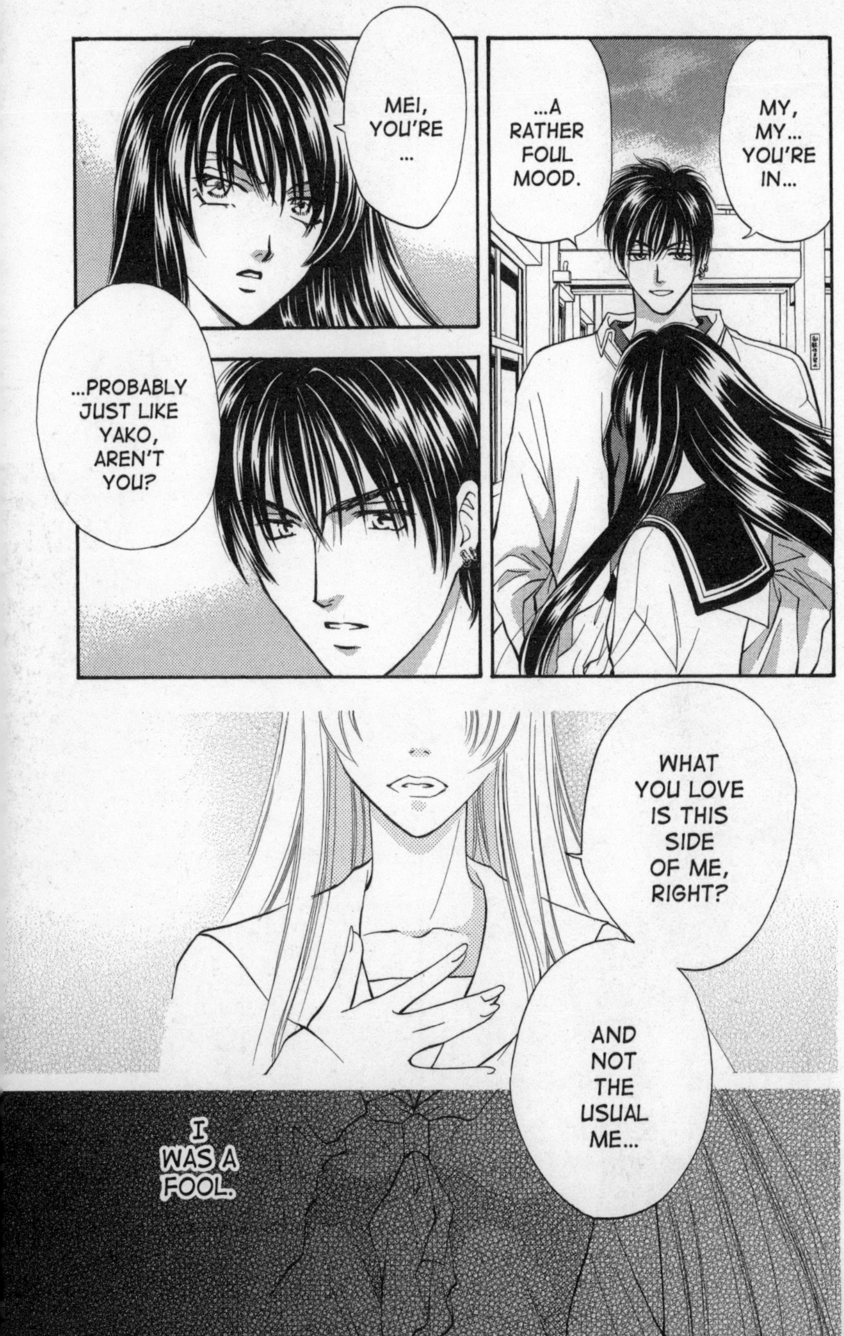
MY, MY... YOU'RE IN...
...A RATHER FOUL MOOD.
MEI, YOU'RE ...
...PROBABLY JUST LIKE YAKO, AREN'T YOU?
WHAT YOU LOVE IS THIS SIDE OF ME, RIGHT?
AND NOT THE USUAL ME...
I WAS A FOOL.

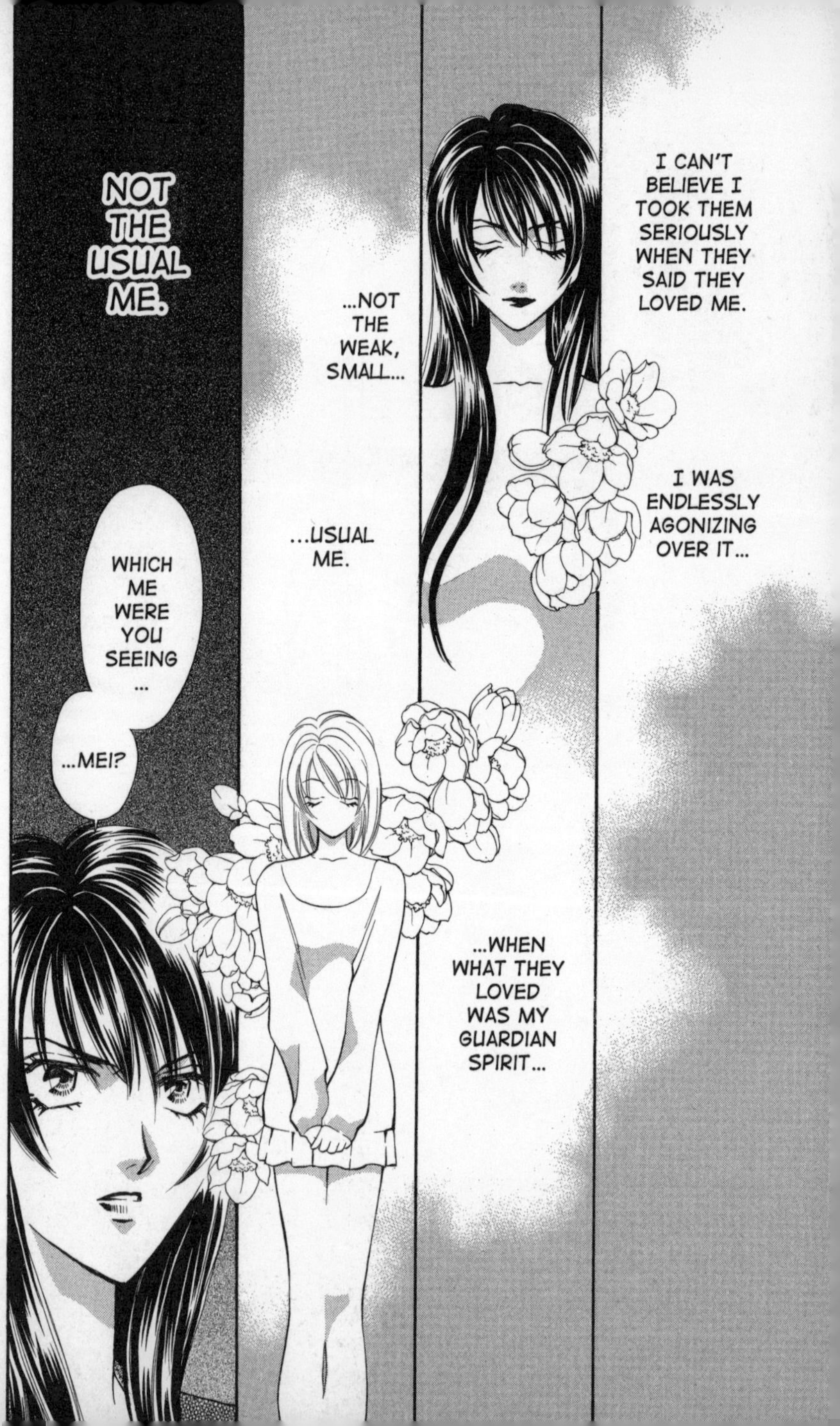
I CAN'T BELIEVE I TOOK THEM SERIOUSLY WHEN THEY SAID THEY LOVED ME.
I WAS ENDLESSLY AGONIZING OVER IT...
...WHEN WHAT THEY LOVED WAS MY GUARDIAN SPIRIT...
...NOT THE WEAK, SMALL...
...USUAL ME.
NOT THE USUAL ME.
WHICH ME WERE YOU SEEING...
...MEI?

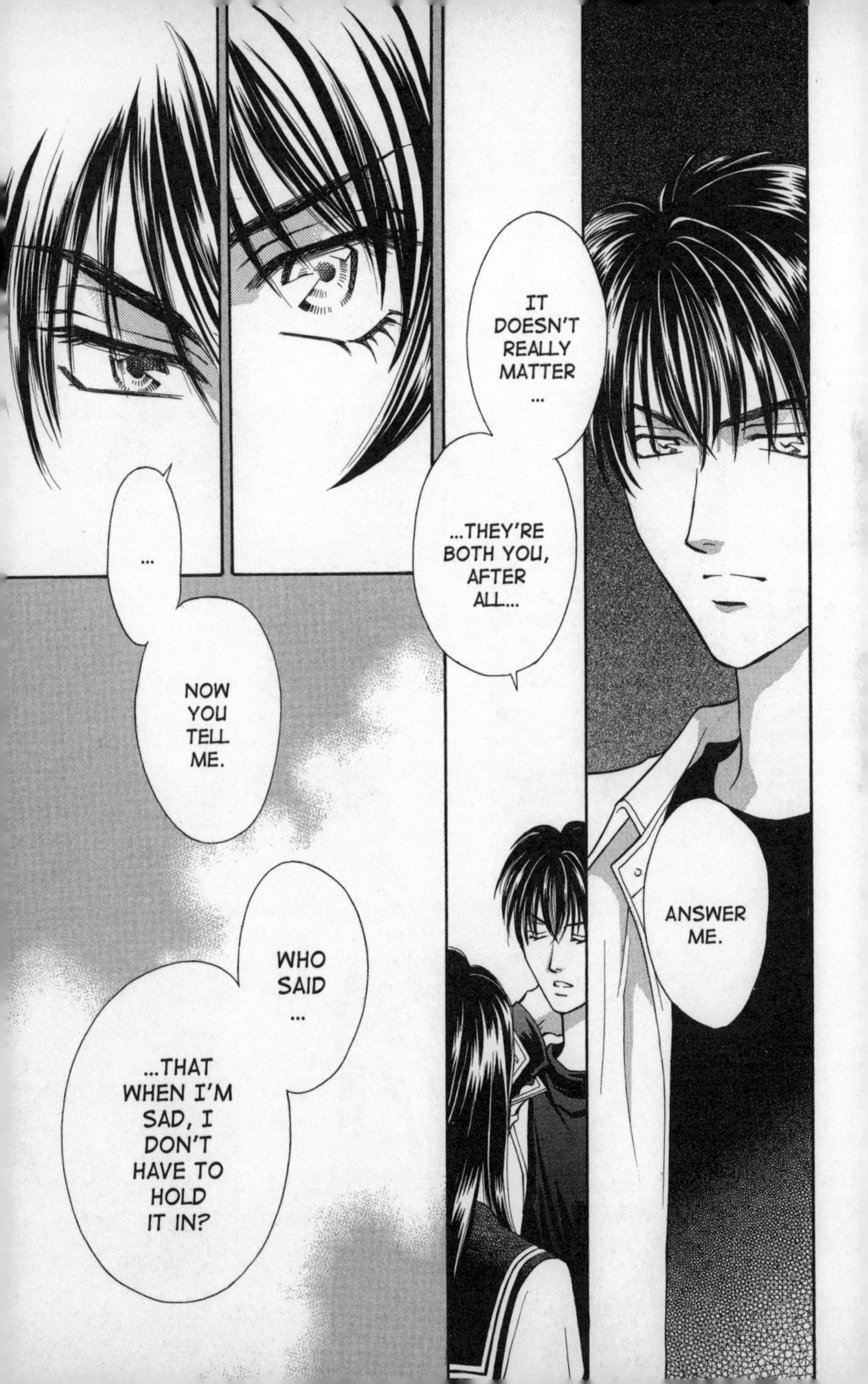
ANSWER ME.
IT DOESN'T REALLY MATTER ...
...THEY'RE BOTH YOU, AFTER ALL...
...
NOW YOU TELL ME.
WHO SAID ...
...THAT WHEN I'M SAD, I DON'T HAVE TO HOLD IT IN?

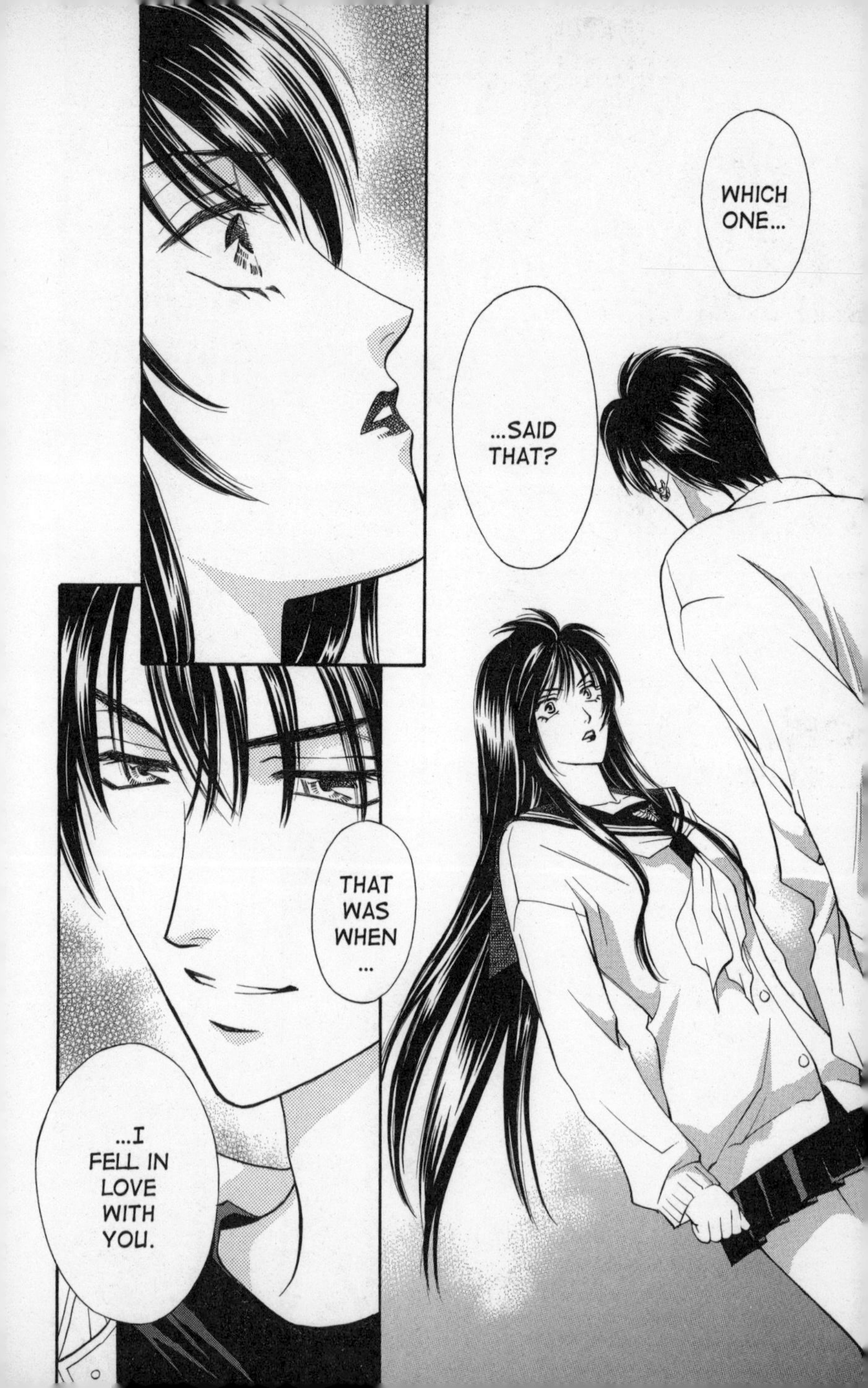
WHICH ONE...
...SAID THAT?
THAT WAS WHEN ...
...I FELL IN LOVE WITH YOU.

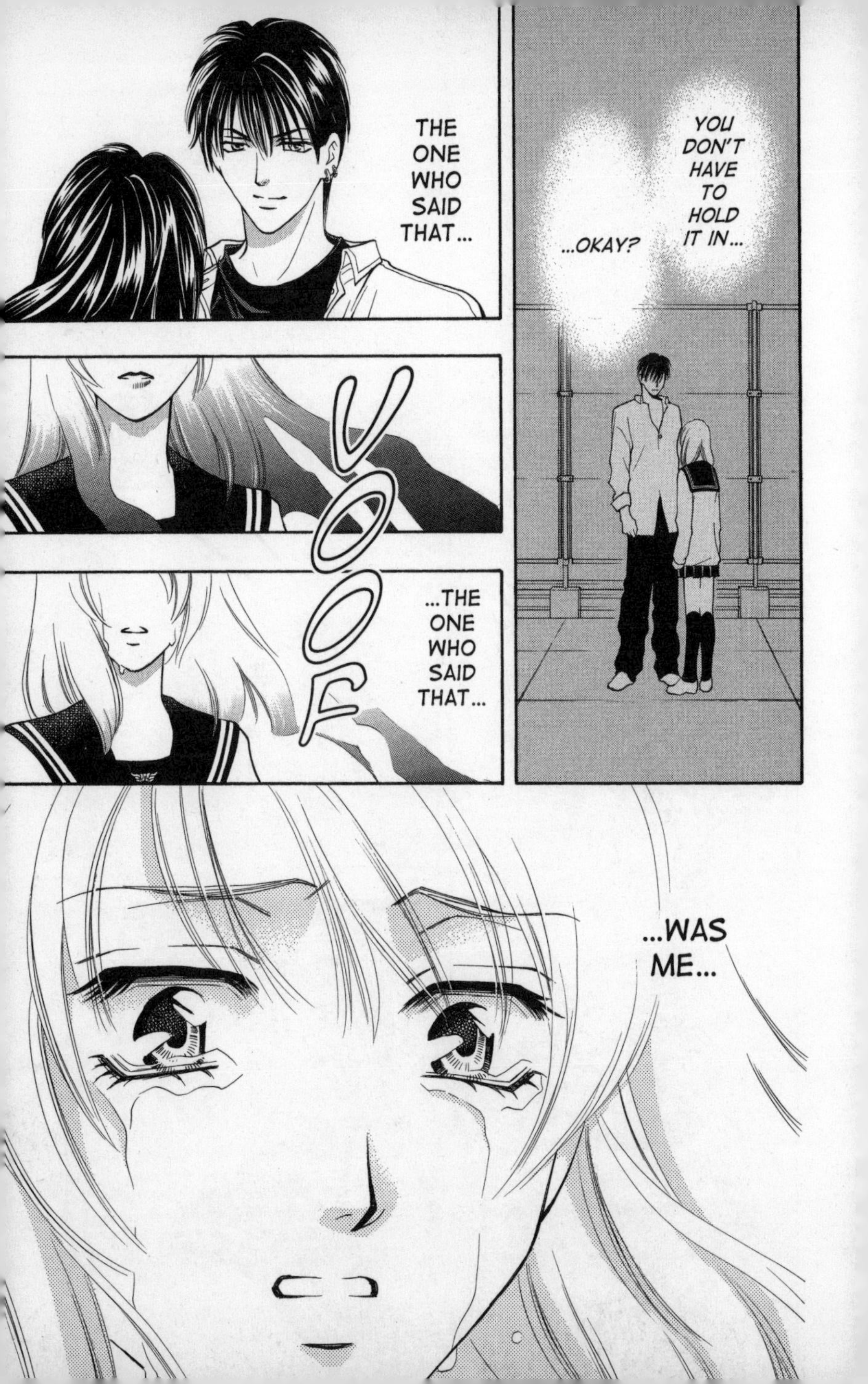
YOU DON'T HAVE TO HOLD IT IN...
...OKAY?
THE ONE WHO SAID THAT...
VOOF
...THE ONE WHO SAID THAT...
...WAS ME...

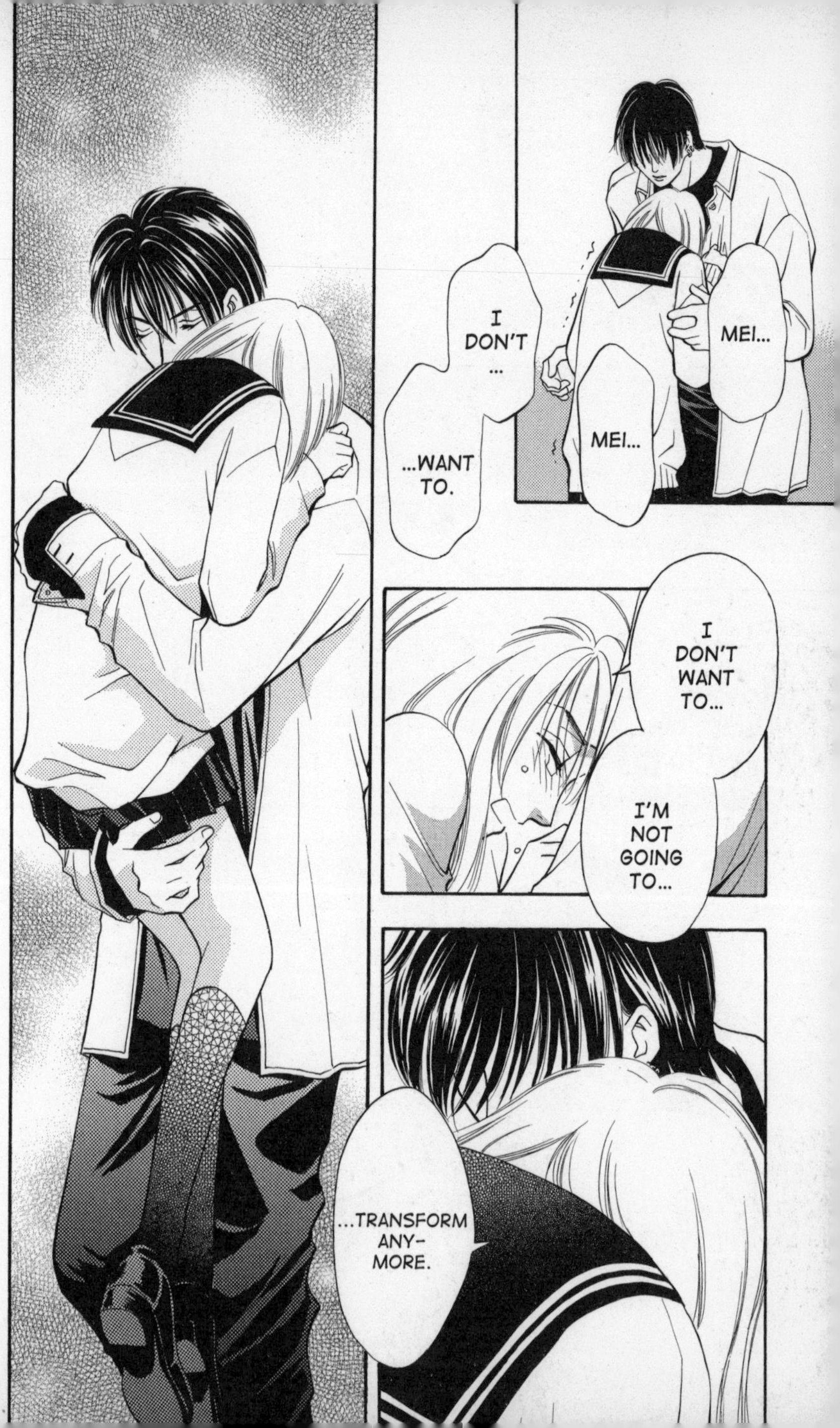
MEI...
MEI...
I DON'T ...
...WANT TO.
I DON'T WANT TO...
I'M NOT GOING TO...
...TRANSFORM ANY-MORE.

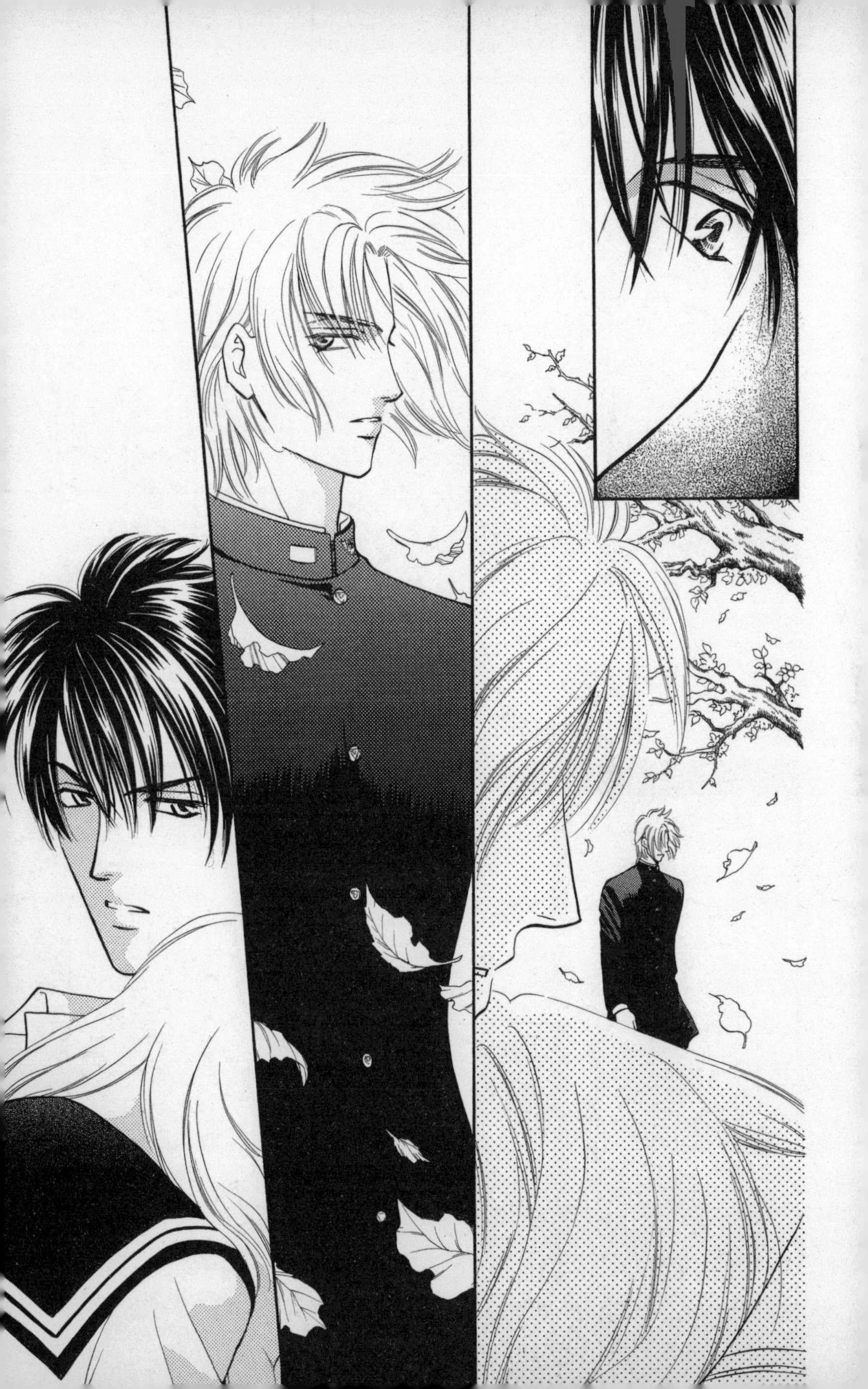

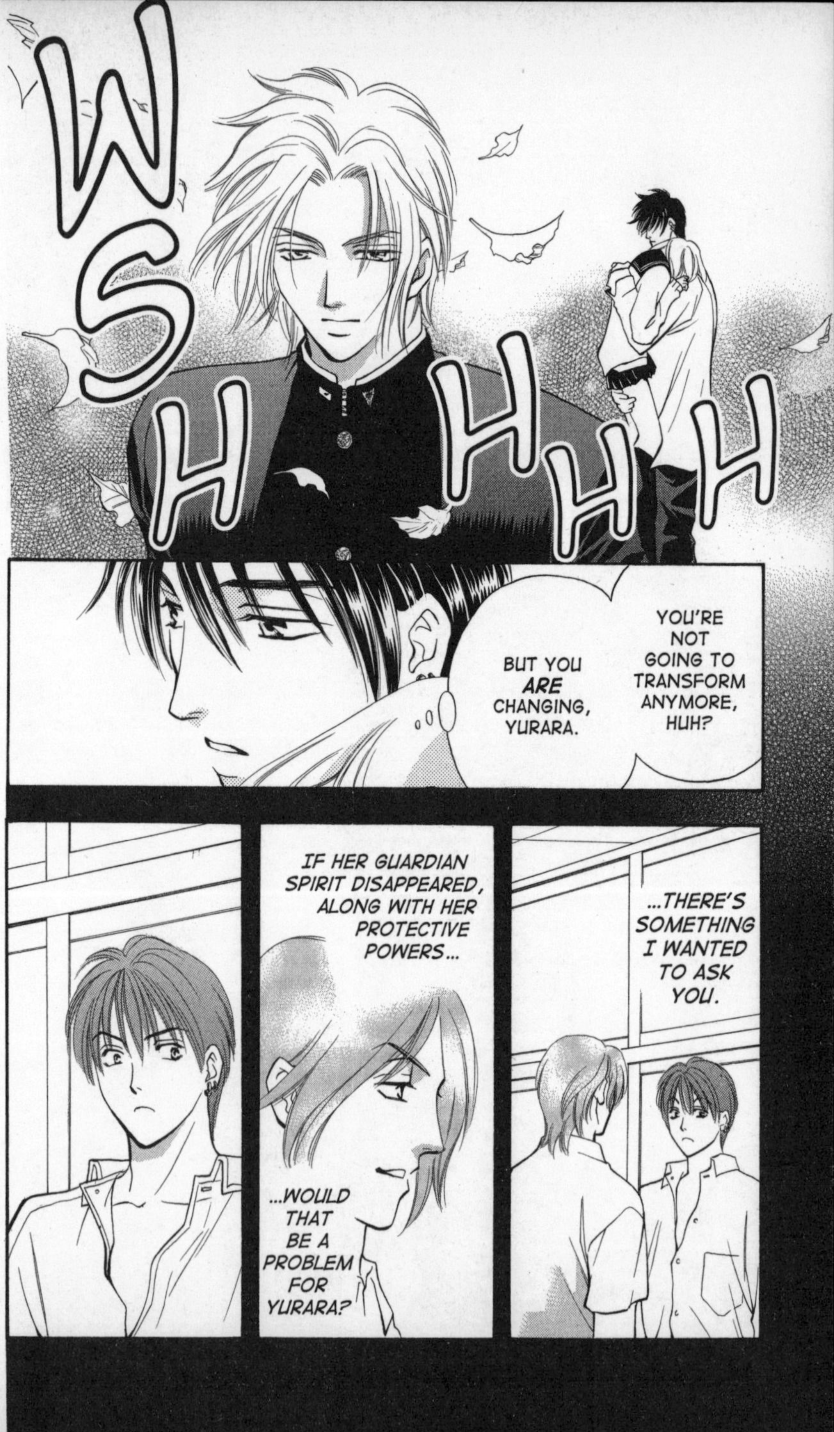
WSHHHHH
YOU'RE NOT GOING TO TRANSFORM ANYMORE, HUH?
BUT YOU *ARE* CHANGING, YURARA.
...THERE'S SOMETHING I WANTED TO ASK YOU.
IF HER GUARDIAN SPIRIT DISAPPEARED, ALONG WITH HER PROTECTIVE POWERS...
...WOULD THAT BE A PROBLEM FOR YURARA?

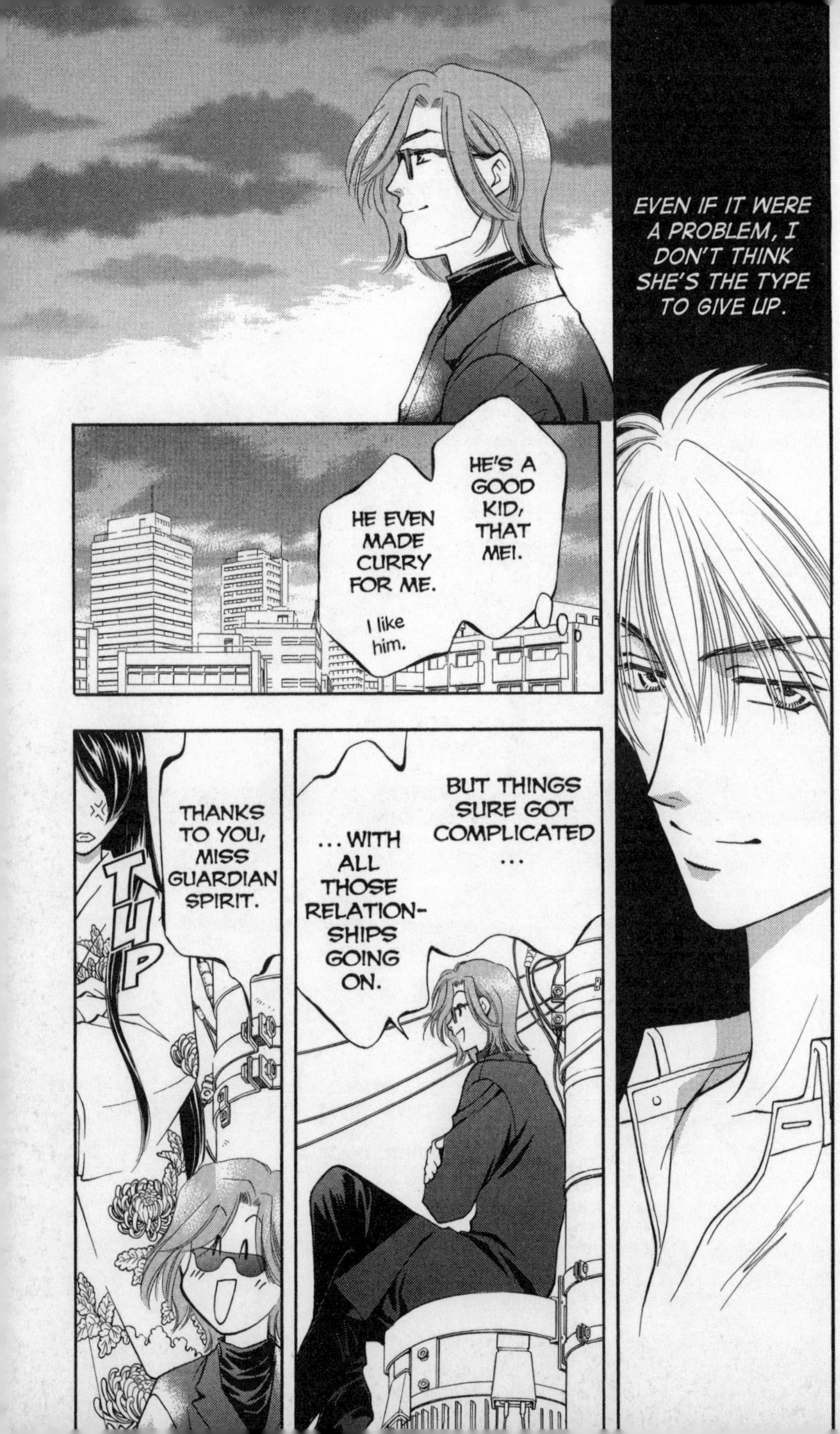
EVEN IF IT WERE A PROBLEM, I DON'T THINK SHE'S THE TYPE TO GIVE UP.
HE'S A GOOD KID, THAT MEI.
HE EVEN MADE CURRY FOR ME.
I like him.
BUT THINGS SURE GOT COMPLICATED...
...WITH ALL THOSE RELATIONSHIPS GOING ON.
THANKS TO YOU, MISS GUARDIAN SPIRIT.
TUP

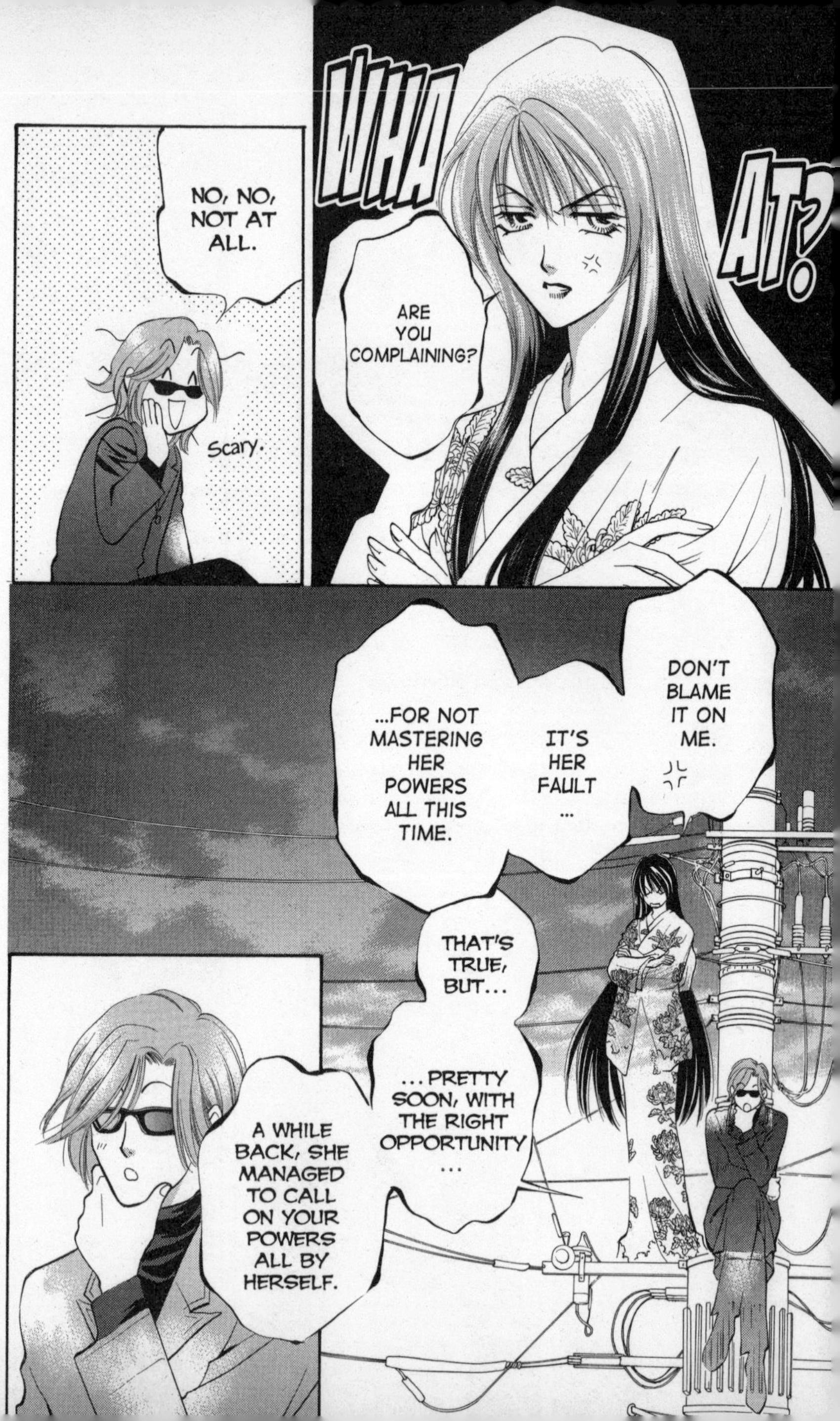
WHAAT?
ARE YOU COMPLAINING?
NO, NO, NOT AT ALL.
Scary.
DON'T BLAME IT ON ME.
IT'S HER FAULT...
...FOR NOT MASTERING HER POWERS ALL THIS TIME.
THAT'S TRUE, BUT...
A WHILE BACK, SHE MANAGED TO CALL ON YOUR POWERS ALL BY HERSELF.
...PRETTY SOON, WITH THE RIGHT OPPORTUNITY...

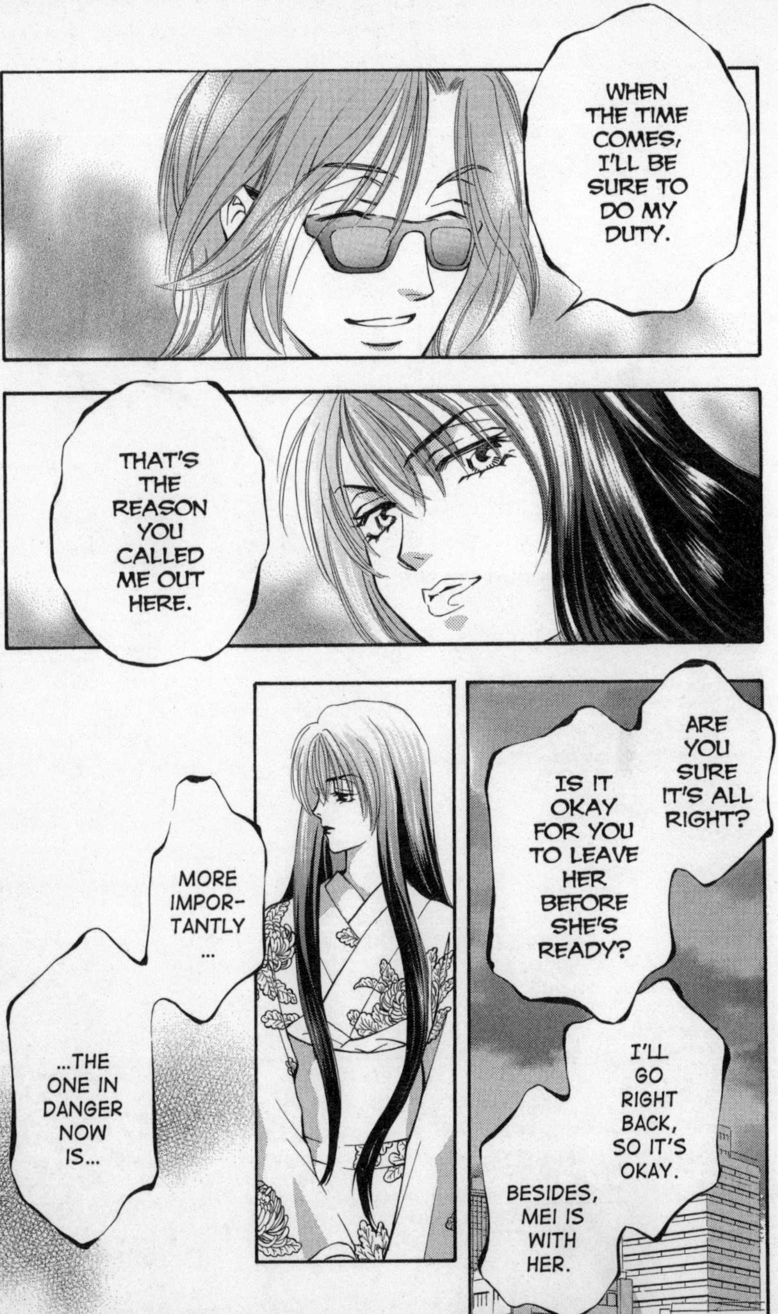
WHEN THE TIME COMES, I'LL BE SURE TO DO MY DUTY.
THAT'S THE REASON YOU CALLED ME OUT HERE.
ARE YOU SURE IT'S ALL RIGHT?
IS IT OKAY FOR YOU TO LEAVE HER BEFORE SHE'S READY?
I'LL GO RIGHT BACK, SO IT'S OKAY.
BESIDES, MEI IS WITH HER.
MORE IMPORTANTLY...
...THE ONE IN DANGER NOW IS...

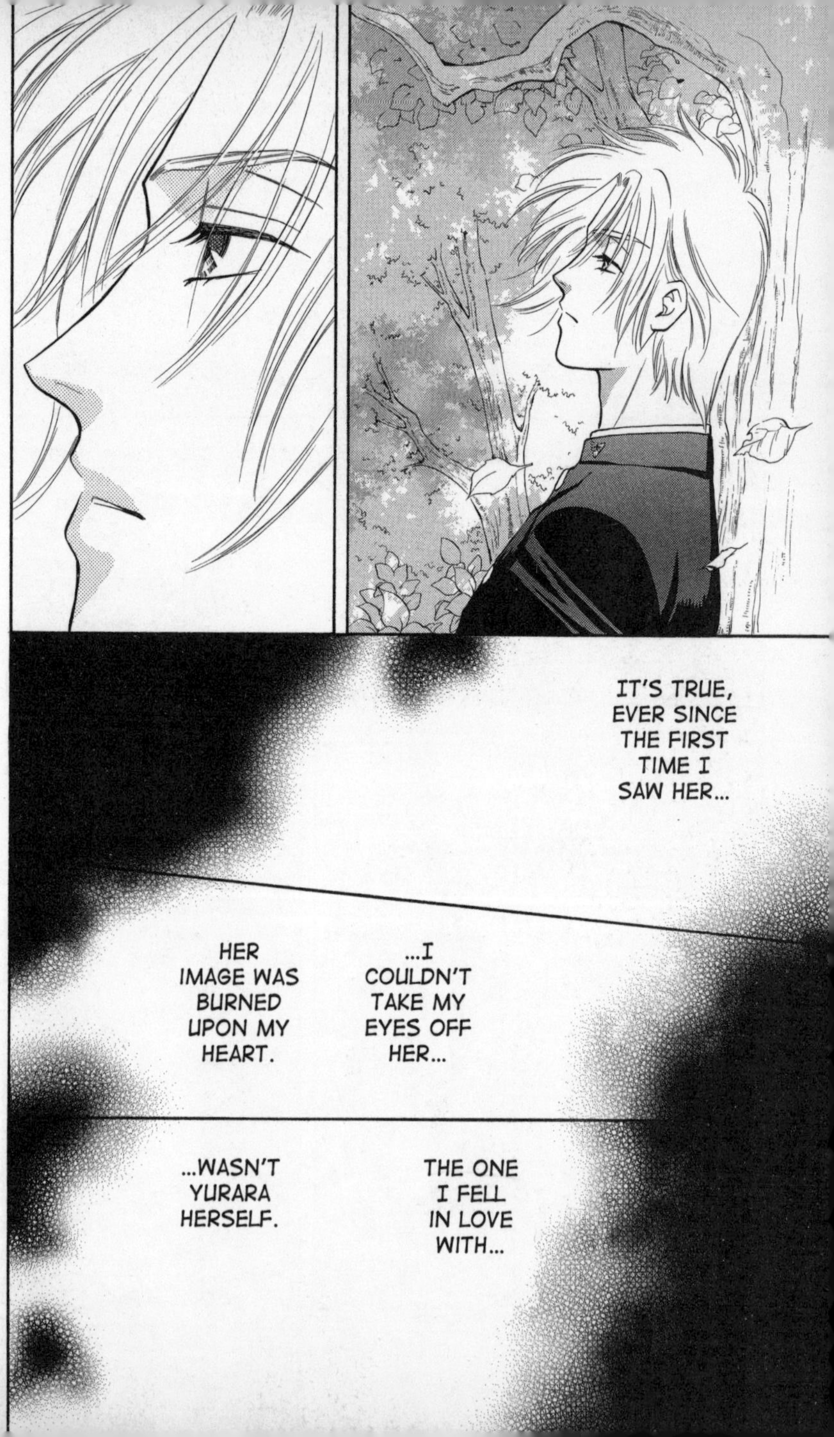
IT'S TRUE, EVER SINCE THE FIRST TIME I SAW HER...
...I COULDN'T TAKE MY EYES OFF HER...
HER IMAGE WAS BURNED UPON MY HEART.
THE ONE I FELL IN LOVE WITH...
...WASN'T YURARA HERSELF.

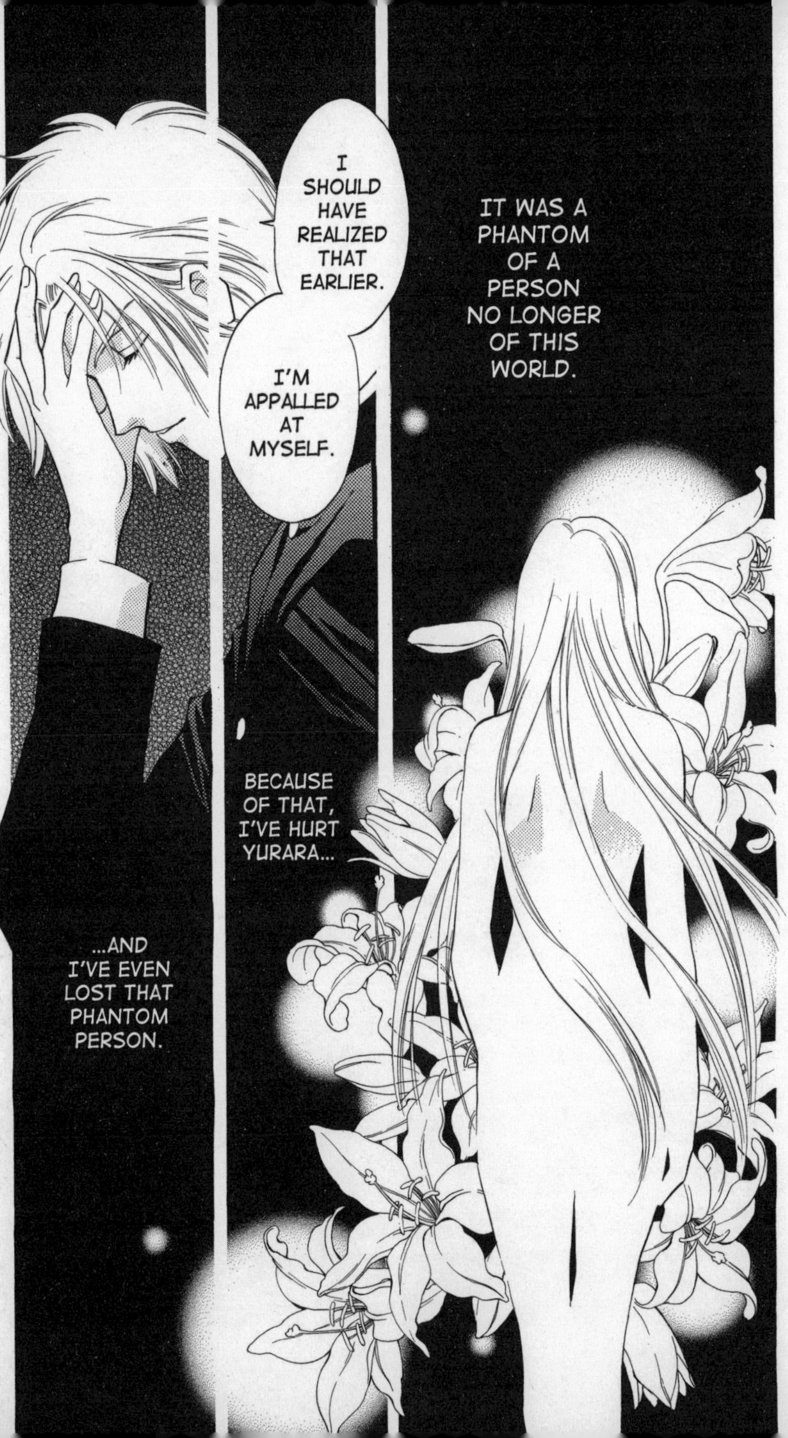
IT WAS A PHANTOM OF A PERSON NO LONGER OF THIS WORLD.
I SHOULD HAVE REALIZED THAT EARLIER.
I'M APPALLED AT MYSELF.
BECAUSE OF THAT, I'VE HURT YURARA...
...AND I'VE EVEN LOST THAT PHANTOM PERSON.

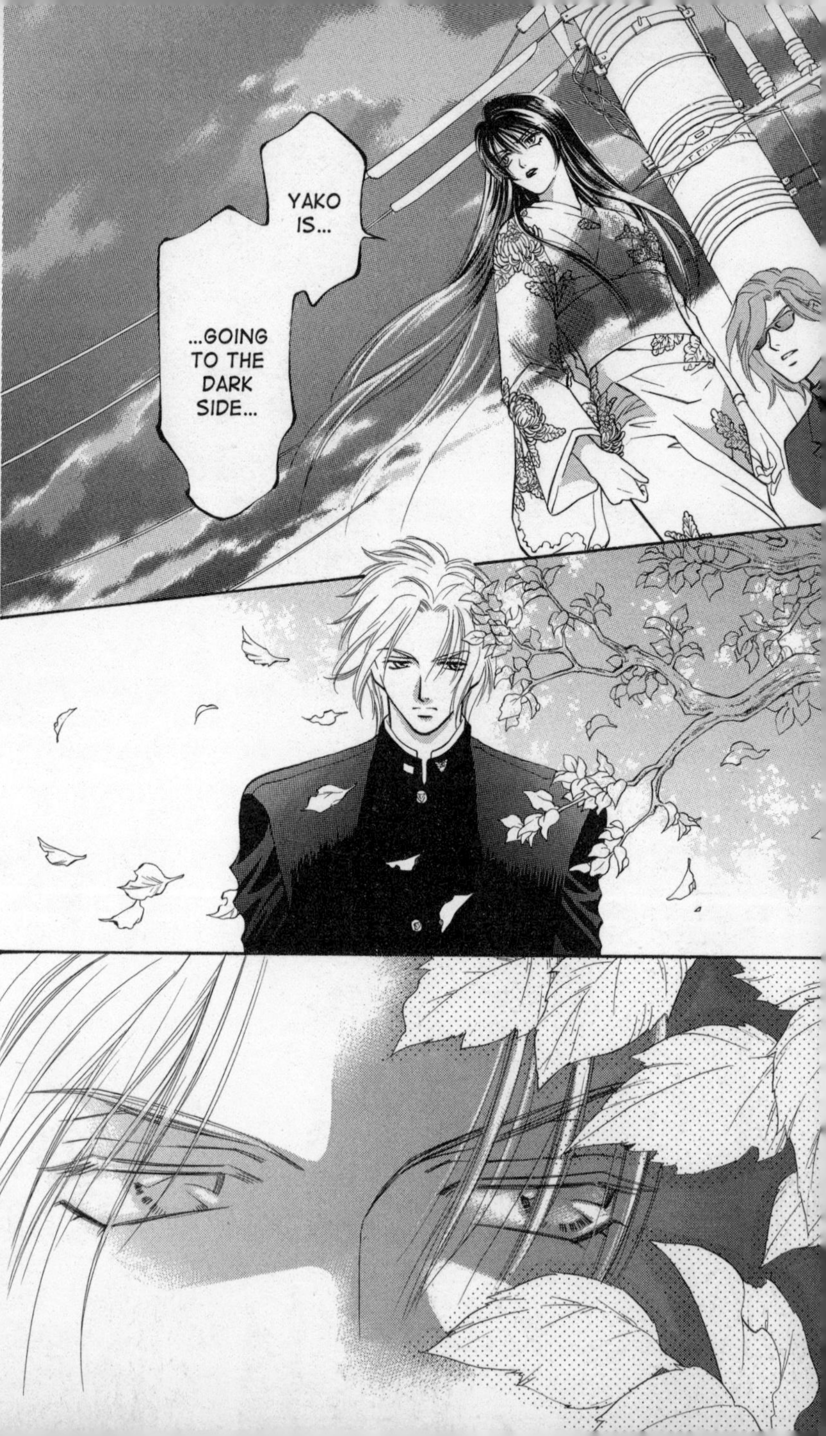
YAKO IS...
...GOING TO THE DARK SIDE...

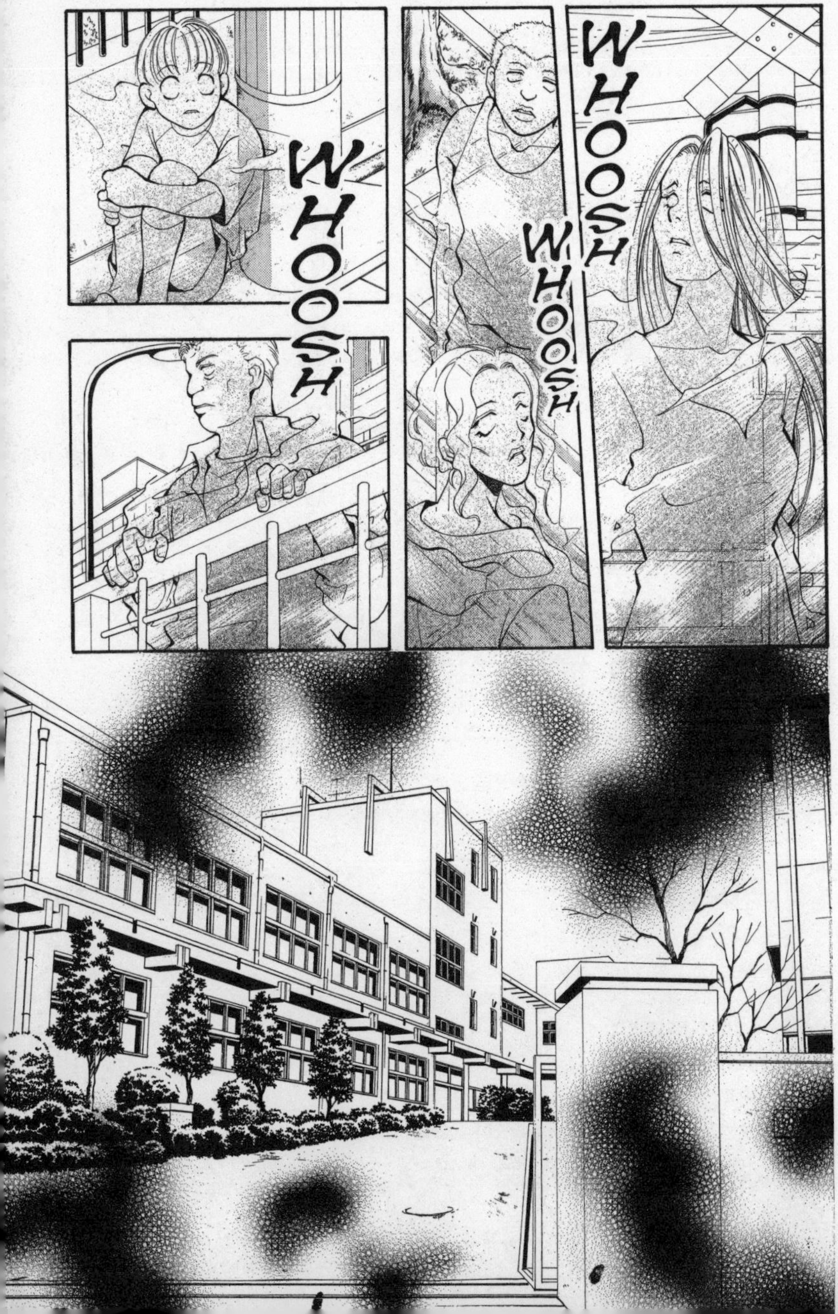
WHOOSH
WHOOSH
WHOOSH

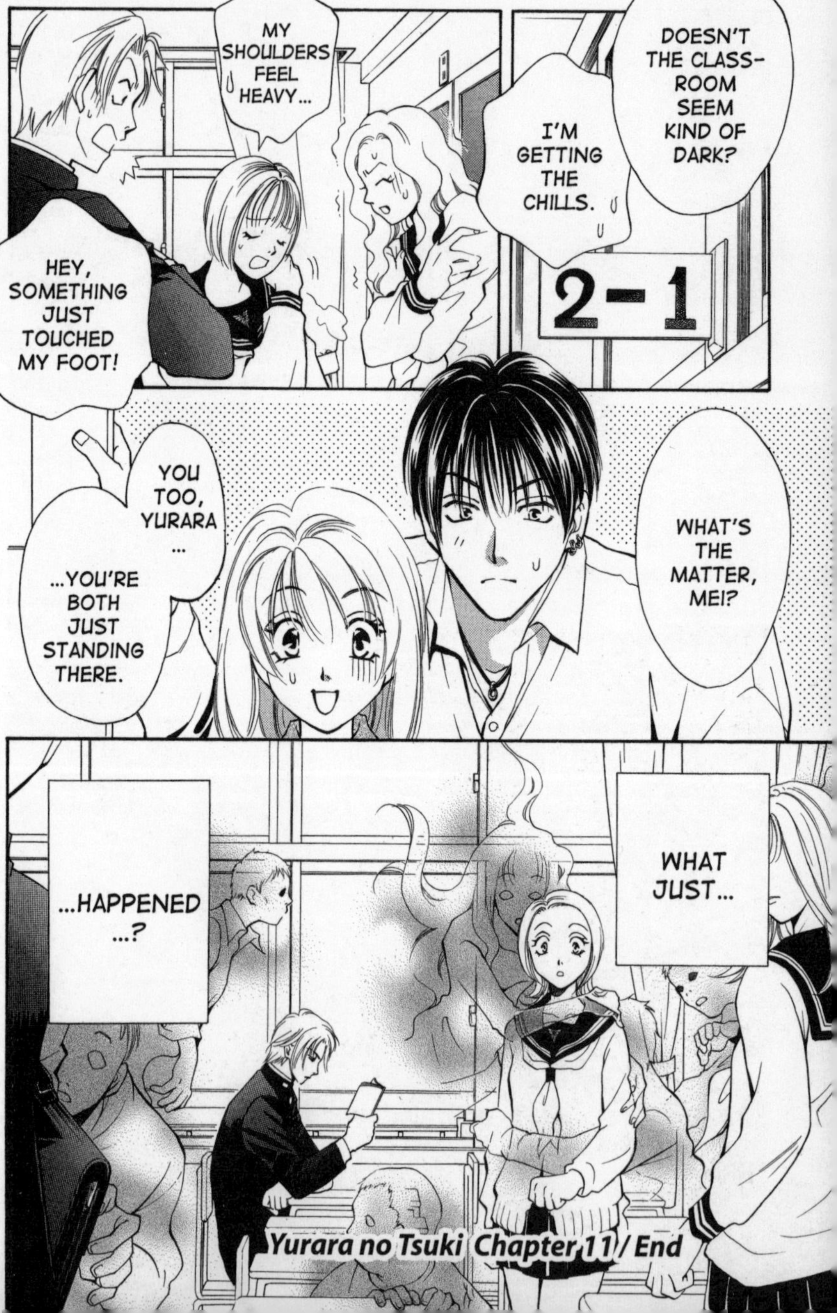
DOESN'T THE CLASS-ROOM SEEM KIND OF DARK?
I'M GETTING THE CHILLS.
MY SHOULDERS FEEL HEAVY...
HEY, SOMETHING JUST TOUCHED MY FOOT!
WHAT'S THE MATTER, MEI?
YOU TOO, YURARA...
...YOU'RE BOTH JUST STANDING THERE.
WHAT JUST...
...HAPPENED...?
Yurara no Tsuki Chapter 11 / End

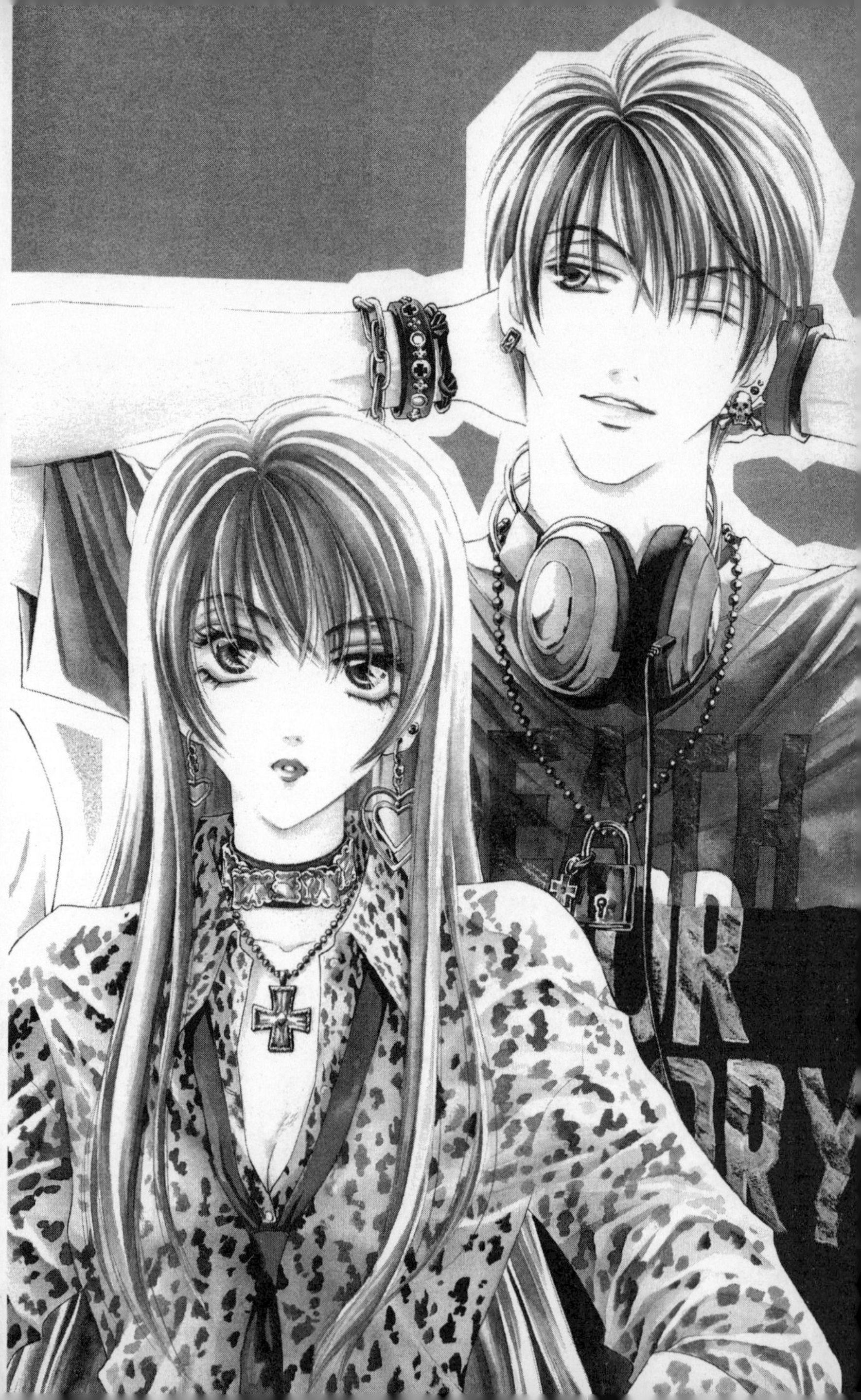

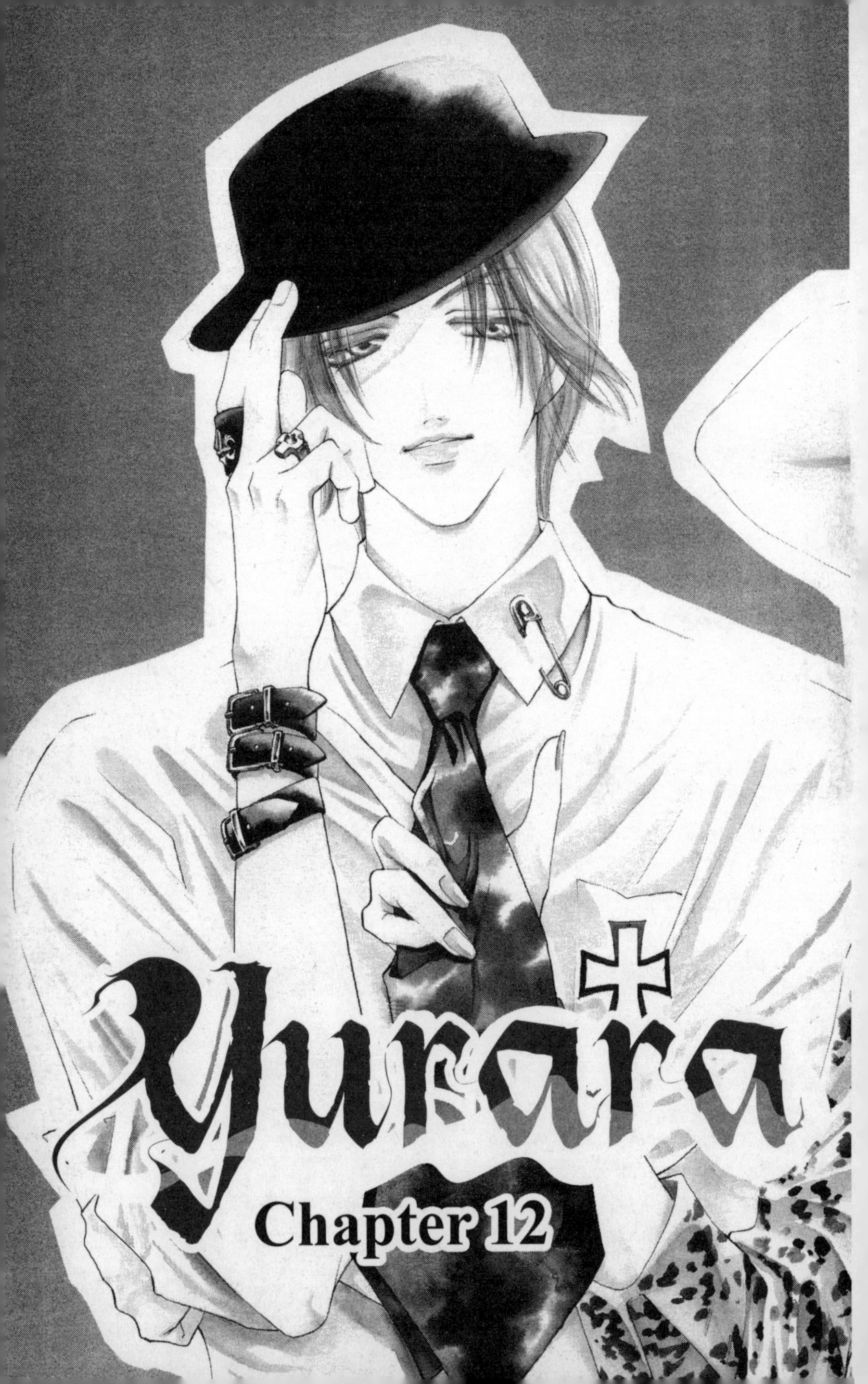
Yurara
Chapter 12

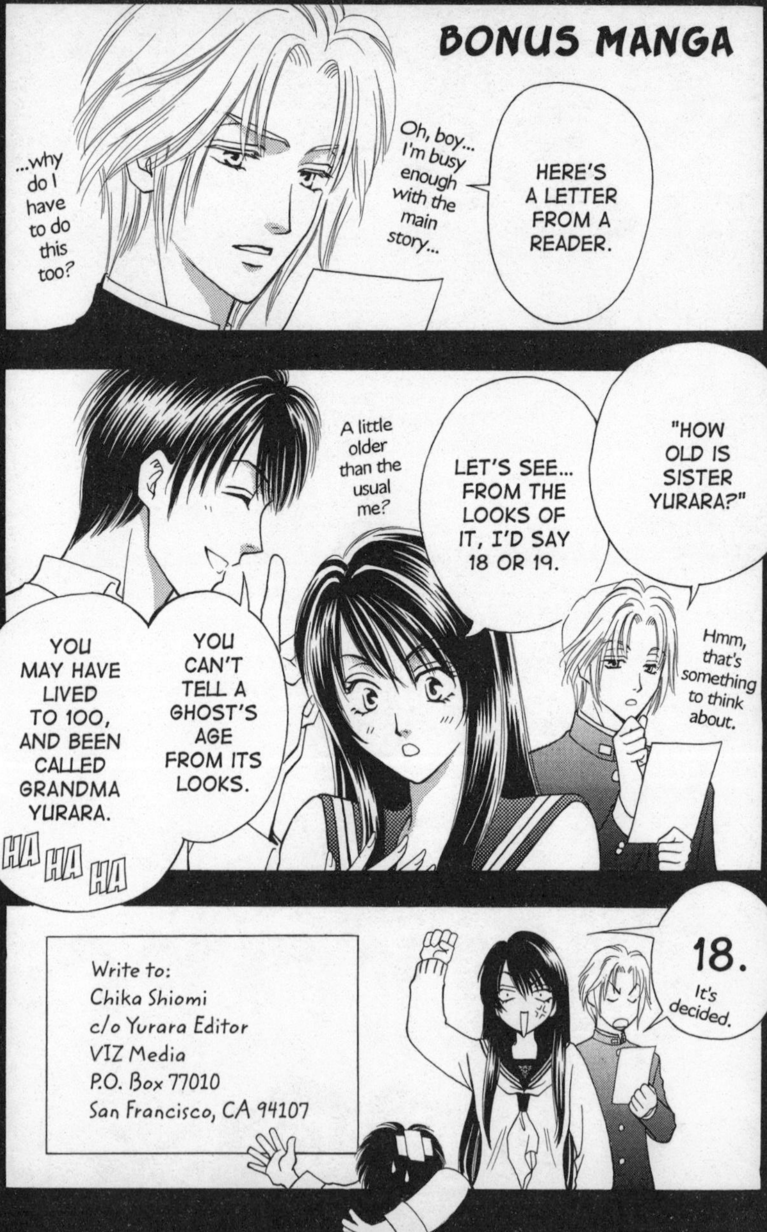
BONUS MANGA
HERE'S A LETTER FROM A READER.
Oh, boy... I'm busy enough with the main story...
...why do I have to do this too?
"HOW OLD IS SISTER YURARA?"
Hmm, that's something to think about.
LET'S SEE... FROM THE LOOKS OF IT, I'D SAY 18 OR 19.
A little older than the usual me?
YOU CAN'T TELL A GHOST'S AGE FROM ITS LOOKS.
YOU MAY HAVE LIVED TO 100, AND BEEN CALLED GRANDMA YURARA.
HA HA HA
18.
It's decided.
Write to:
Chika Shiomi
c/o Yurara Editor
VIZ Media
P.O. Box 77010
San Francisco, CA 94107

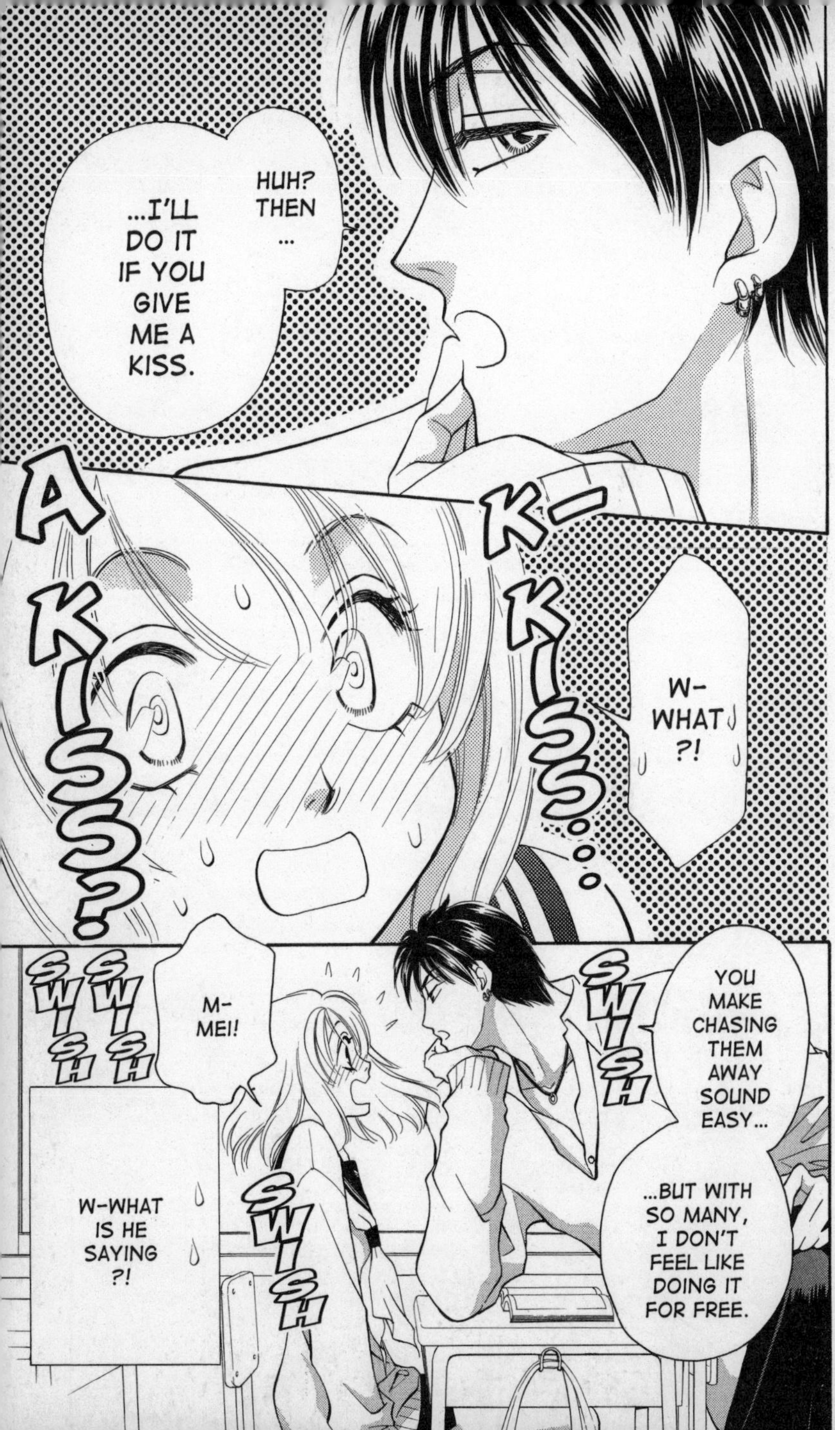
HUH? THEN ...
...I'LL DO IT IF YOU GIVE ME A KISS.
W-WHAT?!
K-K-KISS...
A KISS?
YOU MAKE CHASING THEM AWAY SOUND EASY...
SWISH
...BUT WITH SO MANY, I DON'T FEEL LIKE DOING IT FOR FREE.
SWISH
M-MEI!
SWISH SWISH
W-WHAT IS HE SAYING?!

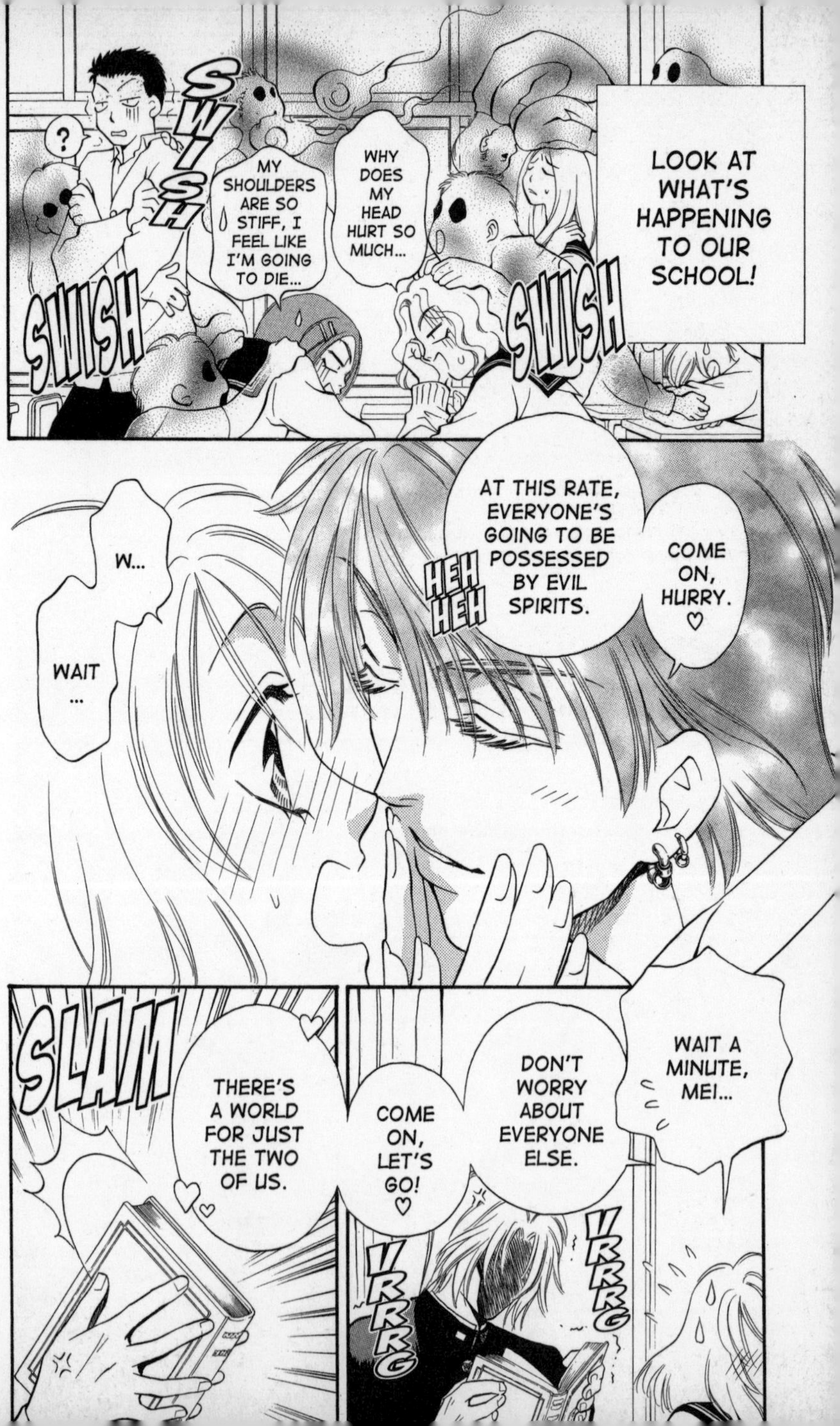
LOOK AT WHAT'S HAPPENING TO OUR SCHOOL!
SWISH
WHY DOES MY HEAD HURT SO MUCH...
MY SHOULDERS ARE SO STIFF, I FEEL LIKE I'M GOING TO DIE...
SWISH
?
SWISH
COME ON, HURRY. ♡
AT THIS RATE, EVERYONE'S GOING TO BE POSSESSED BY EVIL SPIRITS.
HEH HEH
W...
WAIT ...
WAIT A MINUTE, MEI...
DON'T WORRY ABOUT EVERYONE ELSE.
VRRRG
VRRRG
COME ON, LET'S GO! ♡
THERE'S A WORLD FOR JUST THE TWO OF US.
SLAM

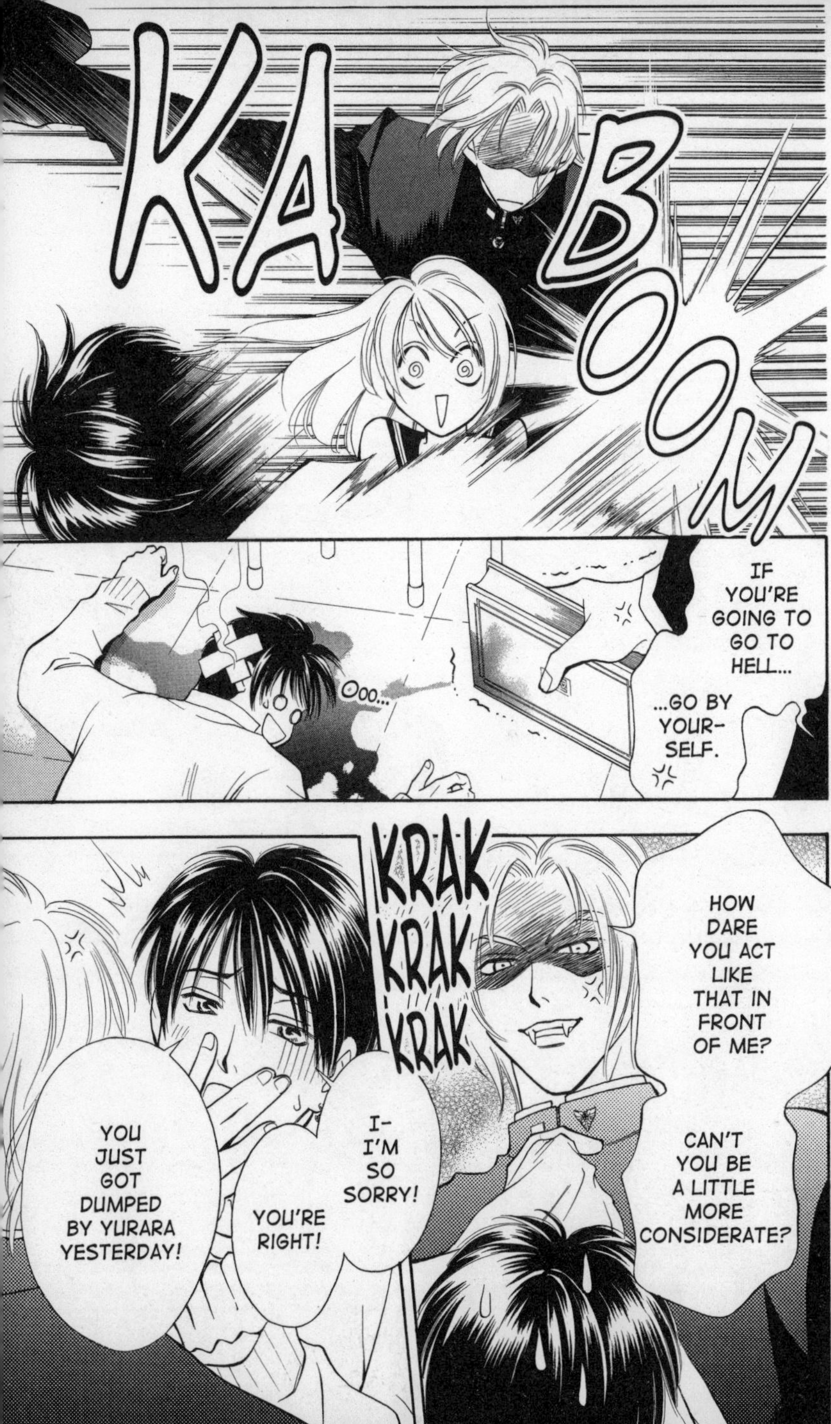
KA-BOOM
IF YOU'RE GOING TO GO TO HELL...
...GO BY YOURSELF.
Ooo...
KRAK KRAK KRAK
HOW DARE YOU ACT LIKE THAT IN FRONT OF ME?
CAN'T YOU BE A LITTLE MORE CONSIDERATE?
I- I'M SO SORRY!
YOU'RE RIGHT!
YOU JUST GOT DUMPED BY YURARA YESTERDAY!

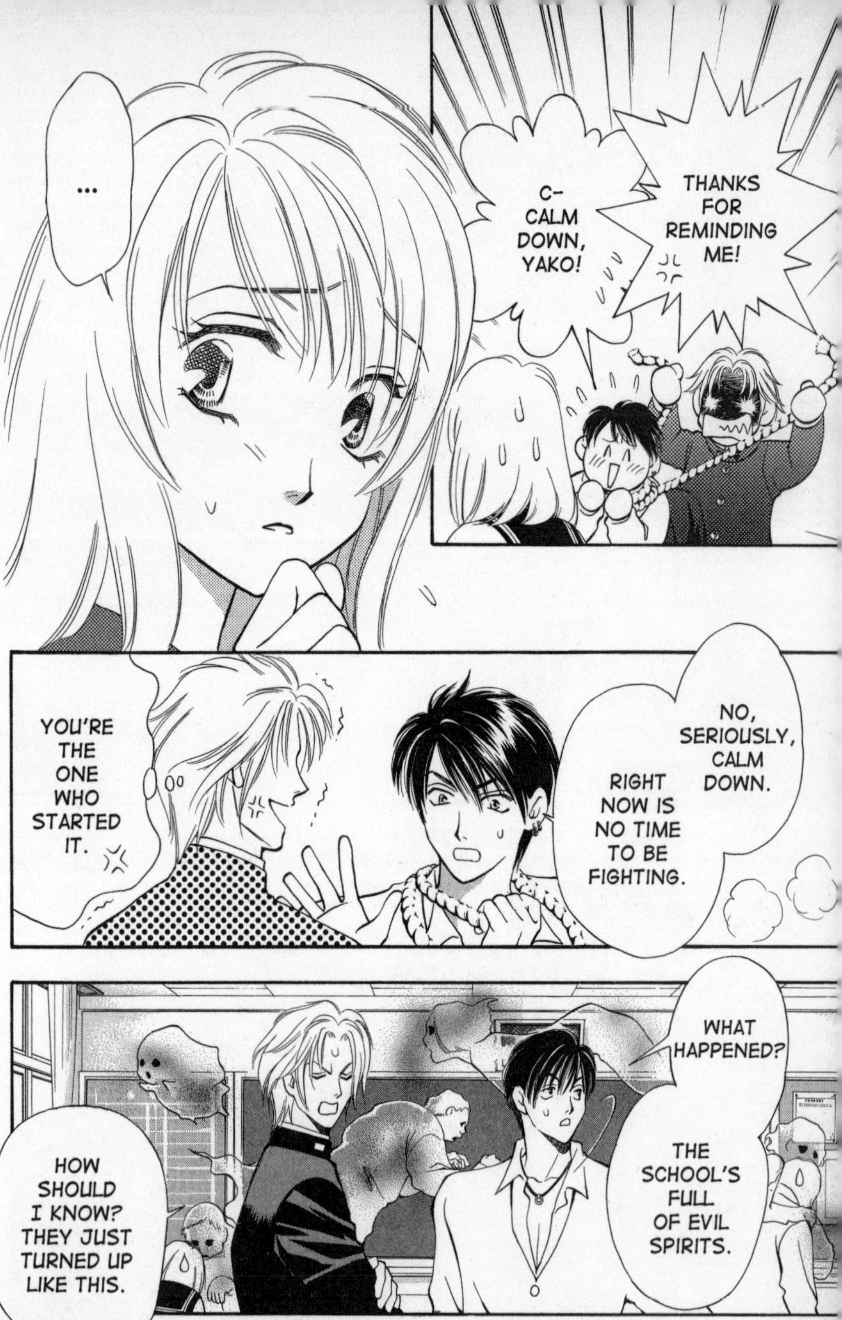

THANKS FOR REMINDING ME!
C-CALM DOWN, YAKO!
...
NO, SERIOUSLY, CALM DOWN.
RIGHT NOW IS NO TIME TO BE FIGHTING.
YOU'RE THE ONE WHO STARTED IT.
WHAT HAPPENED?
THE SCHOOL'S FULL OF EVIL SPIRITS.
HOW SHOULD I KNOW? THEY JUST TURNED UP LIKE THIS.

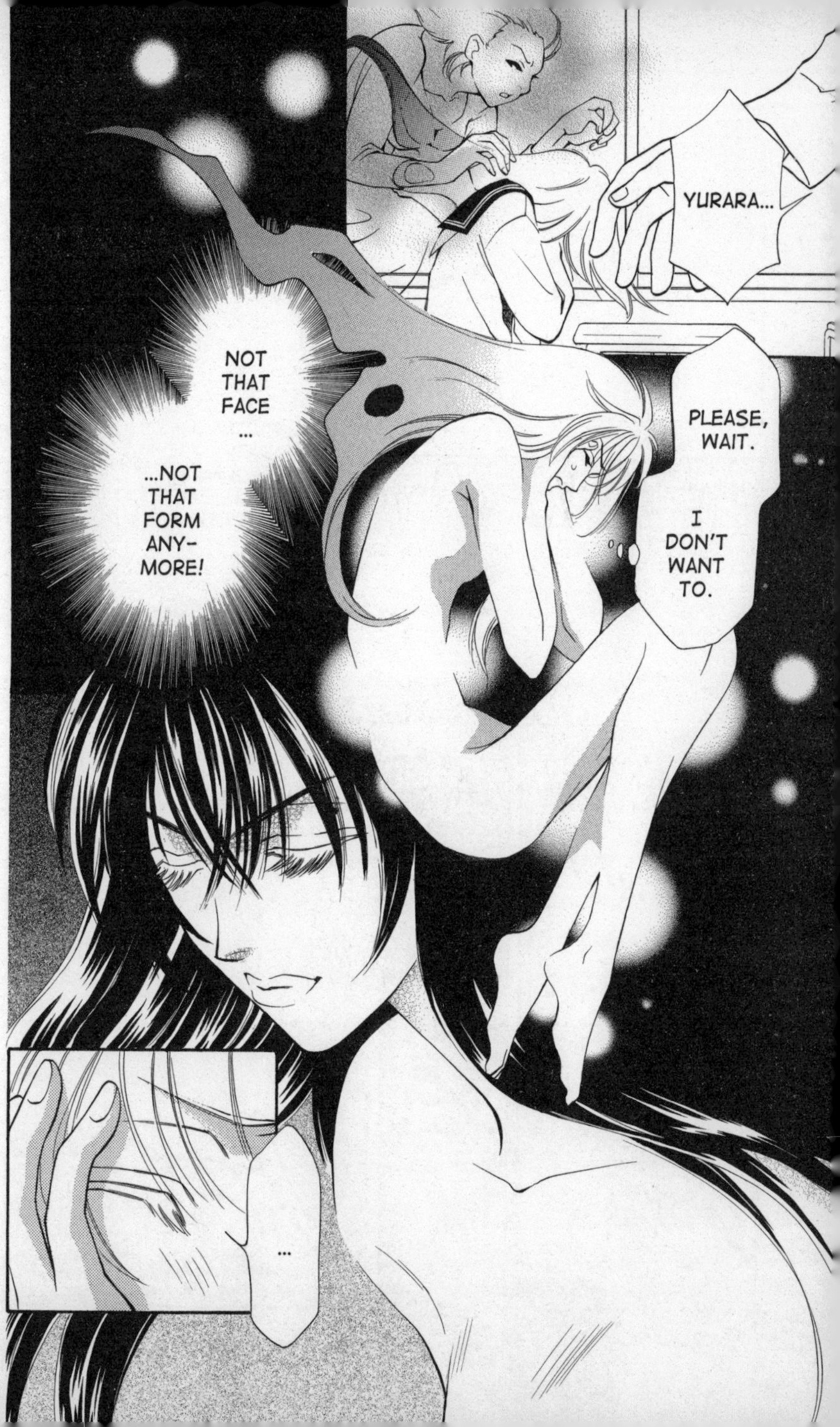
YURARA...
PLEASE, WAIT.
I DON'T WANT TO.
NOT THAT FACE ...
...NOT THAT FORM ANY-MORE!
...

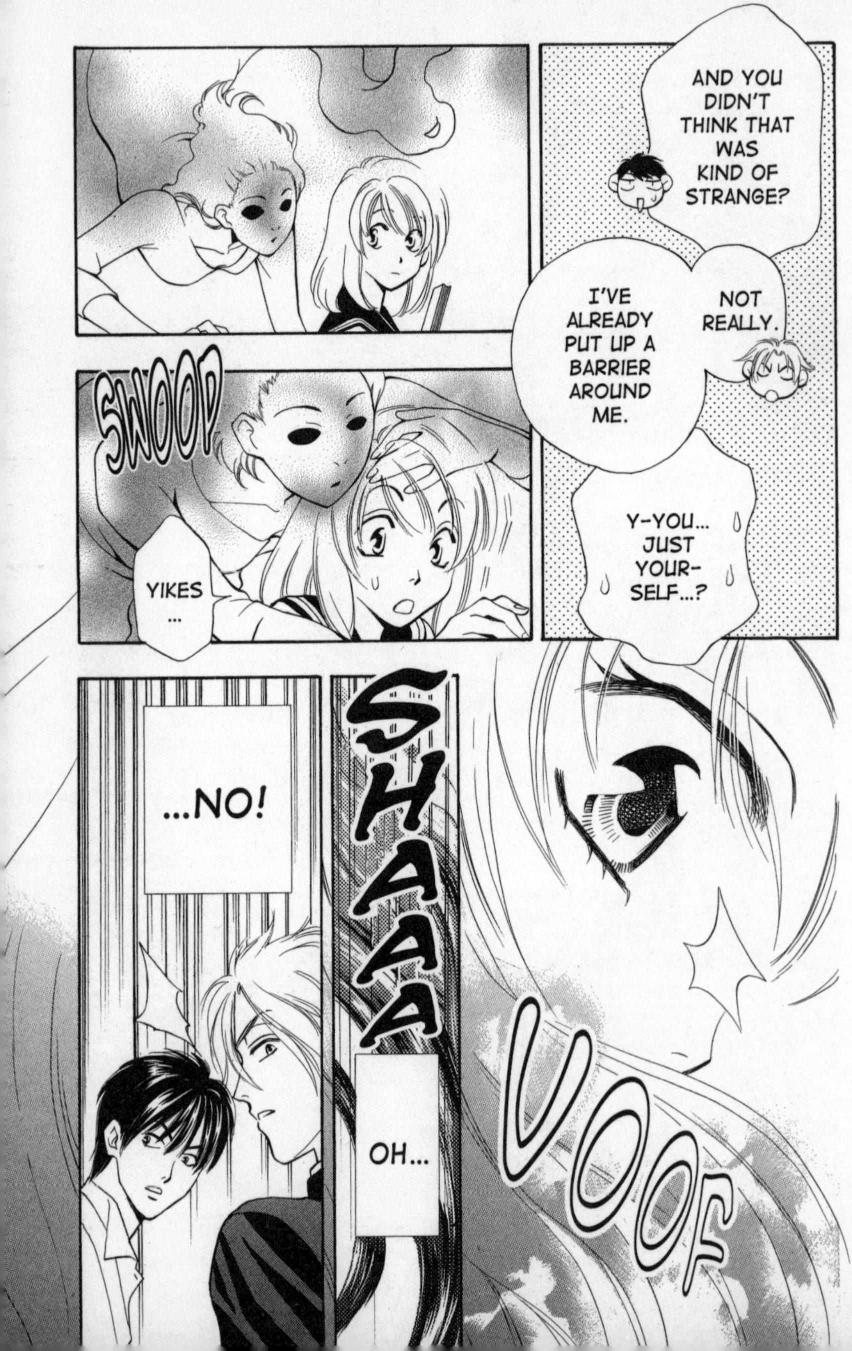
AND YOU DIDN'T THINK THAT WAS KIND OF STRANGE?
NOT REALLY.
I'VE ALREADY PUT UP A BARRIER AROUND ME.
Y-YOU... JUST YOUR-SELF...?
SWOOP
YIKES ...
VOOF
SHAAA
OH...
...NO!

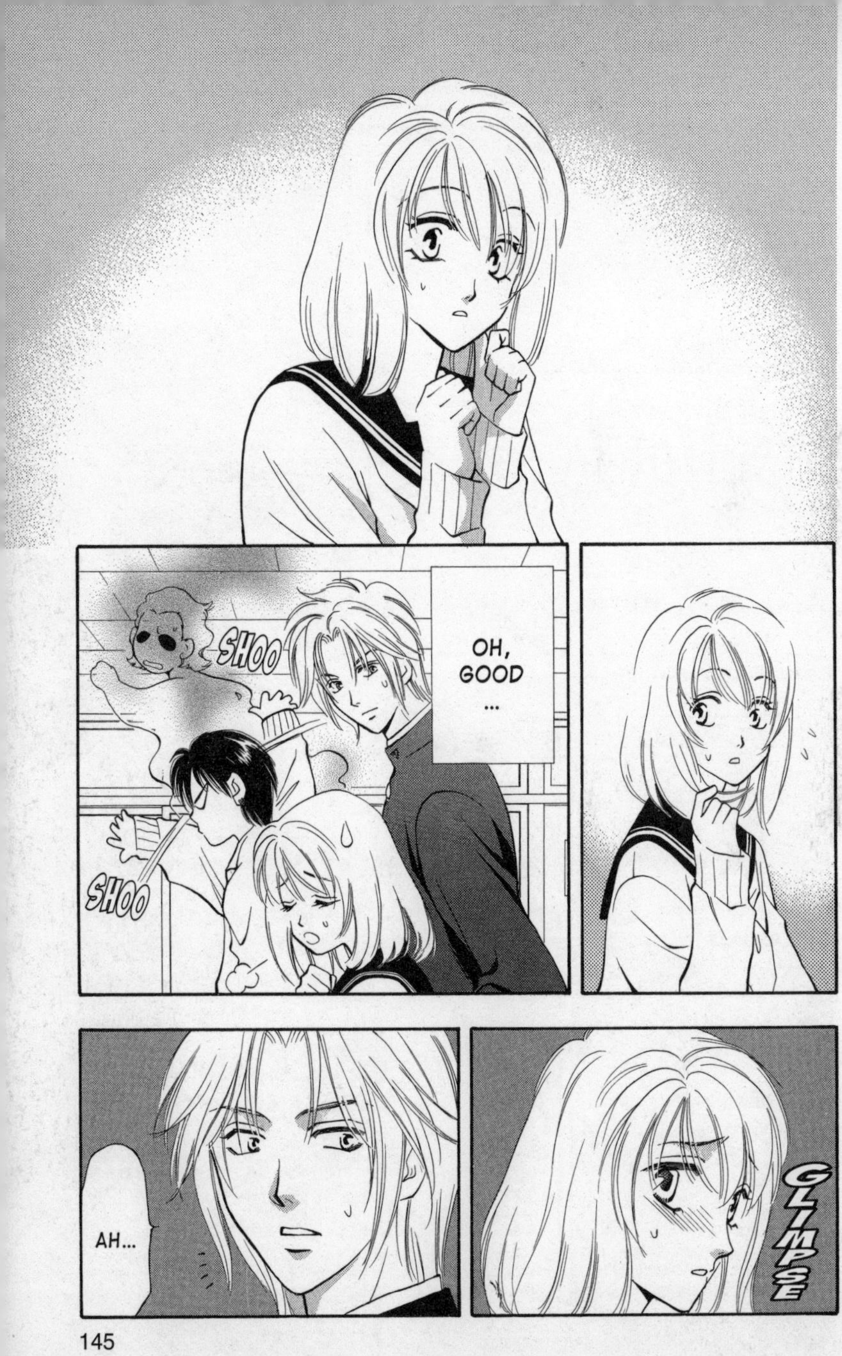
OH, GOOD ...
SHOO
SHOO
GLIMPSE
AH...

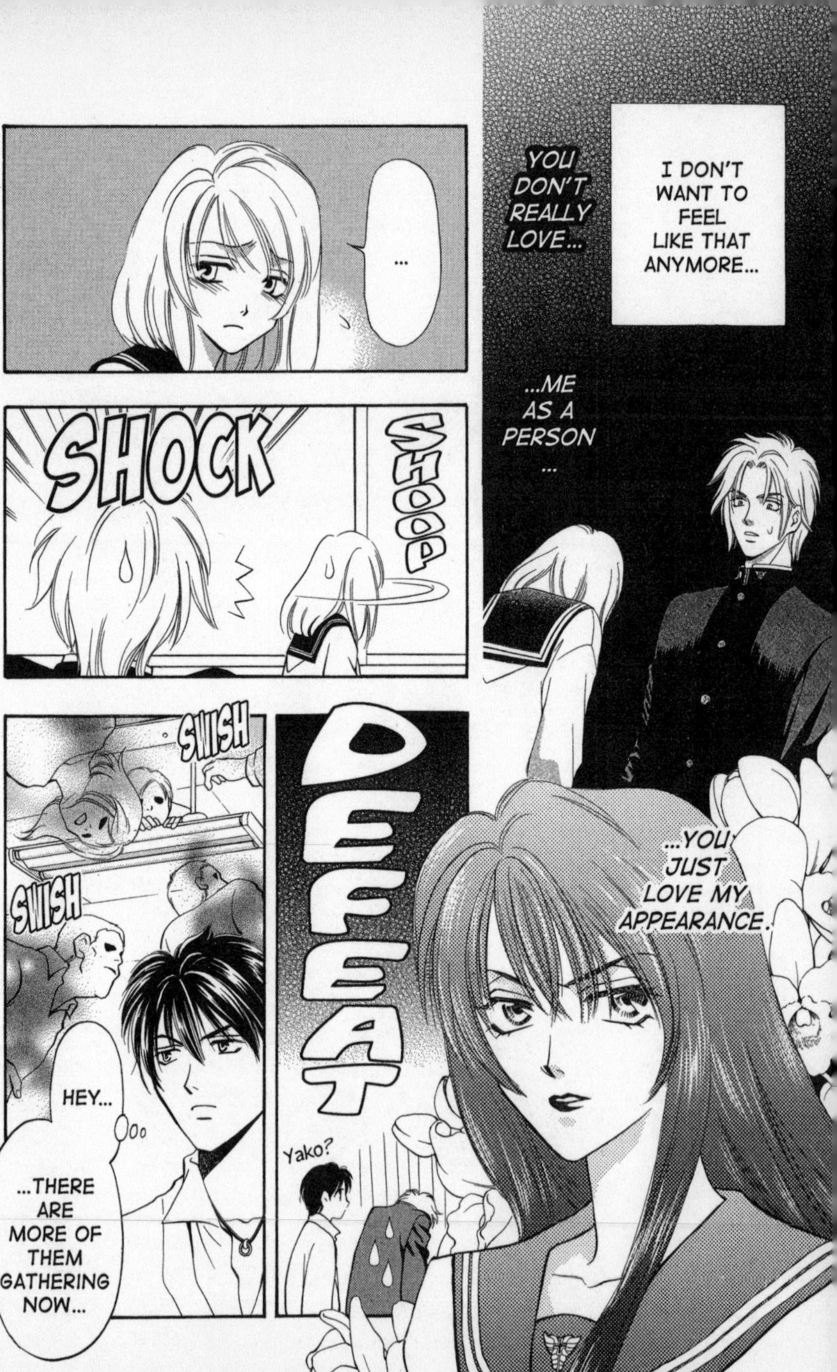
I DON'T WANT TO FEEL LIKE THAT ANYMORE...
YOU DON'T REALLY LOVE...
...ME AS A PERSON...
...YOU JUST LOVE MY APPEARANCE.
...
SHOOP
SHOCK
DEFEAT
Yako?
SWISH
SWISH
HEY...
...THERE ARE MORE OF THEM GATHERING NOW...

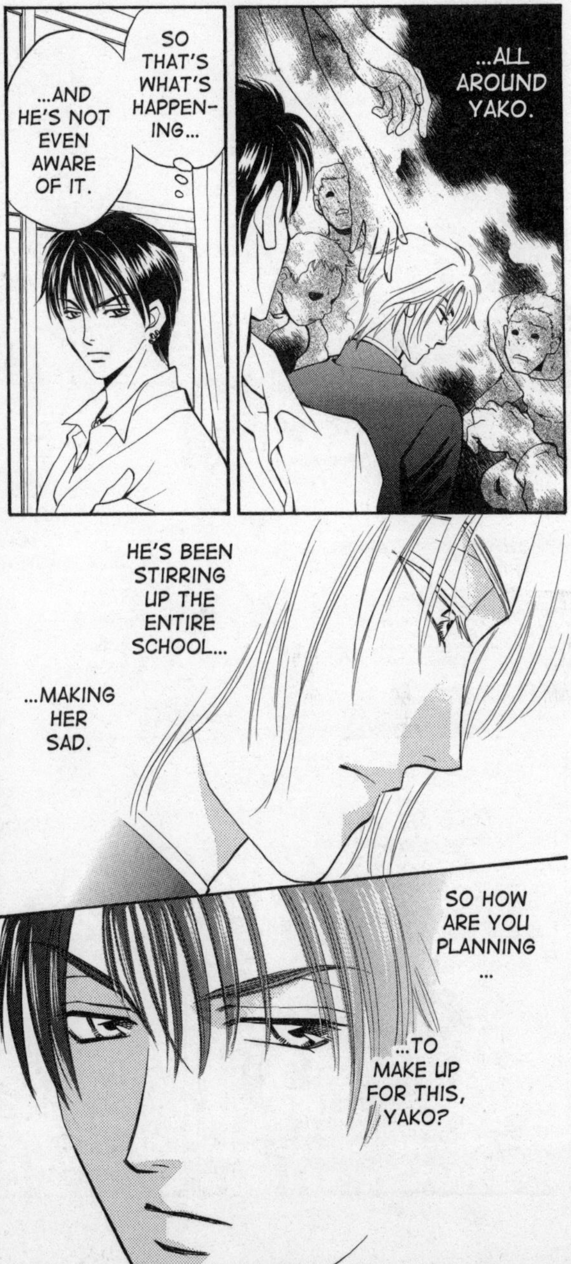
...ALL AROUND YAKO.
SO THAT'S WHAT'S HAPPENING...
...AND HE'S NOT EVEN AWARE OF IT.
HE'S BEEN STIRRING UP THE ENTIRE SCHOOL...
...MAKING HER SAD.
SO HOW ARE YOU PLANNING ...
...TO MAKE UP FOR THIS, YAKO?

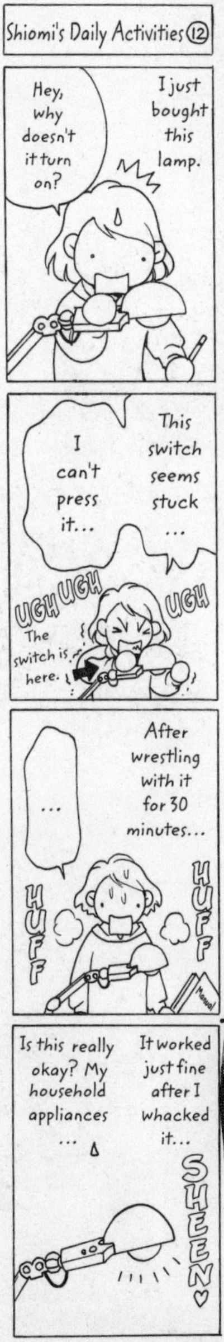
Shiomi's Daily Activities 12
I just bought this lamp.
Hey, why doesn't it turn on?
This switch seems stuck ...
I can't press it...
UGH UGH
UGH
The switch is here.
After wrestling with it for 30 minutes...
...
HUFF
HUFF
It worked just fine after I whacked it...
Is this really okay? My household appliances ...
SHEEN♡

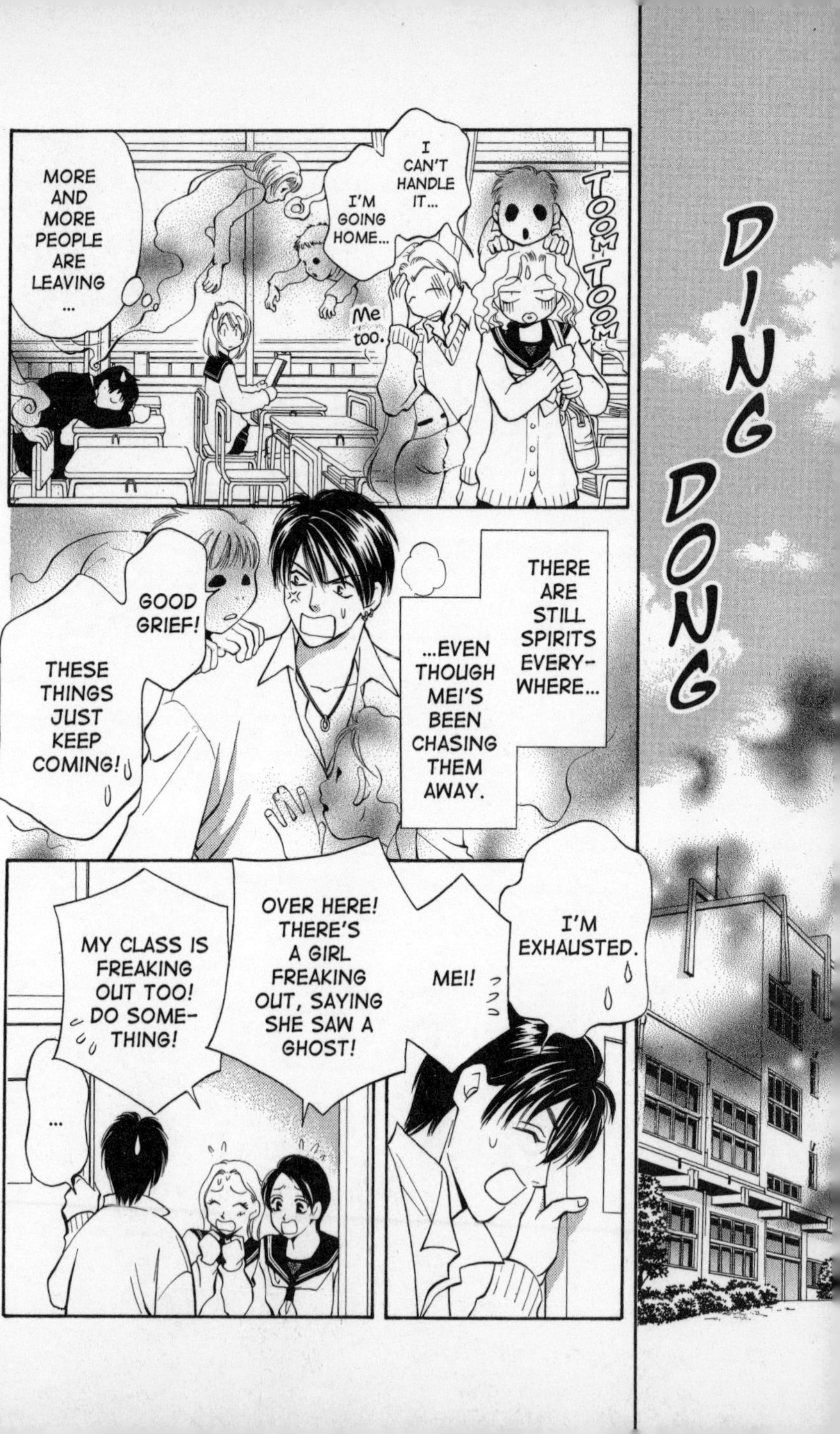
DING DONG
TOOM TOOM TOOM
I CAN'T HANDLE IT...
I'M GOING HOME...
MORE AND MORE PEOPLE ARE LEAVING...
Me too.
THERE ARE STILL SPIRITS EVERY-WHERE...
...EVEN THOUGH MEI'S BEEN CHASING THEM AWAY.
GOOD GRIEF!
THESE THINGS JUST KEEP COMING!
I'M EXHAUSTED.
MEI!
OVER HERE! THERE'S A GIRL FREAKING OUT, SAYING SHE SAW A GHOST!
MY CLASS IS FREAKING OUT TOO! DO SOME-THING!
...

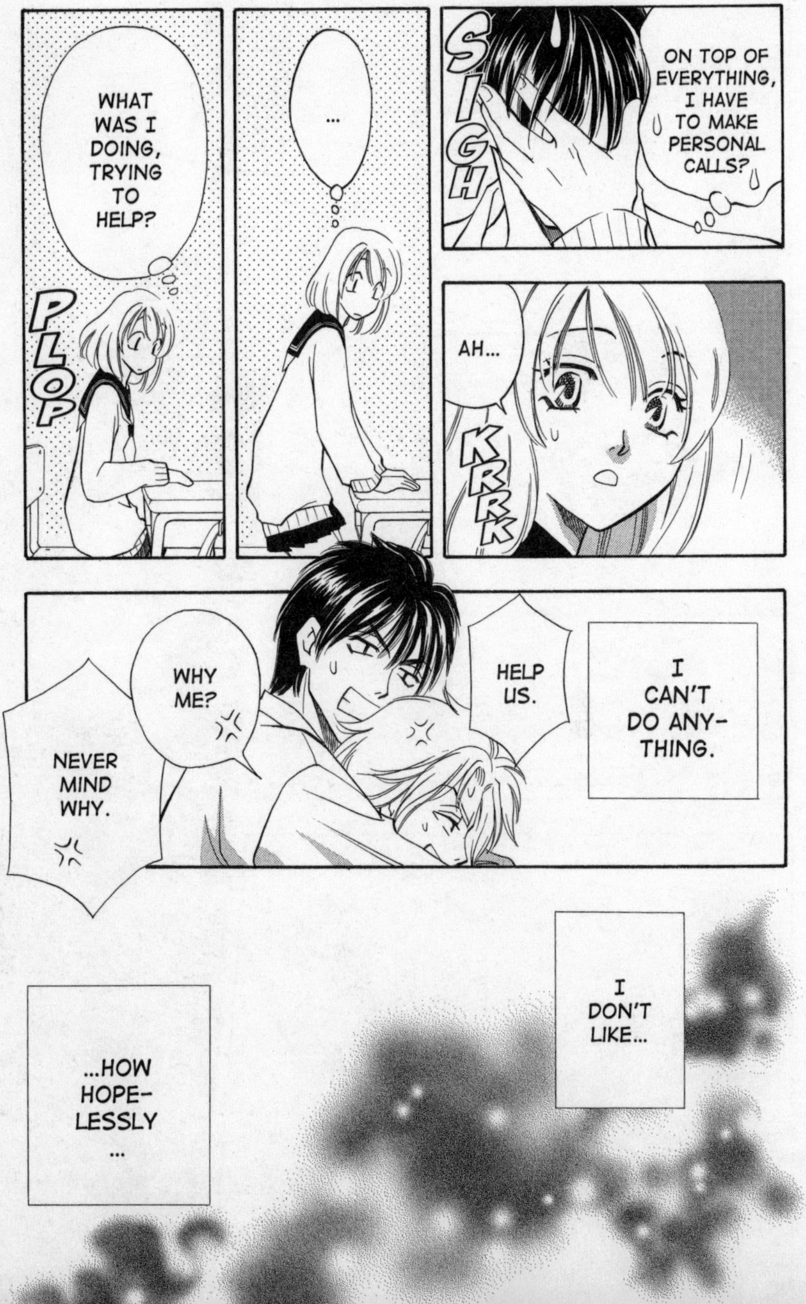
SIGH
ON TOP OF EVERYTHING, I HAVE TO MAKE PERSONAL CALLS?
AH...
KRRK
...
WHAT WAS I DOING, TRYING TO HELP?
PLOP
I CAN'T DO ANY-THING.
HELP US.
WHY ME?
NEVER MIND WHY.
I DON'T LIKE...
...HOW HOPE-LESSLY ...

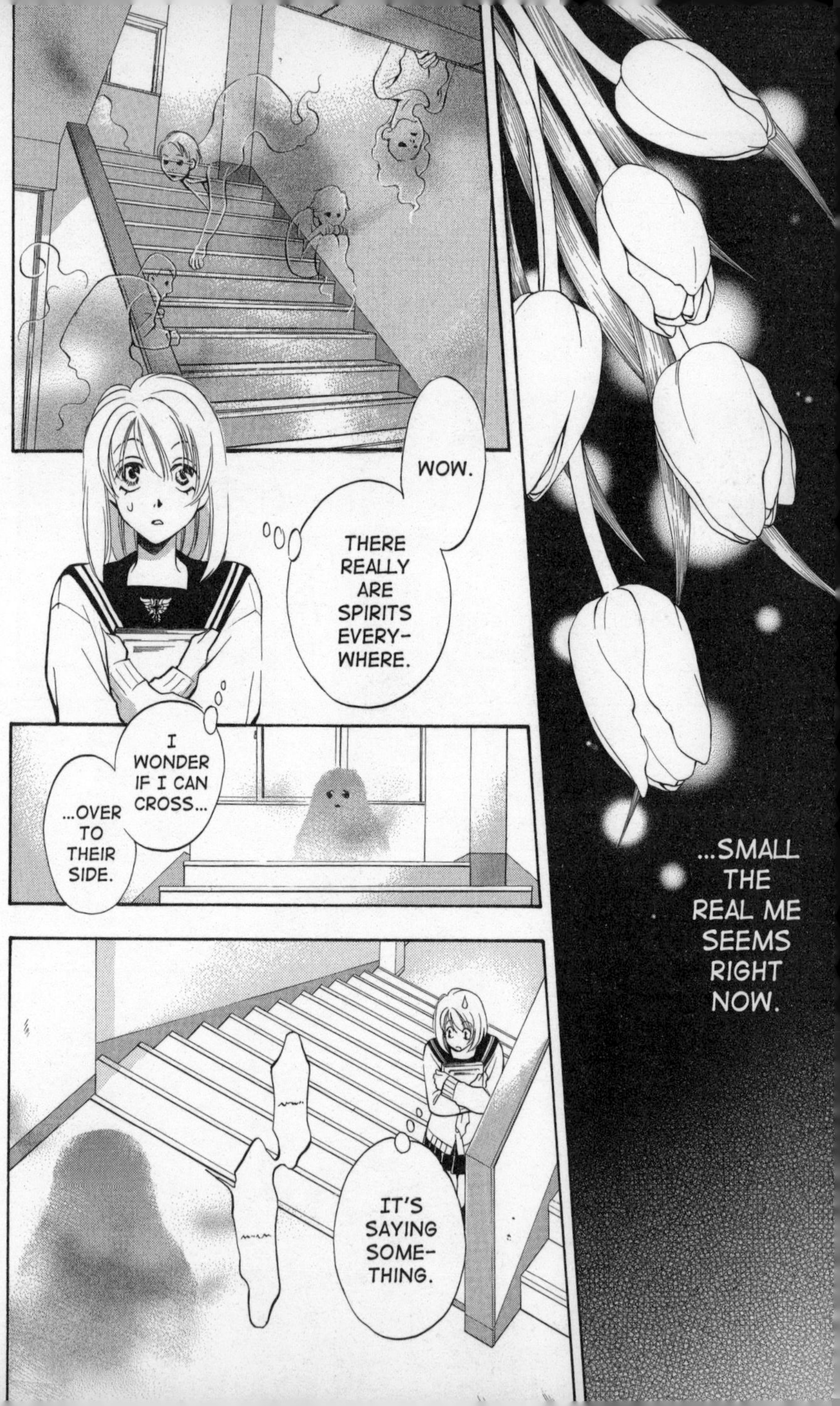
...SMALL THE REAL ME SEEMS RIGHT NOW.
WOW.
THERE REALLY ARE SPIRITS EVERYWHERE.
I WONDER IF I CAN CROSS...
...OVER TO THEIR SIDE.
IT'S SAYING SOMETHING.

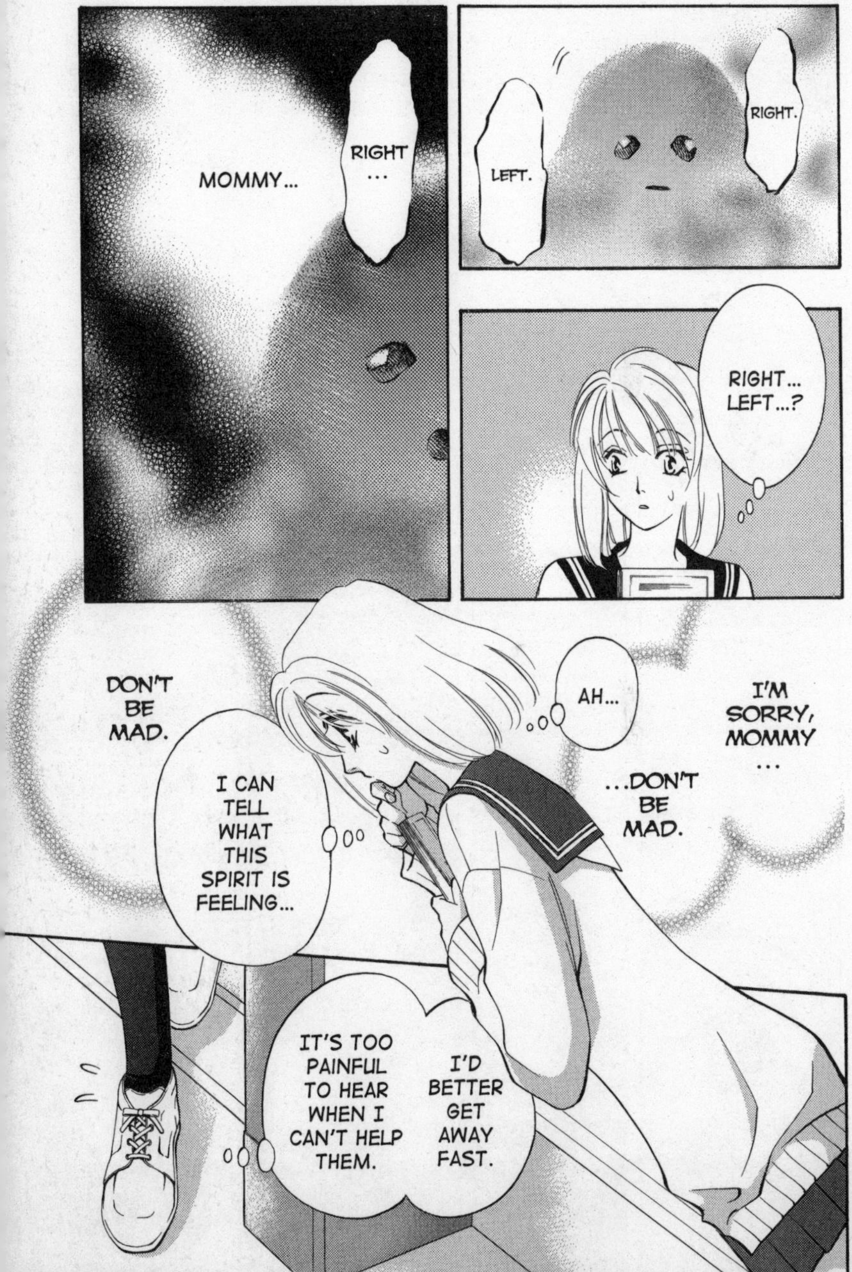
RIGHT.
LEFT.
RIGHT... LEFT...?
RIGHT ...
MOMMY...
I'M SORRY, MOMMY ...
AH...
...DON'T BE MAD.
DON'T BE MAD.
I CAN TELL WHAT THIS SPIRIT IS FEELING...
I'D BETTER GET AWAY FAST.
IT'S TOO PAINFUL TO HEAR WHEN I CAN'T HELP THEM.

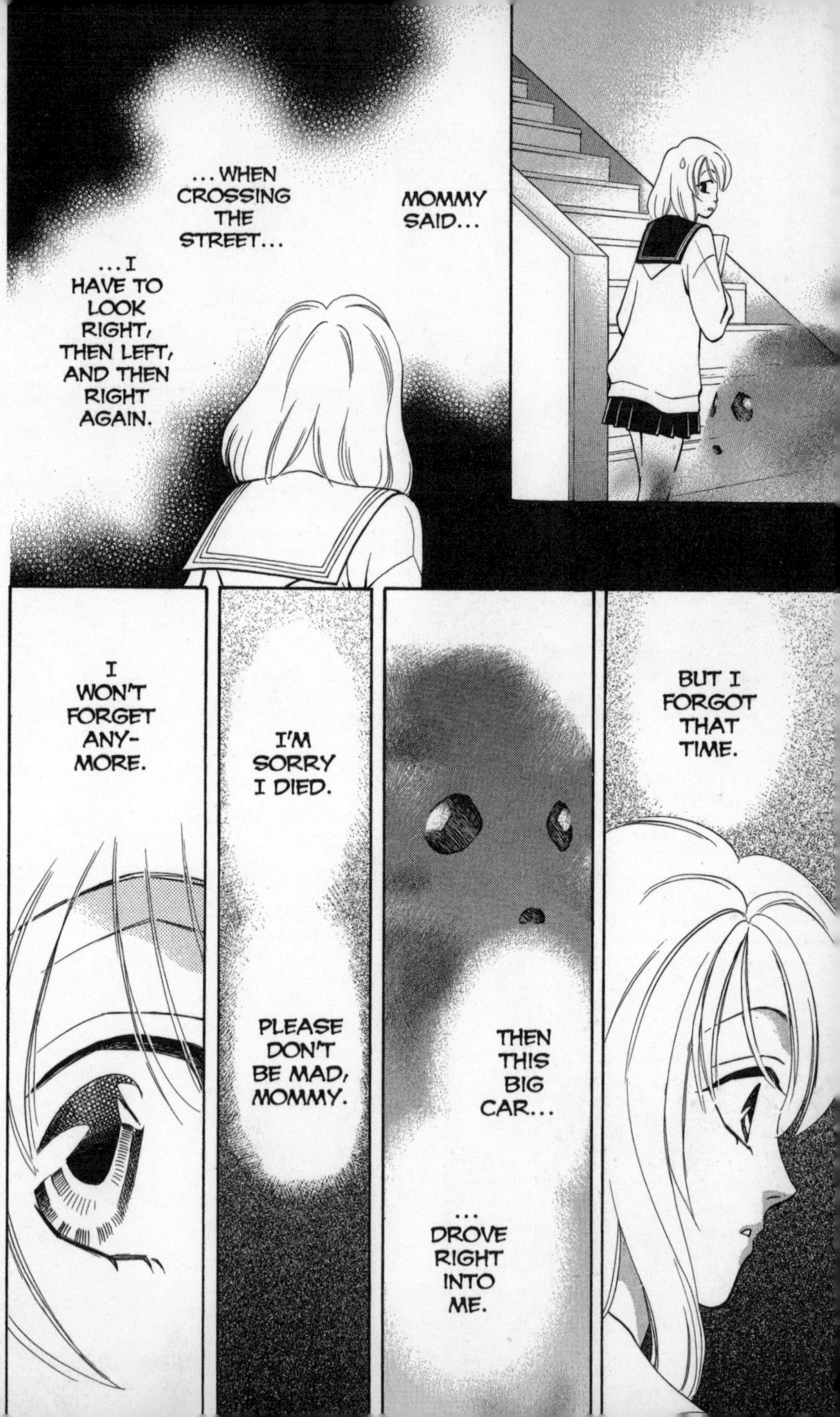
MOMMY SAID...
...WHEN CROSSING THE STREET...
...I HAVE TO LOOK RIGHT, THEN LEFT, AND THEN RIGHT AGAIN.
BUT I FORGOT THAT TIME.
THEN THIS BIG CAR...
...DROVE RIGHT INTO ME.
I'M SORRY I DIED.
PLEASE DON'T BE MAD, MOMMY.
I WON'T FORGET ANYMORE.

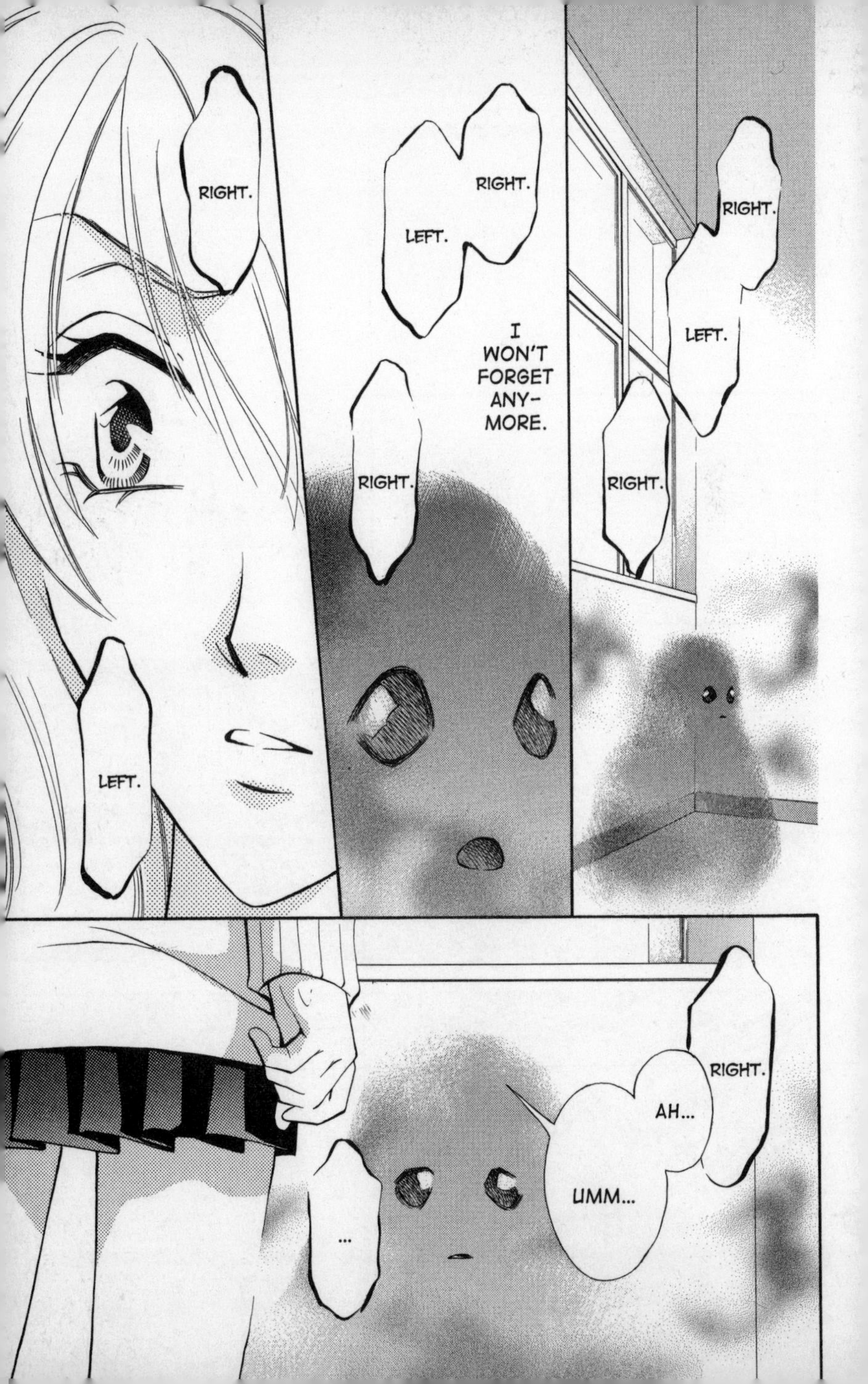
RIGHT.
LEFT.
RIGHT.
RIGHT.
LEFT.
I WON'T FORGET ANYMORE.
RIGHT.
RIGHT.
LEFT.
RIGHT.
AH...
UMM...
...

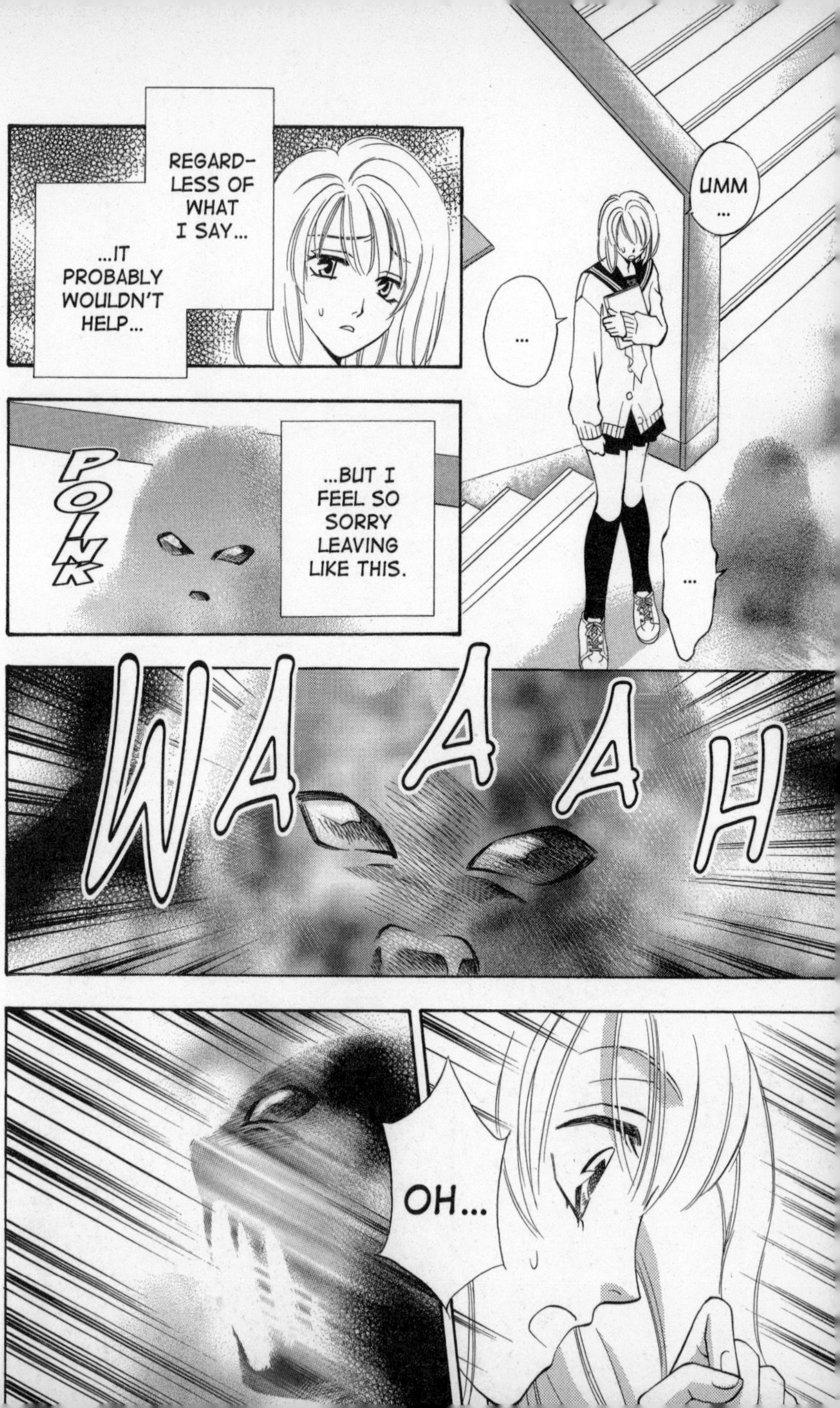
UMM ...
...
...
REGARD-LESS OF WHAT I SAY...
...IT PROBABLY WOULDN'T HELP...
POINK
...BUT I FEEL SO SORRY LEAVING LIKE THIS.
WAAAH
OH...

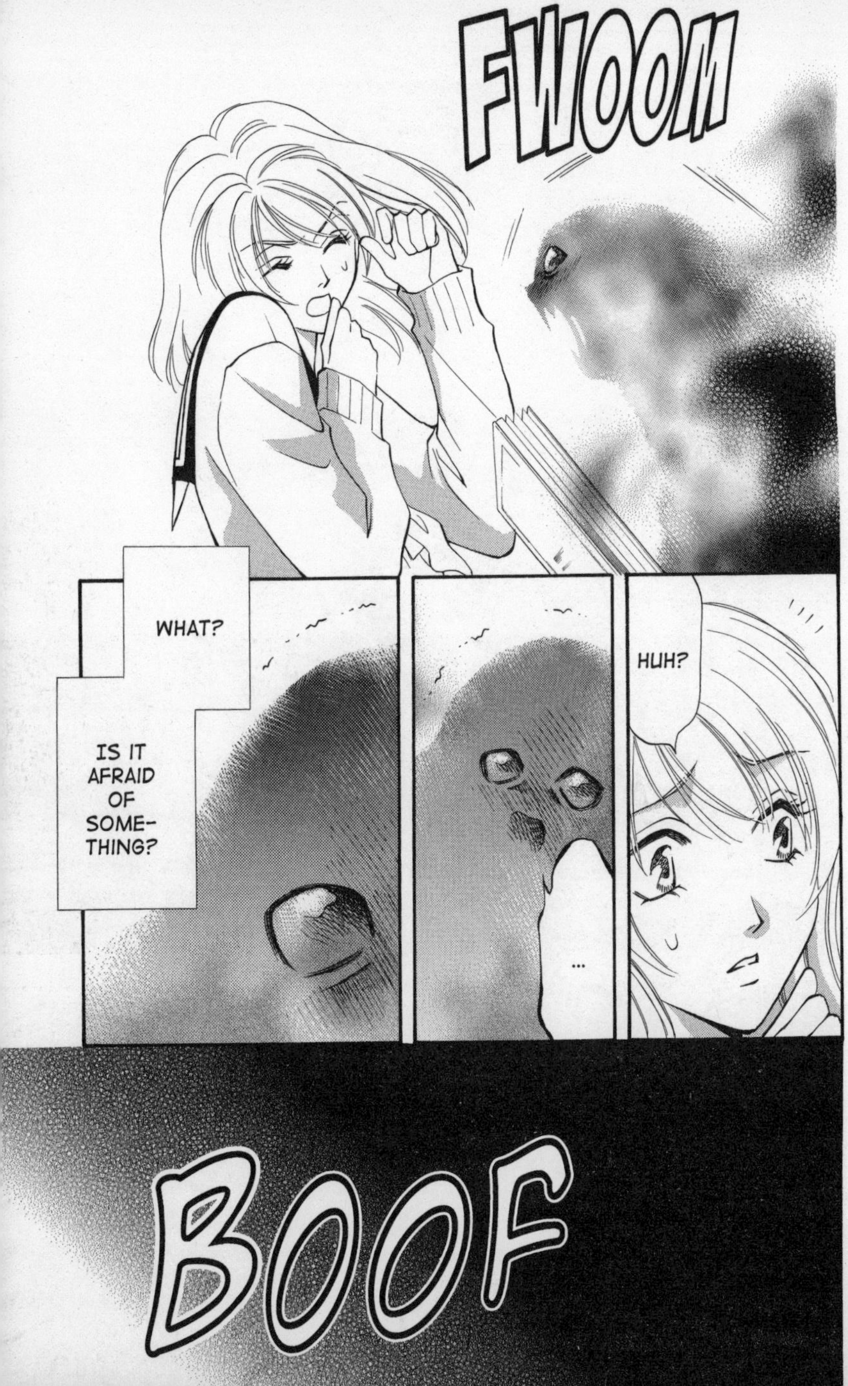
FWOOM
HUH?
...
WHAT?
IS IT AFRAID OF SOME-THING?
BOOF

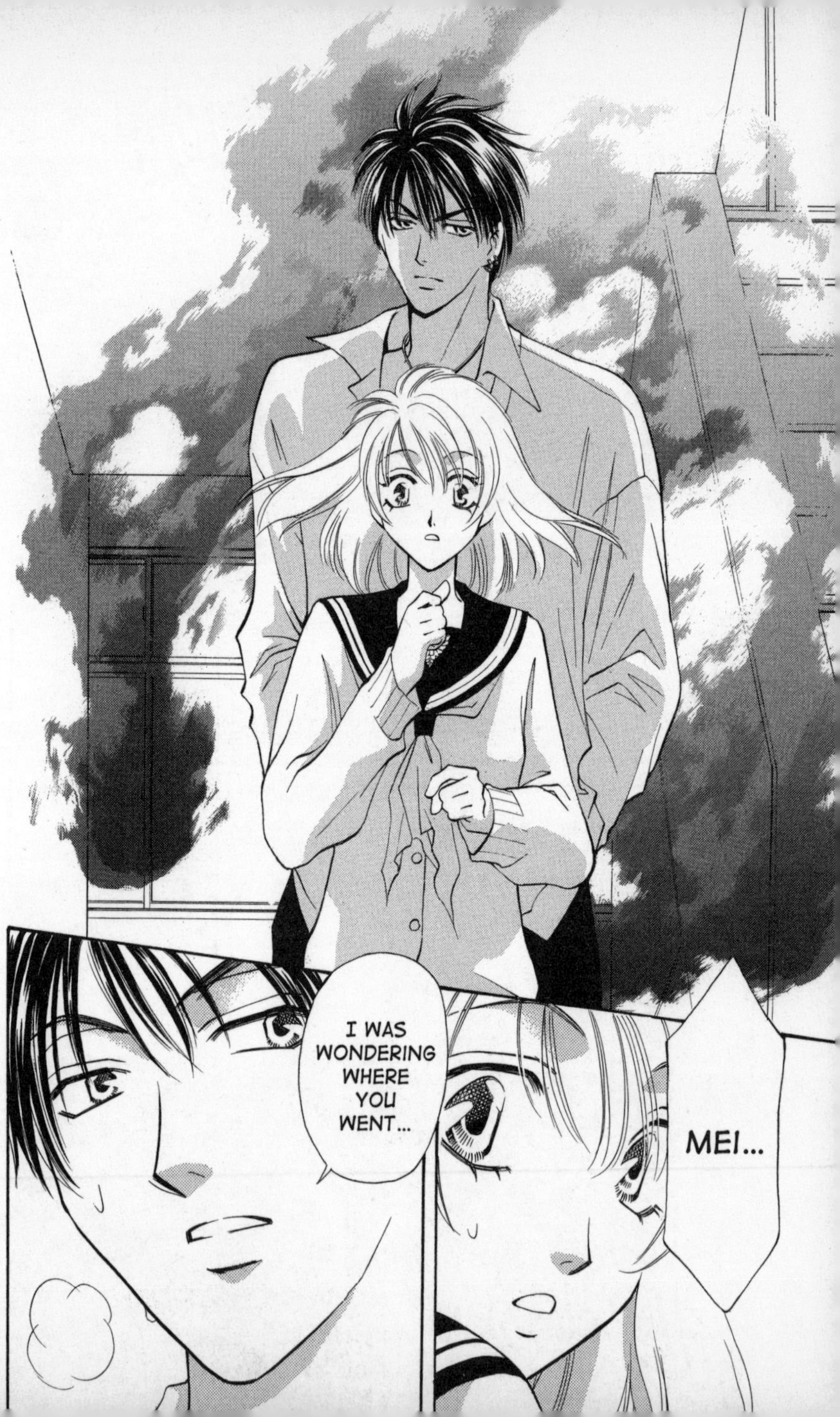
MEI...
I WAS WONDERING WHERE YOU WENT...

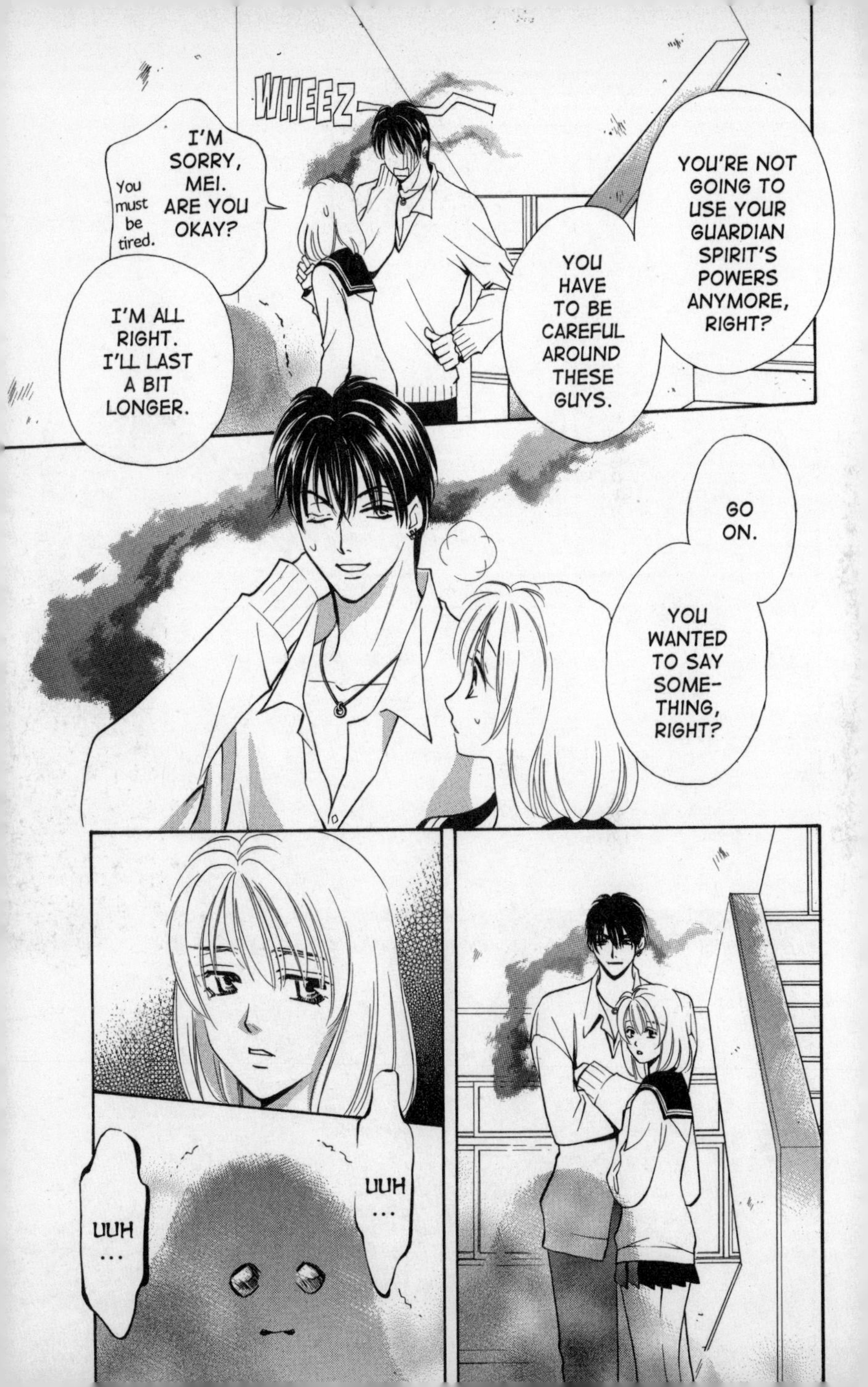

YOU'RE NOT GOING TO USE YOUR GUARDIAN SPIRIT'S POWERS ANYMORE, RIGHT?
YOU HAVE TO BE CAREFUL AROUND THESE GUYS.
WHEEZ
I'M SORRY, MEI. ARE YOU OKAY?
You must be tired.
I'M ALL RIGHT. I'LL LAST A BIT LONGER.
GO ON.
YOU WANTED TO SAY SOME-THING, RIGHT?
UUH ...
UUH ...

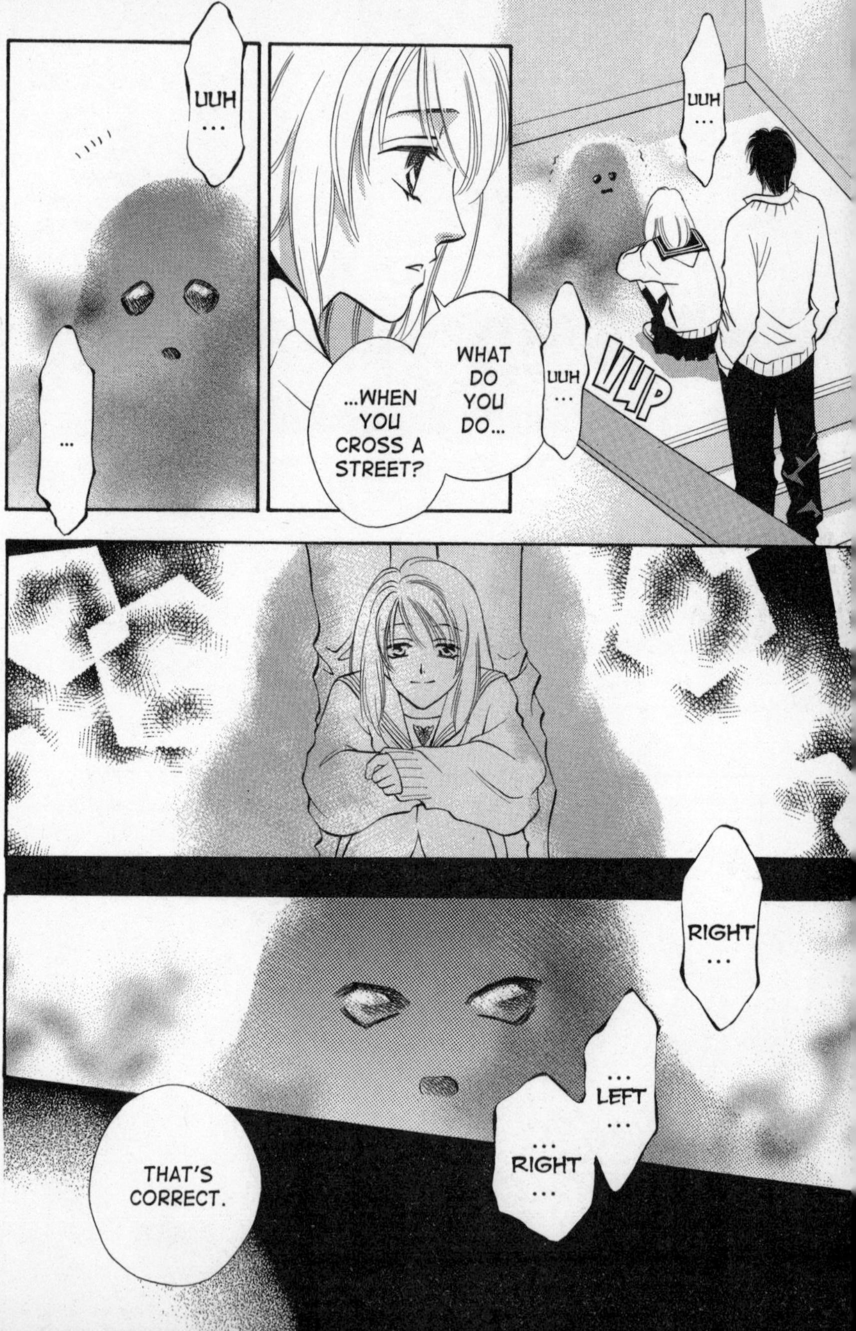
UUH ...
VUP
UUH ...
WHAT DO YOU DO...
...WHEN YOU CROSS A STREET?
UUH ...
...
RIGHT ...
... LEFT ...
... RIGHT ...
THAT'S CORRECT.

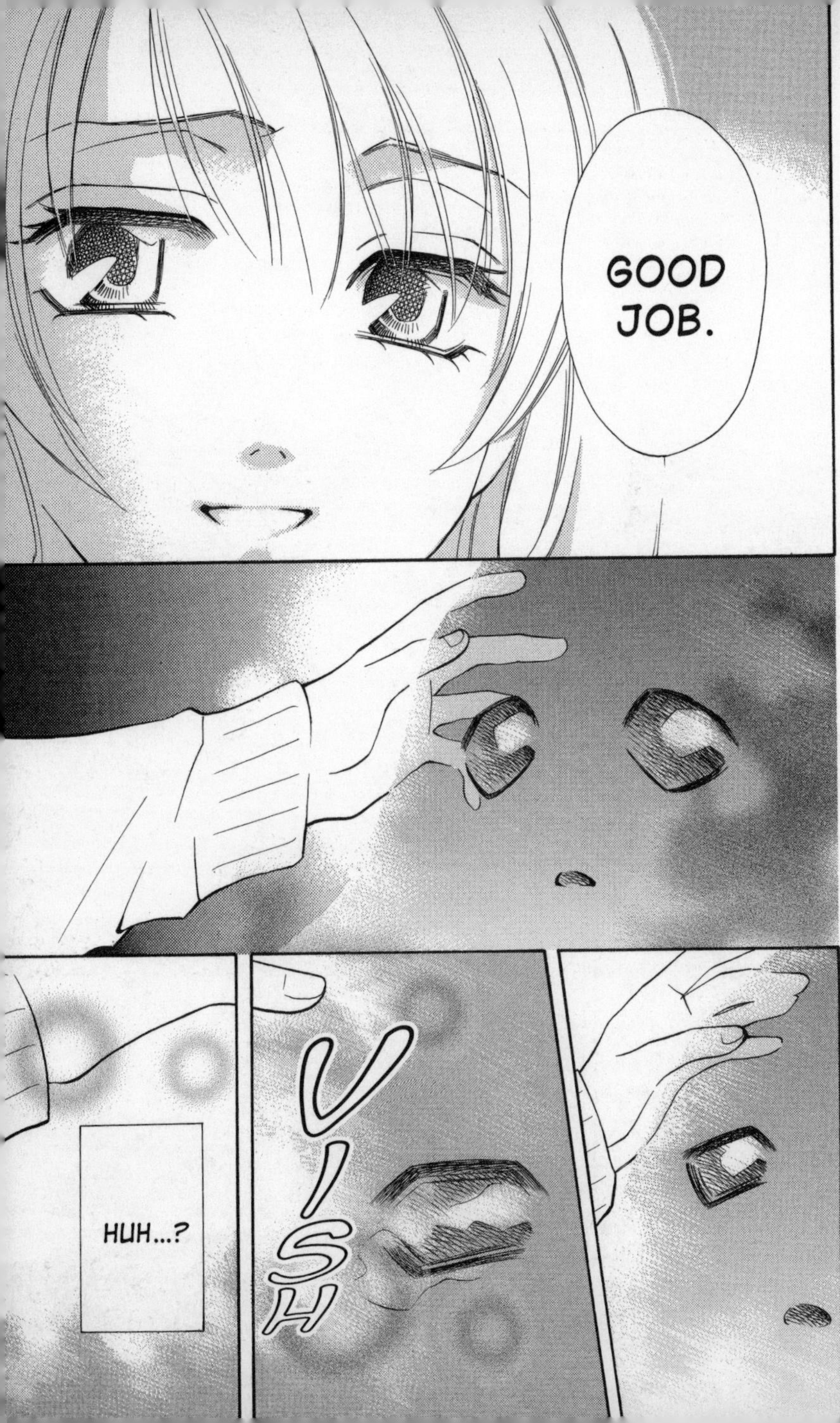
GOOD JOB.
VWISH
HUH...?

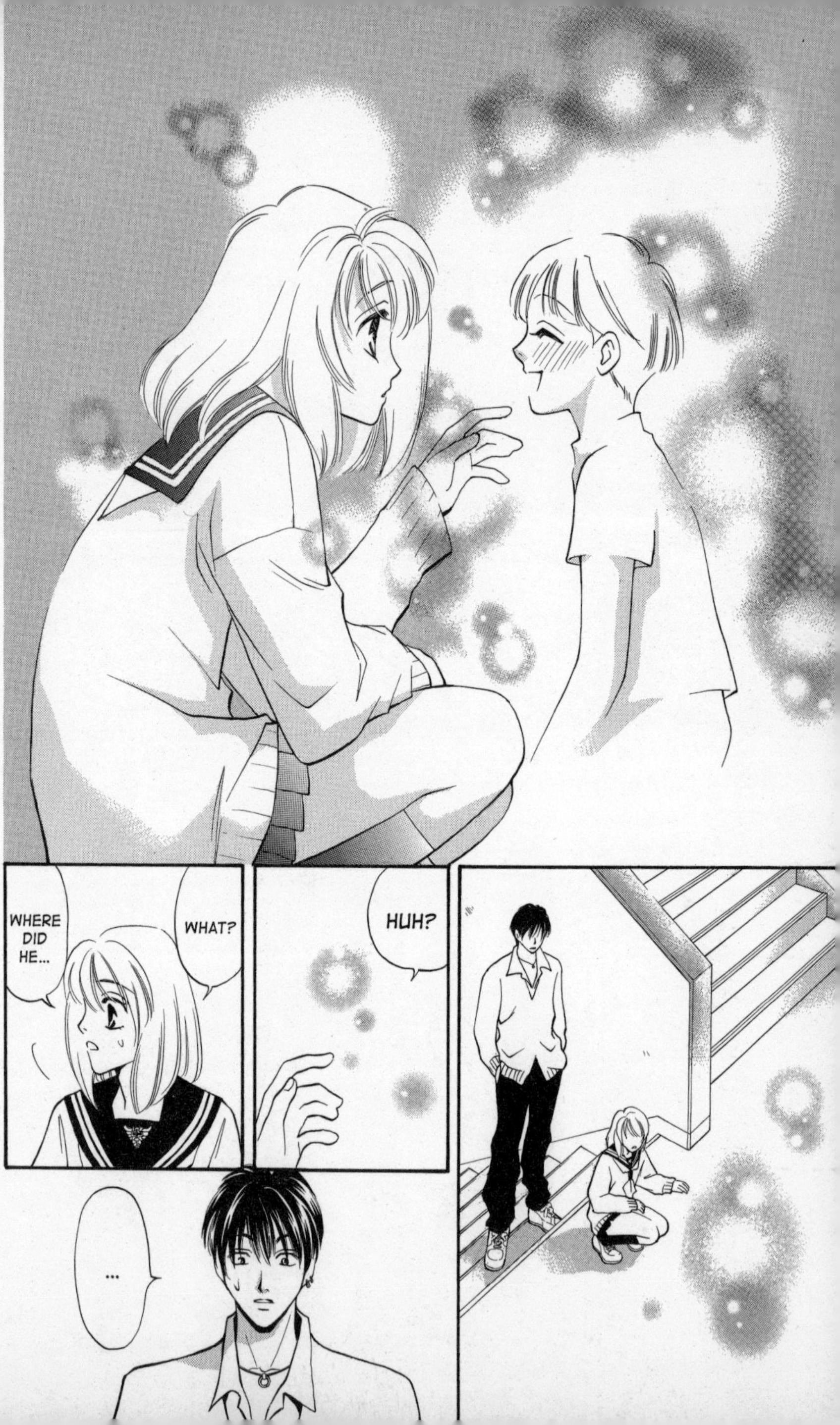
HUH?
WHAT?
WHERE DID HE...
...

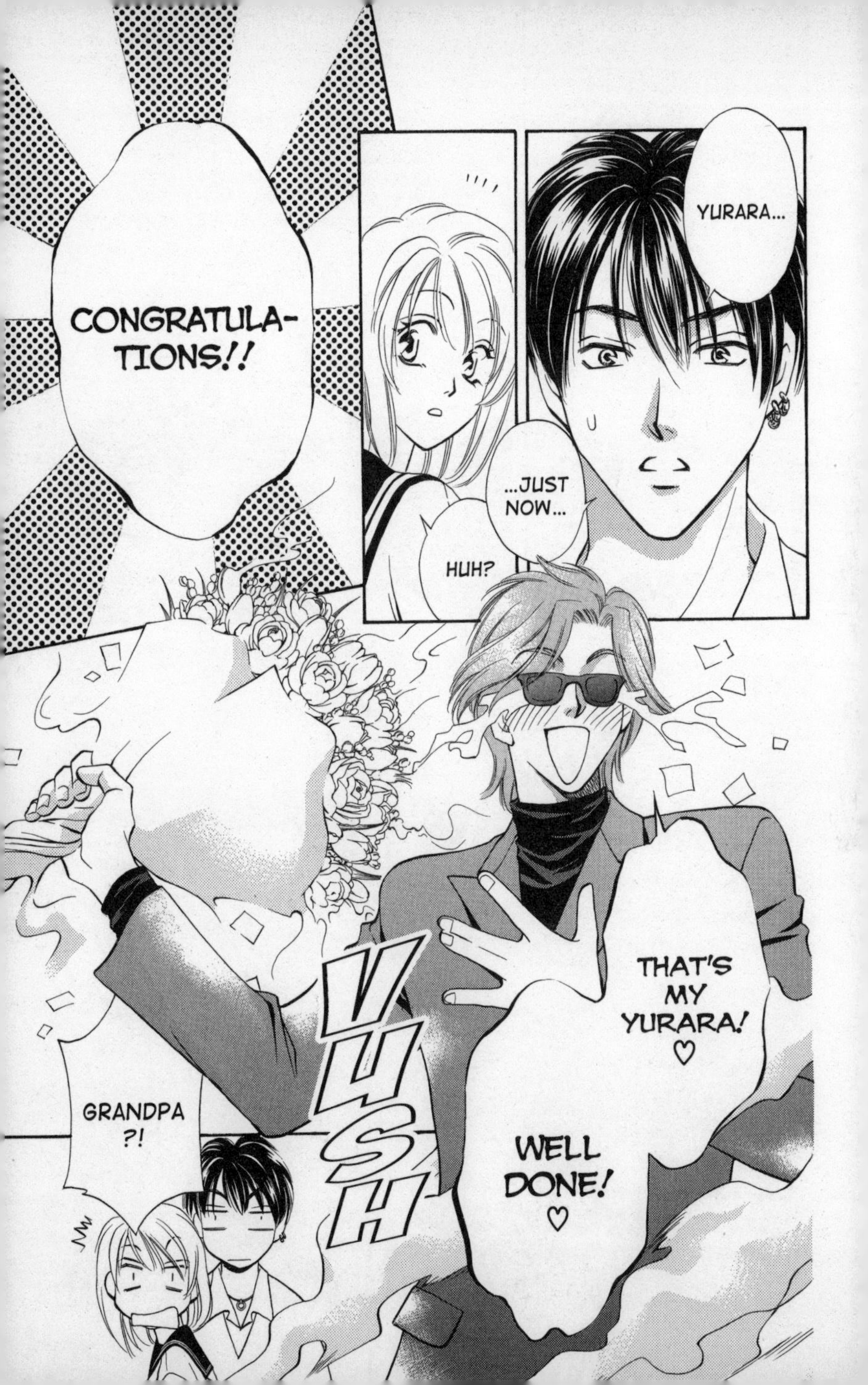
YURARA...
...JUST NOW...
HUH?
CONGRATULA-TIONS!!
VUSH
THAT'S MY YURARA! ♡
WELL DONE! ♡
GRANDPA ?!

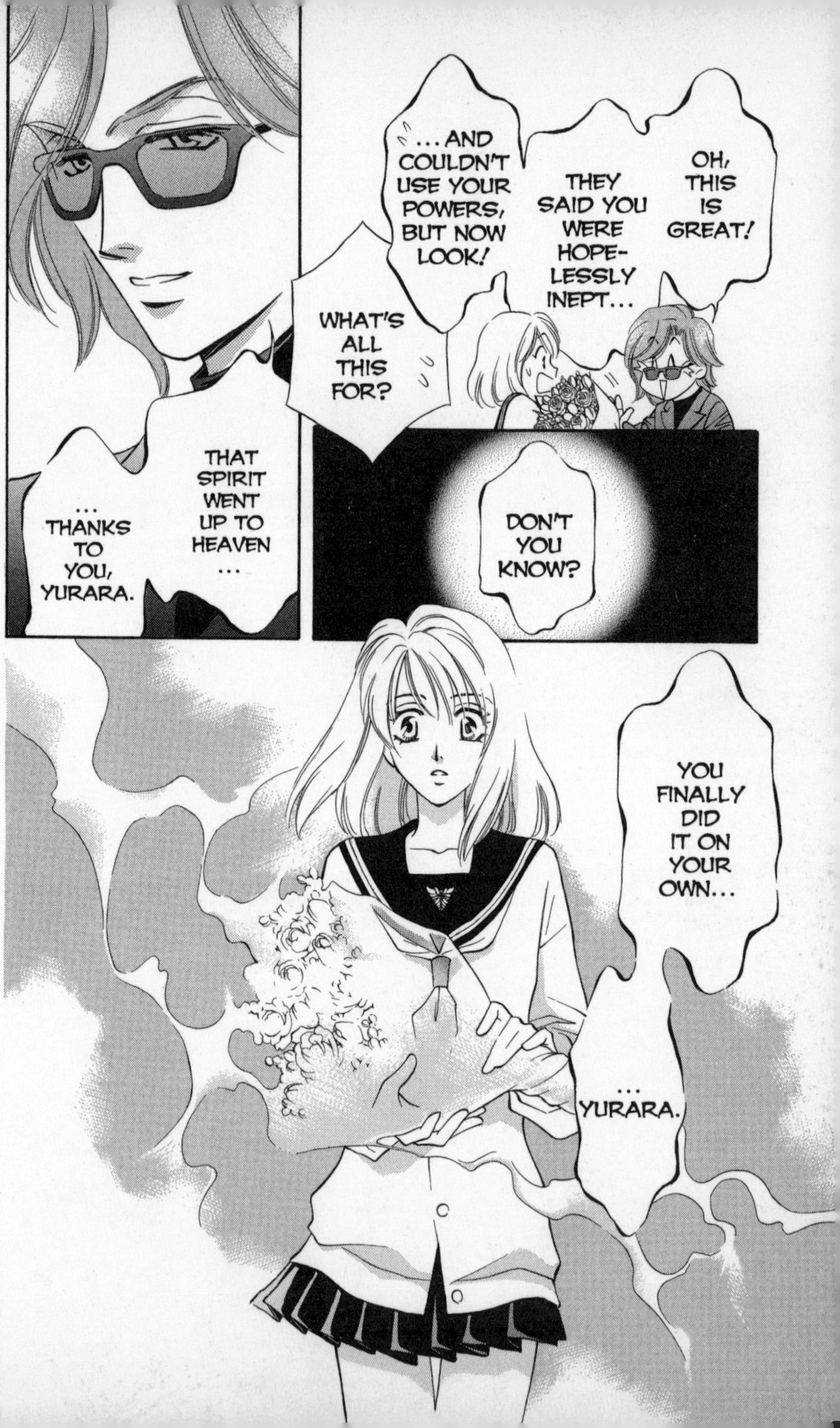
OH, THIS IS GREAT!
THEY SAID YOU WERE HOPE-LESSLY INEPT...
...AND COULDN'T USE YOUR POWERS, BUT NOW LOOK!
WHAT'S ALL THIS FOR?
DON'T YOU KNOW?
THAT SPIRIT WENT UP TO HEAVEN...
...THANKS TO YOU, YURARA.
YOU FINALLY DID IT ON YOUR OWN...
...YURARA.

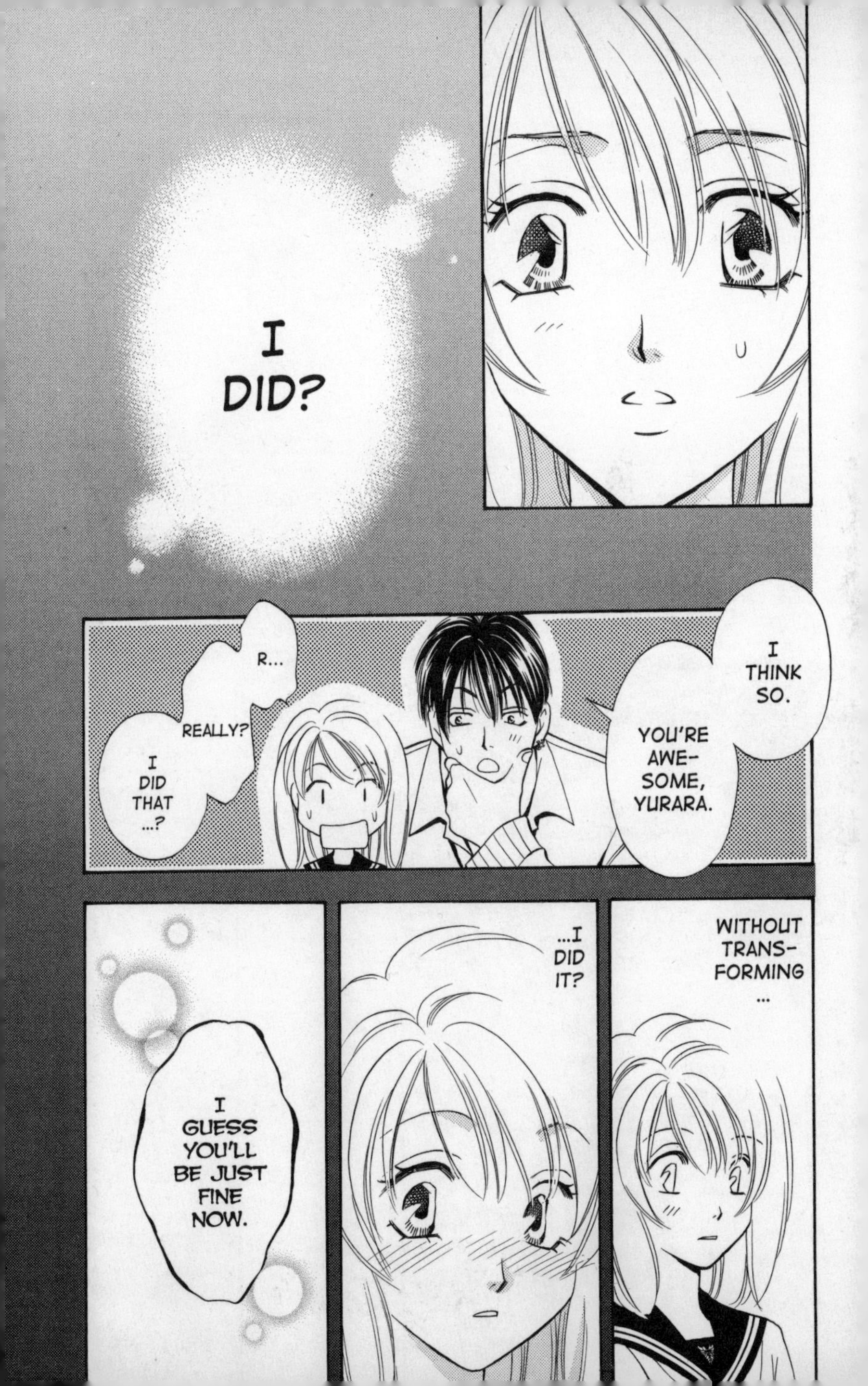
I DID?
I THINK SO.
YOU'RE AWE-SOME, YURARA.
R...
REALLY?
I DID THAT ...?
WITHOUT TRANS-FORMING ...
...I DID IT?
I GUESS YOU'LL BE JUST FINE NOW.

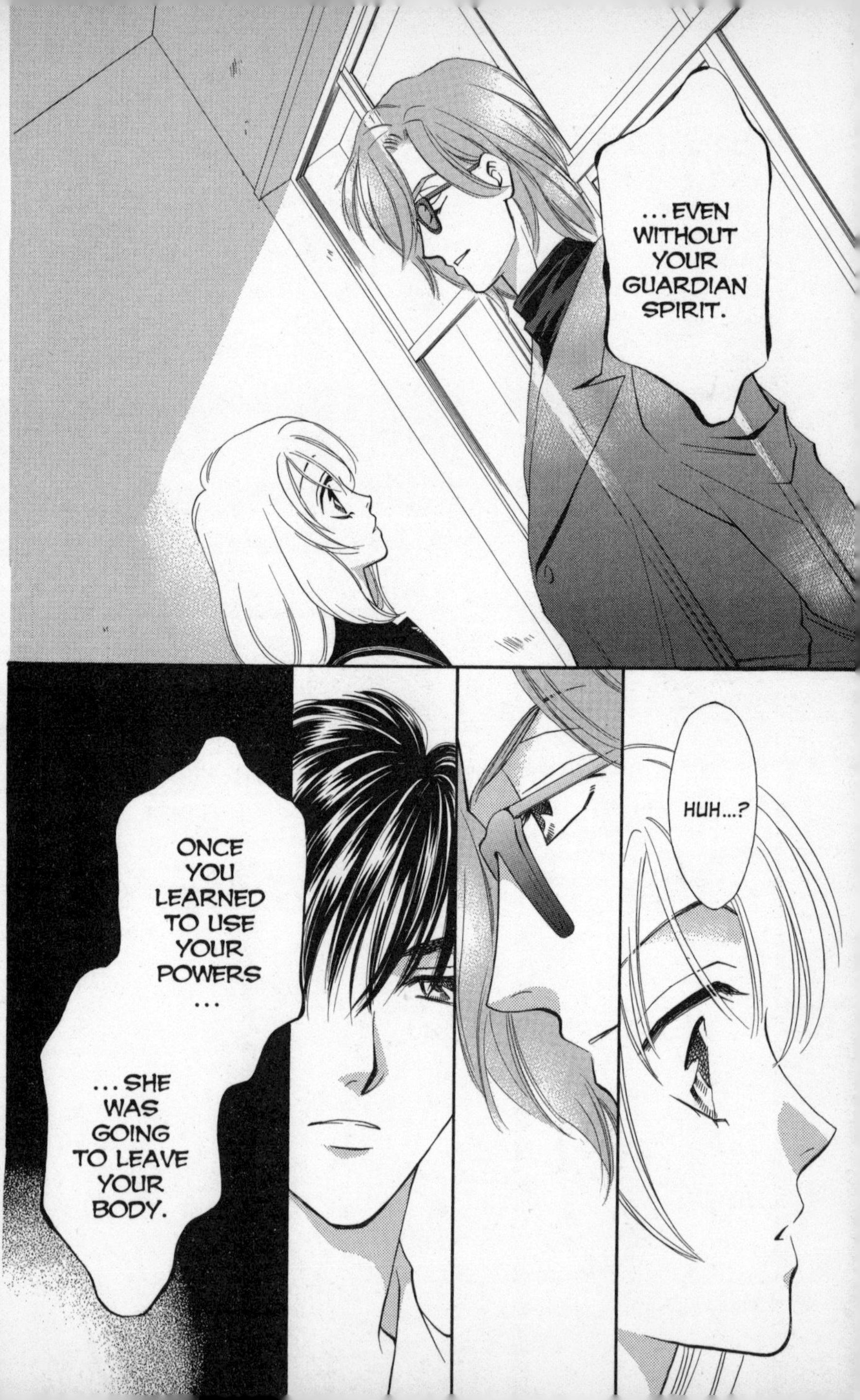
...EVEN WITHOUT YOUR GUARDIAN SPIRIT.
HUH...?
ONCE YOU LEARNED TO USE YOUR POWERS ...
...SHE WAS GOING TO LEAVE YOUR BODY.

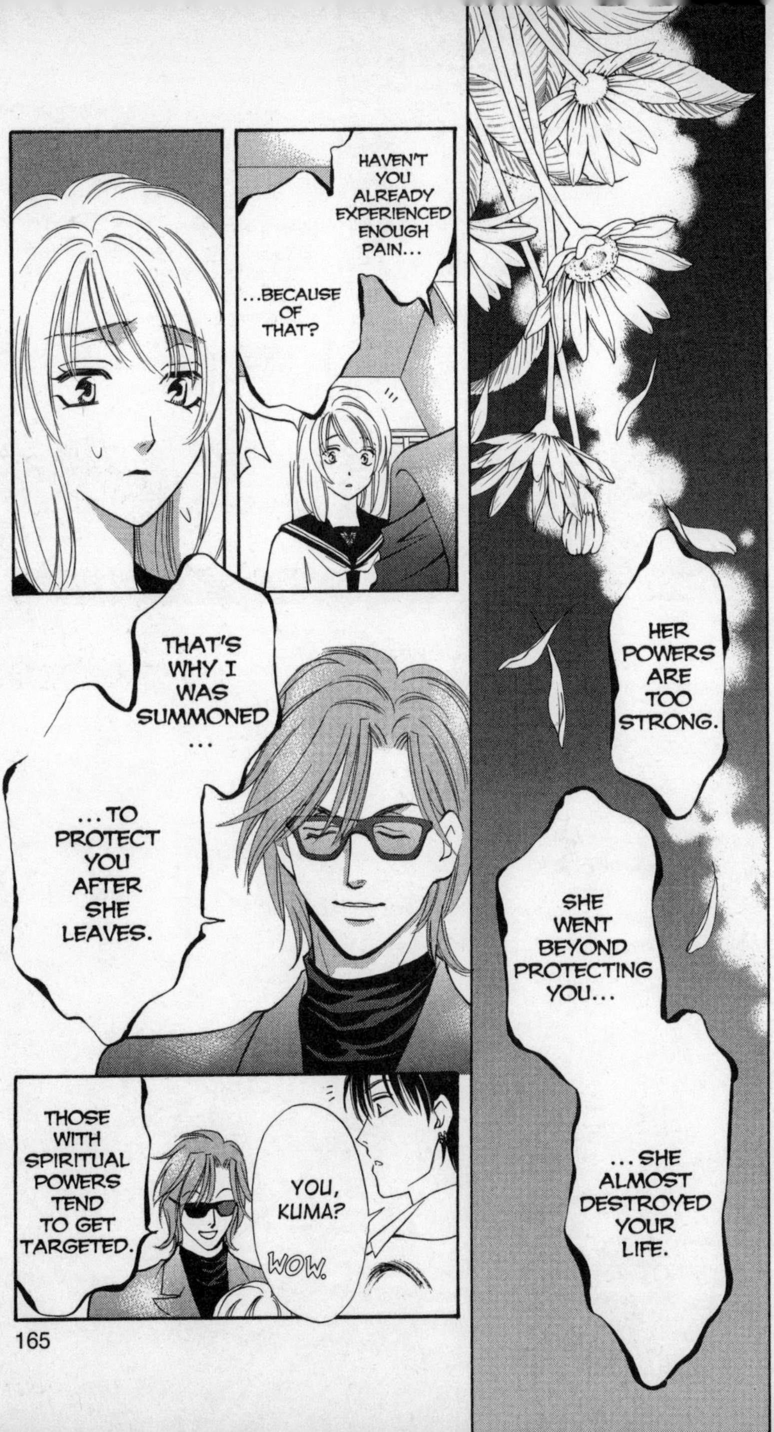
HER POWERS ARE TOO STRONG.
SHE WENT BEYOND PROTECTING YOU...
...SHE ALMOST DESTROYED YOUR LIFE.
HAVEN'T YOU ALREADY EXPERIENCED ENOUGH PAIN...
...BECAUSE OF THAT?
THAT'S WHY I WAS SUMMONED ...
...TO PROTECT YOU AFTER SHE LEAVES.
YOU, KUMA?
WOW.
THOSE WITH SPIRITUAL POWERS TEND TO GET TARGETED.

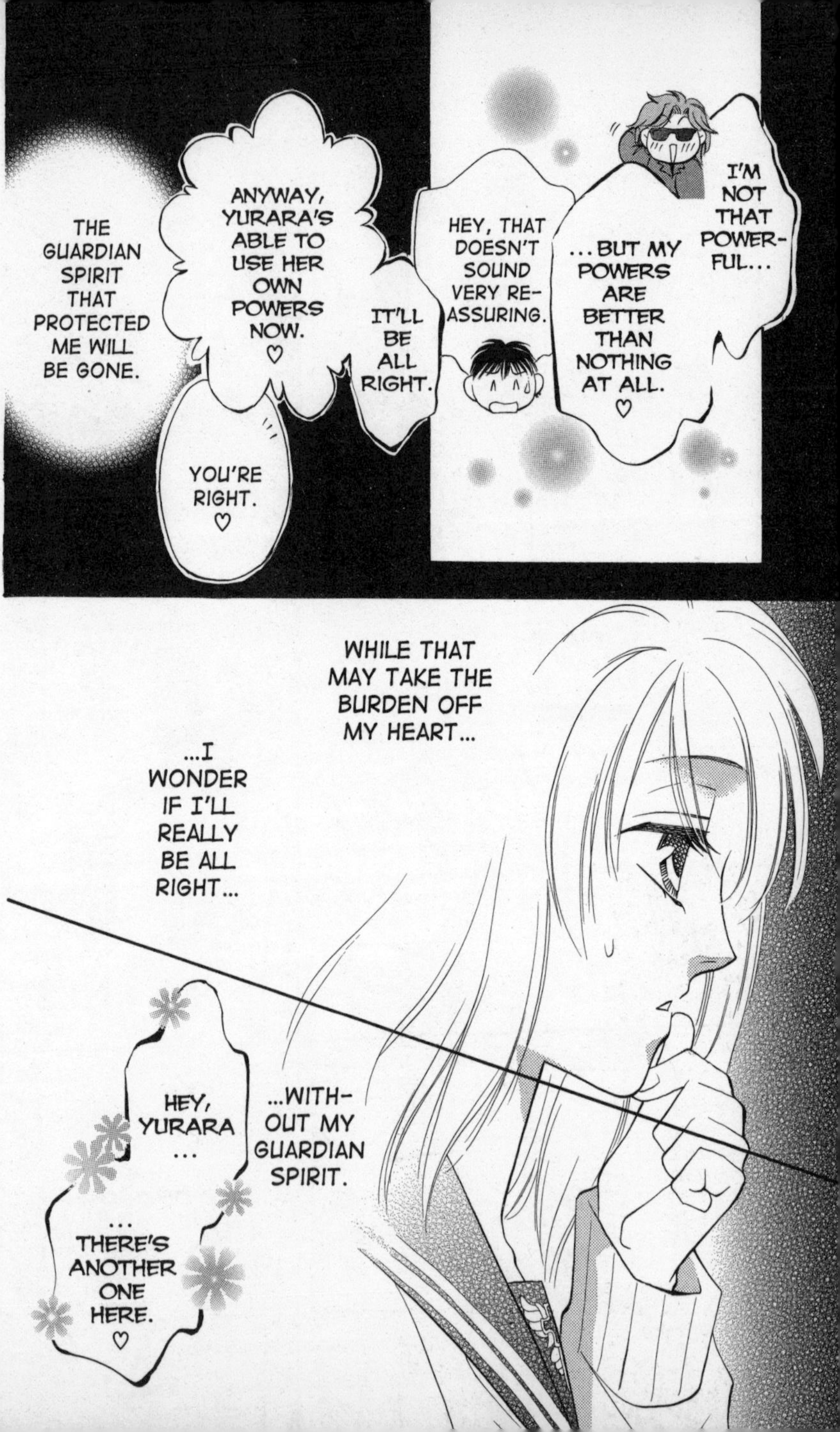
I'M NOT THAT POWER-FUL...
...BUT MY POWERS ARE BETTER THAN NOTHING AT ALL. ♡
HEY, THAT DOESN'T SOUND VERY RE-ASSURING.
IT'LL BE ALL RIGHT.
ANYWAY, YURARA'S ABLE TO USE HER OWN POWERS NOW. ♡
THE GUARDIAN SPIRIT THAT PROTECTED ME WILL BE GONE.
YOU'RE RIGHT. ♡
WHILE THAT MAY TAKE THE BURDEN OFF MY HEART...
...I WONDER IF I'LL REALLY BE ALL RIGHT...
...WITH-OUT MY GUARDIAN SPIRIT.
HEY, YURARA ...
... THERE'S ANOTHER ONE HERE. ♡

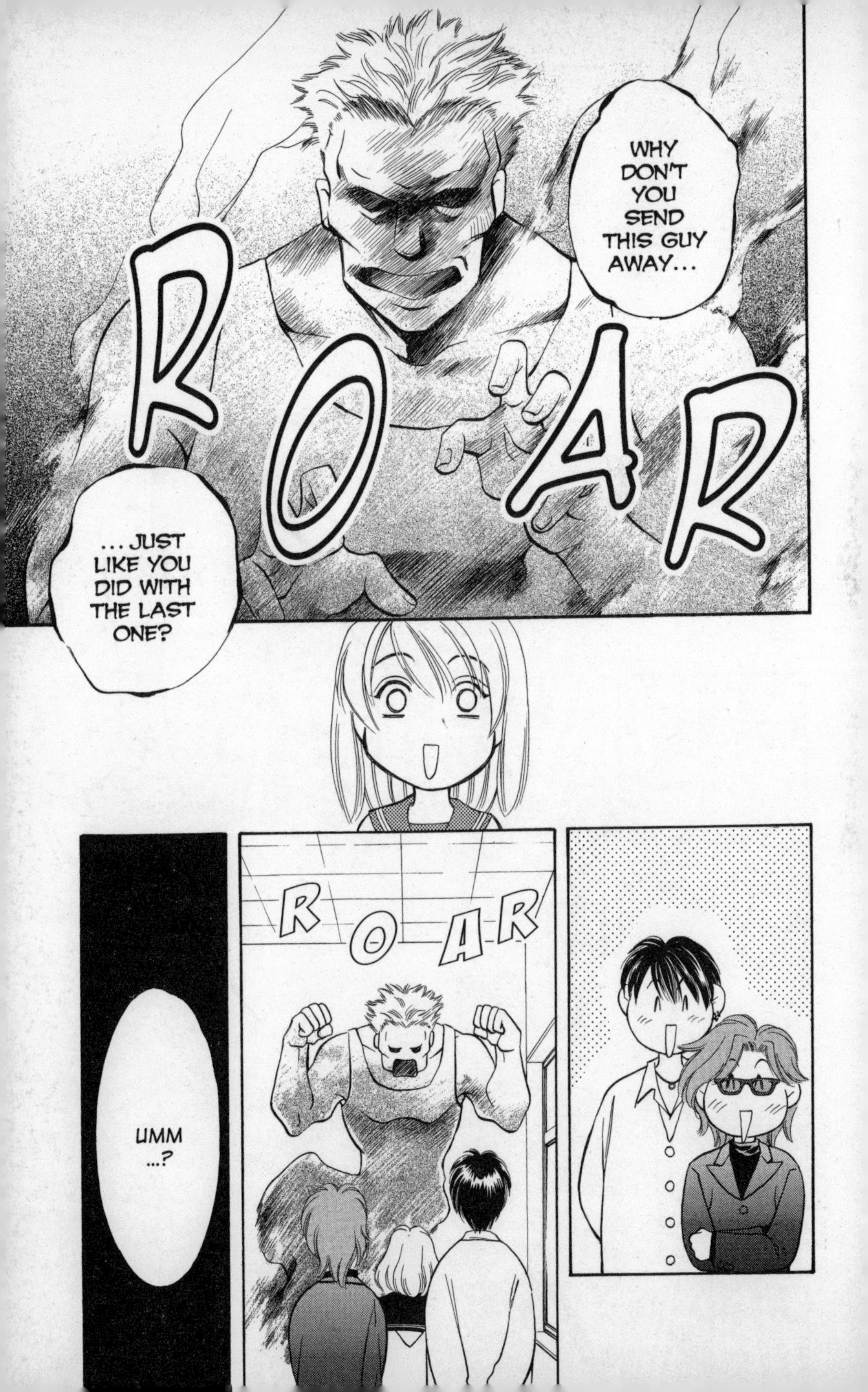
WHY DON'T YOU SEND THIS GUY AWAY...
ROAR
...JUST LIKE YOU DID WITH THE LAST ONE?
ROAR
UMM ...?

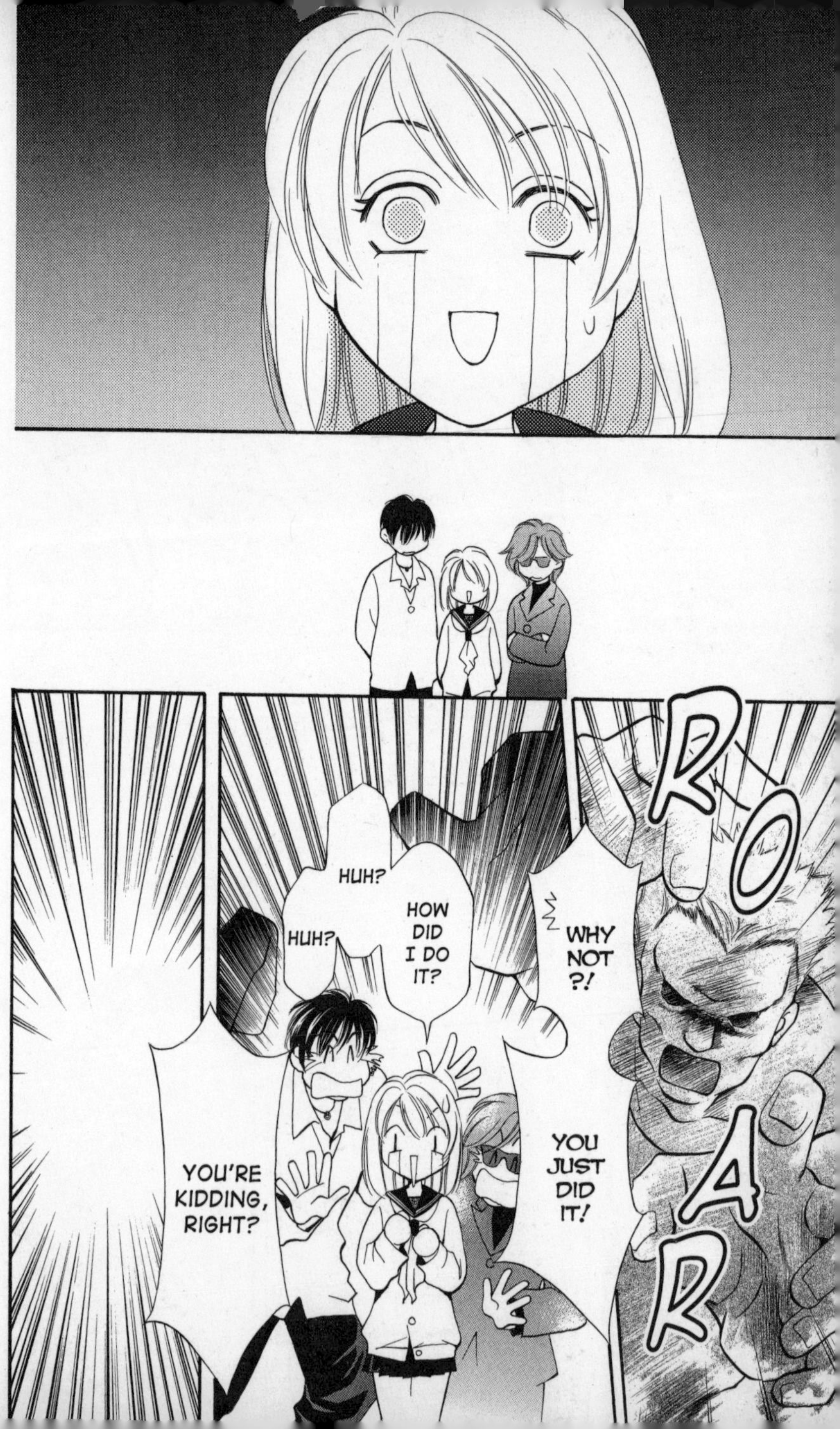
ROAR
WHY NOT?!
HUH?
HUH?
HOW DID I DO IT?
YOU JUST DID IT!
YOU'RE KIDDING, RIGHT?

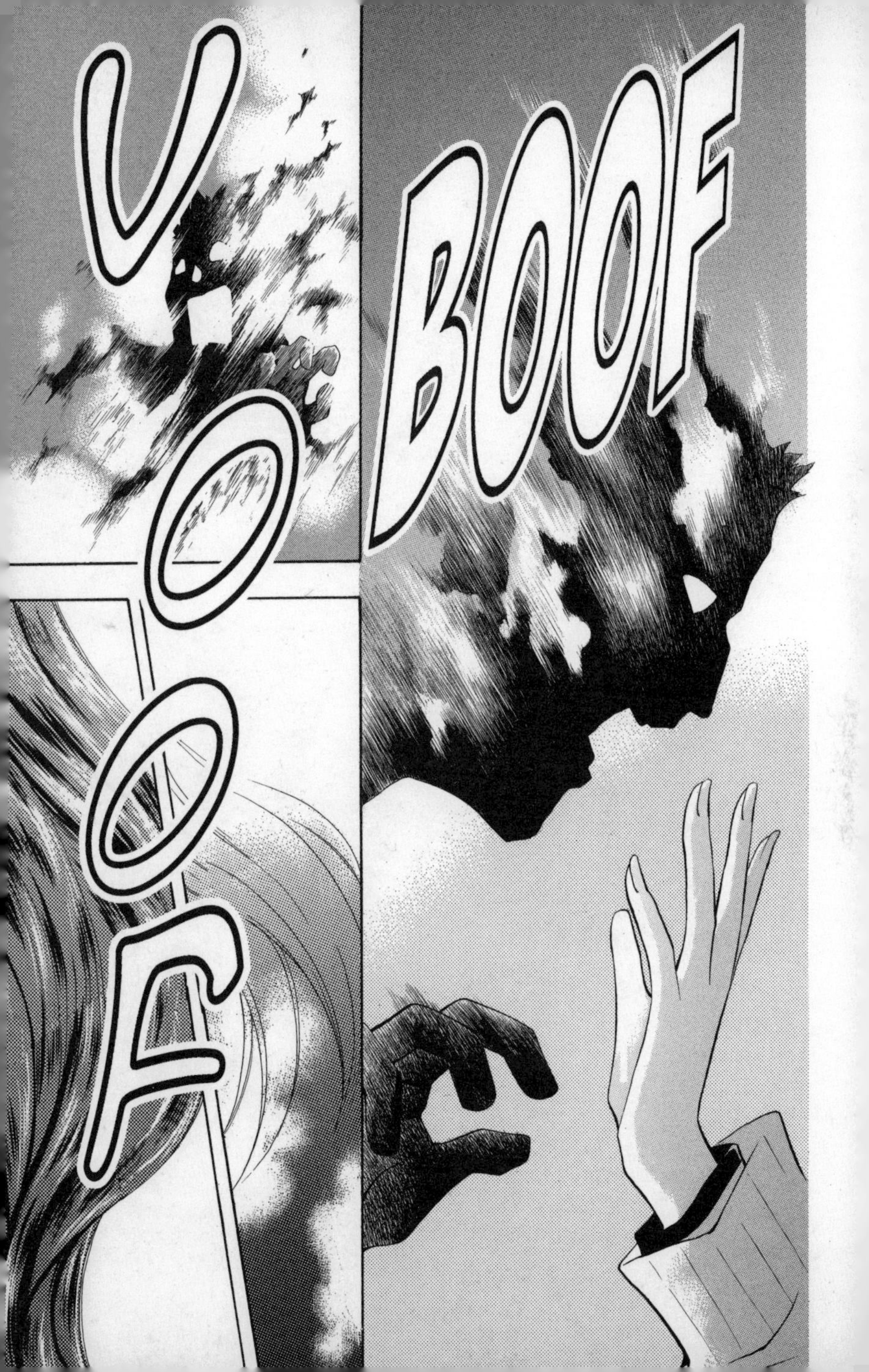
BOOF
VOOF

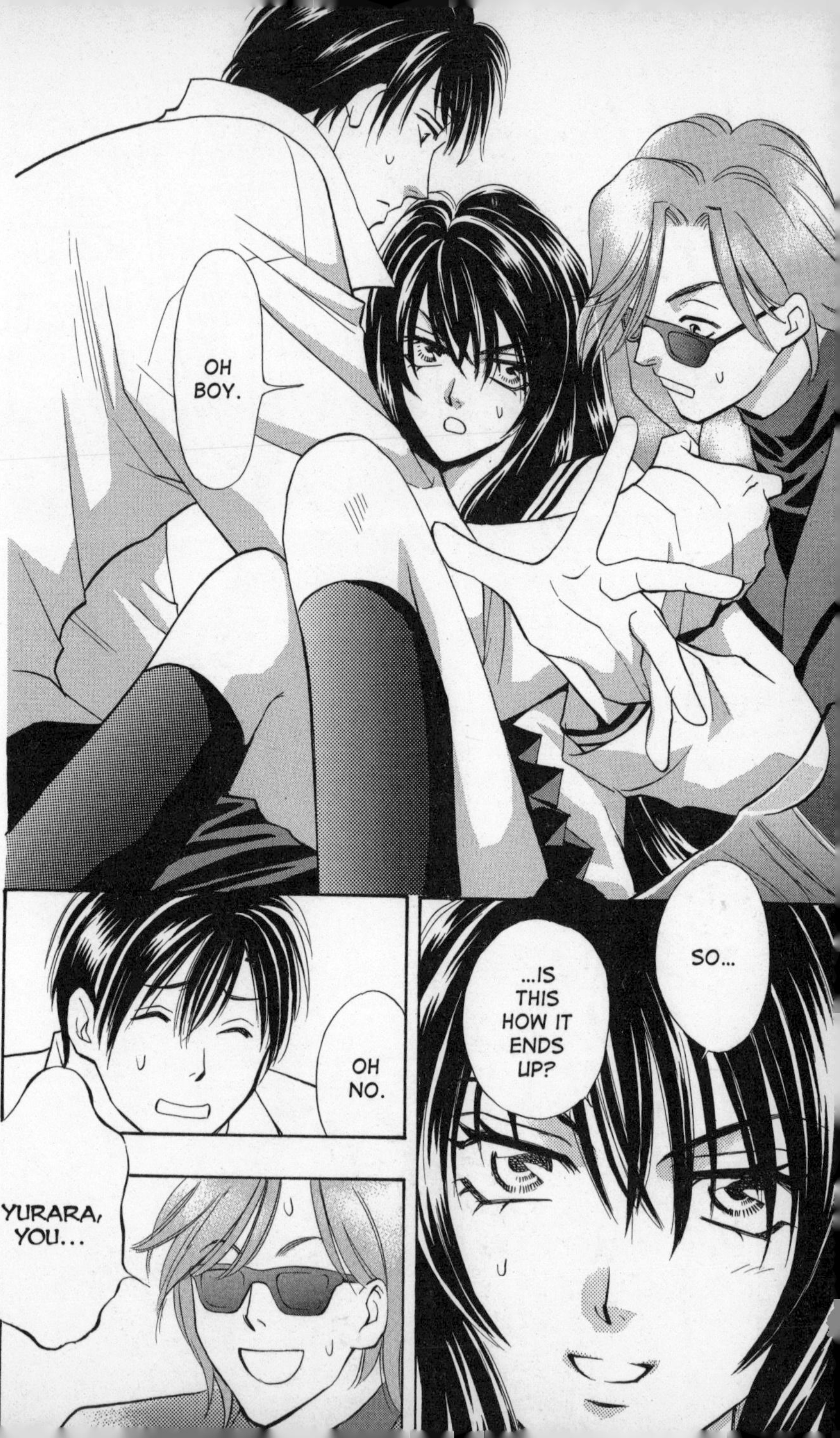
OH BOY.
SO...
...IS THIS HOW IT ENDS UP?
OH NO.
YURARA, YOU...

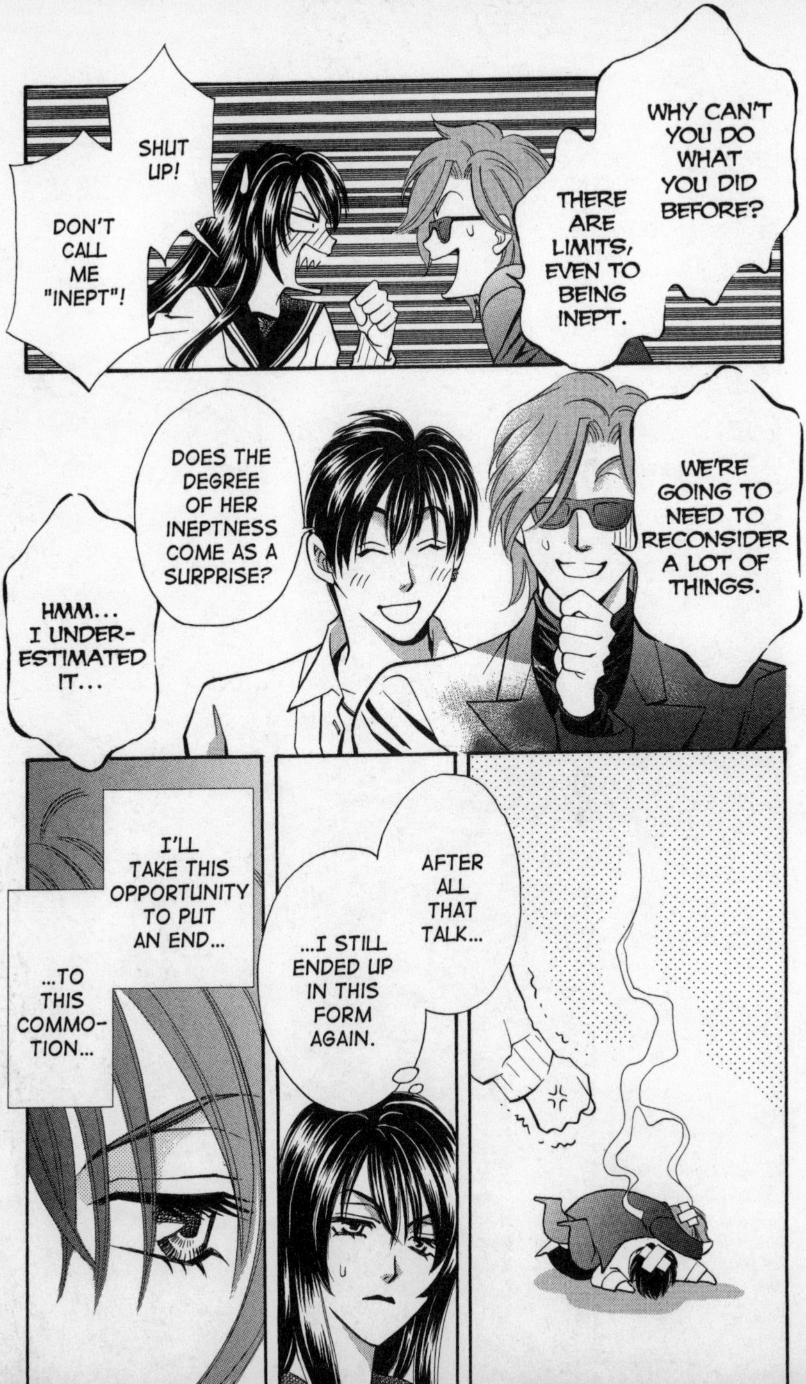
WHY CAN'T YOU DO WHAT YOU DID BEFORE?
THERE ARE LIMITS, EVEN TO BEING INEPT.
SHUT UP!
DON'T CALL ME "INEPT"!
WE'RE GOING TO NEED TO RECONSIDER A LOT OF THINGS.
DOES THE DEGREE OF HER INEPTNESS COME AS A SURPRISE?
HMM... I UNDER-ESTIMATED IT...
AFTER ALL THAT TALK...
...I STILL ENDED UP IN THIS FORM AGAIN.
I'LL TAKE THIS OPPORTUNITY TO PUT AN END...
...TO THIS COMMOTION...

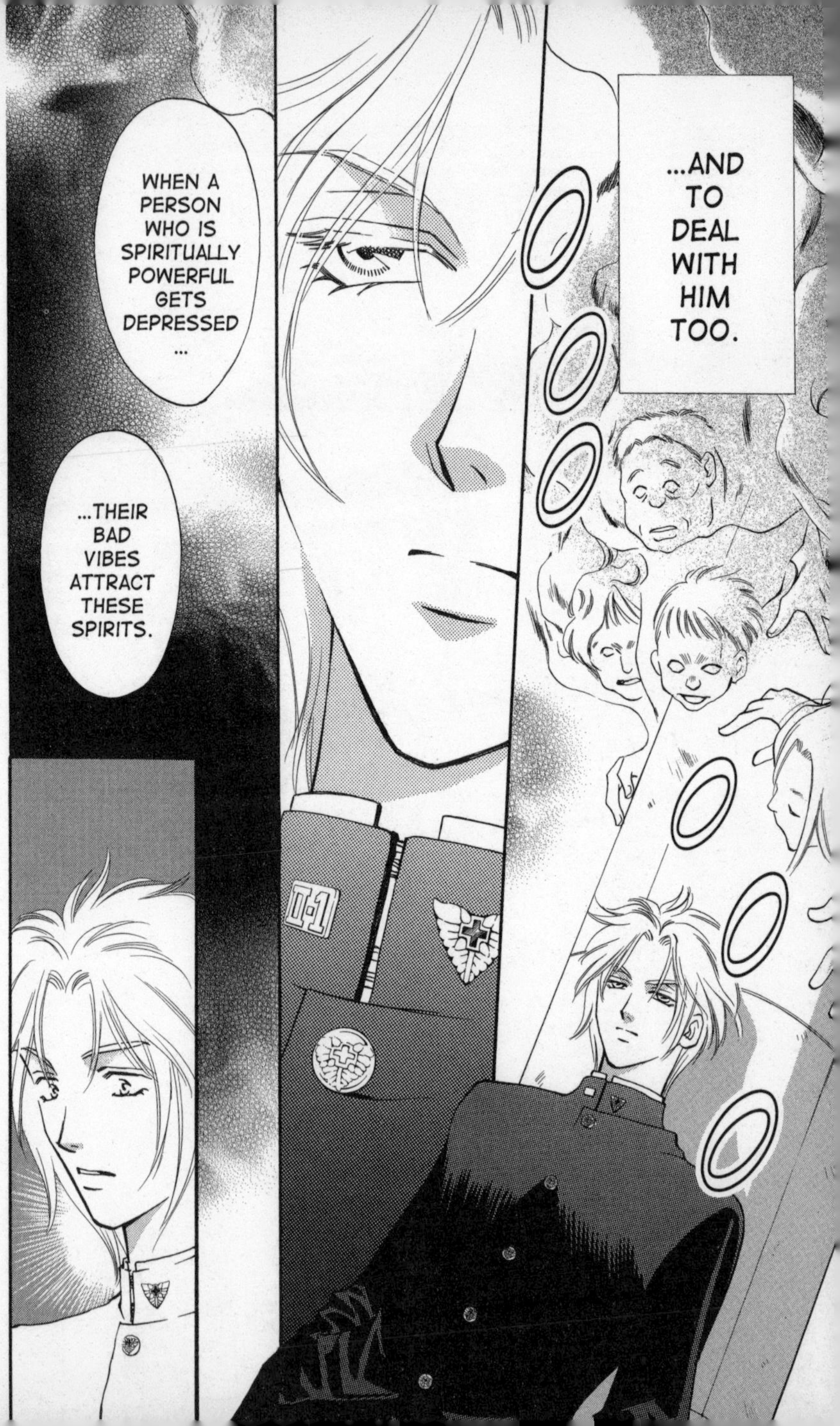
...AND TO DEAL WITH HIM TOO.
WHEN A PERSON WHO IS SPIRITUALLY POWERFUL GETS DEPRESSED ...
...THEIR BAD VIBES ATTRACT THESE SPIRITS.

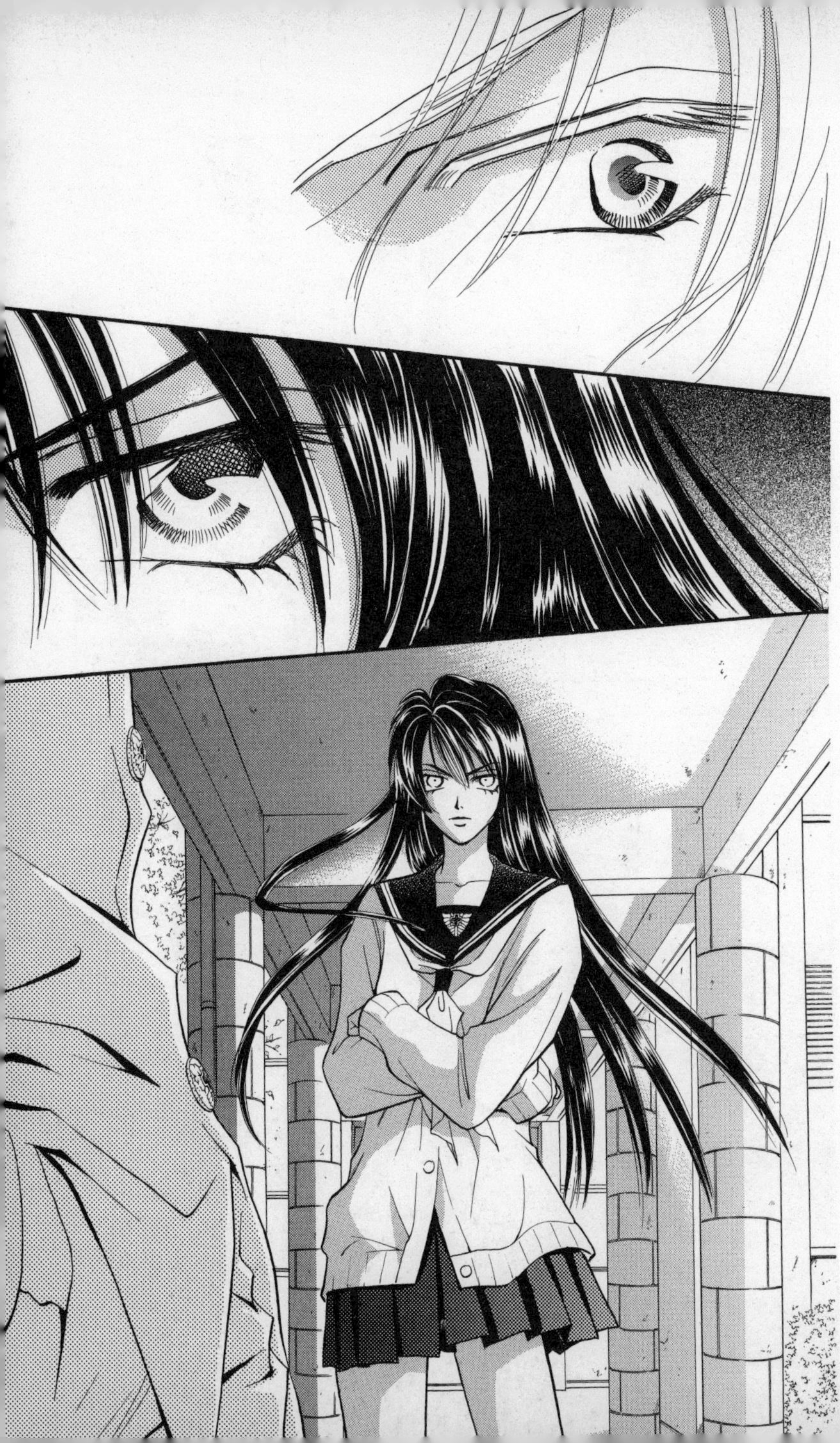

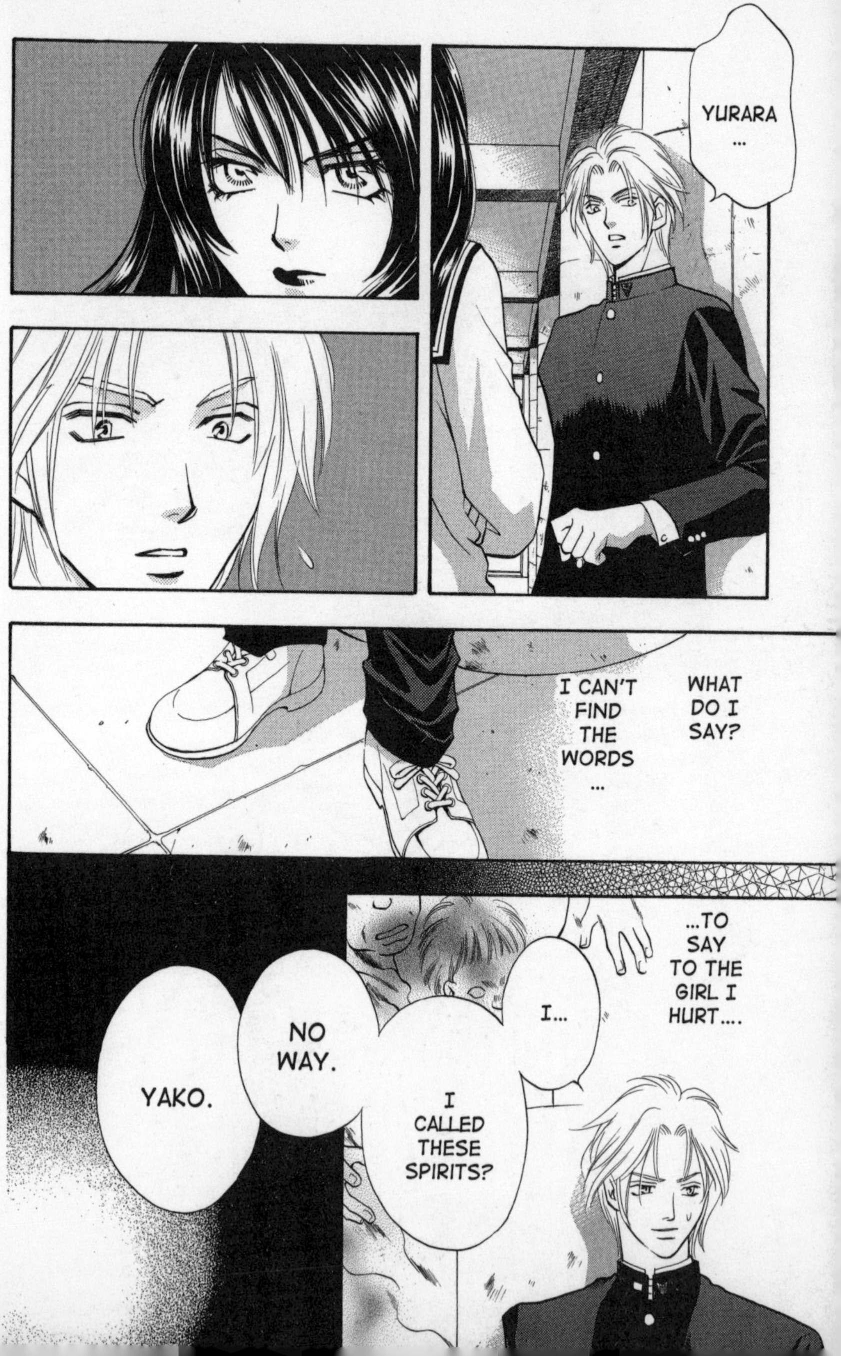
YURARA ...
WHAT DO I SAY?
I CAN'T FIND THE WORDS ...
...TO SAY TO THE GIRL I HURT....
I...
I CALLED THESE SPIRITS?
NO WAY.
YAKO.

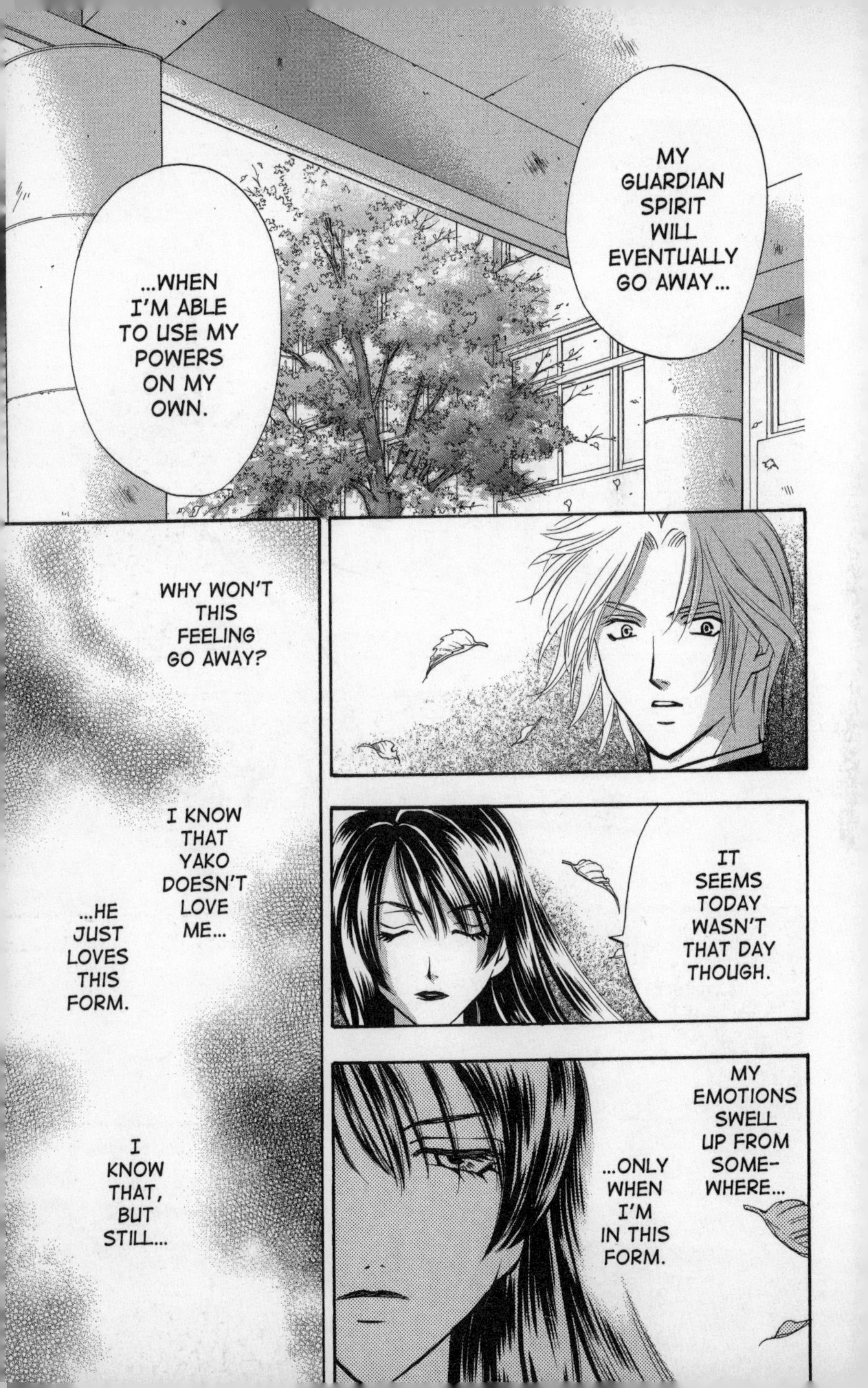
MY GUARDIAN SPIRIT WILL EVENTUALLY GO AWAY...
...WHEN I'M ABLE TO USE MY POWERS ON MY OWN.
IT SEEMS TODAY WASN'T THAT DAY THOUGH.
MY EMOTIONS SWELL UP FROM SOME-WHERE...
...ONLY WHEN I'M IN THIS FORM.
WHY WON'T THIS FEELING GO AWAY?
I KNOW THAT YAKO DOESN'T LOVE ME...
...HE JUST LOVES THIS FORM.
I KNOW THAT, BUT STILL...

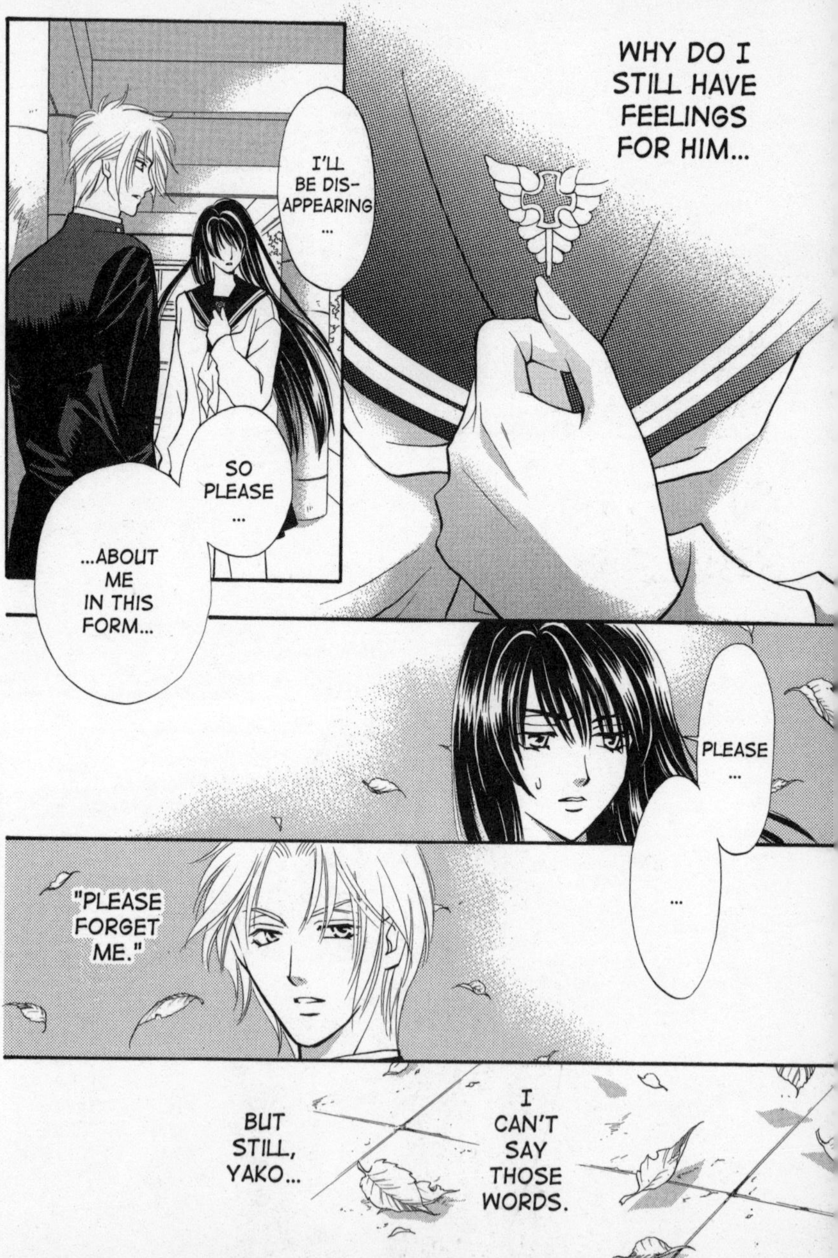
WHY DO I STILL HAVE FEELINGS FOR HIM...
I'LL BE DIS-APPEARING ...
SO PLEASE ...
...ABOUT ME IN THIS FORM...
PLEASE ...
...
"PLEASE FORGET ME."
I CAN'T SAY THOSE WORDS.
BUT STILL, YAKO...

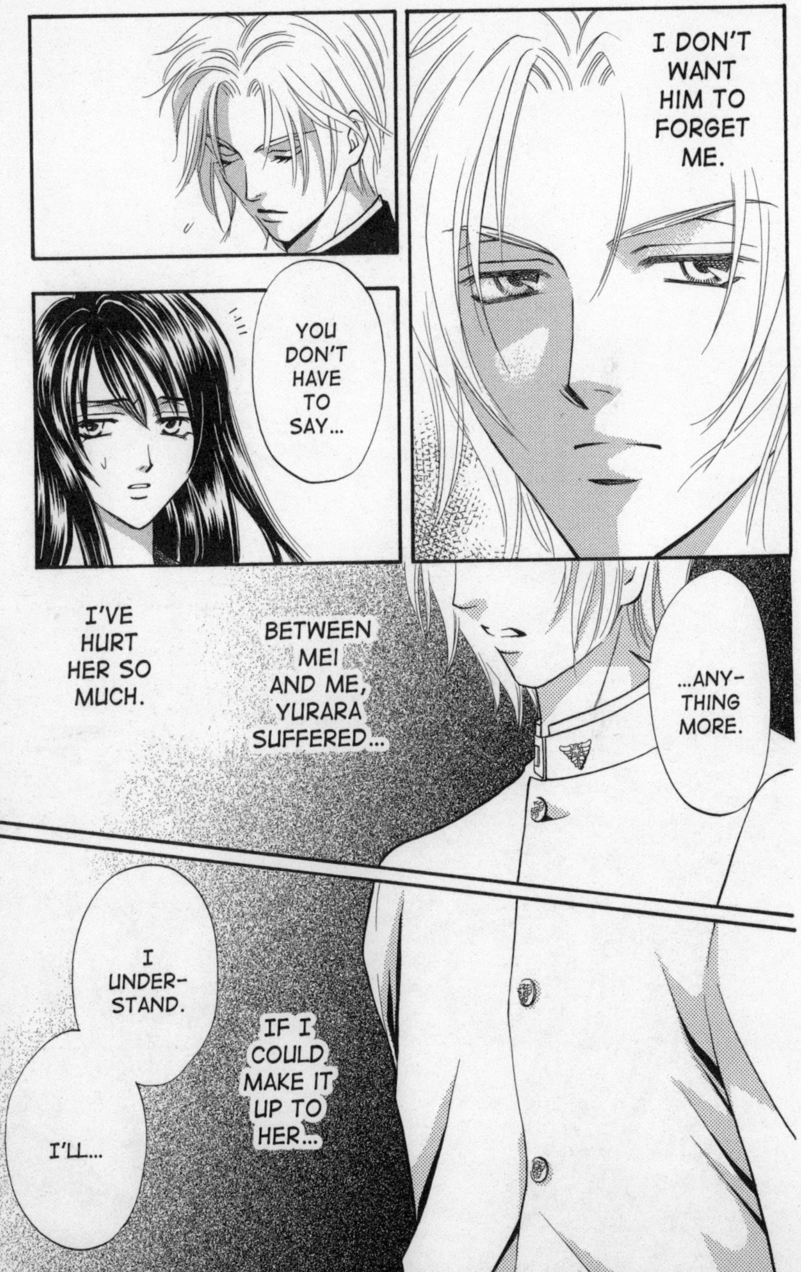
I DON'T WANT HIM TO FORGET ME.
YOU DON'T HAVE TO SAY...
...ANY-THING MORE.
BETWEEN MEI AND ME, YURARA SUFFERED...
I'VE HURT HER SO MUCH.
IF I COULD MAKE IT UP TO HER...
I UNDER-STAND.
I'LL...

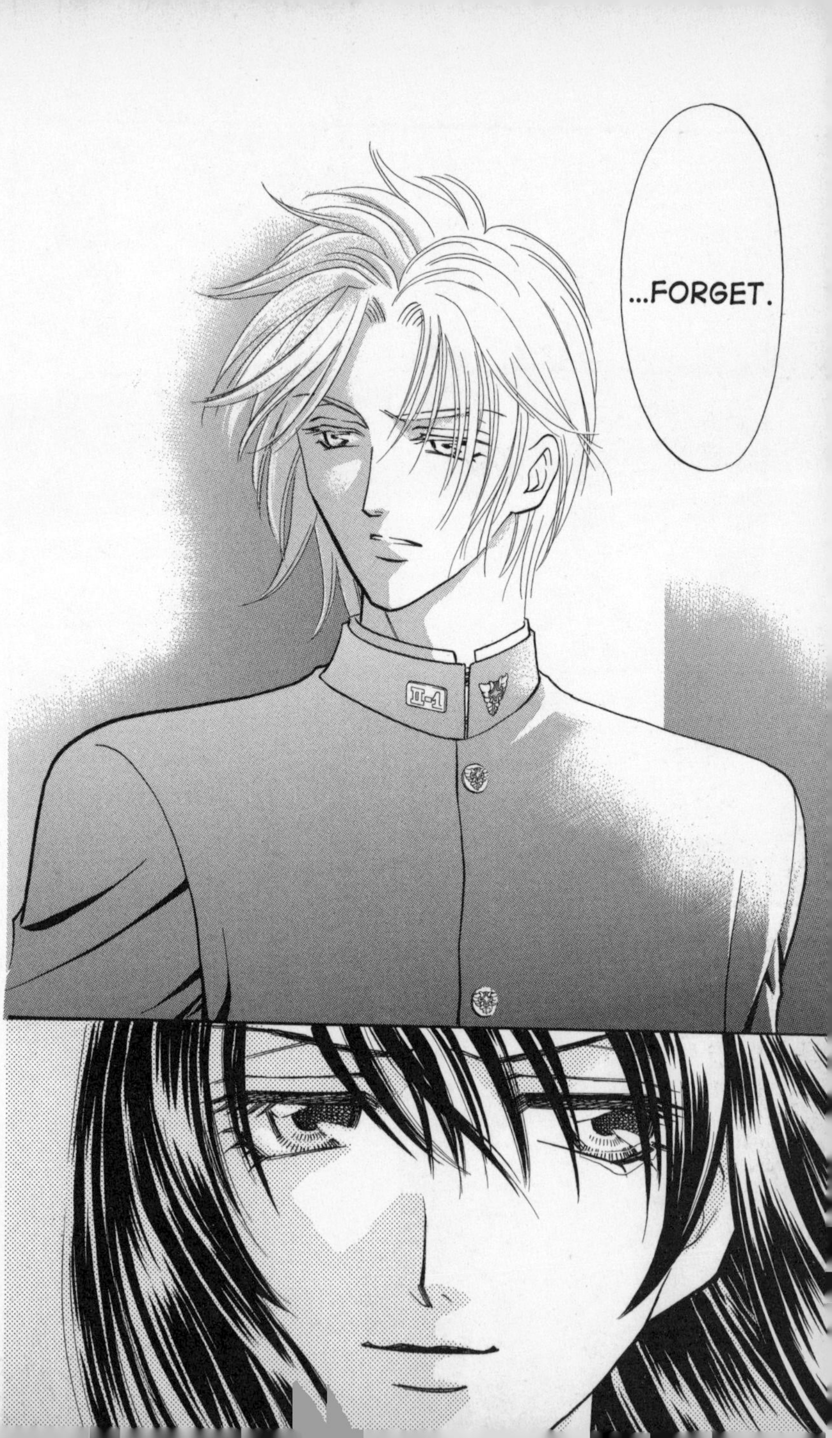
...FORGET.

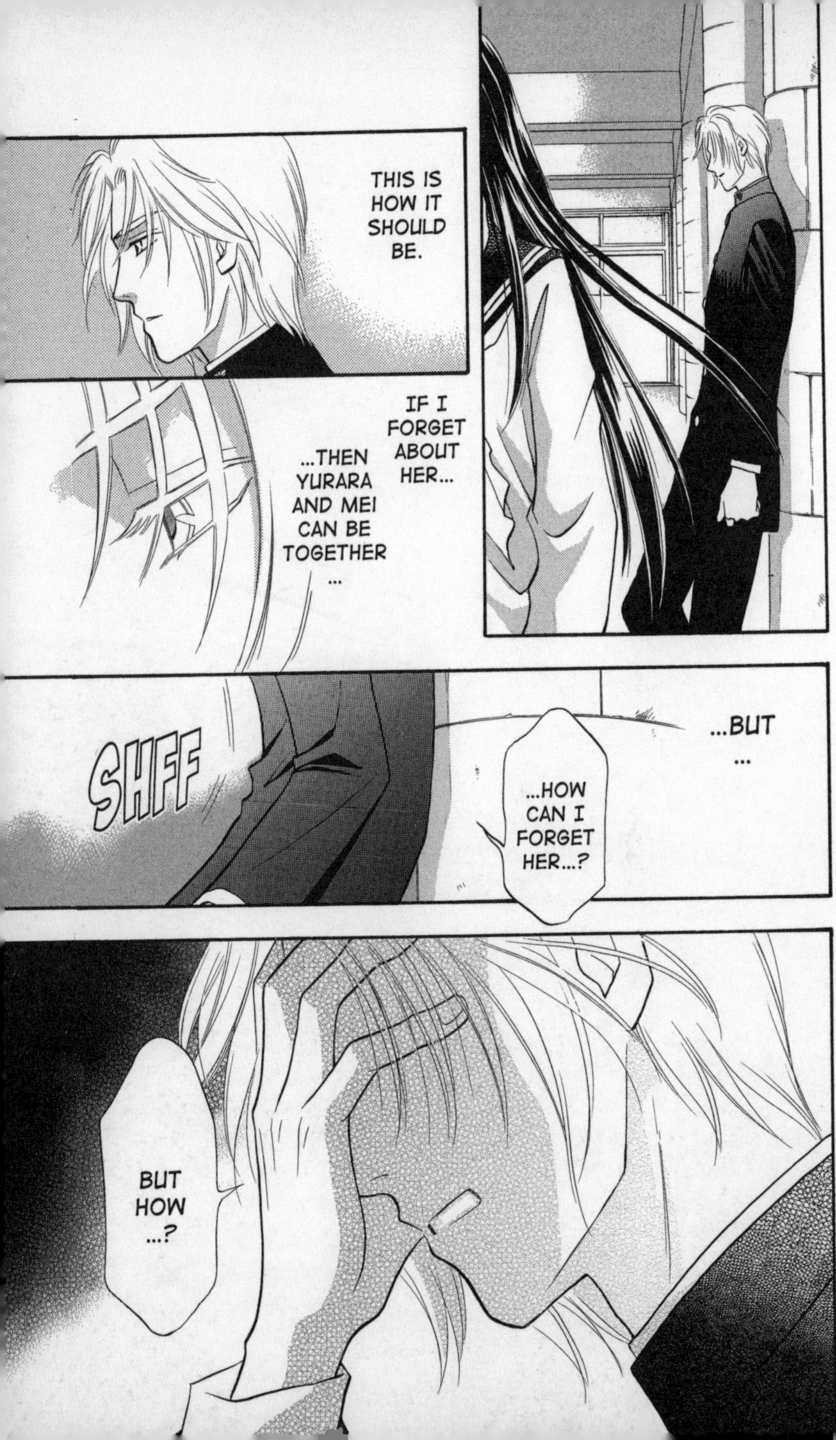
THIS IS HOW IT SHOULD BE.
IF I FORGET ABOUT HER...
...THEN YURARA AND MEI CAN BE TOGETHER ...
...BUT ...
...HOW CAN I FORGET HER...?
SHFF
BUT HOW ...?

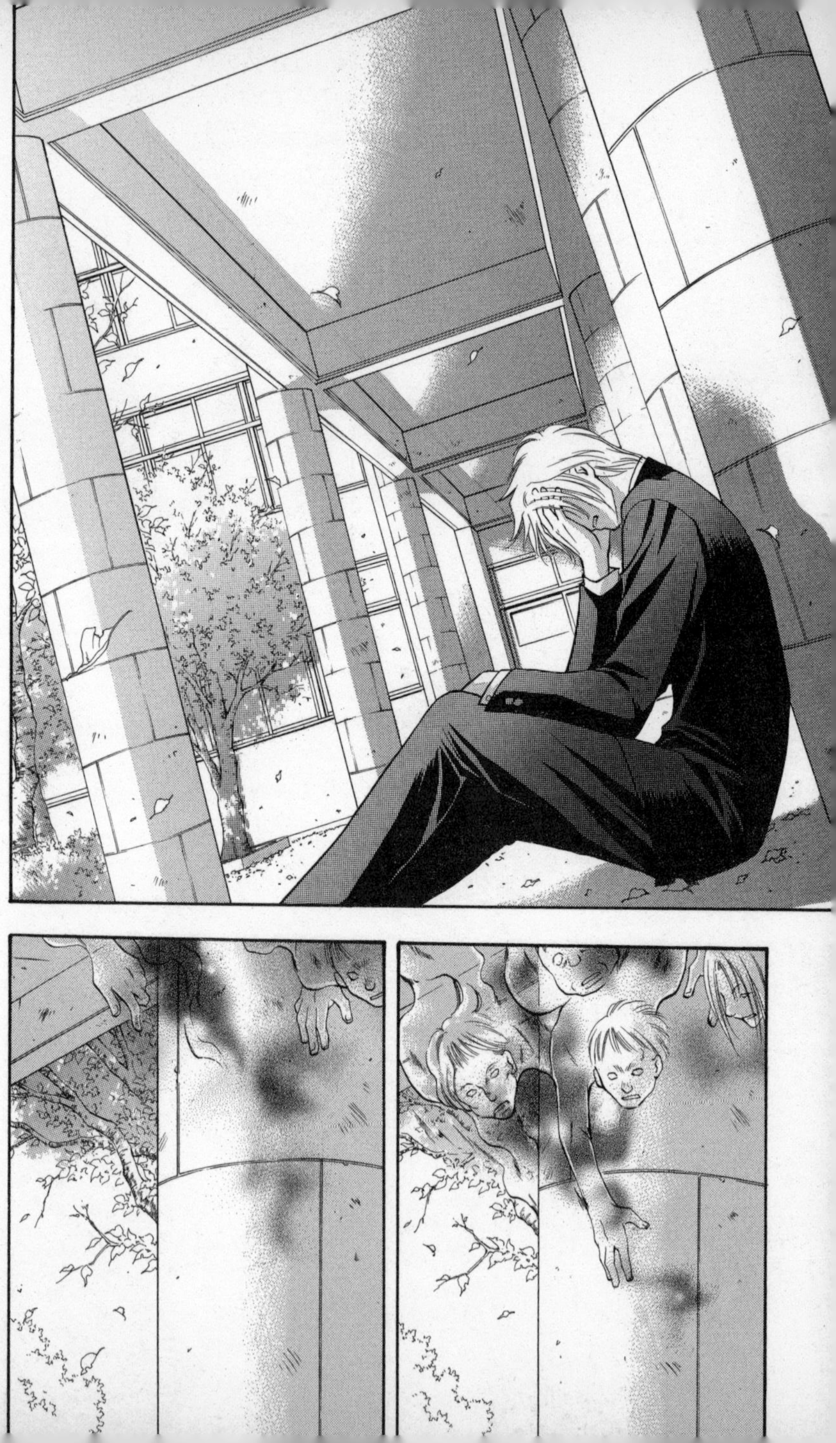

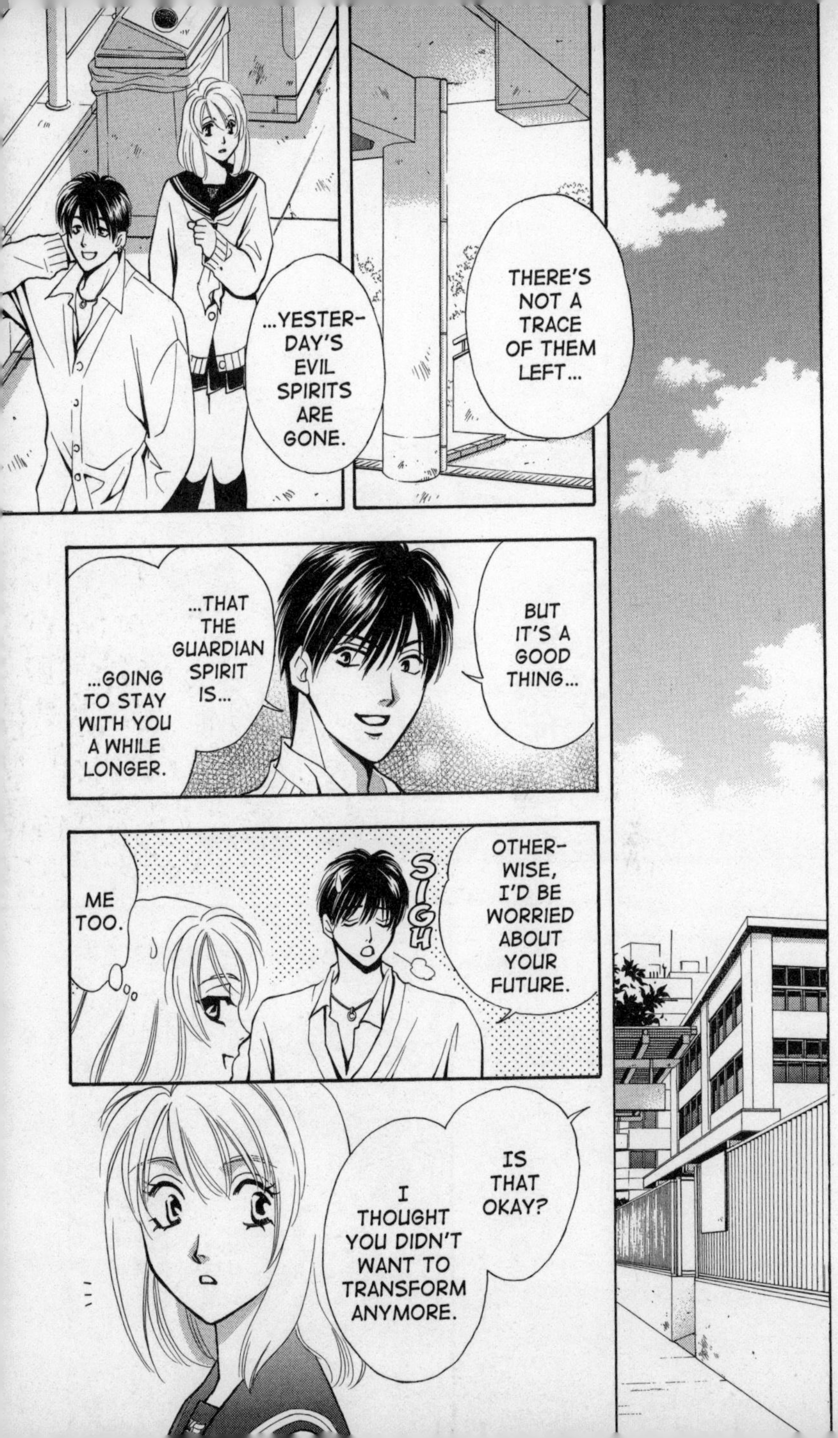
THERE'S NOT A TRACE OF THEM LEFT...
...YESTER-DAY'S EVIL SPIRITS ARE GONE.
BUT IT'S A GOOD THING...
...THAT THE GUARDIAN SPIRIT IS...
...GOING TO STAY WITH YOU A WHILE LONGER.
OTHER-WISE, I'D BE WORRIED ABOUT YOUR FUTURE.
SIGH
ME TOO.
IS THAT OKAY?
I THOUGHT YOU DIDN'T WANT TO TRANSFORM ANYMORE.

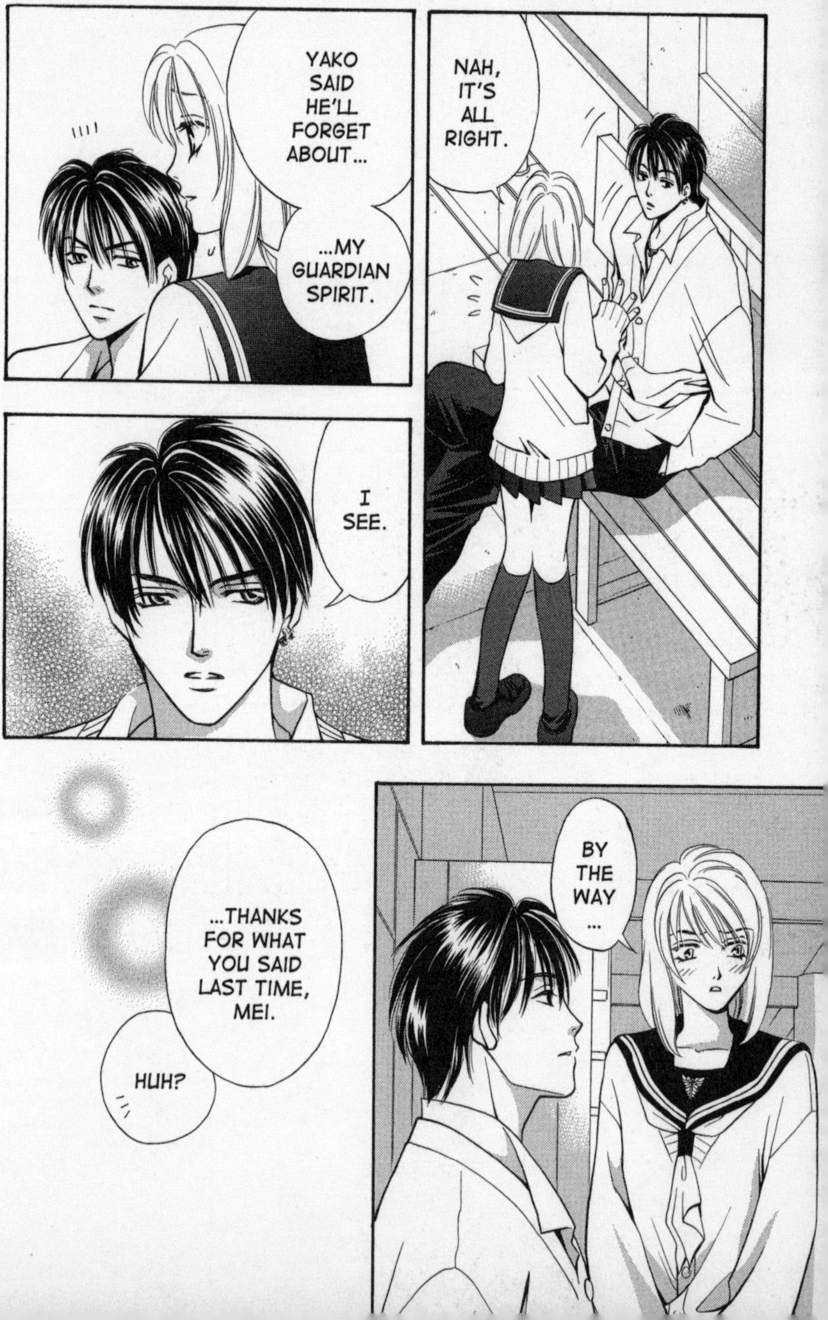
NAH, IT'S ALL RIGHT.
YAKO SAID HE'LL FORGET ABOUT...
...MY GUARDIAN SPIRIT.
I SEE.
BY THE WAY...
...THANKS FOR WHAT YOU SAID LAST TIME, MEI.
HUH?

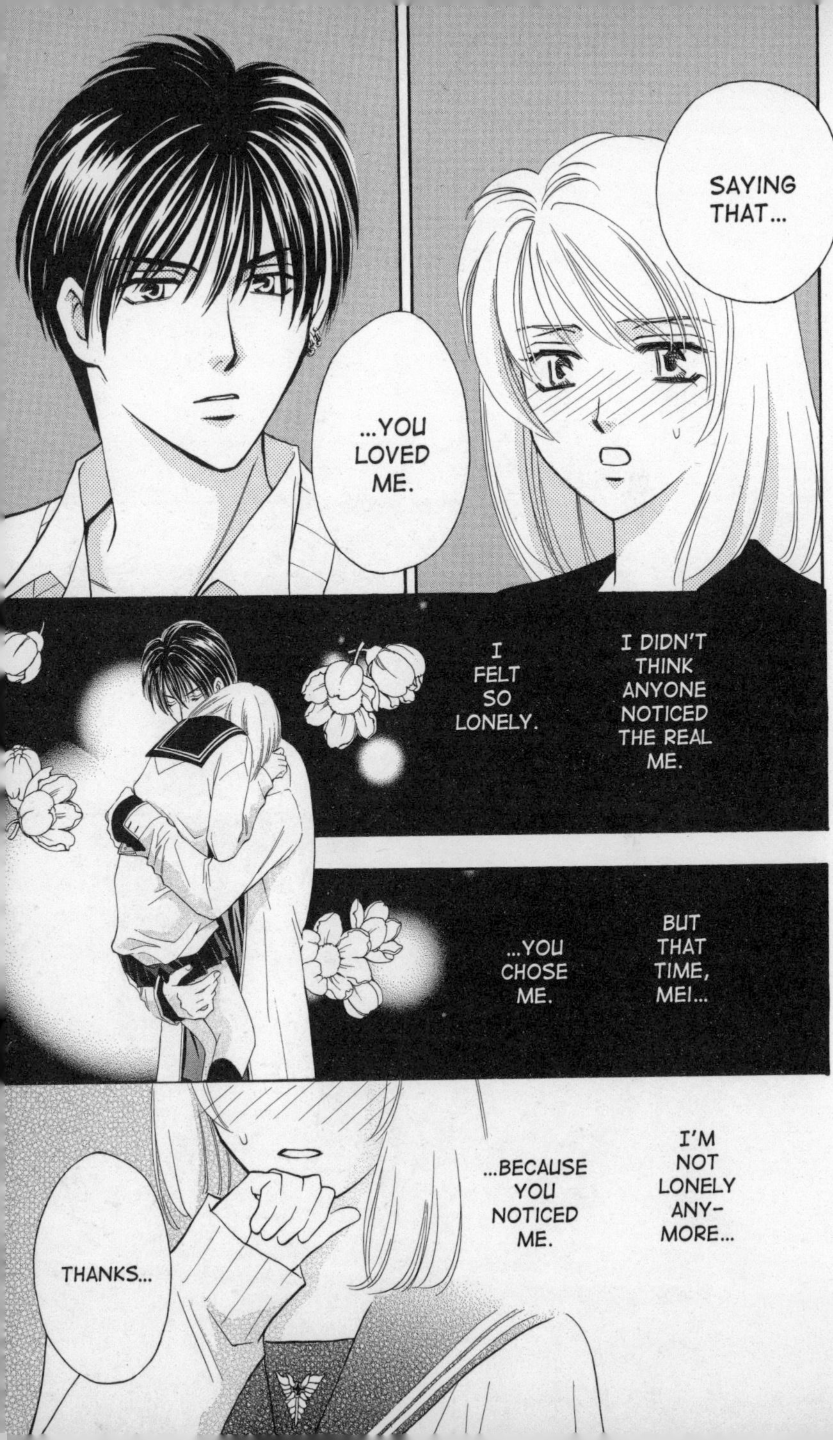
SAYING THAT...
...YOU LOVED ME.
I DIDN'T THINK ANYONE NOTICED THE REAL ME.
I FELT SO LONELY.
BUT THAT TIME, MEI...
...YOU CHOSE ME.
I'M NOT LONELY ANY-MORE...
...BECAUSE YOU NOTICED ME.
THANKS...

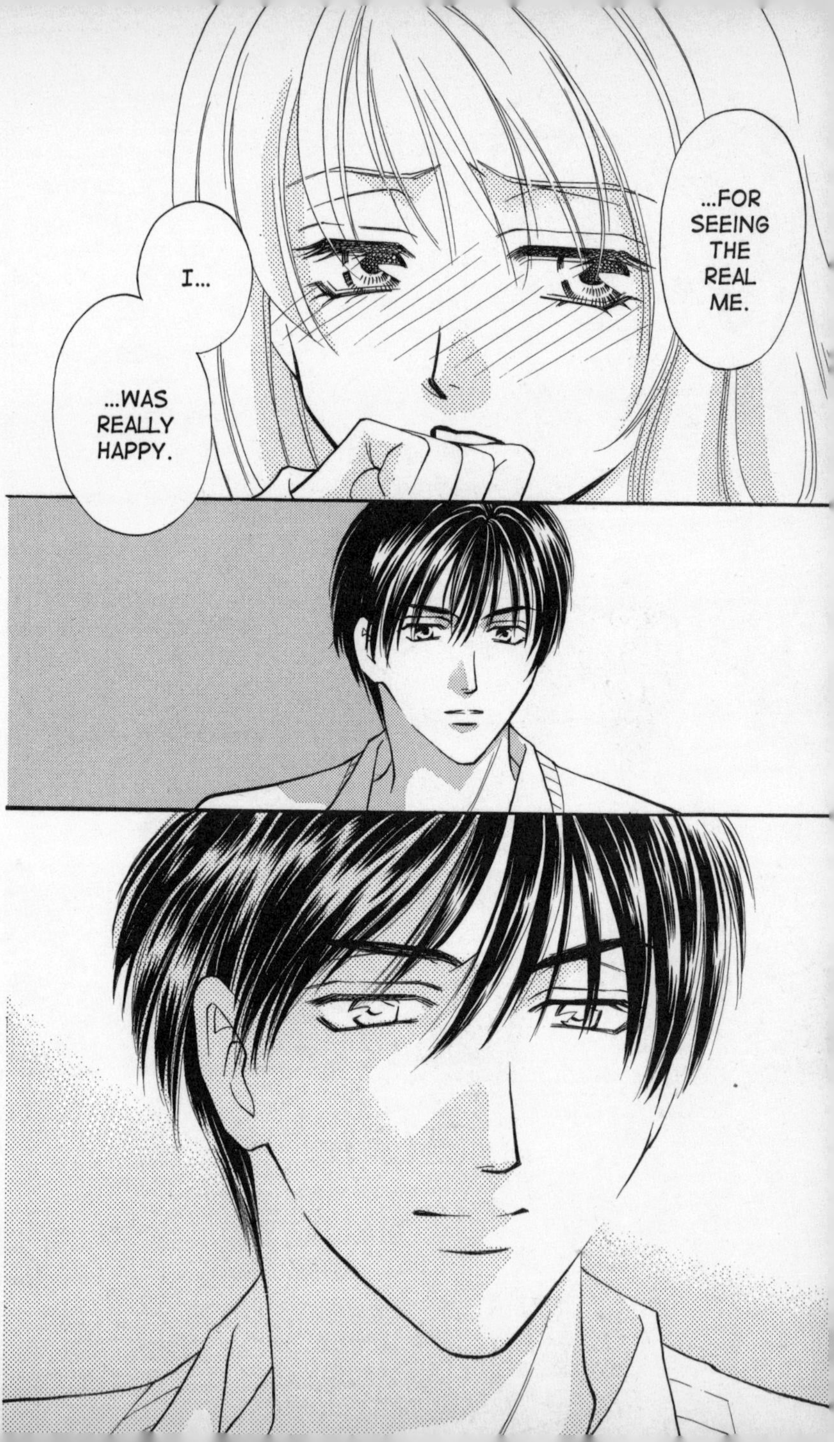
...FOR SEEING THE REAL ME.
I...
...WAS REALLY HAPPY.

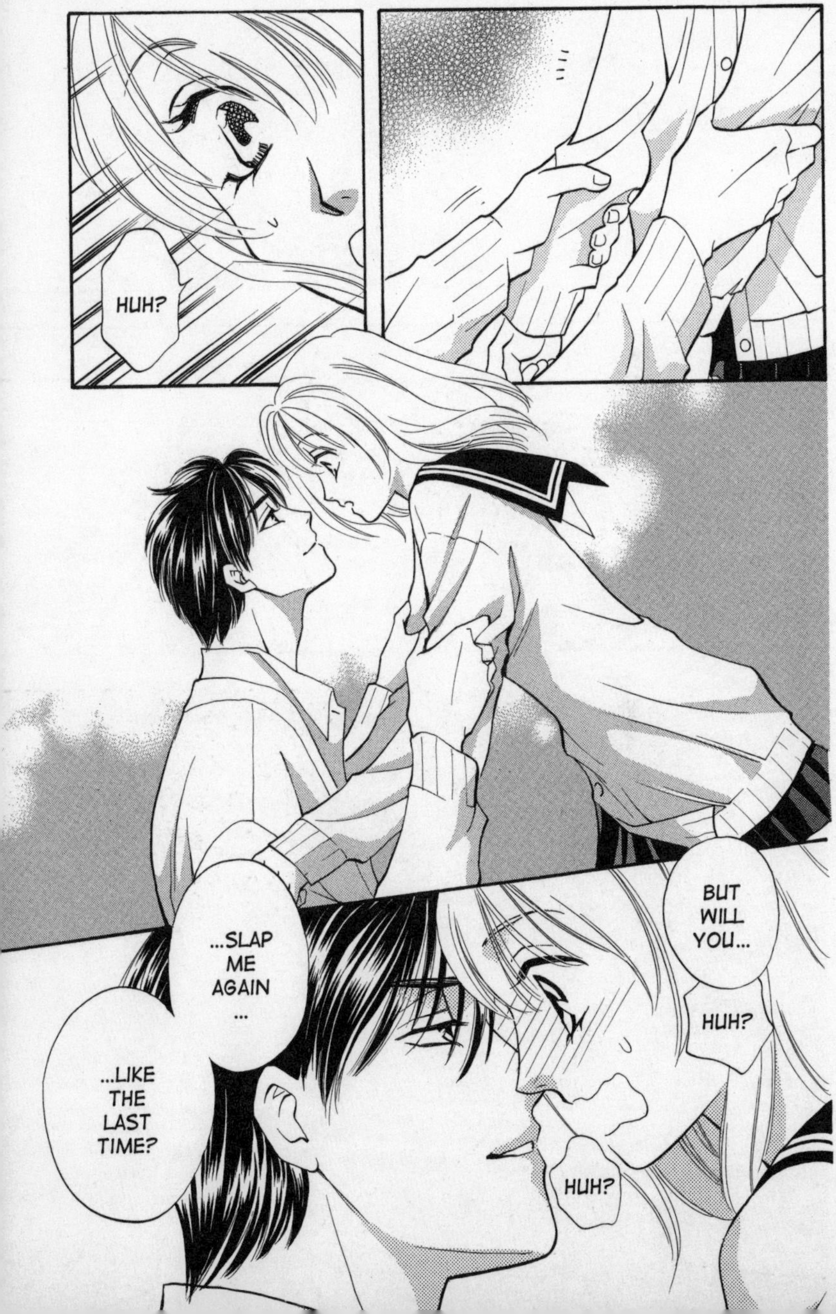
HUH?
BUT WILL YOU...
HUH?
...SLAP ME AGAIN ...
...LIKE THE LAST TIME?
HUH?

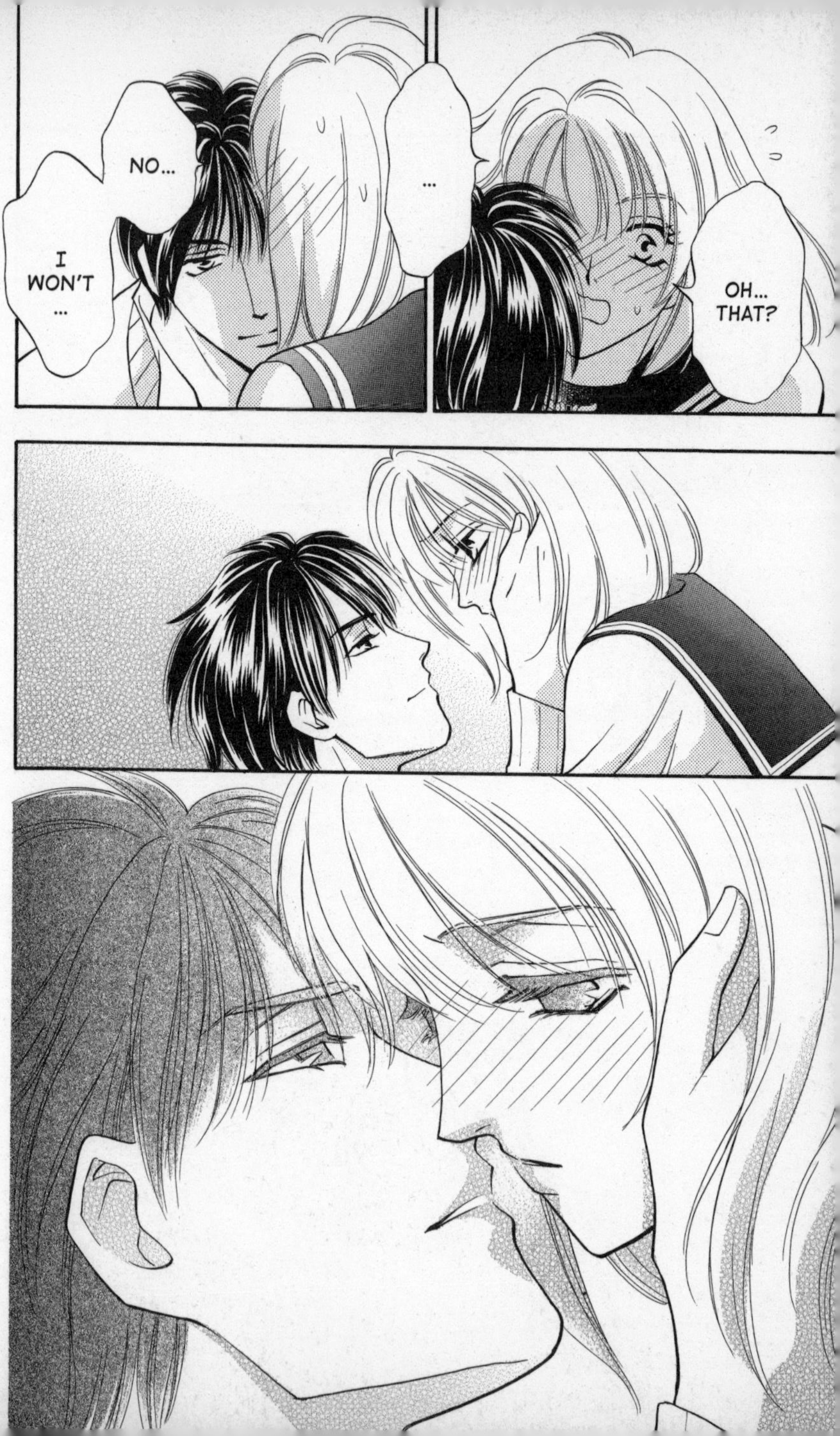
OH... THAT?
...
NO...
I WON'T ...

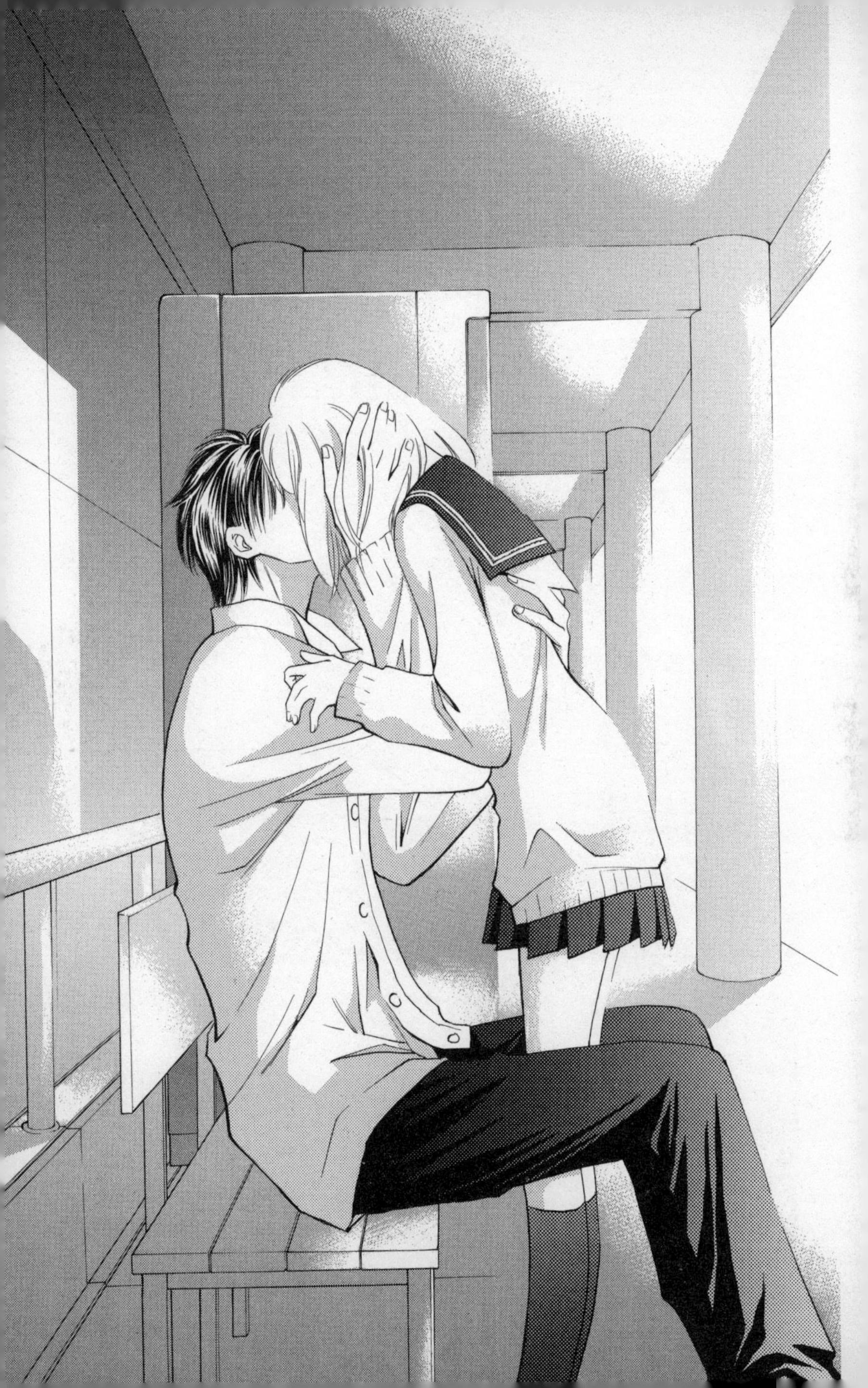

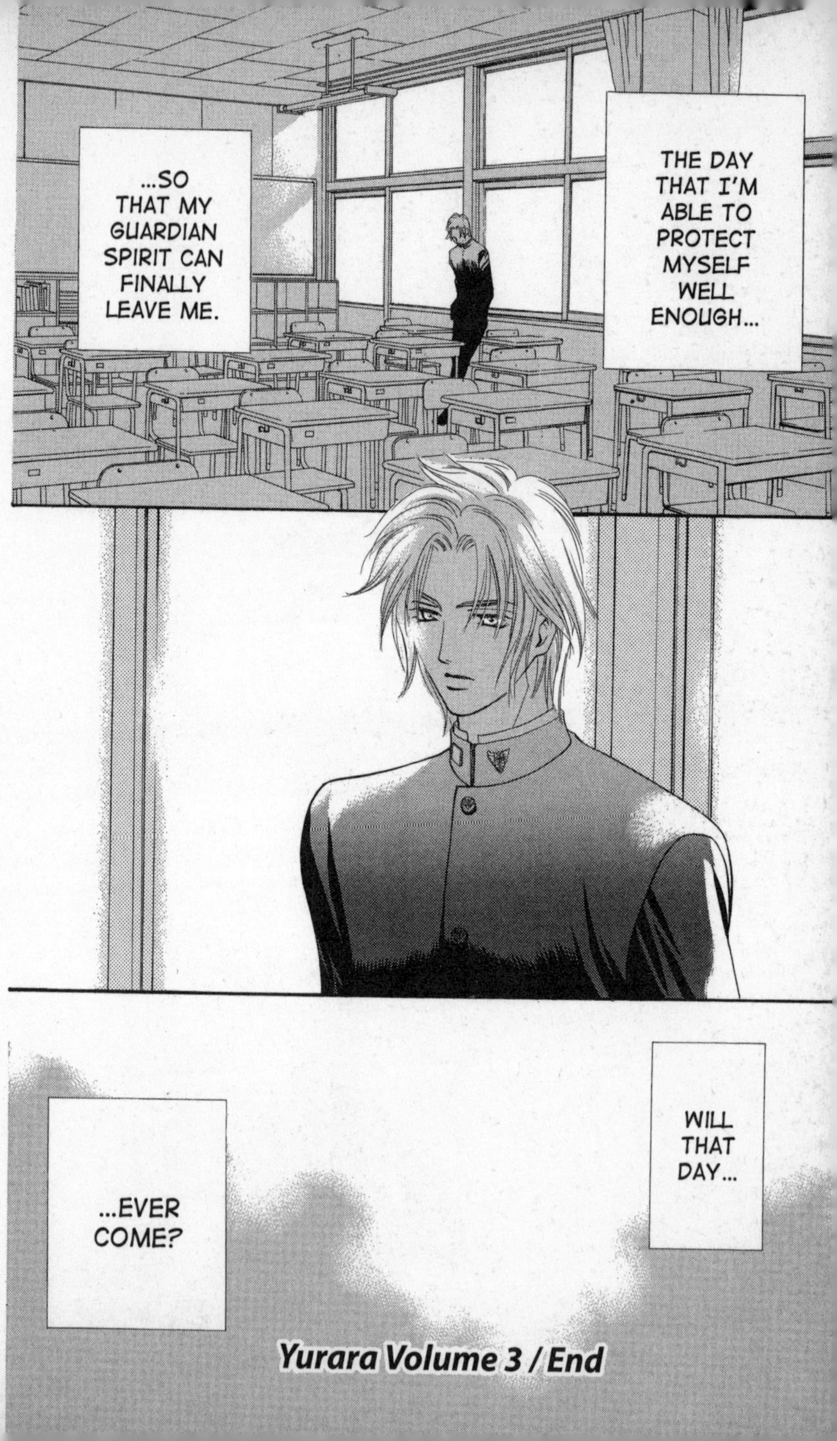
THE DAY THAT I'M ABLE TO PROTECT MYSELF WELL ENOUGH...
...SO THAT MY GUARDIAN SPIRIT CAN FINALLY LEAVE ME.
WILL THAT DAY...
...EVER COME?
Yurara Volume 3 / End

Chika Shiomi lives in the Aichi Prefecture
of Japan. She debuted with the manga
Todokeru Toki o Sugitemo (Even if the
Time for Deliverance Passes), and her work
is currently running in two magazines,
Bessatsu Hana to Yume and *Mystery Bonita*.
She loves reading manga, traveling, and
listening to music by Aerosmith, Hyde, and
Guns N' Roses. Her favorite artists include
Michelangelo, Hokusai, Bernini, and Gustav
Klimt.

Yurara

Vol. 3
The Shojo Beat Manga Edition

STORY & ART BY
CHIKA SHIOMI

English Adaptation/Heidi Vivolo
Translation/JN Productions
Touch-up Art & Lettering/Freeman Wong
Design/Izumi Hirayama
Editor/Mike Montesa

Editor in Chief, Books/Alvin Lu
Editor in Chief, Magazines/Marc Weidenbaum
VP of Publishing Licensing/Rika Inouye
VP of Sales/Gonzalo Ferreyra
Sr. VP of Marketing/Liza Coppola
Publisher/Hyoe Narita

Printed in Canada

Published by VIZ Media, LLC
P.O. Box 77064
San Francisco, CA 94107

Shojo Beat Manga Edition
10 9 8 7 6 5 4 3 2 1
First printing, December 2007

www.viz.com

store.viz.com

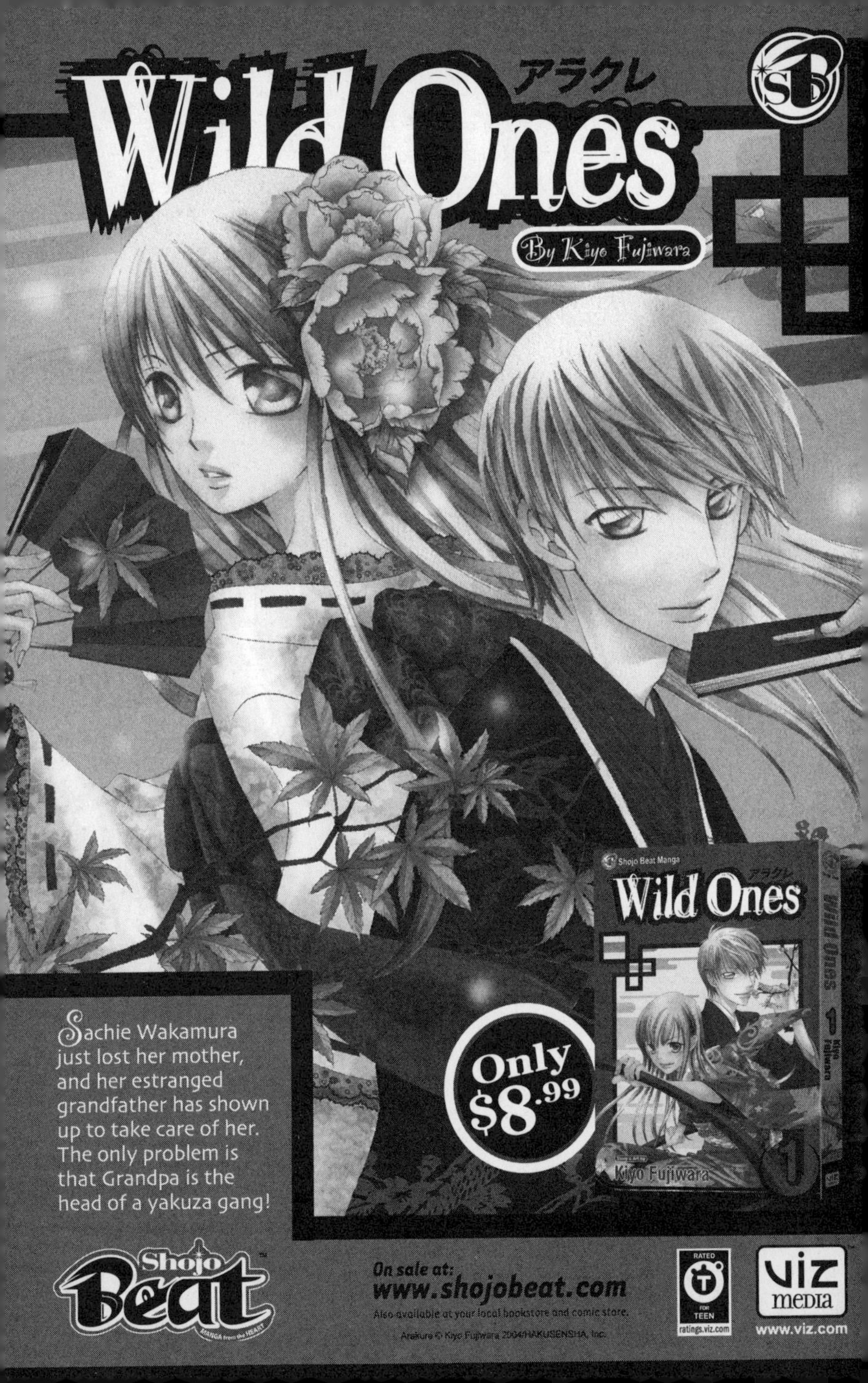
Wild Ones
アラクレ
By Kiyo Fujiwara
Sachie Wakamura just lost her mother, and her estranged grandfather has shown up to take care of her. The only problem is that Grandpa is the head of a yakuza gang!
Shojo Beat Manga
Wild Ones
Kiyo Fujiwara
Only $8.99
Shojo Beat
On sale at:
www.shojobeat.com
Also available at your local bookstore and comic store.
Arakure © Kiyo Fujiwara 2004/HAKUSENSHA, Inc.
RATED T FOR TEEN
ratings.viz.com
VIZ MEDIA
www.viz.com

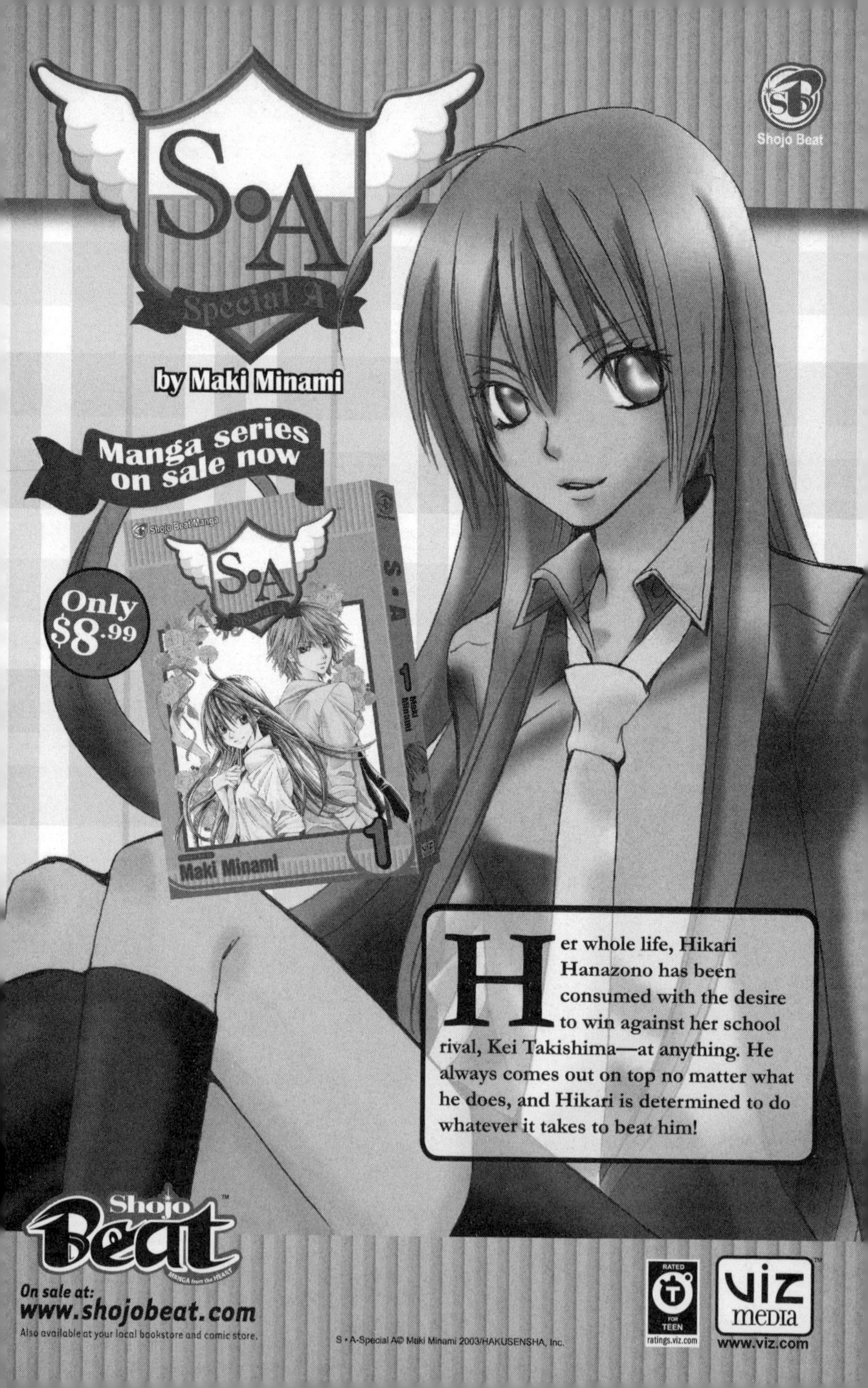
Shojo Beat
S•A
Special A
by Maki Minami
Manga series on sale now
Shojo Beat Manga
S•A
Only $8.99
1
Maki Minami
Her whole life, Hikari Hanazono has been consumed with the desire to win against her school rival, Kei Takishima—at anything. He always comes out on top no matter what he does, and Hikari is determined to do whatever it takes to beat him!
Shojo Beat
MANGA from the HEART
On sale at:
www.shojobeat.com
Also available at your local bookstore and comic store.
S • A-Special A© Maki Minami 2003/HAKUSENSHA, Inc.
RATED T FOR TEEN
ratings.viz.com
VIZ media
www.viz.com

Crimson Hero ™

By Mitsuba Takanashi

Only $8⁹⁹

All that matters to 15-year-old Nobara Sumiyoshi is volleyball—she's an awesome player with big-time ambitions. But sometimes it seems like a girl just can't get a break in the competitive world of high school volleyball. When Nobara transfers to Crimson Field High School, known for its top-notch volleyball team, she decides to start playing offense!

Shojo Beat™
MANGA from the HEART

On sale at:
www.shojobeat.com
Also available at your local bookstore and comic store.

Tail of the Moon

By Rinko Ueda

Only $**8**^{99}

Despite her ninja family lineage, Usagi is hopeless as a ninja. But what she lacks in ninja skill she makes up for in determination, and sets off to win the heart and bear the children of Hanzo Hattori, local lord and revered ninja!

Shojo Beat

MANGA from the HEART

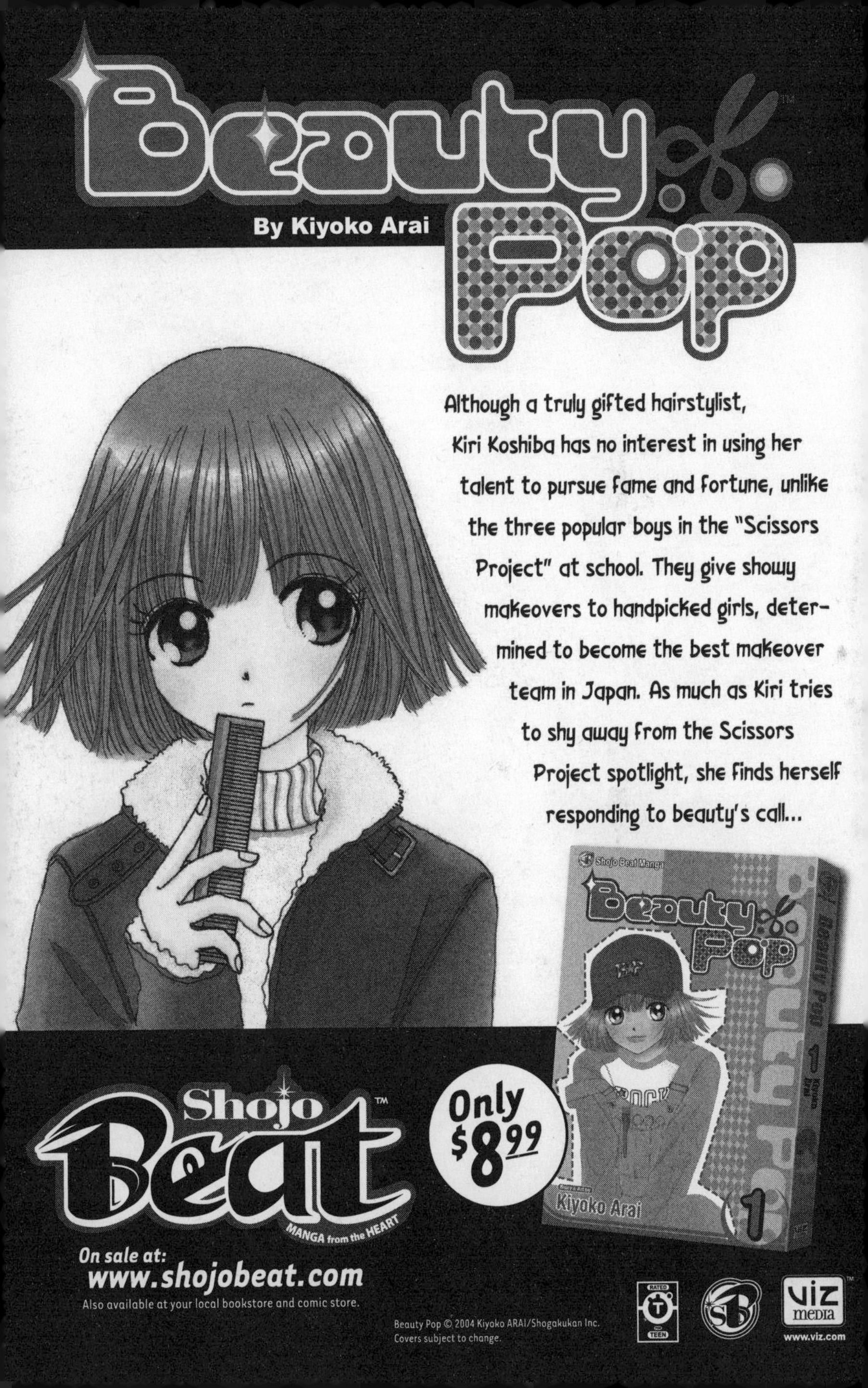

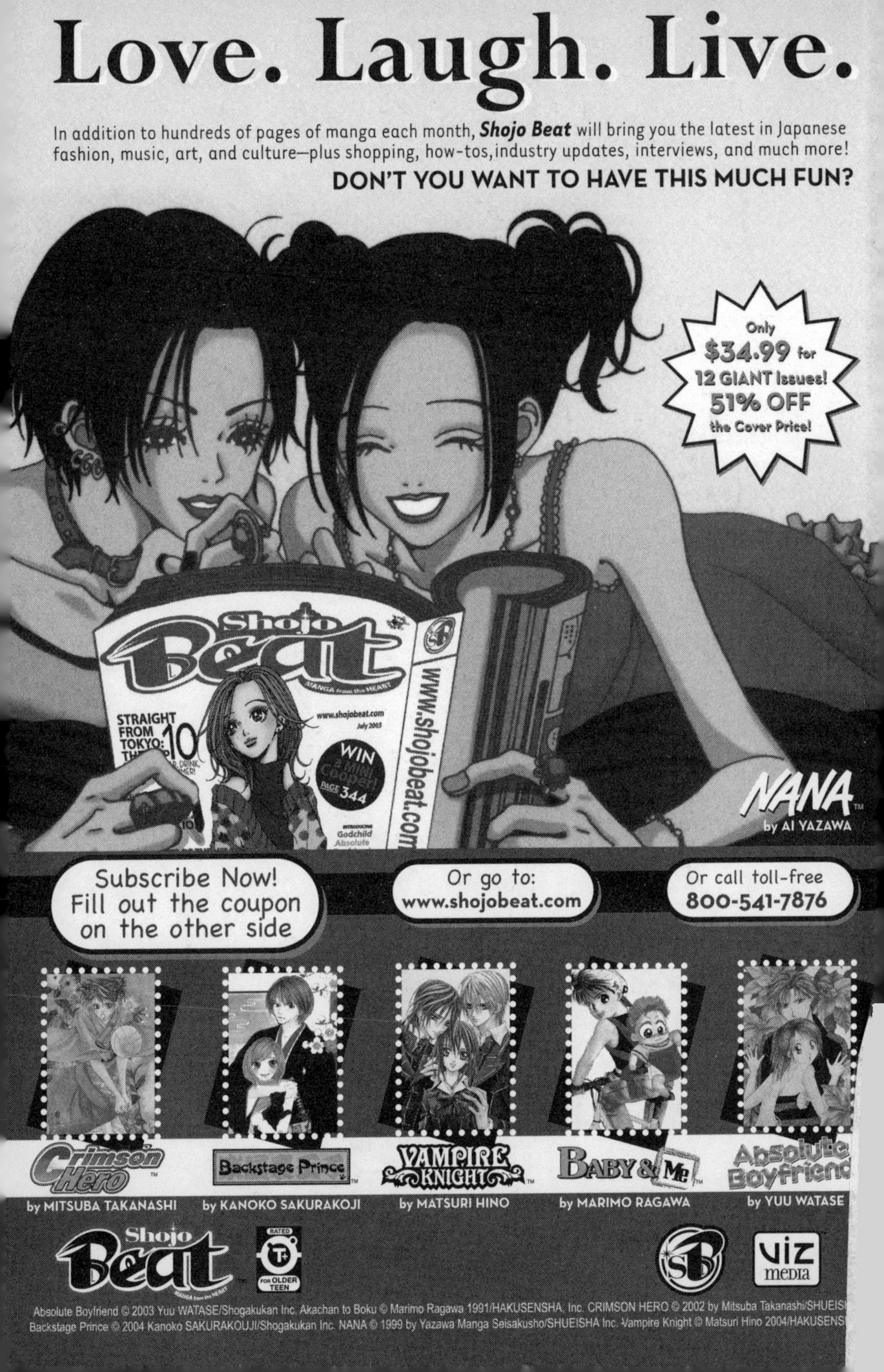
Love. Laugh. Live.
In addition to hundreds of pages of manga each month, Shojo Beat will bring you the latest in Japanese fashion, music, art, and culture—plus shopping, how-tos, industry updates, interviews, and much more!
DON'T YOU WANT TO HAVE THIS MUCH FUN?
Only $34.99 for 12 GIANT Issues! 51% OFF the Cover Price!
Shojo Beat
MANGA from the HEART
www.shojobeat.com
July 2005
STRAIGHT FROM TOKYO:
10
WIN a MINI Cooper!
PAGE 344
Godchild
Absolute
www.shojobeat.com
NANA™
by AI YAZAWA
Subscribe Now! Fill out the coupon on the other side
Or go to: www.shojobeat.com
Or call toll-free 800-541-7876
Crimson Hero™
by MITSUBA TAKANASHI
Backstage Prince™
by KANOKO SAKURAKOJI
VAMPIRE KNIGHT™
by MATSURI HINO
BABY & Me™
by MARIMO RAGAWA
Absolute Boyfriend
by YUU WATASE
Shojo Beat™
RATED T+ FOR OLDER TEEN
SB
VIZ media
Absolute Boyfriend © 2003 Yuu WATASE/Shogakukan Inc. Akachan to Boku © Marimo Ragawa 1991/HAKUSENSHA, Inc. CRIMSON HERO © 2002 by Mitsuba Takanashi/SHUEIS
Backstage Prince © 2004 Kanoko SAKURAKOUJI/Shogakukan Inc. NANA © 1999 by Yazawa Manga Seisakusho/SHUEISHA Inc. Vampire Knight © Matsuri Hino 2004/HAKUSENS